THE PATHWAY to FLOW

The Pathway to Flow

The New Science of Harnessing Creativity
to Heal and Unwind the Body & Mind

DR JULIA F. CHRISTENSEN

SQUARE PEG

1 3 5 7 9 10 8 6 4 2

Square Peg, an imprint of Vintage, is part of the Penguin Random House group of
companies whose addresses can be found at global.penguinrandomhouse.com

First published in the UK by Square Peg in 2024

Copyright © Julia F. Christensen 2024

Julia F. Christensen has asserted her right to be identified as the author of this
Work in accordance with the Copyright, Designs and Patents Act 1988

penguin.co.uk/vintage

Typeset in 11.5/14.25pt Bembo Book MT Pro by Jouve (UK), Milton Keynes
Printed and bound in Great Britain by Clays Ltd, Elcograf S.p.A.

The authorised representative in the EEA is Penguin Random House Ireland,
Morrison Chambers, 32 Nassau Street, Dublin D02 YH68

A CIP catalogue record for this book is available from the British Library

HB ISBN 9781529912296
TPB ISBN 9781529912302

Penguin Random House is committed to a sustainable future
for our business, our readers and our planet. This book is made
from Forest Stewardship Council® certified paper.

To my parents

Contents

Disclaimer   ix

Introduction: The New Science of Why we Can't
Stop Thinking   I

PART I: THE RESTLESS MIND

The neuroscience of habits and overthinking

1. Mind-*full*-ness   II

2. Mind Hooks   34

3. Pink Elephant Ballet   66

4. The Porcupine Dilemma   89

5. How and When to Set Boundaries   114

PART II: BREAKING THE LOOP

Brain-based solutions to the restless mind problem – with the arts

6. Mind Expansions – Create how you feel by what you *do*   135

7. Mind Liberators – Six Strategies to unwind your mind   162

8. Process Over Progress – How we learn a new skill   191

9. Modern Problems, Ancient Solutions?   221

10. Getting Started – And off you go, *flow*   232

Conclusion: Art Matters   257

Acknowledgements   263

References   267

Index   333

Disclaimer

A little warning before we begin: The brain and its interrelations with the rest of the body, with our behaviour and the environment, are very complex. They are systems within systems that connect, engage, disengage and jam with one another. There are thousands of scientific papers about all the specifics – and there is still very much that we don't know. If I were to write about all of it here, this book would simply be too long, and not very interesting. Therefore, for the purposes of this guide, I will do my best to stay away from too much scientific jargon. I'll prioritise the information in a nutshell, over lengthy specifics. This means of course that, understandably, my science colleagues may wish for more formal detail and terminology here and there, but I hope that they can bear with me, while you and I explore our pathway to flow in a way that is practical, memorable, and useful for readers of all stripes.

This book is not a substitute for medical or therapeutic attention, and it is important to remember that this field of research is still very much in its infancy. If you are suffering from psychological distress, mental health, or medical issues, consider speaking to your appointed doctor or mental health practitioners and follow their advice.

Introduction: The New Science of Why we Can't Stop Thinking

The fact that you are holding this book in your hands is the wildest example of how life sometimes redirects us in ways we'd never imagined. I'm a former professional dance student from Denmark, turned neuroscientist via France, Spain and the UK. Years ago, a serious back injury made a professional dance career impossible and I had to completely rethink my life. However, instead of picking at that scar, I'd like to share how I dealt with the aftermath of it. After hanging up my pointe shoes, I soon discovered that there was a limit to how still I could keep my mind, and I deeply missed the feeling of connection and expression that I had tapped into through dance – regularly, and without having to think about it. So I decided to embark on a scientific career to discover what we know about how our brain works, to better understand this feeling. Drawing and writing became my creative outlets and my tools to fight restlessness. In these pages I will share how I learned to unlock my own, new pathway to flow and how you can discover yours too.

Would you like to develop a calm, poised focus, a state where you feel entirely absorbed and productive, without any effort at all, whenever you need it? If so, this book is for you. It will give you an overview of the science that will help you tap into the flow state too. Do you remember hours spent drawing as a child, lost in blissful oblivion? That's flow. Or the way it feels to be absorbed in a good novel, in a dance, in martial arts or yoga practice, in playing your favourite instrument or cooking while listening to a good album? Whatever it is, this is your you-time. You may not even see time pass once you're in that zone. You may even forget about that one urgent thing on your to-do list you really want to sort out before the weekend. Such is the power of the flow state – all-consuming, soothing, and totally free!

The late Hungarian scientist Mihaly Csíkszentmihályi who pioneered this concept,[1] refers to 'flow' as a much-cherished state of recovery and relaxation for our body, both physical and mental, that activates the brain in a very special way. People may experience it when reading,[2] submerging themselves into the zone of a story,[3,4] when listening to or making music,[5,6] dancing,[7] or when doing photography, making art, creating a film or listening to an audiobook. There have been accounts for centuries, if not millennia, from artists about the benefits of this trance-like state, and now evidence is starting to emerge from the sciences that regularly experiencing flow may even be related to good health outcomes for all of us – not least because it reliably unwinds our mind.

Yet, there are many reasons why such a focus is difficult to harness. Among them are the fact that we live in a rapidly evolving modern world but our brain's operating system is about 300,000 years old, with no USB port for updates to modern world v.2.0. All we can do is learn as much as we can about how it works and how to use it – and that's where this book comes in.

Our brains evolved in a harsh, prehistoric world and developed to be sensitively attuned to identifying potential threats and potential pleasures – this radar has kept us alive, but in today's world we're exposed to a lot of stimuli *all the time*. Our environment is scattered with signals that promise pleasure and we live in large, interconnected societies where interpersonal conflicts and risks (real and perceived) happen by the minute, both in person and via our ever-present screens. Whether our brain is telling us to move swiftly towards food, sex or a notification icon or to immediately engage in fight, flight or freeze, neurobiological processes will trigger a state of *high alert* in the body. This in turn activates the memory systems in our brain in order to serve up information about past experiences. These systems evolved to protect us by having information about previous dangers and reward sources readily available, but in practice it is now more likely to serve up negative memories, anxieties, concerns and distractions. If, when presented with this parade of negative thoughts, we don't know what to do to help our body re-establish a balance, the mind can spin into a loop of rumination. The good news is this same mechanism also holds the key to setting your mind free and generating *positive* thoughts. We can lead our bodies into a relaxation state that will activate memories of calm, joy and positivity inside our brain.

In building a toolbox of knowledge about this special edition brain of ours, we can use simple strategies in our everyday lives to feel relaxed, solve problems and steer clear of behaviours that make us feel like we aren't achieving our potential. And with that, we will be building our pathway to flow . . .

→

Today I'm a scientist researching the arts, creativity and the brain, currently at the Max Planck Institute for Empirical Aesthetics in Frankfurt am Main, Germany. And scientists do experiments. So, let's start with a quick one:

Imagine a pink elephant. Imagine it vividly, dancing . . .

Do you see it? Okay.

Now, for sixty seconds, try *not* to think of this pink elephant. Give it a go.

Did you succeed? Did you fail?

I should tell you now – if you didn't manage it, you're not the only one. In fact, it's nigh on impossible. You can't stop thinking.

Why not? Because, our mind is never empty. In fact, our mind wants to be full all the time. We can't get rid of thoughts by just deciding to stop thinking them. This is not a symptom of a lack of willpower, it's a fundamental feature of how the brain works. As long as a brain is alive, it keeps itself busy with impressions from our environment, sensations from our body and thoughts that are already in our head. This is an unstoppable process, and an absolutely necessary one on an evolutionary level. Neuroscientists have previously shown that there are systems in our brain that work fast and automatically, and which ensure that we can't stop our brain with our conscious will. The reason seems to be that it would be quite unhealthy for us if we did. Imagine if the brain suddenly stopped processing, or decided to empty itself without warning. It would be a disaster. So don't worry if you have never been able to empty your mind of thought – 'like a bathtub when you pull the plug', as they say in meditation class. This just means that your brain is functioning in the way that it was wired.

But what to do when our thoughts turn into grinding torture instruments that stress us out and threaten to steal our sleep and peace of mind, and even mindfulness and meditation can't help? What to do when we can't seem to focus on any one thing? According to Oliver Burkeman's eponymous bestselling book, all being well, we get about *Four Thousand Weeks* on earth. How do we want to spend ours? Ruminating?

As a dancer-turned-neuroscientist, my curious mind has been trained to look for new solutions to old problems and to translate them into something that can be applied to make our brains, and our lives, happier and more productive. Like *Kintsugi* (金継ぎ, 'golden joinery'), the Japanese art of creating something new and beautiful out of broken pottery, I'm convinced that we can transcend the roles our personal tragedies have forced upon us and repair our lives instead, creatively joining our broken edges with lacquer laced with gold – creative energy. Whoever you are, whether what sends your thoughts spinning is life-changing trauma or 'just' everyday worries, I believe we can all lace our thoughts and actions with beauty and precious, creative energy, and heal. Many professional artists cope with deeply traumatic childhoods, neurodiversity, mental health and identity issues, and so on, through the act of creating. Just like our ancestors before us, who naturally sought the arts to cope with a world so much harsher than that in which most of us live today.

My own fruitless attempts at harnessing spinning unproductive thoughts set me on a quest to explore scientific findings from all over the world with a simple objective: I wanted to know why a state of flow is so hard to reach, why mindfulness meditation just doesn't seem to work for everyone and, most importantly, I wanted to find an alternative solution that works for those of us with persistently full minds. During this search, I found that modern neuroscience holds the key to why so many of us struggle and why it isn't just about trying harder. I also discovered a scientific explanation for how we can find and use a reliable shortcut to get to that elusive state of peaceful focus whenever we want. When we embrace a recreational artistic practice – whether it be dancing, painting, sewing, cooking, sketching, playing the guitar or making jewellery, it activates systems in the brain that produce a sense of all-encompassing calm. Regular practice can create incredible changes in how you work, think and feel, increasing your concentration, productivity and patience. But you need to know *how*. As a starting point for *your* Pathway to Flow, I reveal what Pathway Prompts are in Chapter 8, to get you started off on your path.

There is a huge amount of research about the thoughts that populate our minds and steal our concentration, sleep and peace of mind. Unfortunately, the information about these intrusive thoughts, why we have them, and what we can do about them is slumbering in academic journals, hidden behind walls of scientific jargon. With this book, I would like to translate that knowledge and introduce an alternative to rumination and the frustration of trying and failing to master looping thoughts. Aided by cutting-edge neuroscience and a close look at artistic impulses humans have embraced since time immemorial, we will learn to guide our wandering minds into healthy, peaceful, sustainable thought patterns, to make us calmer, more productive – and even more likable. A regular creative practice conditions the mind to find that flow state more easily, enabling us to find our way back there, even when we don't have a paintbrush in hand. You just need to see, hear, smell, taste or feel an element of your practice – and off flows your mind, emerging refreshed and energised on the other side. This is an easy-to-read, science-backed guide, with actionable advice. It worked for me, and I'm hoping parts of it will work for you too.

One important point to understand is that our body is a system of many interconnected organs, tissues and neural pathways. More often than not, we're unaware of how our thoughts develop, but there are neurocognitive mechanisms by which our thoughts are linked to processes in the body. We see this when our brain detects rewards, danger, or when it simply needs us to move.

Building a reliable pathway to flow doesn't mean that we have to exist in perfect yogic harmony and avoid all ups and downs. Our brain and body's systems very much like to be used. They want to be thrilled and excited, as much as calmed and soothed. That keeps them in training, just as our muscles stay strong through regular exercise. The best behaviour or activity that I've found to offer the safe space where all this can happen is a creative practice. Modern neuroscience shows that artistic practice is the ideal guide, whether that is as a creator or a spectator. In fact, archaeologists have found evidence that humans may have been using what we today refer to as 'the arts' as a beneficial practice since the dawn of civilisation. Why? Because of the powerful opportunities for imagery, meaning-making, self-expression and communication that they afford. If we choose the right art form for *us*, it transforms a ruminating mind and makes flow possible. We can be lost in thought – with helpful, healthy direction.

You may be thinking that you're not an artist and this can't possibly be for you. But, as long as you have a human brain, an artistic practice can be *your* guide to a peaceful mind. Regular flow with a creative practice can be linked to increases in our creativity, productivity, even our likability. And the more we do it, the easier it becomes to tap into that state of flow. The key strength of this approach lies in identifying a creative pursuit we enjoy and that we can engage in without getting caught up in perfectionism and the drive to create something grand, or memorable, or worthy of praise. It should, first and foremost, be a personal creative practice which, almost as a side-effect, fosters healthy activations in the brain (and, as a consequence, in the wider body) during the process of creating. This means that the *outcome* of our practice is unimportant. If we end up with an object, painting, dance or text that does not meet current aesthetic expectations, it should not worry us. It's the neurobiological changes in our brain and body that happen during the process of immersing ourselves in our art that matters. So, join me on this journey to finding your flow.

→

Pathway to Flow is made up of two sections, to reflect the theory and the more practical aspects of the practice. In Part One, we'll explore the neuroscience of habits and rumination – this section will help you to understand the key processes that keep your brain alert at all times and why they can sometimes work against the things that you want more consciously, such as being productive, or relaxing. In Part Two, we will explore science-based, art-led solutions to rumination, from practical hacks to use in your work to case studies of individuals and communities who have embraced artistic practices as a way to overcome a wide range of personal or systemic challenges, from anxiety and depression to more severe traumas. We will meet filmmaker Susana, who uses photography on her Instagram as a pathway to flow; Jamie Oliver, who finds flow with cooking while also using it as a respite from the crippling feeling of being neurodiverse in a world that is not; Nazanin Zaghari-Ratcliffe, who knitted a 'freedom dress' for her daughter Gabriella while arbitrarily incarcerated in Iran and thus stepping into a cocoon of colours, textures and movements on repeat that filled her time and spun her thoughts in healthy directions, until freedom really came. And we'll meet many more, including some small examples of my own pathway to flow with drawing and dancing Argentine tango.

Soon, you will be one of us, finding your flow with your art! I hope this book can remind us of what our ancestors knew all those years ago: self-expression is not just fanciful – it's core to our humanity and can be the key to healing.

PART I

THE RESTLESS MIND

The neuroscience of habits and overthinking

1. Mind-*full*-ness

If you're human and alive, you have a brain. And this is a very special brain, unique in the animal kingdom. It has very basic neural systems in place that allow you to survive in the wild, while, at the same time, it also has neural systems that can write poetry, fairy tales, dance ballet on pointe, play improv on a saxophone, and create a delicious dish of pasta as an expression of love. Bizarrely, or, wonderfully, these systems overlap. And we can use this to our advantage to reach flow.

Yet, we mostly know very little about this special edition brain of ours – how it works, how to engage or appease it. In order to learn how we can access flow states reliably and manage our brains in a way that improves our wellbeing, we first need to understand more about how it all works.

Your Body-Orchestra

Imagine your body as an orchestra. Touch your chest and picture an orchestra pit just there. Do you see it? Your organs, tissues and muscles are instruments now. There are string players, gently striking their bows, easing your blood around your body. Violins, cellos and guitars play your tune. And there are brass instruments like trumpets, and some cymbals. They take care of the strong oomph of undertones when hormones jump into your blood as it passes through spleen and liver. There are also instruments that your body-orchestra only has one or two of: one heart, one spleen, two lungs. You can think of them as the instruments that there are only a few of in an orchestra and that set important accents; a drum, a harp, two bandoneons. And, there are always some maracas in the corner, sprinkling notes in between the main notes. Cha cha

cha . . . these are the messenger substances, like endorphins and bonding hormones, that travel through our body when things get exciting or when we calm down.

The reason I want you to think of the organs, tissues and bio-chemical transmitters of our inner body as the instruments of an orchestra is:

1. because both organs and instruments are precious, sometimes irreplaceable, and deserve our utmost care, and
2. because I would like you to understand that you can control more of what is going on in your body than you think.

The long and short of it is, you can have a say in what kind of music your body-orchestra plays – a bit like the way you can choose to go to a live concert where they play Brahms, or to one where you can enjoy Metallica. Depending on your taste, one may bore you to pieces, while the other might entice and calm you down at the same time – maybe even give you flow. As you grew up, you'll have learned how different music makes you feel, and that you can choose which record you load into your stereo, or which playlist you pick on Spotify. The music that rises to your ears, depending on your choice, kicks off a whole wealth of biochemical processes between your ears and your brain before you even become aware of it.

This starts with the physiological processes that allow you to hear the music. Via little hairs in your ears that vibrate with the rhythm of the tune, the music is 'translated' to tiny electrical impulses in the auditory cortices of your brain. These then propagate all the way to the broader neural circuitries that give rise to your feelings, in the limbic system. These processes happen automatically and instantly as you listen to the music and they will change how you feel. The neural activity will also resonate with the memory systems at your temples. The memories that are stored there give the music that special tinge of feeling, that special deep feeling of 'me'. And as you become fully aware of the music, it may make you want to cry, dance . . . or both. We've all experienced the way listening to different kinds of music, in different kinds of formats and moments, makes us feel, well, differently.

So, for the purpose of this book, take this view of your body: It's an orchestra made up of precious instruments and you can have a say in what music it is playing within you, rising to your awareness through biochemical processes ('biochemical process' just means that there is a chemical reaction inside your body with biological ingredients from your inner medium). By making different choices about what you *do* with your body in the world, you can, to a certain extent, stir these processes and affect how you feel.

But how does this orchestra work? The instruments of our body-orchestra play by their own inertia, and they play all the time. Our organs are similar, and luckily so, provided that all is in order, and that all the connections between the conductor (the brain) and the orchestra are working, we don't have to think about having to 'play' each of them. Our heart beats, our lungs fill themselves with air every four seconds thanks to automatic systems in our brain, and we are spared from consciously having to keep time.

If every musician was playing their instrument just the way they wanted, at some point, it would be quite chaotic. Nature, therefore, made sure that there are neurobiological mechanisms in place that ensure our body-orchestra plays the right symphony *together*. These basic mechanisms are taken care of by our brain stem, a neural system sitting deep down in our brain, just over the spinal cord. It is one of the oldest structures of our brain – we even share it with most animals, and everything about it is automatic and instinctive. If you make a fist and hold it up so your thumb faces you, you can imagine that your arm is the spinal cord leading down into your body, and inside your fist you're holding the brain stem and its tender folds. This brain stem of ours is located just above the nape of our neck and approximately 2.5 centimetres towards our nose. Layers of brain systems have been added to that basic structure as we evolved and ultimately, this resulted in the

brain as it is today, but everything starts from this instinctive, automatically functioning brain stem.

Crucially, these layers are connected. It's not like they are just
lying one on top of the other. If you added your other hand to the
fist now, imagine that neural *pathways* are connecting the layers –
from one hand to the other – and are telling one hand what the
other is doing. Neural pathways are a bit like motorways with multiple lanes that information can travel by efficiently. They connect
different parts of the brain so they can communicate easily. So,
while the brain stem is working automatically, it is also talking to
other brain systems constantly. It is exchanging information with
brain structures that are older, phylogenetically speaking (meaning
that these structures also existed in beings that lived before *Homo
sapiens* evolved), like our memory systems and all the sensory systems we use for seeing, hearing, smelling, touching and tasting, as
well as with some slightly more modern parts of our brain that we
share with other mammals. These include the insular and limbic
system where social information, our emotions and homeostatic
information (sensory updates about things like our body temperature that help our brains keep our body environment consistent)
are processed.

Of course, there are also connections with the most modern
parts of our brain, the prefrontal cortices that sit close behind our
forehead, that are responsible for our ability to reason, think,
imagine, plan for the future and to perform complex decision-
making tasks. These systems are fairly unique in the animal
kingdom, but never forget: all of it builds on very basic survival
mechanisms in the brain stem.[1] Even the most modern parts of the
brain, the prefrontal systems that make us so distinctively human,
receive information from this very basic and automatic system via
relay stations throughout the brain.[2–4]

We are rarely aware of what these basic survival mechanisms are
whispering into our prefrontal brain systems and, from there, into
our awareness.[5–8] But they are affecting our behaviour[9,10] – including
our ability to experience flow – so let's understand a little more
about these whispers.

Golden Threads: How Mind and Body Connect

The brain stem's primary job is to take care of the basic constants of our body, like our heartbeat, our breathing and our hormone levels. We can imagine the brain stem as a jukebox with pre-recorded discs. It takes care of biological processes that are genetically pre-programmed to happen, like our breathing, our heart rate, or our hormonal changes for the day-and-night rhythm. We don't have any conscious control over these songs, and the various pre-recorded songs each make us feel a certain way. They are life-saving discs, stored in the genes that 'make' our brain after our conception, for each of our basic needs: sleep, food, water, air, shelter, reproduction, and so on. When we repeatedly disturb these automatic functions with our chosen behaviour, a spinning mind is the result. The discipline called psychoneuroendocrinology studies these interactions between our behaviour and our inner medium.[11,12] 'Psycho' means psychological, so everything to do with what we think, feel, or refer to as our 'mind'. 'Neuro' is, well, our brain's actions. 'Endocrine' is another word for hormones. Hence, psychoneuroendocrinology is the science that is concerned with understanding the interactions between what our brain does, our hormones, our behaviour and how we feel.

For example, we feel sleepy when, rather than a pop song, our jukebox plays a lullaby. That song – the sleep hormone melatonin, when it rises in our blood – makes our whole body slow down.[13,14]

While we cannot change the songs that are recorded on these discs, we can sometimes have a say in which one we play. If we notice that our heart is pounding, and we feel scared, angry or stressed, we should know that the song that is playing inside us is often the result of something that we are doing or exposing ourselves to. This 'doing' can be active, or it can be just thinking stressful, threatening thoughts, sitting still for too long, or interacting with an annoying colleague. In all these scenarios we are enacting, or enabling, a behaviour. Now, as soon as we notice our pounding heart and looping thoughts, we have the power to choose to act out a different behaviour, or to choose a different environment to be in, or alter our present one. Thanks to the modern prefrontal cortices of our brain, we can make conscious decisions about what we want, and what we don't want, to *do*. And through the body-brain connection, this new behaviour will help us load a different disc into the jukebox – and appease the heart rate, making us feel less scared, angry or stressed.

It is possible for a decision to influence the way we feel physically because our body and brain are intimately linked.[4,15] If you touch your hairline at the back of your neck now, and let your fingers slide down your neck, you can imagine the spinal cord being protected by the vertebrae, those hard bones that you feel in your neck. Inside the spinal cord, long nerve cells, called ganglia, flow down into our body. Like long golden threads of yarn, they are connecting the neural systems of our brain with organs, muscles and tissues throughout our body so they can play their tune when needed.[6,10,16] These golden threads continue all the way out into the outmost tips of our fingers and the skin on the tips of our toes so we can touch and feel – and stand on our tippy-toes if we're a ballet dancer. Via these connections between brain and body, information flows. Back and forth. This happens through what scientists call *neural transmission*.[17-19] This is a complex biochemical process that we won't go into but the important message to remember is that information can flow *from* our brain, to our body. And the information also flows *from* our body, *to* our brain.

To summarise; there are channels of communication between our brain and our body. With our behaviour and the movements of our body, to a certain extent, we can modify some of what's going on in our brain. For good, and for bad.

There are specific discs with pre-recorded symphonies for different basic needs, like for when we're going to sleep and for when we're hungry. Let's take a closer look at two examples.

The Sleep Symphony

The sleep symphony is automatically loaded into the jukebox of our brain stem when night falls. Receptors in our eyes and skin note the fading light and send messenger substances towards the brain-stem systems, telling them to get ready for sleeping.[14] Composed and pre-recorded during evolution and then stored in our genes, this song automatically lulls us to sleep following a fixed pattern, orchestrated by the brain stem. As the comforting notes of the pineal gland sprinkle the hormone melatonin into our bloodstream, our eyes start itching, we start to feel drowsy, and we slowly glide into dreamland as our heart rate falls and our blood pressure decreases. All of this happens automatically – if we let it, with our behaviour. For example, if we let our body relax while reading or knitting or listening to music before going to sleep, the sleep symphony in our body plays undisturbed. If, however, we expose our body to blue light sources, do high-energy sport, or consume things that frighten or anger us like thriller movies, social media or news about war, our body's sleep symphony can't play properly. Blue light, fear and anger tell our jukebox to load discs that release a different set of hormones and neurotransmitters into our bloodstream.[20-22] And these have absolutely nothing to do with sleep. Rather, they prompt wakefulness, or activate the fight or flight response. Then, we can't sleep.

In the worst case, we repeat this behaviour (for example, *always* watch TV before bed, or *consistently* doom scroll before sleep), and this causes the disc with the sleep symphony to get scratches that need mending. Doctors would call this *disturbed sleep patterns*.

The prefrontal cortex of the human brain is a unique piece of machinery in the animal kingdom. It allows humans to retain control over our behaviour through the choices we make. For example, we can choose to watch TV, or to do something else that is more conducive to sleeping.

If only it were that easy, right? We'll get to the part about why those choices in the *right* direction are sometimes so hard to make . . .

Hungry Eyes

Now, consider this second example. The disc with the hunger symphony is automatically loaded into the jukebox in our brain stem as soon as receptors in our gut, our pancreas, and in the fat of our body detect low levels of nutrients or energy. Compared to the sleep symphony, the organs that play a role when we're hungry release a whole different set of messenger substances into our blood to inform our brain-stem systems about the low levels of energy. The appetite hormone ghrelin – grumpy and menacing – comes rushing through our blood, making us hungry. And it doesn't stop rushing around until we've eaten. This hunger symphony may sound a little discordant at times, but it's incredibly effective at making us keep the energy supplies of our body stocked up.

Again, we can derail this prehistoric tune with our chosen behaviour. For example, if we eat food with sweetener, messages are sent to our gut informing it that a lot of sugar is coming. The taste buds in our mouth send these signals to the gut via our brain stem, down the ganglia in our spinal cord. These signals, in the case of artificial sweetener, cause our gut to produce far too much digestive fluid. If this remains unused, which it does, as sweetener doesn't contain any real energy like natural sugar would, signals are sent to the brain that nutrients and energy are still needed to balance the amount of digestive fluid. As a result, we never stop feeling hungry and overeating is the logical consequence.

The basic knowledge to grasp here is this: it's a two-way process. While our automatic brain and body systems make our organs function from the inside, what we *do* in the outside world with our behaviour, and what we expose ourselves to can impact our internal systems and organs just as much. We have immense power to trigger good or bad things in our body and brain. Once we understand which discs we have in our brain-stem jukebox, and how we can tailor our behaviour to support our body-orchestra instead of sending it into imbalance with our behaviour, we'll be on a path to success.

Strike a (Thinker's) Pose

When it comes to our emotions, the science seems to point one way: how we feel depends on the choices we make because our brain and behaviour have a symbiotic relationship. With our choices, we can impact our moods. Raise your hand and make a thinker's pose. At the tip of your fingers, behind your forehead, is your prefrontal cortex. These folds of grey and white matter allow us to do something unique in the animal kingdom: think, imagine, symbolise, be creative, reason, make decisions, take *informed* action, and have agency in what happens to us. But, unlike those brain-stem jukebox discs that play just one song, the music that our behaviour can make our brain play is more susceptible to change, and to mistakes, but also to doing good. We can compose the song that plays in our head – our thoughts – with our behaviour.

As we know, our behaviour is part of what guides the processes in our brain, our heart, lungs, spleen, liver and all our other organs, which in turn direct the messenger substances and hormones that populate our blood. And all this happens on top of the base-rhythms and melodies that are taken care of by the jukebox in our brain stem. Sometimes, our behaviour is powerful enough to influence even those basic processes, for better or for worse. Our heartbeat accelerates, or decelerates, the thyroid glands play hormone songs that make us feel certain ways, depending on the tune that we have started with our *behaviour*. Sometimes it's good, sometimes it's not. Let's look at a couple more examples.

Still Life

Sitting is a behaviour. Even if it is very still. For those of us with full mobility, it's something we instruct our body to do. Most of us sit loads. At work, in front of the TV, while gaming, browsing social media, and so on. One study shows that on average, middle-aged people sit for around 597 minutes per day (give or take 122 min/day) – that's almost ten hours. This behaviour can make our organs play a symphony that wreaks havoc in our body, and there-fore in our mind too. For example, when we sit our blood pressure is higher than when we stand,[23] and this can develop into a health hazard. Research shows that having 2.5 hours of standing or light exercise interwoven into an 8-hour work day would decrease general blood pressure significantly.[24,25] Even being active just twice a week lowers risk of coronary heart disease by 41 per cent.[26] Yet, most of us sit. This could be because we don't realise that the looping pink elephant thoughts that populate our minds are sometimes caused, at least in part, by the neurobiological consequences such as this sitting choice.

Sitting for too long can catapult our body into a full-blown stress response. This means our body releases a cocktail of 'action' hormones and neurotransmitters into the blood (cortisol, adrenaline, dopamine, etc).

As soon as I found this evidence, I understood why my mind was going astray in ways that I hadn't experienced while being a dancer. As a dancer, I didn't sit very much. Now, as a scientist, I do. Of course, these messenger substances aren't bad in themselves, in fact they're exactly what we need if we are running away from a lion. However, if they remain in the body too long *and we don't use them,* they cook the body in its own broth, making our veins porous and breaking down our body's immune defences against viruses, instead of protecting it. Professional dancing obviously also has a lot to do with stress hormones. However, dancers have one advantage – they get up and dance it out. Physical exercise gets rid of the stress hormones (be physical – that's what these hormones were for in the first place). Sitting, however, does not make use of the cocktail of the stress response. And, according to the evidence, if it persists over longer periods of time, this stress symphony wears out the organs of our body-orchestra, which are playing their instruments at top levels of exertion, preparing the body for imminent action – which never comes. We just keep sitting.

I got so startled by this evidence that I now keep a timer that reminds me to get up from my desk and move around each hour.

Here's what the science shows us: leaving our spine in one position for long periods of time stresses the position of the hips that are bent forward in an unnatural way, it impacts our shoulders and neck. Receptors all over our body are in charge of detecting when there is danger of injury in the body and they funnel this information to our brain, when something is not right. When our brain receives information about the problem, it sends signals to different parts of the body to solve the problem via the ganglia in the spinal cord: for example, it stirs the strings of our adrenal gland (which sits behind our waistline) to release the stress hormone cortisol into our bloodstream. Cortisol is a hormone of action. It rushes through the blood in our immobile body singing *move move move*! At this point, we may start feeling restless. If we keep sitting and sitting, our brain thinks that it's failing to protect us and our thoughts move into dangerous waters instead. So how then do we convince our body-orchestra to play in the right way? First, we must understand why the stress symphony works the way it does.

The Stress Symphony

The stress symphony was composed during our evolution to protect us from prehistoric lions and other dangers in our ancestors' scary world. It is a life-saving disc in the brain-stem jukebox. It sends messenger substances shrilling through every vein at high speed and sends our blood rushing around out into the periphery of the body, into our arms and legs. This is so that oxygen is available in the large muscles, in case we need to run away from a lion or fight an adversary. The breathing rate of our lungs increases, the adrenal gland pumps out cortisol, and our heart pounds. In this state, our attention is a tunnel, focused only on the threat. Our memory and ability to think is impaired, and we may even struggle to formulate words into a coherent sentence. Our body is in a biological state of alarm.

All of this is to protect us, but the state is exhausting for our body, and when the stress has passed, we need recovery.

The 'advantage' when it's a real lion that's making our organs play the stress symphony is that we get up and run away or fight. Running, also a behaviour, has specific effects on our body. Due to the energy expenditure, the use of oxygen and the exhaustion that it produces in the wider body, we get rid of that stress-related hormone cocktail. This is how it was planned by nature. That's what these hormones are for: action. Afterwards the hormones dissipate because now they've done their duty, making us *act*. At the end of the tune of the stress symphony in our brain stem, the release of endorphins is also pre-programmed, which gives us a comforting feeling of relief. This is the ointment as our body shifts into a recovery state, managed by the final verses of the stress symphony. This endorphin response is also the reason for the 'runner's high',[27] a state of elation that some people experience when they run, pushing their body to the limits. (Not all runners and athletes experience runner's high; studies show only about two thirds of them do,[28] and even that comes with drawbacks, but more on that later.)

Neuroendocrinological research shows that the stress symphony can start reverberating through our body for many reasons. It may be because we really spot a lion or an adversary in the wild, or because we've sat for too long before a continuously rising inbox, an aggressive colleague, or upcoming assignments.

For most of us, continuing to sit in a situation where cortisol is high in our blood and our body is ready to run, lungs filled with air, legs pumped with oxygenated blood, won't help us, even if we are doing mindfulness meditation. Importantly, these stress hormones, like cortisol, are neurotoxic (unhealthy for our neurons) if in our body for too long. The body basically attacks itself after a while, and this makes our thoughts spin even further out of control.

Mind Control

Never forget that we have a brutal survival artist between our ears, as much as a consummate poet. The delicate meanderings of the prefrontal cortices are preoccupied with symbolic thought, creativity, abstraction and ideas, but they depend on survival mechanisms that function according to some very binary, basic premises like reward or punishment, like or dislike, yes or no, friend or foe, threat or safety, fight or flight.

What enters our senses is very quickly evaluated according to these opposites by basic sensory systems of the brain and brain stem.[29] There is no avoiding that. Depending on the outcome of this first, fast and unconscious processing, the information is then sent on for further processing.[30,31]

These fast and basic systems are all about 'me, me, me': safety and survival – act first, think later. That's how they kept us safe throughout evolution, in a difficult and dangerous terrain. In our modern world of abundance, however, you may see the advantage of learning to think first, but due to how these basic systems work, the only way we can achieve this is by changing our behaviour. These basic systems are simply too fast to catch up with our thoughts.

The Resting Brain

This brings us to why the activation patterns in our body are linked to what is going on in the mind. We've already discussed the close connection between the body and the brain. So how exactly does the mind fit in? In psychology, taken really broadly, the *mind* refers to our conscious experience. It's what we think and feel: our perceptions, memories, beliefs. It's something ephemeral, not unlike the hard-to-grasp-concept of the 'soul'. There are vast research fields across philosophy, anthropology, psychology, neuroscience and even computer science that are grappling with the concept of consciousness. For the purposes of finding a practical solution, let's simplify. In short, the music of our body-orchestra, at least in part, creates our thoughts. And our thoughts may dance gracefully to that music, or they may not. That depends on whether the music is a gentle, harmonious hum or a stress symphony. Do you remember the pink elephants, those thoughts we cannot let go of? A stress symphony is likely to make unpleasant pink elephant thoughts start practising pirouettes and other loops to that tune, stealing our concentration. This is when we are most desperate to switch off and just stop thinking for a moment.

It was when I was ruminating about my own inability to switch off my unwanted thoughts that I came across a paper about the 'resting brain'. In 2001, Marcus Raichle and his colleagues from the Washington University School of Medicine, St Louis, used functional magnetic resonance imagery to scan participants' brains.[32,33] And they did something slightly unusual for neuroscientists. Usually, neuroscientists analyse the brain's activity while participants are doing a specific task. Raichle and colleagues, instead, analysed the brain activity of their participants while they were *not* doing a task, studying them while they were *resting* between tasks.

The results were astonishing.

When participants were apparently doing nothing at all, their brains weren't doing nothing. On the contrary. The results from the brain scans showed that *resting* is very much a behaviour too, and our brain remains very active. The researchers found that, during rest, a specific network of brain regions was notably active.

Raichle and colleagues nicknamed this network the brain's *default mode network* because further research showed that this network was always active, even when participants were asked to rest, and the network seemed 'on' by default.

Imagine the default mode network like a golden network of nerve cells inside your brain. A network that consists of interconnected parts of the brain, pulsing with activity while we are resting, and letting our mind wander. Raichle and his colleagues, and many researchers since then, have shown that this network touches on brain regions that are active when we think about ourselves and on different brain regions that are active when we think about others. Glittering bursts of activity also span the regions that the brain needs to create imagery, our sense of self, and to help us remember the past and plan for the future. Remember the last time you sat and listened to your favourite song? Your thoughts were connecting you with the present moment, as well as travelling back and forth in time, imagining situations, people, and yourself, all at once? This was your default mode network at play. And now hold your breath – researchers have found out that when we contemplate artworks that we really like – the default mode network is *on*.[34-36]

→

Our brain is never off, even when we're resting. So, trying to 'just stop thinking' is doomed from the outset. There is this beautiful music reverberating through our body, brain – and consequently, our thoughts – all the time.

So what is it doing? We know that about 20 per cent of our body's overall energy is nibbled away by the brain and, when at rest, the energy expenditure of the brain is only 5 per cent less, so not only is the resting brain still active, it is still doing a lot of work.

It is probably busy creating what we experience as 'consciousness'. But that's not all. A study in 2008 by Fei Du and colleagues from the University of Minnesota Medical School provided another tentative answer to this question . . . housekeeping.[37] The brain needs a large amount of energy for *neural communication* – to send neural signals during its various functions via complicated biochemical processes – but it also needs a lot of energy for maintenance. According to the authors, one third of the entire expenditure of the brain goes to housekeeping. Research shows that large parts of the brain's energy expenditure go to eliminate toxins, repair damaged nerve cells, get rid of cell debris, etc. When we allow our brains to exist in this state it could be like spring-cleaning a house, or opening a window on a winter's day to let a fresh draft get rid of stale air in a room.

These are recent discoveries, but it is possible that the default mode network has a restorative function for our brain. This idea finds some support in the finding that the network isn't functioning properly in the brains of people who suffer from depression, Alzheimer's, Parkinson's, schizophrenia and epilepsy. In some of these conditions, the default mode network is hyperactive, while in others, it isn't active enough. In people with depression and anxiety disorders, the default mode network's activity is unstable, or abnormal, and often some of the network's subsystems' interactions are disrupted. This clinical evidence suggests that our brains need this network to be activated regularly, and in the right kind of way, in order to function healthily. It also means that 'switching off' our brain would be a really bad idea.

→

If we can't switch off our brain, what are we to do when our thoughts start looping? We now know that they are often caused by letting our body-orchestra play symphonies like the stress symphony for too long. The good news is we can combat this torment if we choose the right *behaviour*. It's all about choosing the behaviour that will help us change songs, instead of trying to 'switch off' the thoughts with our mental biceps.

Throughout human history different techniques for controlling rampaging pink elephants and restless minds have fallen in and out of favour. Like mindfulness, these techniques presuppose that we can work on our thoughts alone. For many of us, however, this is a bit like trying to put a harness on a pink elephant and make it do as we want. Pink elephants are not a 'thing' that we can control. If we try, they'll slip through our fingers like smoke, because they are exactly that: the smoky fog of our thoughts tinted pink. If we don't have the right behaviour to channel our thoughts into a different direction than the one that is hurting us, attempts to control where our mind goes are usually in vain.

Let's take a look at three of these classic mind-control techniques and why, from a neuroscientific point of view, they won't work. Unlike mindfulness (which works for some people and not for others), these techniques for mind control simply do not, and cannot, work because of how our brain functions. The important point to keep in mind is that we're seeking a behaviour that will allow important restorative processes in body and brain to take place without triggering other effects that might be counterproductive to peace of mind, and these next methods won't help us do this.

Suppression

In the 1984 *Ghostbusters* movie there is a moment when Gozer, the God of Destruction, is about to arrive on earth to destroy it. However, the God of Destruction has a weakness: he needs his victims to imagine him first. He cannot destroy people who don't have him clearly visible in their mind, they have to *visualise* him. So the God of Destruction first appears as an immaterial voice ordering the Ghostbusters to 'choose the shape of their destructor'. The audience of course knows how destruction can be avoided: just think of nothing! However, you, dear reader, know better by now; thinking of nothing is impossible. Once a thought – pink elephants and Gods of Destruction alike – has been conjured up in our mind, it is here to stay. So when Ray thinks of the Stay Puft Marshmallow Man from his childhood, Gozer simply materialises in the shape of a giant Stay Puft Marshmallow Man, spreading destruction at every step.

The social psychologist Daniel Wegner and his colleagues from Trinity University in San Antonio conducted a series of experiments about thought control.[38,39] They asked participants to try not to think. Perhaps unsurprisingly, people couldn't do it. In the past thirty years, social psychologists have uncovered a whole string of evidence that shows that it is even more difficult to think of nothing if we tell the person *what* we want them to stop thinking about.

Although I used pink elephants in the introduction, this struggle is known as *The White Bear Problem* in social psychology.[40,41] The research was inspired by a story about the Russian writer Fyodor Dostoevsky, who as a teenager played a trick on his little brother. Tired of looking after his brother, Dostoevsky told him to raise one hand in the air. The challenge was that he could only take it down the moment he managed to stop thinking about a white polar bear.[42] The poor boy stood there with his hand heroically raised for hours. When the hand finally came down, it was through exhaustion. This polar bear was haunting Dostoevsky's poor little brother's mind until the end of his days. So if you have some daunting, painful or otherwise unwanted thoughts in your head, the very fact that you are aware of them will make it impossible to just stop thinking about them. The moment we ask our brain to stop thinking about something, it will do everything it can to comply. For this, it divides itself in two. One part stops thinking about 'it'. The trouble is that the other part keeps checking on the first part, making sure that it is not starting to think about 'it' again. In the case of Dostoevsky's little brother, the task of *not thinking of a white bear* activated the pattern for *white bear* in the language systems of his brain. At the same time, his memory systems were reminding him what a white bear looks like. On the other hand, the executive control systems of his brain (the prefrontal cortex) and perhaps his decision-making systems (regions known as the orbitofrontal cortex and ventromedial prefrontal cortex), were activated with an order to *suppress the white bear.*

This means that when we attempt to suppress a thought, our brain needs to activate (and maintain), both the systems representing the thought that it should suppress (via the language and memory systems), and the systems for suppression (executive control and decision-making systems). Do you see the dilemma? The suppression behaviour keeps catapulting the unwanted thought back and forth through our awareness.

Avoidance

Often, when we realise it's not possible to suppress a thought, we try the next best thing . . . we run from it. We all have our own techniques for avoidance: we work more, we exercise, we party, we help others, we watch one cliff-hanger soap opera episode after the other, gamble another round, or we clean or organise obsessively. Busy-ness is a very common, if entirely useless, approach to combatting pink elephants. We find ourselves fleeing whatever it is, but soon realise we can't. These behaviours won't dissolve pink elephant assemblies in our mind, nor resolve a task waiting for us; our thoughts will still be there waiting to assault us, when we come back up for air.

By indulging in avoidance behaviours, we ignore the fact that the thought we are trying to run away from travels with us in the language and memory systems in our brain, no matter how fast we run or how long we scroll. Getting busy to avoid your pink elephants is a bit like getting on a merry-go-round at a funfair. While you're spinning round and round, providing your brain with one pleasure burst after the other, your pink elephant thoughts are simply squeezing into the backseat of the wagon. They're not gone and they'll rush back to the forefront of your mind as soon as you get off the ride.

Psychologists refer to these types of behaviours as avoidance behaviours – procrastination, psychological flight or denial – and there is a huge amount of research about why people do it, and why it doesn't work.

Avoidance behaviours give us a little (temporary) respite. This is because they tend to be quite frantic (like a merry-go-round), so they produce something similar to a stress response in our body, with loads of little dopamine kicks. As I explained earlier, the stress response narrows our attention to a tunnel and impairs our memory. So avoidance behaviours leave us – for a short period of time – in a blissful forgetful state, focused on the here and now.

Let me explain one beat more. The symphony that avoidance behaviours ask our body-orchestra to play is a demanding one. Many different processes are running at the same time, and they are mostly completely unrelated to one another. Maybe we start exercising, but then we start browsing social media because we have the phone next to us on the mat. While we swipe and like, we suddenly remember work, so we start composing an email, and from there we're one click away from Amazon. Back to the mat, in between the push-ups and the squats, we spy that cupboard in the corner that needs tidying.

All of this may be keeping our minds away from whatever we're hoping to avoid, but it's chaos. It requires performance of the highest skill, releasing different neurohormones related to all of these various and unrelated behaviours. As a result, our internal systems look much as they do during the stress symphony, except that unlike natural stress, this avoidance symphony has no end. Workaholic, helpaholic, and cleanaholic behaviours are not better for us just because they have an apparently positive output. The avoidance symphony drowns our body in a broth of clashing hormones and other messenger substances. This wears down our veins and tires our organs, and the moment we pause to recover from this chaos, the unwanted thought pops straight back to the front of our mind.

Distraction

When they had verified that avoidance didn't work, social psychologist Daniel Wegner and his colleagues attempted to find another remedy to the white bear problem: they went on to research the usefulness of distractions. A distraction is when we try *thinking* of something other than what is bothering us.

The basic premise of the researchers' new experiments was this: If we want to stop thinking about something, say pink elephants in our case, then simply set your mind to think *of something else*. Yet – as you probably know by now, your mental biceps won't do the job. Because your mind doesn't have biceps. The force to flex your biceps is in your body; and you can only work them with your body, through your *behaviour*. I'll explain what works, but first, let's watch Wegner's participants fail at flexing their mental biceps.

Daniel Wegner and his colleagues told their participants to *not* think about a white polar bear and to think about a red sports car *instead*. What they found was this: their research participants found it incredibly difficult to glue their mind to the new object or thought that the researchers had proposed. Their minds simply bounced back and forth. Some of them told the researcher that a red sports car simply wasn't very interesting for them and, therefore, their mind somehow didn't know what to do with it and the white polar bear kept inserting itself into their thoughts – for some, even after the experiment had ended! What the researchers hadn't considered was that the brain can never be still. From the moment we're born, our brains have basic objectives: to move, to explore, to learn – and to enjoy. As the research participants in Wegner's study threw their thoughts from one part of the semantic language network in their brain (*white polar bear*) to another one (*red sports car*) their mind couldn't just stay there as it was told.

To keep our attention on something (for example, a red sports car), our brain needs a motivation to do so, a reward. Think of all the things you think about – they all have an intrinsic reward for you, something that attracts your attention to that thought. And remember what some of the participants in Wegner's experiments said: it was simply too boring for them to keep thinking of a red sports car. The brain needs little dopamine showers for our attention to stay glued to something. If it's too boring, we'll struggle to keep our attention motivated to stay. What we focus on needs to matter to us. The brain loves emotions, it feeds on them, even the negative ones. The reason for this probably lies in our evolutionary history. Of course, no one would admit that they love drama, feeling sad, fearful, disgusted, or that they like watching those emotions in other people. However, the viewing numbers of YouTube and Facebook videos of precisely that kind tell a different story. Our attention is immediately trapped when there's some drama looming.

In a dangerous prehistoric world, it was a huge advantage to be able to detect quickly if someone else was fearful, angry, sad, disgusted or otherwise in a drama because whatever was causing it could also be dangerous for us. Hence our brain developed these threat-detection mechanisms in the systems of our brain that we don't have so much control over. Our conscious mind can estimate that what we're watching doesn't contain any direct threat for us; however, that doesn't prevent our brain-stem systems from gluing our attention to the drama.

Hence, if there is a thought that has some juicy dramatic emotion attached to it, our mind will latch on to it and stay there. You might say that a white polar bear isn't particularly exciting, so why should our mind latch back on to it? Well, the white polar bear itself may not be exciting for the brain, but a *prohibition* is. The forbidden fruit metaphor is a big thing in Western thought because it illustrates precisely this: our brain craves anything forbidden. If you really want someone to think about something endlessly, prohibit it. Prohibitions are dramatic, and hugely alluring to our brain – just think of the last time you heard a parent prohibit something to their offspring, and the drama that ensued. Prohibitions have a special effect on the brain; they can make any thought irresistible, especially if it has something to do with our basic needs like, food, sex, status, shelter. Forget that doughnut! No sex before marriage! But even completely abstract thoughts like a white polar bear can haunt us forever if someone just forbids it. When you drag your mind towards another thought, some mental image that you've conjured up to replace the forbidden fruit, your mind hits the new thought . . . and immediately rebounds like a ping pong ball.

Your Working Memory

Trying to suppress, stop, prohibit, or distract ourselves from thoughts doesn't work. Very few people can successfully divert unwanted thoughts with the force of their mind alone (among them are a small number of experienced mindfulness meditators). When we try not to think about something, we're trying to ignore our body-orchestra. As we know by now, it's going to play no matter how pointedly we look in the other direction.

The effect of this can also be summarised by what psychologists call the *Zeigarnik effect*.[43,44] Early in the twentieth century, the psychologist Bluma Zeigarnik conducted a series of experiments about a curious effect. People remember details of *unfinished* tasks better than details of finished tasks. Unfinished tasks seem to load our working memory and keep it occupied until we finalise it. And this is not necessarily a good thing.[45] Research shows that unfinished tasks cause bad sleep quality in employees, and may contribute to pathological worrying.[46,47] In one study, tasks that were left unfinished by employees before the weekend caused them to ruminate and struggle to fall asleep.[48] Bad sleep quality was the consequence.[49] So – *what* you load your working memory with matters. Soap opera cliff-hanger endings use precisely this effect. They leave the story unfinished, and with that, use your brain's need to solve and finish tasks to keep you hooked inside the story.

Your working memory keeps catapulting the contents and the drama of the soap through your conscious mind in perpetuity – until you finally click 'next' to see the subsequent episode.

Direct Your Mind, but Don't Try to Trick It –
It's Cleverer Than You

So, what we need to do is to *direct* our mind, because flexing our mental biceps trying to control it via our thoughts alone won't work. It won't 'stop'. Our only hope is to keep our mind *moving*; but to make sure that it is in the right direction, we need to find alternative behaviours to direct our body-orchestra.

You should now be familiar with your body-orchestra, and the intimate connection between body, brain and mind. You understand it's impossible to stop thinking or avoid, suppress or forbid a thought once it's in there. Just remember that the Zeigarnik effect will make sure all is rehearsed over and over again in your memory and language systems, and will load your working memory, catapulting what you least want in and out of your awareness, like a ping pong ball. So if we know that the key to a calm, happy, peaceful mind is the right behaviour, and we know that we have the power to choose that behaviour, it should be a straightforward fix, right? If only it was that easy!

2. Mind Hooks

On the Isle of Corfu in the Ionian Sea, hidden away behind massive stone walls, there is a garden. It is the garden of Palace Achilleon, created in 1889 by Empress Elisabeth of Austria, who many of us know as Princess Sisi. In the grip of a terrible, inescapable grief, Princess Sisi boarded a boat to Corfu. She was fleeing toxic court life and a great personal tragedy. Her son, Crown Prince Rudolf, had killed himself and his mistress when faced with the reality that they would never be allowed to be together. She arrived in Greece in pursuit of change, and a cure for her tormented mind, but no matter how far she travelled from the court, her mind remained stuck on looping thoughts of grief and betrayal, and terrible memories she'd rather forget.

Floods of Negative Thoughts

Imagine that you are in the grip of unbearable grief. Whatever it is, allow yourself to picture it there, conjure it up from your memory, grasp it with your heart, hold on to it. You're so incredibly deep into that grief that you cannot think about anything but *it*. When we experience sorrow and other negative feelings, the parts of our brain that are responsible for physical pain ignite themselves. To the brain, emotional pain is as strong as physical pain. The pain symphony, like so many other symphonies in our mind that aren't so pleasing, evolved to keep us safe. As we touched on in Chapter 1, the pain system is linked to our memory systems. This connection ensures we remember what behaviour caused us pain or sorrow in the past so that we can avoid it in the future. This works by selectively activating memories that match pain; which is why we specifically remember sad experiences and feelings when we are already experiencing pain.

I once met a man called Erol, who works as a translator for the military of a European nation, and was stationed in Hatay after the devastating earthquake in Southeast Turkey and Western Syria in spring 2023. He helped European doctors and Turkish victims of the earthquake communicate in the field hospitals. His messages during his month there were deeply sad.

'I've seen people who lost their spouses and children, their mums and dads. I've seen the emptiness, the loneliness in them. They felt their bodies didn't belong to them anymore. How unfair they thought all this is cause they're still alive and left here alone.'

This testimony from the frontline of suffering is straight out of the trauma literature. Depersonalisation and derealisation are other common symptoms of overwhelming grief. It is likely a flight or fight reaction of our mind. Faced with an overpowering threat, the brain alienates itself from the source of suffering – and if the suffering is in the body and in the world around you, well, that's what your brain alienates you from. And, while getting back into that body and that reality is the only way forward – giving your body new, positive experiences of trust and wellbeing – this is also where the guilt resides. Survivor's guilt is a term that is well known in communities that have suffered, and it was first described in the 1960s in the clinical psychology realm. 'Survivor's syndrome' was something therapists diagnosed over and again in the survivors of the concentration camps in Germany. Research with victims of terrorism, natural disasters, combat, accidents, etc, has shown that about 60 per cent of survivors suffer from survivor's guilt.[1]

What is more, because the brain stem is an ancient system, it doesn't always restrict this process to strictly sorrowful experiences. It is more a good-bad, like-dislike kind of operation. So sometimes sad, excited, angry and fearful thoughts are all rolled into one. Even just excitement can get the wheel spinning in our mind. And this co-activation of the memory system kicks in when we're in emotional turmoil, flooding us with negative thoughts at the strangest of times.

As we know now, suppressing, avoiding, prohibiting or distracting ourselves from this carousel of negative thoughts simply does not work. For Princess Sisi, undertaking an ocean voyage in an attempt to outrun her pain was probably a good first step to get away from a terrible situation, but as an attempt to manage her thoughts? The voyage was doomed from the outset. What she needed – and what we all need when our thoughts loop – is to find the right behaviour to direct our body-orchestra to activate *change* in our body and brain . . .

Choosing the 'right' behaviours, however, is difficult for a very specific reason. We have an Achilles heel, or rather, the brain does. Achilles was the greatest warrior in Ancient Greece, unstoppable and unbeatable . . . except for a single vulnerable spot on his heel, which ultimately became his downfall. Similarly, our brains are strong and awe-inspiring things, designed to survive a harsh pre-historic world. But in our modern world, that same cave-brain, especially the basic systems of our brain-stem jukebox that play automatically, has a dangerous tendency to urge us to choose the wrong behaviours that shatter our peace of mind even more. These behaviours hook our mind because they are addictive and so deliciously moreish. They stimulate the brain-stem jukebox's songs, which makes them so hard to control. This is our Achilles heel.

Two Neural Systems That Regulate Our Decisions

In Chapter 1, we used our fists to imagine different parts of our brain. The limbic system is the second layer of that fist. This evolutionarily ancient system is incredibly important for our ability to choose between different options. Roughly speaking, it helps us to 'feel' the value of each option, to then choose the 'best'. It does this in a wonderfully orchestrated way that lies mostly outside of our awareness.[2-6] What we don't realise is that different layers of our brain engage in a philosophic debate of a sort each time we have a choice: should we choose the quick pleasure, or wait, and build something that gives us a much bigger reward later?

→

As far as pleasure and meaning are concerned, roughly speaking, there were two schools of philosophers in Ancient Greece. School 1 were the hedonists, who sought happiness through pleasure-seeking. School 2 were the eudemonists, led by Epicure, who sought happiness through meaning-making. It so happens that these two schools of thought quite clearly map onto two interrelated systems of our limbic system that are as diametrically opposed as these two schools of philosophy were. One is basically constantly shouting, 'I want pleasure NOW,' while the other is cautioning, 'No, wait, defer gratification, and later, later you will have even more satisfaction. If you wait now, you'll be rewarded big time, you will have a meaningful life!'

Inside our brain, the first system includes the amygdala, the posterior ventromedial prefrontal cortex (VMPFC), and the striatum, including also the nucleus accumbens. They're the hedonic hotspots of our brain. The second system includes the insula, the anterior VMPFC, hippocampus, dorsolateral prefrontal cortex (DLPFC), and the anterior cingulate (ACC).[7–9] This second system connects with the meaning-making parts of our brain – much like the eudemonist philosophers in Ancient Greece.

I could draw you a picture, to illustrate where these different parts are in our brain. However, that will make us none the wiser when it comes to balancing out how we feel. It's not like with dancing, for example, where I can tell you which body part to focus on to make your movement more harmonious. I can tell you to make sure that, generally, when you walk, you should focus on rolling your foot from the inside (heel) to the outside of your foot (toes), and not outside-in. The former (inside-out) makes you more stable in your dance moves. If the final part of your step has you 'lean' on the full fan of your toes, that's much better than going towards the big toe, which is just one toe to rely on for balance. By describing the physical parts of your body and how the movement feels, you can focus on those parts and use the words to guide your movement. The brain is different. Calling out brain parts won't help us change how we feel. That's why we're trying to get at these brain parts indirectly, through our behaviour and sometimes by envisioning them through metaphors.

Let's think of these two schools of philosophy and of the two brain systems as two camps. Two divisive and quarrelling camps of philosophers that argue a lot. The philosophers lived in different parts of ancient Athens; one up-town (the eudemonists) and one down-town (the hedonists), and the two neural systems are located in two different parts of the brain; the hedonic one is deep down, the meaning-making one a little higher up – but they are all part of one reward system.

In Ancient Greece, there were narrow, earthy paths between the two camps. The more frequently the philosophers walked on the paths between the two camps to visit each other and discuss their philosophies, the wider and more street-like the paths became – today they are motorways. It's similar for our brain's reward system. Its sub-systems are connected via neural pathways, [10–12] and they exchange information between them[13,14] and with the homeostatic systems.[15] We're born with those systems and pathways in place, but what I want to propose to you here is that you can have some say in how these systems jam with each other, and maybe also in how strong the pathways *between* the two neural systems are. With the behaviours that you choose to do in the world, you can take advantage of your brain's neuroplasticity[16] and strengthen your neural pathways. Now venture a guess about why this book is called the *pathway* to flow.

Connections

Stay with this basic idea: Camp 1, the hedonists, are concerned with maximising immediate reward. Camp 2, the eudemonists, are concerned with maximising future reward and prosperity. Camp 1 sits deeper in the brain, closer to the brain-stem jukebox and is more edgy, compelling us to approach or to avoid whatever presents itself to our senses, depending on its usefulness for our physiological state.[17–19] For this, it triggers the neurochemistry that regulates our autonomous nervous system. We'll be ready to react in no time.[20–23] These are not very conscious processes, which explains why it matters what we expose our senses to.

Camp 2's circuits receive input from homeostatic systems in our body (for example, about lack of nutrients or fluids, sleep, etc). Information is funnelled up to the insula, and via our interoception (the sense of our body from within), we may become aware of it. Some of the information that Camp 2 has access to is from Camp 1. Importantly, however, Camp 2 links the information that it receives from all these sources to previous experiences, memories and the possible long-term value and consequences – this is how meaning about something that enters our senses is created in our brain. Camp 2 will also push us to action or inaction, but it will do so 'all things considered'. This is how we're able to defer gratification, wait for a bigger reward later, and ultimately build a more lasting experience of pleasure. This is how a simple sensory pattern that our senses perceive can suddenly become meaningful.[17,24–26]

The Three Mind Hooks

We need our reward system for our body to survive, and we need it for learning new things, to feel intrinsically rewarded, and we need it for enjoying what I call 'pleasure-plus' behaviours – behaviours that give us both delicious immediate pleasures *and* lasting joy in life. Therefore, the reward system and its connections are key to creating our pathway to flow. However, this same reward system of ours is also involved in rumination and in bad habits. And rumination is a bad 'habit' for our brain. The good news is that, even if this is sometimes very difficult, we can unlearn bad habits, and forge better ones. Remember, it's all about turning our weaknesses into strengths. You can use your reward system to create your pathway to flow, or, simply put, you can use it to chase quick highs and end up ruminating.

With that in mind, I would like to introduce you to three behaviours that hook our minds. They are behaviours that we can choose to do, but we should know that they have the power to lure our body-orchestra into seemingly inescapable ruminative loops, because they feel so gratifying – at first. And that's the trap.

Mind Hook Behaviour 1: Competitiveness

In early 2020, a study about stress hormones and football hit the headlines.[27] During the 2014 FIFA World Cup, Martha Newsom and her colleagues from Oxford University collected saliva samples from Brazilian fans while they were watching games. In the lab, they measured the concentration of the stress hormone, cortisol, in the samples. They found that the spectators of the match had dangerous levels of cortisol in their body from just *watching* their team lose. During the epic loss against Germany, researchers found that fans' cortisol skyrocketed to a point that would actually increase the risk of falling ill after watching the match.

Competitive Sports

Football is the world's most popular sport and a number of research groups have rallied to investigate its effect on cortisol levels in our blood. What symphony does this popular behaviour direct our body-orchestra to play? In 2017, Maamer Slimani and his colleagues from the National Centre of Medicine and Science in Sport in Tunisia analysed seventeen peer-reviewed articles.[28] The researchers compared players' and spectators' cortisol levels while they engaged in two different types of games: competitive and friendly tournaments. The scientists also differentiated between situations where teams were winning versus losing the game. The outcome of this analysis was bad news: cortisol levels increase in players and spectators during *all* matches, even if they are just friendly games. In addition, results from several studies show that if a match is *lost,* cortisol skyrockets even further.

A high level of cortisol means that our immune response is switched from what immunologists call a *Th-1 response* ('cellular immunity) to a *Th-2 response* ('humoral immunity').[29,30] How this works is all rather complicated, but we can stay with this basic idea: the Th-1 immune response is 'on' when we're in a normal state of relaxation. It keeps us safe from viruses and other pathogens. Th-2, however, is activated by the stress symphony in our brain stem. It's designed to keep us safe if we're in a fight or flight situation.

When we are in immediate danger of injury, the Th-2 immune response is ready to protect the outer shell of our body if we suffer a wound to our skin, or we need to otherwise protect the body from invasion of pathogens from the outside world through mucosities and orifices. It produces a barrier. You may have noticed that you sneeze more or develop skin problems during prolonged periods of stress. This may just be your body setting up a line of defence against possible invasion from the outside.

The stress symphony controls the switch of our immune response from Th-1 to Th-2. This is perfect, if we really are in physical danger, but as the study of Brazilian football fans showed, we can activate that stress symphony (and flick on Th-2) just by *watching* competitive sport. One study even found that fans of competitive football, baseball and rugby matches are at risk for cardiovascular events, especially when their team is on the losing side.

Besides the negative health effects for the individual, there is another sad side to this. Remember what we said earlier about excitement leading to a co-activation of all sorts of negative memories in our brain? You won't be surprised to learn then that this evidence of heightened stress hormones is likely linked to the aggressive behaviours that are much too often observed around sport by both winning and losing teams. There is a line of research that has shown how explosive the aggression is that builds up during a match, and how it persists beyond the match. Several research teams have looked at US and UK police records. According to these records, on days of large sporting events, the incidence of reported domestic violence incidents increases by around 10 per cent.[31,32] Sure, domestic violence has also been found to increase with events like natural disasters, economic crises, hot weather and public holidays. The point is that some (though not all[32,33]) types of sporting events can have this effect *too*. Cortisol in blood means we get hot-headed and we lash out – an effect called 'arousal misattribution', which we will discuss later (see page 61). Sometimes this has devastating consequences for those closest to us, and for society as a whole.

What does this have to do with flow? These studies show us that if the behaviour you choose has strongly competitive elements, meaning you can *lose* something (a match, money, status, etc) from *doing* it, that behaviour is likely to result in increased stress hormone levels. When the brain receives the message that there is cortisol in the blood, it will trigger a state of high alert. This state can automatically activate negative memories and, as a result, we interpret what we see in a negative way.[34-36] We're likely to leave with minds full of pink elephants, ready to attack our thoughts the moment we sit down to work or try to fall asleep.

In the introduction to this book, I promised to show you how the arts – be it through artistic practice or as a spectator of the arts – can be *your* personal pathway to regular moments of refreshing experiences of flow. But, will any artistic practice or consumption do? No. Arts practice and consumption are behaviours, and it is about choosing the right one if what you want is to free yourself from intrusive thoughts.

Competitive Arts

When co-writing my first book, *Dancing is the Best Medicine*,[37] I was in a conflict of conscience. The message of the book was to highlight all the wonderful health effects of dancing. And the title definitely reflected that. Yet, this title suggests that dancing is, regardless of how you engage in this behaviour, the best 'medicine'. Here I was, a former dancer, with a broken spine and a broken soul, advocating that dancing is the best medicine. I am profoundly grateful that with this book, *The Pathway to Flow*, I've been given the opportunity to tell you, finally, the whole story.

Here, there's one bit of research that is particularly helpful in showcasing how competitiveness affects us: Nicolas Rohleder and his colleagues from Dresden University were interested in measuring the health effects of dancing, so they attended training sessions of ballroom dancers and set up back-stage during competitions.[38] The researchers were interested in whether or not there was a difference between a competitive situation and a training situation in terms of the dancers' cortisol levels. After having read the first part of this section, you will now have a hunch about what the researchers found. The measures of cortisol on the day of the competition showed extremely high levels in the dancers after the competition. And this couldn't be due to the physical exertion of the movement itself, because the researchers had also collected cortisol on a normal training day, when no such increase was recorded. These findings were replicated by another group of researchers. Eleanor Quested and her colleagues from the University of Birmingham also measured cortisol levels, this time of ballet dancers after a solo performance for an exam. As compared to a normal training day, the dancers' cortisol levels had skyrocketed after dancing on the exam day.[39]

In a third study, another group of scientists was interested in the stress-hormone-health effects of dancing. Tudor Vrinceanu and his colleagues from the University of Montreal invited participants to practise one of three different activities for three months.[40] One group of participants took part in a dance class three times a week, another group did spinning, and a third group just followed their normal schedules. The researchers measured cortisol levels at predetermined times after the dance and spinning sessions throughout the three months, just like the other researchers had done. The results surprised the researchers. They found that dancers' cortisol levels fell significantly after the training sessions, spinners skyrocketed, and the control group showed no change.

What was going on here?

What the researchers of the first two studies hadn't considered was that competition itself is incredibly stressful for our mind and body. It isn't about the activity in which we're competing, it's the competing itself that makes the difference. Competition ignites a particular type of fear in the part of our brain that scientists call 'the social brain': the fear of losing. And we know from a ton of neuroscientific research: the fear symphony makes cortisol levels skyrocket, because it activates the fight or flight system in the brain.

As soon as there is a competitive element in your practice, your artistic practice is unlikely to work as a pathway to flow.

A Threat to the System

The social brain is located on top of the brain-stem jukebox, with very strong connections to the basic processes. This is because 'being social' helped us to survive in a dangerous prehistoric world: we were able to live in large social groups that protected us. So it's not only official competition that increases cortisol levels. Human brains are naturally primed to seek to overcome social adversaries – even imagined ones – and that can make us terribly judgemental and competitive.

These automatic social processes often happen outside of our awareness and come with a pitfall. On the one hand, evolutionarily speaking, when we were still living in caves and had to struggle for survival each day, this competitive drive helped us survive. On the other hand, however, these basic instincts push us to be competitive, even when there is no reason for being competitive. Today we're competitive *for fun*, not because we need it to survive. Winning, rising to power, glory, activate our reward system. We like it. But it won't give us a calm mind.

As we've already covered, our brain has not changed significantly since then and carries with it all the same virtues, and all the same vices. What others think about us matters tremendously to our brain. Our brain perceives glances and body movements from others automatically. And *losing* is, above all, a social phenomenon. And it's a threat to the system. If there was no one around, it wouldn't matter if we fail, we'd just carry on practising what we're doing until we do it well. However, if our practice doesn't happen outside the 'social gaze', or within a space where non-judgement and kind consideration is the norm, losing is risky. Psychologists studying this have identified what they call *social comparison processes*, which cover everything from jealously admiring someone's beauty, comparing what they have to what we have, to FOMO. They happen in families, at work, in sports and, yes, also in the arts if we let competitiveness take over. We evolved to take particular note of each other's successes. Even in today's world of abundance, our cave-brain is often jealous of others: their beauty, their possessions, their skill, their happiness; we want it, and our first impulse is to compete. This is why social competitions are a very stressful environment for our body-orchestra, even if the competition is part of a recreational activity like dancing, running, or even yoga that, in principle, should make us feel zen.

I think this is a good moment to say that it is not that I want to stop you from being competitive. Being competitive serves a purpose in our lives. In life and in business, we may need to strive towards a goal, we may have to compete with others to win money, admiration or status. Some striving is, of course, a good thing. Unsurprisingly, throughout our lives, we're taught to compete, to strive, to always attempt to outperform others, and ourselves. What we're not taught, however, is that too much competition, too much focus on winning, and on *extrinsic* rewards, can be perilous in the long run. The downside is a restless mind.

To find flow, competitiveness will be in your way because of what it does to your body and mind. Any behaviour can become stressful when it becomes a competition, even dance, or any other art form, but there is one key difference that sets the arts apart. Some behaviours are *inherently* competitive, and thus inherently stressful, whereas the arts don't *need* to be, as we will see in the next chapters.

What we can do is choose to avoid high-stakes competition, and try to stay away from situations in which we will be driven to compare ourselves (or our hair, our salaries, our bodies, our clothes), but we cannot always control our broader environments. Others may force behaviours on us that make our body and brain ring out in competitive battle songs and we can't always escape them – whether it's in the office or at a family Christmas or Diwali celebration – even if we'd like to. Most of us have experienced a competitive environment we couldn't control and couldn't escape. During the Covid pandemic, social media turned toxic with debates over infection numbers, hospitalisation rates, vaccination, and so on. Wherever you stood, the heat of anxiety, anger and depressive rumination was as unavoidable as the blame and condemnation as we all competed to be *right*. The endless loops of these debates, without any final insight or relief, were pure rumination. This behaviour (whether participating in the debate ourselves or passively consuming it) directed our body-orchestra into terrifying symphonies, and the neurobiological cocktail it conjured up was harming our bodies and our minds. Consider this when checking social media to 'switch off' – it is unlikely to free you from unwanted thoughts. Stress isn't a nice feeling. So we may ask: why are we so drawn to competitive behaviours that create stress? Because of the reward. Because of the dizzying pleasure kick in the reward systems of our brain that we get *when we win*.

So what are we to do? If we are programmed to seek out competition and are surrounded by endless opportunities to do so, are we doomed to be stressed forever with judgemental pink elephants spinning in ruminative loops? Must we abandon our favourite football team and spend time only with people we feel no desire to compare ourselves to? Of course not.

As I said, competition is not, in itself, harmful. In fact, practising competitiveness with games and sports hones our ability to strive towards a goal, deal with adversity and adversaries. The world is not perfect, and competition for resources is a fact of life. When we compete, competition hormones, otherwise known as stress hormones, jump into our blood. They help us to strive higher, better, faster. Competitiveness can be a good thing – but it can tip, as it happened to the football fans.

It is only becoming *hooked* on competition that's the problem.

Competition is a behaviour and we must be mindful of the fact that our body is experiencing competition even when we are engaging in behaviours we don't think of as competitive. It's when we fail to acknowledge the heightened stress hormones pumping through our blood, and fail to give ourselves a reprieve from them, that we run into trouble. We know by now that we are not powerless. When we acknowledge that this stress symphony is playing, we can make active choices to direct our body-orchestra into healthier symphonies and free up our mind-space.

So here is the first key to our pathway to flow: if we want our body-orchestra to play a soothing symphony, we must avoid behaviours that include competitiveness, judgement, or comparison. These are behaviours which involve a battle between us and someone else, or with ourselves, or which involve negative evaluation or judgement of any kind, whether it's a literal grade or just performing for the praise of others. This is one of the mind hooks that keep our brains stuck and prevents us from finding flow. When competitiveness kicks in, the levels of our stress hormones ascend. Feel free to do that when you need it – but it won't result in your thoughts pleasantly flowing along, making your mind and body healthier.

Mind Hook Behaviour 2: Pleasure-Seeking

Let me tell you about a rat named Barnaby. Professor Burrhus Frederic Skinner, an American psychologist active in the 1950s, coined the term *operant conditioning*.[41] He seemed convinced that free will is an illusion: that we're not free to choose our behaviour. We're controlled by the reward system in our brains. Rewards catch us like a rat in a trap. Skinner proposed that he could control people's behaviours simply by keeping a close eye on the contingencies of their behaviours. *Contingencies* refer to the immediate consequences of our behaviour. Do we get pleasure or punishment? Do we get attention? A like? A treat? Do we get nothing at all out of the behaviour? It boils down to a basic premise: we repeat what caused pleasure in the past, and we avoid what caused pain.

Professor Skinner demonstrated, in his famous rat experiments, that rats would be happy little creatures if they could press a lever on a dispenser in their cage whenever they wanted and get a little food pellet in return. For the rest of the day, they'd go about their business in the cage, as rats do. Conversely, if pressing the lever resulted in an electrical shock, they'd never press the lever again. They'd even avoid that corner of the cage for the rest of their days. One day, Skinner reprogrammed the system of the food-pellet dispenser so that the rats only received one, say, 30 per cent of the times they pressed the lever. Every third press would result in a pellet. This caused some stress in the cage. Not a lot, but a bit. Not because they didn't have enough food. The rats seemed to become a little obsessed with the pellets from the lever if they didn't get them at every attempt.

The real shift happened, however, when Skinner reprogrammed the system of the dispenser again, to make the occurrence of the food pellet entirely variable. It was still at, say, 30 per cent, but now it didn't happen at every third lever press anymore, but entirely at random. This is what psychologists call *intermittent reinforcement*. Rat Barnaby and his comrade rats in the cage became frantic. This uncertainty was a killer. Now Skinner was indeed in perfect control of the rats' behaviour. They were entirely hooked on pressing that lever. They forgot all about their other business in the cage, forgot about mating and about grooming, about drinking and eating things other than pellets. All that mattered was the lever. The beautiful magnificent lever! This definitely meant goodbye to free will for these rats.

Intermittent Reinforcement

This type of experiment has been replicated endlessly. With different types of rewards, different types of animals, humans, and so on. Rats, humans and other mammals, even reptiles, share those ancient basic circuitries around their brain's reward system because these are so key to survival in a harsh world. *Opening Skinner's Box: Great Psychological Experiments of the Twentieth Century* is a wonderful book by Lauren Slater that describes those experiments beautifully, but I can give you a sneak preview: the result is always the same. We all *lose it* when intermittent reinforcement is applied to us. You think you're in control, but you're not.

This is the way bad habits take over: we tend to repeat even dysfunctional behaviours if they have been rewarded in the past. A child having a temper tantrum at the supermarket checkout to get *that sweet* will perform the same tantrum again if their dad once bought them the sweet (reward) in the past. A one-time giving in to buy the kid a sweet is enough for the kid's brain to have experienced intermittent reinforcement, and to crave the sweet more than ever in the future.

We repeat what caused pleasure in the past, but even more so if the pleasure is only obtained on some of the attempts to obtain it, *and* when the ratio of success is variable and unpredictable (sometimes Dad is tired and buys the sweet, sometimes he can resist the embarrassment of the tantrum and doesn't buy it = variable intermittent ratio of reinforcement).

We are all affected by this. Receiving a WhatsApp message, a social media notification, gambling, or checking a sports score are all events that can cause pleasurable dopamine releases, but they're also unpredictable and bring pleasure on a variable basis, intermittently. Some potential suitors are more or less exactly replicating the lever experiment when they text inconsistently, and we end up hooked on them – not because they are so wonderful, but because they've hooked our reward system with their inconsistent behaviour.

To see the lasting effect of these intermittent dopamine kicks, consider how often you pick up your phone for no reason, open a new browser, check for notifications, check your emails, and put it back down, only to do it again minutes later. That's your bad habit right there. But what is it about these activities that is so addictive, so enticing for our pink elephants that they seek out yet another stampede in our mind? And how do we protect ourselves against it? Well, for a start, we can educate ourselves about what psychologists call hedonic behaviours and their delights.

Senses, Emotions and Habits

In 2020, during the Covid pandemic, my colleagues and I felt increasingly outraged as we observed our friends, colleagues – and ourselves(!) becoming increasingly hooked on network tools. We decided to do a review of the scientific literature about how some consumer neuroscientists exploit the hook of intermittent rewards to sell us things and to keep us hooked on their products.[42] We found that the tricks they use roughly fall into three categories;

they entice our *senses*, trigger our *emotions* and spin our behaviour into *habits*. Skinner's experiments with Rat Barnaby showed how pure hedonism, that is, chasing after pleasure only, creates bad habits in our brain through intermittent reinforcement. Let's now take a quick look at what it does to our brain when we shatter our concentration over and again by allowing our senses and emotions to be pulled at constantly. Our behaviour gets looped into bad habits and we feel increasingly helpless and frustrated because we can't focus on any one thing.

Neuroscientific experiments show that when our senses perceive images, words, sounds and smells of natural rewards, we automatically turn towards them. Natural rewards are things like sugar, fat, sex, shelter, status. They are important for survival in the wild and our brains, unchanged for about 300,000 years, are hard-wired to respond to them. Psychologists call these *orienting responses*. They use eye-tracking technology to measure rapid eye movements towards an item. These glances towards natural rewards last only milliseconds. That's how scientists know that we're not doing this *consciously*. It just happens. You think you're in control, but you're not.

For example, strings of nerve cells are connected to the muscles that control our eye movements. Our sense of vision, like all our senses, has been crafted by evolution to *automatically* take stock of the shapes and movements that promise natural pleasure sources in our surroundings. This ability to quickly detect potential natural rewards nearby is another incredible advantage for survival in the wild. But in a modern landscape scattered with potential pleasure sources, our attention is constantly pulled away from what we are doing. Our eyes register a burger on a dashboard, our nose detects the smell of an enticing perfume, our ears tune into the sound of a splashy bubbly drink being poured, and our attention is hooked. Beyond that, anything that just *reminds* us of the prospect of that pleasure to our senses is enough to conjure up pink elephants on a rampaging quest for dopamine. It's the red sports car all over again: as soon as we try to disengage from a thought about imminent pleasure, and cast it toward a distraction, it rebounds. If we, with our behaviour, expose ourselves to pleasure prospects, these will automatically trigger craving pink elephant thoughts in our brain and shatter our attention. We can't help it.

In addition, dopamine, adrenaline, and other excitement neurotransmitters and hormones are out and about when we have strong, unpredictable bursts of emotions like joy, chills, or being moved, and even when we have negative emotions like fear, anger, sadness, even disgust. Some emotions like curiosity, surprise or feeling moved are so-called *attachment emotions*. They 'attach' us to the person, object or experience that caused us to have these juicy feelings in the first place. And because this excitement feels so good and usually comes to us unpredictably (on an intermittent reinforcement schedule), we want it again.

This is how soap operas play on our emotions. When we choose to watch a soap, we experience emotions triggered by the content. Not all of these emotions are positive, they trigger sorrow, drama, fear, but we like to experience them . . . they rustle up the excitement messenger substances in our brains, and that's how we get attached emotionally to the story, the characters. If it is well-made, watching one episode will make us crave more, their cliff-hanger endings will make us want to watch the next episode, and the next, and the next . . . voila, the Netflix effect.

That is why you can't stop binge-watching. Even though you *know* it's a bad habit, it's making you restless, stealing your focus and your sleep. Episodic series are designed to make our body-orchestra play the final verse of the pleasure symphony on repeat, to make you crave *more*. Besides, the Zeigarnik effect we spoke about in Chapter 1 is doing its work to keep the unfinished story at the forefront of your mind.

Your brain is working exactly as it was designed to, the feelings of anticipation and yawning curiosity are enticing, entirely human, and absolutely okay. But if you want a calm mind, intermittent reinforcement is not helping, even if it is exciting.

With every beat of pleasure, brain structures including the substantia nigra and the hypothalamus release dopamine and related messenger substances. These signal pleasure and then, after consumption, satiety, to our conscious mind. Yet, depending on the situation, they can also signal *anticipation* of pleasure. This anticipation can lead us to develop what is commonly understood as a feeling of *craving*. Craving is a portal to stress and gets in the way of finding flow. Our brain is at risk of developing cravings when we pursue a behaviour for the sole purpose of experiencing pleasure and we are only able to attain that pleasure intermittently.

There are behaviours that let our body-orchestra play its pleasure symphony and end it in satiety and relaxation, while there are also behaviours which trap us in an endless pleasure-seeking loop. We'll call these latter 'pleasure-seeking behaviours'.

➤

We can learn about the complexities of our brain's reward system from a surprising source: people struggling with depression. One symptom of people who suffer from depression is *anhedonia*: the inability to feel pleasure, to learn from a reward, or to feel motivated to seek out something that gave them pleasure in the past. Put very simply, people with anhedonia don't learn from rewards like Rat Barnaby and other mammals like we humans usually do; their brain simply doesn't make a link between pleasure that was obtained in the past and how to get that again. But researchers have found a surprising fact: while people suffering from depression may not experience pleasure from things like a night out, a boat trip, or dinner with friends, they do experience the same level of pleasure from a piece of chocolate as non-depressed individuals do. This is one reason why some people with depression may also suffer from obesity: sugar and fat are among the only rewards that still give them pleasure and satisfaction.[43–46] This type of research shows how complex the neural systems that make pleasure in our brain are. Yes, we get a fleeting feeling of pleasure from a soap opera or a notification on social media, but it's just the quick hit in your reward systems like when you've eaten a piece of milk chocolate. These systems are involved in so many important things for our pathway to flow – they ensure that we can learn (remember that the basic learning principle is that we repeat what gave us pleasure in the past), can be creative, feel a sense of self and achievement, and that our life and what we do is *meaningful*. To find our pathway to flow and a life we perceive as meaningful, we need to cultivate behaviours that engage *both* the low-level reward circuitries and the broader systems of our conscious brain that create meaning – together. For now, remember this second key to finding our pathway to flow: if we crave a bit of peace of mind, we must ask ourselves whether the behaviour that we're about to choose is likely to result in a situation leading to a strong but unpredictable reward. If we seek a behaviour that will allow us to build a pathway to flow, intermittent reinforcement will not help us.

After one year of studying psychology in France, I decided to move. I liked France, but I found the course I was taking was too singularly focused on social psychology. I find social processes incredibly important and interesting to study, as we will see in Chapter 4, but I've always felt that before we human beings do anything social, a whole load of biological processes must happen in our brain and body first. *That* was what I wanted to learn more about. I had heard that there was a good university on an island in the Mediterranean with a focus on psychobiology and statistics. I didn't know much about the island but if you do, you likely know it for its reputation for parties and questionable behaviour: Mallorca. I had lived a life in a ballet bubble and had never heard of it at all.

When I arrived, I discovered that there are two worlds on the island of Mallorca that just so happen to echo the two philosophical camps: the hedonists and the eudemonists. The first is a world of mass-tourism that is all about booze, boobs and bacchanalia. A never-ending pleasure-seeking crowd disembarks up to a thousand aircraft each day of the week and swarms out to specific stretches of land on the island of Mallorca. In these resorts, you find 100 per cent hedonistic behaviour. Alcohol, drugs, gambling, fries, burgers and sex whenever, wherever and, seemingly, with whoever you want. Research shows that the frequency of use of drugs, unprotected sex, alcohol and gambling behaviour, for many individuals, increases by up to 50 per cent[47] when in these Mediterranean holiday resorts.[48–51] In my first weeks on Mallorca, I remember reading one newspaper article after another about violent behaviour on those beaches and in the nightclubs as a result of the overindulgence in things that ping our reward systems.

In stark contrast to the hedonistic madness and bacchanalia stands the 'other' world of the island: a paradise. The landscape bears the testimony of Roman, Arab and Hispanic presence. Bathed in a unique sienna light all year round, it has a wonderful varied vegetation with a stretch of mountains called La Tramuntana that is protected as a UNESCO World Heritage Site and has long been home to artists seeking solace and inspiration. Mallorca's red earth bears witness to a long cultural, culinary and artistic tradition, dating back about 5,000 years.[52,53] The beauty that awaits you at every corner is breathtaking. Among the more recent foreign sons and daughters who've found both pleasure and meaning on the island and expressed it through their art are Joan Miró, Frederique Chopin, Pablo Picasso, George Sand, Robert Graves, Coll Bardolet and many more. In the capital Palma, there are architectural gems by Antoni Gaudi, statues by Eduardo Chillida – and the university where I studied. I soon discovered that the university is named after Ramón Llull, a medieval philosopher who is also the patron of the island. Thanks to his writings we know that the Catalan language was present in Mallorca before the Spanish language. Some of his famous works from the thirteenth century were written in Catalan, Latin, and probably Arab. His symbol is a quill, symbolising his writings. You can see a statue of him close to the seaside in Palma.

All the knowledge nuggets above are now somehow connected in your brain, and the one connection point between them is the island Mallorca. You now have a 'deeper' meaning about Mallorca stored in your brain, quite literally. Apart from the sensory information that you may have about Mallorca, how it looks, how the nature is beautiful and rewarding to look at, how much you can party, and so on, we have now connected this information with other knowledge that was already in *your* memory systems, resonating with your sense of self. The web of knowledge in your brain about Mallorca is now a little bigger, and a little more connected. It's connected both with sensory and reward systems, and, importantly, it is interrelated with your personal life experience. And, surprise: your brain has stored these knowledge nuggets with the help of the reward system. Remember: our reward system is incredibly important for us to learn – thanks to the little dopamine showers that we get *when we learn*.

Booze, Boobs and Bacchanalia

Our brains love pleasure. *We* love pleasure. Sugar, sex, fat, wine, whatever works for us. This is because our brains evolved in a world that was very sparse. Our ancestors needed to fight hard for each calorie, to find shelter, safety and sex. Pleasure kept us going. If we didn't have a dab of pleasure in the reward systems of our brain every time we ate, felt safe or had sex, we wouldn't bother, and our species would have been extinguished long ago. So pleasure-seeking has such a hook on our brain because evolution wouldn't have happened if it didn't. But in affluent modern societies like on Mallorca, we face a different problem. Ours is a world of abundance, and we are not designed to resist pleasure. At the same time, we've designed our lives to give the brain a constant stream of many easy highs. When we let pleasure-seeking behaviours direct our body-orchestra, it's all about quick and easy thrills, strong emotion, pleasure, and sprinkling excitement transmitters everywhere, as they try to get as much pleasure for us as they possibly can. Mindless hedonism destroys brains and, in this way, lives, relationships and societies.

My experience on Mallorca formed my understanding of the brain's reward system. On this island, you can live in extreme hedonism or pursue a life full of meaning and bliss. Our reward system, just like Mallorca, can make you lose it, handing over your free will for the next pleasure hit, gambling, drinking, liking your brain away. In parallel, our reward system is one of the most important systems of our brain that enables us to learn, and to forge healthy habits, and Mallorca offers opportunities for this too, with the knowledge hidden in its centuries-old libraries, its art and its cultural history. The learning signal, when we learn something and do it right, *also* comes from the dopaminergic fireworks in the reward circuits that spark with pleasure.

The important take-home message is that as soon as we experience pleasure-seeking impulses, our excitement hormone levels ascend. It's okay to act on them, but for your pathway to flow, you need something else in addition to pleasure. We need pleasure, and pleasure is good, but if we're able to build connections in our brain between that rush of pleasure and activities that engage those broader uniquely human areas of our brain, that's when we can experience pleasure-*PLUS*, the kind that doesn't trap us in a loop of craving, but leaves us feeling free, satisfied and at peace. As we build our pathway to flow, I'll take you through the moves of how to do that.

For now, remember this: social media, shopping, gaming, gambling, dating apps . . . they're all designed to supply us with quick little pleasure hits. These sweeteners are not inherently problematic, but they provide the brain with frequent bursts of dopamine neurotransmitter activity in the reward systems, deep down in the primal folds of our brain. In excess, these intermittent bursts are addictive, and deeply unhealthy.[54–57] Depending on how we use these behaviours, they can shatter our concentration and tamper with our free will. They lure us into chasing the next dab of pleasure that twinkles seductively around the next corner. We could compare the neural process at play in our brain here to spoiling our body with too much sugar or developing a compulsive drug habit.

Mind Hook Behaviour 3: Sensation-Seeking and Risk-Taking

In 2008, a paper by Siri Leknes and Irene Tracey from Oxford University hit the science news.[58] They had discovered that what we experience as painful and pleasant sensations are made by overlapping circuitries of the brain. But are pain and pleasure not opposites? It turns out it's not that simple. Many studies have followed this path of research, aiming to discover how pain and pleasure are interwoven, but fifteen years on, we still don't fully understand the exact nature of the link. Do we sometimes deliberately provoke pain, in order to experience pleasure afterwards?

Each time we seek adventure, each time we crave some excitement and suspense, we willingly expose ourselves to feeling a little tingling of pain. Think of the last thriller you watched, where your tolerance was stretched and stretched. You may even have felt a pressure on your chest. That was the solar plexus nerve bundle that sits just under our breastbone. When we play a risky symphony with our behaviour (for example, watch a scary movie, bungee jump or gamble), we're directing this nerve bundle to be on high alert through messenger substances of excitement, like adrenaline and dopamine. We feel this pressure, even pain, but still keep watching the film. We like the sensation of tickling our senses in new ways. When our curiosity is right up there on its toes, ears up, tongue out to take in as much exciting newness as possible, the neural systems responsible for the feeling of *wanting* are overactive, and we keep going, step by step, pushing the accelerator. The excitement can be all-absorbing, our heart beats against our chest, a tingling feeling is pulsating just under our skin, and it's almost painful. Often, we don't even enjoy this feeling that much . . . it's the promise of the feeling *afterwards* that keeps us going. The moment when our curiosity has been met, when we've gone over the cliff and lie back, drunk from an inebriating neurohormonal cocktail of body-made opioids, pain-relieving substances that help our muscles relax and give us a feeling of relief. This naturally occurring cocktail rushing into our blood is like being high. Who wouldn't want to seek that pleasant feeling over and again?

Is this a mistake of evolution? Not at all. Once again, we may not even be here if it wasn't for the hook that curiosity has in our mind, or the ability of our reward system to give us the golden feeling that overcomes us as we recover from the thrill of novelty and discovery. Back in the stone age, our ancestors' reward systems compensated them for continuing to explore our world, and this meant being willing to expose themselves to danger and chance. This is the basic drive for innovation, development and progress in all aspects of human life; personal, societal, scientific . . . If our ancestors had totally contented themselves with what they had, it would likely have meant death for humankind. But once again, our lives today are not what they were then. Back in the stone age, danger presented itself naturally, in a way it rarely does for most of us today. Our ancestors didn't need to go out and seek danger and the delicious allure of risk on purpose. We do. Risk keeps tempting us, and in modern Western societies, opportunities for experiencing novelty are overabundant. The result is a sensation-seeking, restless mind.

What Do YOU Load Into Your Working Memory?

We can understand a lot about the impact that risk has on our minds and bodies from studying the effects of something very common in our modern smartphone dominated world: the news. Newsfeeds, headlines, press pictures are everywhere. They catch our attention and the language systems of our brain immediately spring into action and process those headlines at a glance. Did you know that when you see a word, the language systems in your brain responsible for how that word sounds and what it means spur into action automatically? If the word is in a language that you speak, you cannot avoid it.[59] The only way to prevent having your brain 'read' something without you wanting to is by *not* putting text in front of your eyes.

The temptation today is that we can consume news at any time of day, through any medium, and we never need to run out of new news on which to binge.

But we cannot fully control *what* news we see. We don't know what the story holds for us at the end. Some news outlets like the

BBC kindly tell us if 'some readers may find the contents disturb-ing'. However, that just increases the allure of the news-nugget for many. We don't know what we are about to invite into our thoughts, what words and concepts will be loaded into our work-ing memory and language systems, and rebound like ping pong balls in and out of our awareness, as a result of what we'll be read-ing. We may end up jealous, disgusted, anxious, angry, sad, and so on. That's the risk.

More often than not, we see how news can cloud our thoughts as a result of a neurocognitive process that experimental psycholo-gists call *mood induction*. Experimental psychologists use mood induction as a technique to study emotions in a lab setting. For example, a psychologist may be interested in the influence of fear or anger on other cognitive functions like our memory perform-ance or our concentration: are you better at a memory task when you're happy or when you're angry? Or do you perform best if you're in a neutral mood? To test questions like these, psycholo-gists need the participants to feel these emotions before they test memory or concentration.

The most powerful mood-induction techniques to trigger par-ticular emotions in the lab is to have participants read fear-inducing or anger-inducing short stories, or by showing images that trigger fear or anger. Of course, such experiments go through a complex process of ethics approval and experimenters are obliged to ensure participants are guided back to a neutral mood before leaving the lab. This is called the *debrief step* of the experiment. The same con-tent we almost constantly consume – first thing in the morning, right before bed, scrolling on our phones, in breaks between calls or tasks or while on the bus – would be considered as so actively harmful to people's mood that, in the lab, it would be unethical to expose participants to it without carefully undoing the effects before they go out into the world again.

In 1997, Johnston and Davey from the University of Sussex investigated the impact of news watching on looping thoughts.[60] Of course, they didn't ask their participants about 'pink elephants'.

They called it *the impact of negative news bulletins on catastrophising of personal worries*. In their experiment, they divided research participants into three groups and gave them news to watch for fourteen minutes. They set up the experiment a little like in real life: participants didn't know what kind of news they were going to watch. One group got positive news, the second neutral news, and the third group received a negative news bulletin. The researchers measured participants' moods and asked them for their thoughts before and after watching the news. The group that got the negative news bulletin reported sadder and more anxious mood than any of the other groups. Moreover, they reported thoughts full of personal worries that had no relation to the news they were watching.

Results like these were brought together with many other similar results in a review paper that was published in the midst of the Covid pandemic by Pfefferbaum and colleagues from the University of Oklahoma, who warned us against the link between what is now called *mass trauma media contact* and depressive and anxious pink elephants on our mind. Exposing ourselves to the news is a risky behaviour.[61,62]

In 2007, Szabo and Hopkinson from the National Institute for Sport Talent Care in Hungary exposed two groups to a random news bulletin.[63] Mood, thought disturbance and positive and negative effect were measured before and after the news. Both groups had significantly lower levels of positive mood, higher levels of anxiety and thought disturbance. After this, Group 1 underwent a fifteen-minute guided relaxation exercise, while Group 2 was exposed to a fifteen-minute lecture for distraction. Only Group 1 made it back to their pre-news levels of good mood. Yet, in the real world, there is no debrief step. Of course, if news weren't novel, risky and unexpected, it wouldn't be news. But it's important we understand the impact that risky novelty has on our bodies and our minds. It has the power to alter our mood and cloud our minds. And it excites us. It puts us in a state of heightened arousal, ready to rumble. That's when we may succumb to what is known scientifically as *arousal misattribution*.

A Scary Bridge To Cross

Arousal misattribution theory was first described scientifically in 1974 by Dutton and Aron at the University of British Columbia to explain a curious effect.[64] When a group of men met a woman on a perilous bridge, they were more likely to find her sexually attractive than those men who met the same lady on a normal street. Why? Being on a scary bridge at high altitude makes our brain activate our body to be in high alert. And it seems that the brain isn't very good at identifying the *source* of our excitement. If our behaviour directs our body-orchestra into thrilling excitement, this co-activates all sorts of memories and feelings. Of course, finding a stranger attractive isn't generally a problem, but when our brains crave excitement, our inability to distinguish exactly where it's coming from can cause us some issues if what you seek is calm and a peaceful break. You might not know what hit you, but your mind spins away in uncomfortable looping thoughts. This can also be a problem in the work context: some managers think it is a good idea to send people to an escape room for 'team building' purposes. Stoking up arousal level in people's bodies certainly activates excitement substances in the body – people *like* it. However, it also stokes up bonding hormones like oxytocin, and you may have your team 'bond' in sexy ways, which is not very conducive to the mental health of the team members and ultimately team productivity.

Distracting ourselves or just carrying on with our day will not offset the effects of mood induction and arousal misattribution. And we are more likely to experience lower mood, a lack of focus and a parade of overheated negative thoughts unless we actively break out of the loop of endless novelty-seeking. We are seeking that relief, that golden glow, which may never come. We know now that our penchant for sensation-seeking is creating havoc in our mind because it activates all sorts of low-level perceptual processes that were designed by evolution to keep us safe. We also know now that we should limit our news consumption and other arousing behaviours to specific times of the day. However, we also know that our cave-brain craves a little novelty now and then. But how much is just right?

Our brain hates stagnation. But we vary considerably in terms of just how much excitement our brain needs. With functional resonance imagery, neuroscientists have studied the brains of people with different personality profiles, and found that some people's nerve systems simply need more stimulation to maintain happy base levels than others.

The personality feature under scrutiny is known as *sensation-seeking*. Scientists use a cap with electrodes in it, called an electroencephalogram (EEG), to study the neural activity of our brain when we see something new. In an experiment published in 2019 by Xintong Jiang and colleagues,[65] the researchers first used a questionnaire to determine the level of sensation-seeking in their research participants. From these participants they selected two groups, one with people who had high levels and one with low, then exposed these two groups of people to different objects on a computer screen while recording their brains' electric activity. Some objects on the screen were novel, some less so.

When we perceive something new and unexpected, an orienting response appears on the trace of the electroencephalogram as a spike. It's like the brain goes, '*Wow, what's that?*' and as a result, the electrical activity of the brain increases for a moment. What Xintong Jiang and colleagues found was that in the brains of the participants with high sensation-seeking needs that spike went back to normal levels much faster than in the brains of people with low levels. Scientists refer to this as *abnormal fast habituation* to novel events.

Abnormal or not, in some sense it is an advantage to have a high level of sensation-seeking need and a quick habituation to novelty. These people adapt faster to changing, new environments, they recover faster from the almost painful sensations that we experience in unfamiliar, new situations. It makes them good workers who adapt and habituate quickly to unknown situations and cultures. They sense possibilities for new discovery around the next corner quite frequently, they're creative, and they're good at seeking out situations that may contain the lure of risk or something new, and they don't mind taking others along for the ride.

Each of us needs to find out how much stimulation we need to provide our brain with in order to be happy. We test our tolerance to new things, places, people or feelings by what we expose ourselves to, and the behaviours we choose. We may travel or live in a culture that is not our own and find our senses are constantly heightened. We may do extreme sports that thrill our senses or experiment with pain, or we may stay at home and watch horror movies or eat spicy food. In modern life, the opportunities for sensation-seeking abound.

There is nothing wrong with sensation-seeking, or with the feeling of relief that follows, but it is impossible to ignore the science suggesting that too much sensation-seeking behaviour is unhealthy, for our bodies and for our brains, and it may put others in danger. This is because of the neurohormonal cocktail that is in our blood *during* the risky episode. Its basic ingredients are stress hormones and other excitement messenger substances in our blood. Heart rate and blood pressure increase, we feel the alertness rushing along under our skin, our senses are open wide, we take in all information from our surroundings that we can get, as our body prepares for the impact. Research has found that our blood vessels actually sustain little injuries when we let our behaviour play our body-orchestra's risky symphony too excessively. When we're exposing our heart to this neurohormonal cocktail for too long, it makes the heart walls porous which increases the risk for heart disease when we get older.[66,67] More immediately, an unhealthy body makes an unhealthy mind. And of course, you risk injuring your body with some of these behaviours.

Balconing

While I lived on Mallorca in the 2010s, a strange risk-taking behaviour started to hype in the island's hedonic hotspots: Balconing.[68] German and British tourists jump from balcony to balcony, for fun. Many a life-changing injury and even deaths are reported each year. Jumping from balcony to balcony is treacherous. Especially if it's dark, you've drunk alcohol or taken other drugs and you're driven by a competitive drive to impress others. It is likely that you will misjudge the distance and your capabilities. We know that people regularly overestimate themselves in such situations.

Risk-taking is an effective system for keeping us progressing as individuals and as a species; but it does add fuel to pink elephants in our minds if we overindulge in it. Pink elephants feed on fear, anger and frustration and, more generally, on excitement. And given our brain's tendency for arousal misattribution, it is unlikely that in seeking out novelty we wanted to reactivate memories of past fears and frustrations, but this is the price we pay. It makes us edgy; we may lash out in anger and frustration at people around us, we may provoke arguments and worries in ourselves and others due to the effects that risky behaviour has on our brain. Risk, like pleasure and competition, is thrilling. The feeling of relief that follows risk can be liberating but it is also temporary. Most importantly, it's incredibly moreish and it comes with drawbacks. So here is the third key to building a pathway to flow: if a behaviour can risk our own or others' mental or physical health, it cannot send our mind flowing; we are too busy navigating fears, real and imagined, as the brain prepares to protect itself. As we'll see later on, one important aspect of behaviours that act as a guide to flow is that they offer the right balance between opportunities to feel *excited* and those to feel *in control*. It's about finding the right dosage of this neurohormone cocktail in our brain that works for *us*. You'll discover that the arts can be a safe space where we can experience wonder, awe, fear and delight, but without risking mental and physical balance.

The need for excitement, to escape the familiar and venture into the unknown, to discover or conquer or stand in wonder, is profoundly human. It's when we do this that our brains go into creative mode, find new connections between neurons and practise problem solving. Humans need to take risks.

The key to avoiding sensation-seeking's hook and to finding our pathway to flow, however, is to ensure we do not prioritise excitement *alone*. Due to arousal misattribution, we may get hooked on a risky behaviour that makes us feel good afterwards; however, it's a juicy trap for our mind that will take us nowhere.

Now you know which three behaviours are particularly prone to send your thoughts spinning and block your access to a flow state: when you crave peace of mind, the simple instruction is: stay clear of competitiveness, pleasure-seeking and sensation-seeking.

3.   Pink Elephant Ballet

Our mind doesn't have a back-space key, we cannot unsee, unthink or unfeel things. Once sensory impressions from our inside and outside worlds have been deemed important enough to be processed further by our brain, our memory and language systems hurl things in and out of our awareness. You don't need to be traumatised by a life-changing event to know the devastating effect of thoughts gone astray. The bottom line is this: once we're in a thought loop we are very likely to stay there, and the longer we stay in the loop, the more unwelcome thoughts insert themselves into the spinning blur. Psychologists refer to this as *rumination*.[1-3] I call it the pink elephant ballet.

In the 1940s Disney cartoon *Dumbo*, trauma-induced rumination is cast as, well, a pink elephant ballet. Born with extra-large ears, Dumbo is ridiculed, bullied and bruised. In a failed attempt at finding something Dumbo is good at, Dumbo and his friend, the circus mouse Timothy, end up accidentally drinking water laced with alcohol. There is a burst of pink and we can almost picture a phantasmic circus director gloriously announcing: 'Ladies and Gentlemen: Welcome – THE PINK ELEPHANT BALLET!' Trumpet fanfares . . . and off spins Dumbo's mind. Stirred up by the alcohol, parades of pink elephants trot, canter and pirouette through Dumbo's tormented mind. The merry-go-round explodes into one big pink blur and the next thing we see is Dumbo sleeping on a tree, of all places.

By chance, Dumbo now discovers his superpower: he can fly. *Thanks* to his ears.

Dumbo's is a typical story of 'turning your weakness into a strength'. *Our* weakness is that we have a body with needs and urges, and we 'have a history', meaning that memories may growl under the surface, and reach up into the present. All that pokes at our brain. What we need to do is to spin *that* into a strength: use our body to free our mind – via the behaviours that we choose to do.

Let's keep this idea of a pink elephant ballet as we dive into the science of rumination in this chapter. Rumination isn't a pleasant thing. But I realised that it's helpful to poke a little fun at my own looping thoughts by thinking of them as pink elephants pirouetting about.

For our brain, rumination and overthinking are bad habits. They are behaviours, even if they are behaviours of our mind. And we ourselves *create* those bad habits inside our mind. The good news is that as we have the power to create bad habits, we can also create good ones through the behaviours that we enact with our body.

For my own pink elephants, one remedy that I found was this: *doing* stuff that gave me regular experiences of flow reliably unwound my thoughts and, with time and repetition, improved my focus and my general mood – and I believe I even got healthier from breaking those pink elephant loops.

We Are Decision

'Don't worry, be happy!' is so easily said – but, *done*? Susana Bravo is a living example of how to implement this advice. She is a professional filmmaker, CEO of her own film company. Her life is all about film; about glossy beautiful images and films, showcasing perfection; the perfect coating for weddings, commercials and corporate PR videos. Susana's professional life is one big chase for pleasure and sensation, and the market is very competitive.

To stir herself free of the pull of the perfect, to replenish her energy, Susana uses simple photography with her mobile phone camera as her flow tool. Tucked under blankets on the sofa during rainy Sundays, she lets her mind flow through the lens. On her professional Insta page it's all about perfection, but on her personal Insta, she keeps the deliberately imperfect 'Diary of a Myopic'. Susana is short-sighted and when she takes out her contacts, her world is blurry. For about eight hours of the day, while she wears her contacts, the world is sharp and defined around her. But *her* reality is actually a different one. In the evening, when she takes out her contacts, she returns to her reality. A reality that she has to deal with, and that is difficult for a person that lives for the beauty of creation as an artist, who cherishes the detail of the world which, for a large part of the day, she cannot discern. This worries her. Will her eyesight allow her to keep her job in the long run? Through 'Diary of a Myopic', she expresses this reality, spun into something beautiful.

In moments of intense stress, when work and worries overwhelm her, she opens her Insta and dives back into herself, looking at her flow photographs, recharging her batteries. The photographs are conditioned cues, linked to past feelings of calm and refreshment inside Susana's brain. As soon as her senses perceive the photographs, this conditioned link makes the photos themselves evoke the same feelings in her chest and lets them reverberate through her body. You probably know the feeling of hearing a particular musical piece or smelling something that takes you back in time and makes you so happy. It is remarkable how authentically Susana is able to express herself through photos, just by showing, in a picture, how she literally sees the world. In fact, scientific research shows that even simply recalling moments of being authentic in the past increases wellbeing and happiness.[4] And artworks that mean something to you make recalling those instants easy.

In the summer of 2023, Susana broke some neck vertebrae in a motorcycle accident. Staying immobile in hospital for weeks, delegating work to colleagues, she lost out on the all-important summer income for a filmmaker that usually takes her over the winter months. More spinning worries in Susana's mind were the result. But over a coffee, she showed me her recent flow photographs of her reality during the hospital stay. 'The good thing is that now even a mobile phone camera is enough to do great photos, I didn't even have to move from the hospital bed,' she told me. And she was as optimistic as always. 'We *are* decision,' she said. With her flow tool she chooses actions that make her feel good. She never cares what others may find in these pictures, because the most important thing for her is that during flow, her mind frees up resources and her worries recede. 'Then I gain mental space to create my new path.'

Science does suggest that we *become* who we are and what we care about, depending on the cues that we decide to *act* upon. These cues can be in the world or inside our mind.

In this chapter, we'll look at the neuroscience of why we can get hooked on the wrong behaviours, and we'll discover what behaviours to *choose* instead. These are 'pleasure-plus' behaviours that we spoke about in Chapter 2; behaviours that give both pleasure and meaning to our life – and it so happens that the arts *can* be precisely such pleasure-plus behaviours.

Rewards, Habits, Compulsions and Addiction

During my ballet education, for about six years, I banned sweets and fatty delights from my life. When I re-emerged from the dance world and started to study at university, I rediscovered the world of sweets and culinary joys. Like a kid in a candy shop I stuffed myself with all the bliss I'd denied myself for so long. My Camp 1 was in charge and I was focused on immediate pleasure.

Artificial Rewards

Have you ever wondered why you get hungry, and why you stop getting hungry? Our brain has 'negative feedback loops' in our brain-stem jukebox that usually signal when we've obtained enough to reach the optimal level – enough fat, sugar, warmth, and so on.[5] This stops us from eating more food than we need, or carrying on with an action for longer than really necessary. For example, when we're hungry, the hunger hormone ghrelin rushes through our body.[6] When we've eaten enough, our digestive system sends the pacified satiety hormone leptin to our brain to say 'enough, thank you'.[7–9] That's a 'negative feedback loop' linking brain and body to regulate our behaviour in line with our body's needs: not enough nutrients in the body → feeling hungry → eating → enough nutrients in the body → feeling sated → stopping eating.

So, in principle, it might seem like I was safe eating all these sweets when I stopped dancing professionally. My brain was going to tell me when to stop, thanks to the feedback loops. Unfortunately, this wasn't the case.[10] The problem is that this reward system of ours is very old. Evolutionarily speaking, it came into being long before the first humans. This means that this lizard brain was around *long before* we started to invent artificial rewards. With artificial rewards, I mean things that we can consume that don't have a 'deeper meaning' for our body's survival like sugary foods.[11] Our reward system simply doesn't have any tools to distinguish between natural and artificial rewards. It's a bit dumb. That's how we can be tricked into eating more than we need by what scientists call 'hyperpalatable foods'.[12,13]

Hyperpalatable foods have been designed to be very enticing to our lizard brain,[14,15] but they hold no deeper purpose for our body in terms of nutrients or other useful agents for our health. One such trick to hype our palate is the 'bliss point'.[16] The bliss point is a perfect mix of salt, sugar and fat in a food item – at which point, we humans stop feeling satiated.[17-20] The negative feedback loop doesn't work, and we overeat.[19,21] Another trick is to combine many different ingredients (especially flavours) that don't naturally occur together in a food item to make it hyperpalatable.[22] As a rule of thumb – anything above five ingredients is suspicious.

Too Active, and Not Active Enough

At the height of my newfound indulgence, I came across Dr Antoine Bechara's work on decision-making, impulse control and loss of willpower. I once thought that people who are addicted to drugs could just choose to stop taking the drugs and they'd be okay, but Antoine Bechara's articles told a different story.

In a nutshell, this is the deal: if we keep triggering the hedonic hotspots of our brain – for example, as I was, by eating all that sugar – this causes some parts of our reward system (e.g. the amygdala) to become hyper-activated.[23,24] At the same time, other parts of the reward system, those closely connected with the meaning-making structures of our brain (especially, the insula), are hypo-activated (not activated enough);[25–27] which means those meaning-pathways start wasting away. This imbalance between Camps 1 and 2 is one of the building blocks of addiction.

Why do I mention addiction in the context of eating?[28] Because we only have *one* reward system. And it is structured around the basic mechanisms that help us survive. Hyperpalatable foods entice it, just like other hedonic behaviours like gaming, or substances like heroine and nicotine do, and we can get 'addicted' to hyperpalatable foods with devastating consequences for our health (for example, if we develop obesity). Food is among the most basic things that keep us alive, and the pleasure we get from it is created by the same system in our brain that sustains all other pleasures.

Because of the hyperactivated Camp 1 in addiction – which we have little control over – addicted individuals can't easily just 'snap out of it'. They've inadvertently trained their brain to be all about pleasure. The hedonist philosophers in Camp 1 are excited, craving ever more delights, partying all night. In a healthy brain, the eudemonist philosophers from Camp 2 would help restrain the excitement a little, injecting knowledge about the possible long-term consequences of continuing with this level of consumption.[29] In the addicted brain, however, the pathways between Camps 1 and 2 are simply not strong enough anymore to 'down-regulate' the overly excited Camp 1. These people somehow lose their ability to *choose* their behaviour.[30] This is a shift that happens in our brain as we keep seeking empty pleasures. And this is the scary part: these 'empty pleasures' can be drugs or hyperpalatable foods, but they can also be *behaviours* that excite only Camp 1 over and again.[31–33] And, today, we live in a world infused with possibilities to obtain 'artificial rewards' easily, and they can become mind hooks, as we saw in Chapter 2.

The way substances work as drugs is that they contain agents that act directly on the receptors of the neurotransmitters of pleasure in our brain. Behaviours elicit pleasure by the same process of acting on neurotransmitters, but *via* the behaviours.[34–41]

Argentine Tango

During my PhD, I struggled terribly with a restless mind problem. I was sitting too much, ate too much sugar, and had sad and terrifying memories about a life not lived that kept getting catapulted into my awareness by cues in my surroundings. By indulging in the quick pleasure- and sensation-seeking to distract myself and suppress the unpleasantness, I had taught my mind to be unsteady.

You've probably heard of gaming addiction and heroin addiction, but many other behaviours can also become addictive. To learn more about our brain, let's look at the process of getting addicted to an art. To illustrate this, I'd like to take you on the journey that brought me to Argentine tango.

When I arrived for my first postdoctoral position in London, I gladly joined the magnificent joyride that is London, discovering all sorts of wonderful bizarreness around every corner. One of those wonderfully bizarre things that I discovered was Argentine tango. My back had recovered enough to allow me to move and walk without too much pain, thanks to extensive movement training that built up muscles to compensate for the irreversible part of the damage. One day, a Groupon offer chimed into my inbox: '10 Argentine tango dance classes for £20'.

I felt ready to try to dance again, especially a totally different style in terms of movements and music, so no cues would remind me of *ballet*. Off to my first Argentine tango class I went that same evening. And until the pandemic in 2020, I did not miss a single week without at least one Argentine tango evening, be it a class or a milonga (a milonga is a social dance evening of Argentine tango, where people meet and dance the night away).

I loved everything about it right away. The Argentine tango music with its special rhythm, the movements and the gestures, the sparkling dresses, the shoes, and all those wonderful embraces we shared as we danced and danced.

Our mammal social brain reacts with bursts of bonding hormones to social moments like sharing an embrace and music. Our brain releases endogenous opioids (made by the body itself), and off goes the pleasure symphony in our reward system. Likewise, the aesthetics of the décor, the people and the perfumes, the dresses and the shoes – all of these cues entice our senses, beautify the world. They all ignite our Camp 1 philosophers and stir up our reward system.

Often, it was up to four times a week that I flowed off into the *zone* with my fellow milongueros in this parallel world of the hidden London milonga places. The feeling of everything together reverberated from our senses to our brain and out into our wider body; pulsating with the rhythm of the golden milonga nights.

I'd walk home after milongas feeling happier than ever before in my life. My heart light, my body without any pain at all. Several studies show that dancing has analgesic effects.[42,43] It acts on the pain receptors, and pain dissipates. I experienced this first hand, and I'd greet the cold night like an old friend that picked me up at the milonga exit and walked me home. Even the grey street cats looked as if they were brushed with a golden patina, as they strode past me around the dark corners of London by night. The tango glow engulfed me.

It usually lasted for a few days, protecting me from the gloom of the weather in winter, the years of fiercely competitive and uncertain academic life, the pain in my body, the meek room that I rented for a much-too-large portion of my salary, and from the loneliness of someone uprooted by life. If I needed a moment away from it, I'd briefly close my eyes, hear the music, and I'd be back there again. Or I'd peek into my bag to see the sparkling shoes in their red satin pouch, and the golden glow would return to my chest.

But then the glow would wear off again.

To get it back, off I went again, into the night, completely into my body, to feel, to dance, and to forget.

Stop. Red flag.

Back in Chapter 1, we discussed how avoidance, suppression and distraction won't work to stop ruminative loops.

There were times when I was dancing for what scientists call *extrinsic motivations*. I was dancing to forget the past, to not feel the real world that surrounded me, that seemed populated only by difficult choices and competitive sharks. I was using the zone to escape, to distract myself.

I became aware of this slippery slope with a startle at a café table in Brussels before a milonga, with my tango-friend Hamish.

'Argentine tango – another behavioural addiction?' Hamish flung a paper print-out of a scientific paper onto the table between us. 'You publish research about dance being so healthy and good for us, but what about this?' He pointed at the title, looking fairly outraged. 'This is my life explained,' he continued. 'They describe exactly how I'm feeling.'

At the time of this conversation, Hamish and I had known each other for a couple of years. He is an amazing dancer, always perfectly styled, always there, at every milonga.

However, the paper by Remi Targhetta and his colleagues from 2013 tells a true story.[44] Any behaviour that can lead to strong feelings of pleasure, especially unpredictable episodes of pleasure, have an important addictive potential. They act on the same circuitries as addictive drugs do. Argentine tango, and any art, can trigger the same process. Especially if we use tango, or any art, for an *extrinsic* goal. Like me. I realised I was using tango to forget, to escape, to avoid and suppress.

'I can't stop thinking about tango the whole day,' exclaimed Hamish. 'No matter what I do, I try to distract myself, but I can't help it, my mind is glued to tango!' And he continued, 'The only thing that calms me down is tango. Thinking of tango, watching tango videos, browsing tango stuff to buy online, listening to tango music . . .'

Remember the study where participants' minds sprang back and forth between white polar bears and red sports cars, like a ping pong ball? Something similar was going on in Hamish's mind.

Whenever he tried to focus away from tango in his mind, for example on work, his mind bounced back to tango.

Now I understood some things about Hamish. All the travels for tango events, the fact that you'd meet him at literally *every* milonga all over Europe, always dressed in a different outfit. This did sound like a problem. Hamish's mind seemed to circle around tango in a never-ending pink elephant blur. But even worse, it seemed that he couldn't control these thoughts anymore. They kept circling, no matter what he did. And to *neutralise* them, all he could do was to keep thinking of tango, or do something tango related (watch a tango video on YouTube, go dancing, buy a new outfit).

'I only have tango-friends now. And I'm completely broke.' Hamish ruffled his hair while he said this, looking pretty distressed.

Warning signs for addiction include a drop in productivity, neglecting social contacts that aren't related to the subject of their addiction, and overspending on their addiction. What we focus on and spend time and money on matters when it comes to the direction our brains spin.

Pleasure Addicts

Cues and Their 'Incentive Value'

In 2017, inspired by my first years in London, I undertook research about how certain behaviours that we choose to do, like eating sweets, gambling, social media – and even leisure activities like the arts – affect our brain and our physical and mental health due to their addictiveness. While writing about the research, I quickly realised that an important aspect of the paper would have to be a summary of the science about why some behaviours, *and how we use them*, determines whether they are good or bad for us.[45] To be clear: I am *not* asking you to stop using social media, eating sweets or dancing Argentine tango. I do all of the above myself. But it's all about knowing how your brain works so you can use behaviours wisely.

One important point to know about our brain is its love for *cues*[46–48] that promise that there is pleasure to be had.[23,29,30,33]

For people *en route* to addiction, cues that secretly remind their brain of the drug are like a huge pink elephant balloon that is being blown up to enormous dimensions. For Hamish and me, it was anything that reminded us of tango: the music, the clothes, the perfume, the shoes. For a gambling addict it is the sights and sounds related to the gambling milieu and so on. The more drug-related cues we perceive with our senses, the bigger the pink elephant balloon gets, and soon there isn't room for anything else anymore. That's a hyperactivated Camp 1 – the hedonists are partying full time and have blocked the path uptown, to the eudemonist Camp 2 philosophers.

In the paper about addiction and the brain by Antoine Bechara and his colleagues, this growth of the *incentive value* of cues related to the drug is a real problem. There are different structures in the reward system. Some are responsible for giving us the feeling of pleasure, but other structures give us the feeling of *wanting* something. In Chapter 2, we spoke about this in relation to Rat Barnaby the effect of *intermittent pleasure-cues* on our brain. And that feeling is what scientists also call 'craving'.[47,48] It gets harder and harder to resist our 'drug' and we feel more and more motivated to 'get it',[29,33] and not do anything else.

The Habit Loop

Any artistic practice has specific sounds, movements, gestures, places, thoughts, smells, tastes, sights and touches associated with it – cues.

Those little cues act as magnets for our body to *act*.[49] They are incentives, natural cues that pull us into action. They *motivate us* to *go* for it.

For our brain, a habit is the result of a loop between a cue (see a sparkling dress), a behaviour of our body (get up and prepare for milonga) and the reward that the behaviour triggers in our brain (a wonderful dance, bonding hormones, etc):

Reward   **Cue**

Action
(Behaviour)

A behaviour is always initiated by a **cue** that promises pleasure, continued by an **action** that we do. Then **reward** follows. And that reward pulls us towards any cue associated with the reward we have just had; it *motivates* us to get more.

For Rat Barnaby in Chapter 2, the **cue** was the sight of The Mighty Lever, the **behaviour** he initiated as a result was pressing the lever and the **reward** was the food pellet. If you're a little hooked on social media, the **cue** is the notification icon, the **behaviour** is to pick up the phone and click and scroll, and the **reward** (which doesn't always come) is the Likes/Engagement. For someone who is *en route* to a gambling addiction, the **cue** is the machine, dice, cards, chips of whichever game you play, the **behaviour** is pulling the arm of the jackpot machine, tossing the dice or cards or moving the chips onto the roulette table, etc, and the **reward** is the money that you win – which, as we know, is a star example of an *intermittent* occurrence, a proper Rat Barnaby Lever Experiment on your brain. For this reason, on Mallorca, for example, in recent years, gambling halls have been barred from painting their exteriors in the typical 'gaming' colours, as an attempt to control the cues that initiate the gaming behaviour in the addicts.

Neurotransmitters like dopamine play an important role here, and this is part of the basic principle of learning. If a behaviour is repeatedly rewarded, we learn this behaviour. A habit is quickly formed, as are incentive cues related to your favourite behaviour, be it Argentine tango, social media or gambling. They get etched into the reward systems of our hyperactivated Camp 1. This goes for anything positive, like learning a new skill and good habits. However, it also applies to bad habits. And to addiction. You probably think you're one of these people in control, and maybe you are. But chances are, you're not, and even worse, you don't even know that you're not.[50–52] How to manage our pleasure-seeking brain in a modern world isn't part of our school curriculum. We don't know the warning signs because no one has taught them to us, like they taught us the warning signals of street safety. Even when the loudest pink elephant alarms go off in our brain, many of us calmly keep going, thinking that the alarming lightning over our head is just another type of pretty Christmas decoration.

Silicon Valley Parents

Facebook, Insta and other social media platforms have what psychologists call 'potent secondary reinforcer properties', because of their intermittent reinforcement schedules. We're just like Rat Barnaby, waiting for his delicious pellet: we never know when the notification icon will strike with new messages, likes and hearts, or what new delight will come up next on our feeds.

Besides, research shows that excessive social media use encourages dysfunctional personality styles like narcissism, low self-esteem, shyness and excessive need for confirmation.[53–56] It encourages jealousy,[57–60] dysfunctional social comparison processes[61,62] and mental health problems, especially anxiety and depression. The compulsive use of these platforms exposes us to prolonged and unnatural social and psychological pressure, compelling us to make choices that are not optimal for our own psychological health. In other words, 'social media use' behaviour unleashes *herds* of pink elephants in users' minds.

Silicon Valley parents know of this effect very well. The

powerful Netflix documentary *The Social Dilemma* shows how these parents limit their own children's screen time from early on, while developing ever smarter tech-(tr)apps for the minds of *our* children.[63–65] The Chinese-made app TikTok is heavily restricted inside China itself. The personalised feeds show only fun videos about educationally valuable content including science, gifted pianist-kids and art history.[66] Videos can only be liked, not uploaded or shared, and usage time is limited to a maximum forty minutes per user, *per day*. On the other side of the globe, we allow our children to be sucked down the wormhole-feeds for hours on end.

China provides the minds of their TikTok users with a time-bubble within which the use of the app (use TikTok = a behaviour) is healthy. In the West, we have freedom of choice, and that freedom comes with a responsibility. We have to make our own bubble. Yet, we grow up to be adults with little mental training for how to stay clear of craving and ruminative loops.[67] On the contrary, we are trained early on by the apps to obsess over the icon-pellet. We're at risk of forging bad habits in our brain.

When looking at the brains of addicted people with neuroimaging methods (techniques we can use to see the brain in action), neuroscientists have discovered another terrible thing. As the addiction intensifies, we don't only lose our mind, we lose the pleasure too.[68] The clinical psychologist Frank Tallis cautions that addiction is initially maintained by pleasure, but the intensity of this pleasure is reduced over time and with repeated consumption, and we end up in a situation where the addiction is maintained by the attempt to avoid pain and cravings. 'My life is a mess!' is the last thing Hamish said before we, of course, entered the next milonga after our coffee date. When we're addicted, we eventually use the behaviour to *avoid the bad feeling of craving*, not for causing pleasure. During the milonga, I observed Hamish dance, one dance after the other. He wasn't in a flow, this blissful state of being lost in dance, and he was looking a bit frantic and edgy. There was a huge pink elephant in the room.

Rumination Science

Much of the knowledge that we have today about rumination started to emerge from neuroimaging research with people with addiction, that we have spoken about so far, and from people with obsessive-compulsive disorder (OCD). About 2 to 3 per cent of people may suffer from OCD in their lifetime.[69] These patients are under the constant assault of pink elephants and their reward system shows abnormal patterns of activation, similar to that of an addicted brain.[70–74]

OCD is part of what clinical psychologists refer to as 'anxiety disorders'. Jack Nicholson gives a heart-warming portrayal of OCD in the 1990s romantic comedy *As Good As It Gets*. Melvin's (alias Nicholson) OCD is threatening to get in the way of his romance with the waitress Carol (alias Helen Hunt). We puzzled viewers witness Melvin tuck a little dog down the waste disposal chute because, as he says, it's loud and dirty. He's behaving generally appallingly towards Carol and everyone around him.

This picture, however, looks different through the lens of someone that is simply trying to keep his obsessions, his fears, in check. Melvin's irrational fears and worries urge him to think he *must* perform the compulsions, *no matter what*. His obsession is what clinical psychologists call 'contamination fear', and his compulsion is 'cleaning'. He *has* to make sure everything is clean, orderly, quiet. Otherwise . . . his pink elephants grind on and on. Overstepping others' boundaries and hurting others simply is the lesser evil, considering the imminent doom that lurks in Melvin's mind. While his actions are undeniably awful and cannot be excused, clinical psychology explains why he still performs them over and again: he suffers from OCD; his thoughts keep looping back to something very scary that he *really* wants to avoid. People close to someone suffering from OCD will know very well of the terror that the controlling behaviour can feel like. Let's take a look at the science.

Do You Like To Ruminate?

On our way to discover alternative behaviours that send our minds off into a placid state of flow, we need to acknowledge a seemingly hugely contradictory finding that scientists have recently started to investigate: When people ruminate, they have what scientists call 'abnormal' reward system activation.[75] Does it give us pleasure to ruminate? Before you slam the book shut, outraged because 'rumination certainly is not something I *like* doing', please hear me out.

This can be slightly puzzling to realise. In principle, you'd think that anything that gives us a negative feeling, like things that make us angry, sad, scared . . . in principle, these are punishments to our brain and we should automatically shy away from them by the fight and flight symphony. We saw above that our brain is very skilled at keeping memories about things that caused bad feelings like fear and anger in the past, to enable us to stay away from these things in the future. So why don't we? Well, scientific research into the brains of people who ruminate a lot show abnormal patterns of neural activation in parts of the reward system. What neuroscientists see is that the brain of someone who ruminates a lot looks like the brain of an addicted person.

Addicted to rumination? Can we be addicted to sadness? To anger? To pleasure? To fear? To excitement? This sounds as if we 'like' to ruminate and that we should just flip out of it if we don't like it.

Of course that's *not* what it means.

The reward system 'lights up' on the brain scans of ruminating people because rumination is a habit, and part of that habit loop is the learning signals, and these come, as you well know now, from the reward system.

Rumination is also a behaviour.[76,77] It is a mental behaviour, but a *behaviour* nonetheless. And any behaviours that are rewarded repeatedly get looped into habit loops. The pleasure-promising *cues* around the behaviour pull us towards the behaviour over and again. Once a habit is formed, the pleasure from doing the behaviour diminishes. And, as we've seen before, as paradoxical as this may seem, this is simply the basic principle of how our brain *learns*; the behaviour has passed from explicit to implicit memory systems, so we don't have to think about it anymore. This is because the basic mechanism in our brain that gives us the rewarding feeling is nothing but a learning signal to our brain: repeat what caused pleasure, don't repeat what didn't. Very easy maths here.

The Chewing Jaws of Your Mind

There are different types of rumination.[78] There is angry rumination that is stoked by testosterone and the excitement messenger substances, where we fantasise about the stupid colleague, boss, neighbour, bus driver (etc) who wronged us, and how we are *going to show them*. There is fearful rumination, where pink elephants keep warning us of imminent danger and we obsessively spin the thoughts of 'what if . . .' on repeat.[79] There is sad rumination that makes us descend spiral after spiral into the darkest corners of our mind, where all our most lonely memories live and where the only light we see is the pink blur of our pink elephants – the only creatures that have followed us all that way down here. And there is, strangely enough, a type of rumination that is about pleasure, obtaining pleasure, craving it and all that excitement, *if only I could have . . . just one more . . . oh yes.*

Our brain decides to spin off into ruminative loops due to the formation of a habit loop, which also explains why we keep at this behaviour, although it makes us feel bad and sucked out.[45,80,81] However, why this happens is unclear. Some people start this behaviour when faced with adversity, others don't.[82,83] Trauma is one reason because many scary thoughts make for a good reason to try to avoid them.[84] The scary thoughts are the cue, the behaviour is the rumination, the reward is the relief that the scary thoughts are gone for a moment.[85–87] But also, people without life-changing trauma fall into the enticing trap of rumination.[1,88] Of course, as you flee whatever cue is in your mind ('that stupid colleague!'), with a ruminative behaviour (you play a scene on repeat in your mind, where you 'put them in their place once and for all!'), you have a brief relief ('they are finally where they deserve to be!'). But here we go; you've laid the cornerstone for a rumination habit. You've sent a learning signal to your reward system: do this again.

Mental Health

Research shows that if you ruminate regularly, you're more likely to spiral off into depression, start suffering from anxiety, insomnia or eating disorders, and you may more easily fall into the trap of substance abuse like smoking, or spin off into behavioural addictions. Like a drug, rumination makes us spend more and more time with this behaviour. And with thoughts alone, you cannot solve anything that happens in the outside world, especially if the rumination concerns other people. Other people are 'out there', with their own personalities, opinions and actions. Hence, any problem-solving we ruminate about is bound to fail in the real world.[2,3] Therefore, people who ruminate a lot also spiral further down: they get worse at thinking positive, are crap at solving problems, their creativity decreases and they find themselves involved in more and more interpersonal conflicts. As Mark Twain put it, 'You can't depend on your eyes when your imagination is out of focus.' We misinterpret what we see, get annoyed, lash out. We seem in a vortex of trouble. Until we withdraw. Then we sit and stare into nothingness, seemingly enjoying a pleasant reverie; however, in reality, we're trying to escape a self-made hell, having taught our brain a rumination habit loop.[1,89]

Noteworthy evidence has started to emerge in the past years: people who ruminate regularly have poorer immune markers (e.g. leukocyte and lymphocyte counts, as well as number of B cells).[76,90,91] Although the link between rumination and inflammation in the body is still poorly understood,[92–96] the available evidence invites us, at the very least, to *consider* seeking alternative behaviours.

Yet, a habit is a full circle, hard to break, and it's hard to identify the cue that started it all off. When our habit has to do with an overt behaviour of the body, the cue is easier to identify. You reached for your phone. Why? You saw a notification icon pop up, or you felt an inner urge to check. Those are some cues that can set off a habit loop to do with phone-checking, for example. But ruminations inside the jaws of our mind are hard to spot. On our way to choose an alternative, healthier behaviour, we need to identify the cues of our habit loops.

Spotting your cue is an important labour that *you* need to *choose* to do.★

Masters of Self-Deception

Theoretically, you now know what to do. Find your cues. However, there is a problem. When in the loop, it's hard to get out, and there is another uncomfortable truth: our brain excels at coming up with 'after the fact' justifications for sub-optimal acts and behaviours. 'Mistakes were made, but not by me'[97] – an often-heard sentence. This cognitive behaviour that keeps us repeating bad behaviour is known as *self-justification*.

Cognitive Dissonance

Leo Festinger first proposed the theory of cognitive dissonance when he conducted experiments in the 1950s.[98] Cognitive dissonance happens in the mind when we have two pieces of information about ourselves that contradict each other. For example, we've snapped at someone, piece one. But *actually*, our mind is convinced that we're a good person that does things for good reasons, piece two. To reconcile this conflicting information, we come up with a

---

★ As always, if you have or suspect you could have a clinical mental health condition, you should check in with a professional to ensure that this cue-searching does not become another prompt for your thoughts to spiral out of control.

justification for why we did what we did that is congruent with that belief, e.g. 'they deserved it'.

Our mind is incredibly skilled at streamlining all information so that it fits the story in our mind.[99] 'Everyone *needs* a sweet from time to time,' says our mind after we finish a tub of ice cream, even though we had taken the decision to give up sugar. 'I literally have *nothing* to wear,' it says to our guilty feelings after overdrawing our bank account for an expensive outfit we may never wear. And it gets even worse.

In 2005, scientists played a trick on participants' minds in an experiment.[100] In the first part of the experiment, participants were asked to watch a series of pictures of potential partners and rate their attractiveness. The researchers presented the pictures in pairs and instructed the participants to pick the person that they found most attractive. After many pairs of pictures, part 2 started. The researchers now instructed the participants that they would be seeing the pictures of the people they had chosen in part 1 and ask them to provide justifications for why they had chosen that person, in other words, what made that person attractive to them. Participants gave all the reasons why they had chosen the respective person – they were beautiful, they had a nice smile, kind eyes, good hair. What was the catch?

The researchers didn't show the pictures that the participants had chosen. They showed them those that they *didn't* choose. Still, participants babbled away, giving all their good reasons for making a choice that they had never in fact made.

What was going on here?

The authors of the study, published in *Science*, called the effect 'choice blindness'. And it set off cognitive dissonance and confirmation bias. Confirmation bias is the tendency of our mind to recall and interpret situations and information in a way that confirms the harmonic humming that is already going on in our mind.

Participants' minds received the information 'you have chosen this picture' and in accordance with the harmonic humming of their minds whispering to them that they are rational, congruent people, they proceeded to provide reasons for choosing that person.

How does the brain make such blatant irrationality possible?

During the 2004 US presidential elections, a team of researchers invited people who supported two opposing presidential candidates to participate in an experiment with functional magnetic resonance imagery (fMRI), allowing them to study the participants' brains in action.[101] The researchers showed the participants information that was aligned with their beliefs about their candidate and information that opposed their beliefs. The results were eyewatering: when presented with information that was incongruent with their beliefs, the parts of their brains responsible for rational reasoning, the prefrontal cortices, simply shut down. When supporters received information that was congruent with their positive beliefs about the candidate, deep structures of the brain that are involved in feelings and basic constants of the body were active. The supporters' brains simply did not process the information that was not congruent with their beliefs, while basic structures of their brain hungrily nibbled at everything that confirmed their beliefs – confirmatory bias.

So does that mean we have an excuse when we succumb to the mind hooks? Can we just say, 'My brain made me do it!'? No. What the evidence means is that we need to be prepared for our mind to play those tricks on us.[102] Our brain wants to keep harmonically humming away as it always did, avoiding cognitive dissonance in our mind at all costs. We are not as rational and in control as we'd love to think we are.

Pleasure-Plus Behaviours

Any leisure behaviour can make our brain go astray; even the arts leave us vulnerable to mind hooks that can send our thoughts spinning and even ruin our life. For example, if we develop a behavioural addiction to them, like the tango dancer Hamish did.

If what you're doing is focussed entirely on obtaining some 'prize' in the end, it should set off warning signs in your mind, because this is when the vast neural pathways in our brain responsible for 'wanting' something are active. These are dopamine-fuelled and motivate us to continually chase onwards, seek out that next shot of our thing. This craving-wanting state in our brain *promises* pleasure, but it is, if we listen in, a quite unsatisfying feeling to have. We're never at ease, never still, never enjoying – and flow will not come in that state. The pathways that we want to activate in our brain with what we do are those that fuel our brain with endogenous opioids and endocannabinoids ('endo' just means that they come from inside us).[103] When those systems are 'on', we feel that warm, all-encompassing pleasure. We're satisfied, we're at ease, we enjoy – and this enables flow.

But what calls these wonderful pathways into action? Pleasure-plus behaviours. Those are behaviours you *like* doing (you might also 'want' to do them, but the important point is that you *like* them while you're doing them). So don't choose to do behaviours that you don't *like* much (e.g. 'running') *just* to get something that you *want* (e.g. a thinner waist line).

How do you get to *like* doing something? Well, that's very personal. You need to investigate which behaviour does it for you. Usually, we *like* doing something that is, in some way, meaningful to us – behaviours that activate our feeling of 'me', our memories and preferences. Whether we like a behaviour or not can also depend on the context that we create for our senses while we do that behaviour – sights, smells, tactile sensations, maybe the people we're with. Creative behaviours have a way of enticing our brain (as we will see in the next chapters) and making us *like* them because they can so powerfully link our body movements with thoughts, feelings and concepts that are important to us. As sensory impressions travel through our brain towards our awareness, they collide with our memories, ideas and fantasies. These special 'collisions' between sensory cues and the memories and beliefs that make us *us* have the power to move us, and even to induce transformational experiences.[104–106] And as we explore that path with our creative activity, our brain activates those special neural pathways and suddenly, we just *are* – and our mind flows.

So, remember this liking-wanting principle on your quest for *your* pleasure-plus behaviours as we dive further in. You need your chosen art to engage the personal meaning-making systems of your brain. The thrill or the hook that you might also *want* – that's like candy; a little bit is fine, you can nibble at it as you dive into the deeper layers of the story. Suddenly, as the incoming information gets mixed up with feelings of 'me', together they create meaning in our brain. That's when the eudemonist philosophers in our brain's Camp 2 are finally delighted too.

On our pathway to flow we must choose arts that also appeal to those deeper levels of our brain. That's when we strengthen those neural connections and forge our pathway to flow.

Life can be a tragedy because of our relationships with other people. It can stress us out, keep us awake at night, make us have sad, happy, angry, fearful rumination, and everything at once. As long as there have been humans, life seems to have been like this. Drama makes the world go round. You just need to go to the movies, and you'll see a reflection of that merry-go-round, made by life in human societies.[1,2] In the past chapters, we looked specifically at threats to our physical body, like too much sitting, or straining our body or brain with too much work or exercise, eating too much sugar, not sleeping enough, or spending too much time on our phones. They can all shorten our attention spans and make flow impossible. Now let's add another layer to this: the social layer of our brain – another source of unspeakably grinding pink elephants.

→

The philosopher Arthur Schopenhauer used 'The Porcupine Dilemma' as a metaphor to explain the contradiction of *needing* human connections, while often suffering *because* of these relationships:[3]

Two porcupines in winter need each other's warmth to survive, but when they come too close, they inevitably prick each other.

'Ouch! Get away from me!'

'Ah, but it was you getting closer!'

After pricking each other painfully, they ease away, sometimes disperse completely. Only to then realise again, how cold it is, and that they need each other's warmth and the cycle repeats itself.

Real porcupines know how to cuddle despite their spines, but humans don't. We need others, but whenever humans get together, invariably they create mutual discomfort. There is no avoiding that. The trouble, again, starts with our body; our body needs others to survive.

The Social Brain

Scientists refer to some interrelated systems of our brain as 'the social brain'. That's because of those systems' importance during our social interactions.[4] The social brain includes systems like the amygdala and the nucleus accumbens. These systems process the emotional importance of stuff that is happening around us (amygdala), and whether we're likely to get a social reward from what's happening (a smile, a hug, a pat on the shoulder) (nucleus accumbens).[4] The social brain also includes the insula and the anterior cingulate cortex which are implied in empathy and processing the affective value of social information, plus a 'mentalising network' (precuneus, medial prefrontal cortex and temporoparietal junction) which is implied in understanding other's minds and perspectives.[4,5]

You may now wonder why many of these structures that I now mention as part of the social brain were also part of what I called Camp 1 and Camp 2 in Chapter 3 in relation to reward, choices, learning habits and behavioural addictions. You're right to be confused. The reason is . . . it's complicated.

When scientists study the brain, they try to give names to the subdivisions and systems. This helps us organise the information about the different brain systems and their possible functions. However, there is much overlap between systems and functions. We have only *one* brain, and we realise more and more that what looks like different behaviours on the outside may, in fact, be taken care of by similar brain systems – likely because they have similar survival value for our body.

For our pathway to flow, let's stick with this; whether our brain is taking care of body-survival information or social-survival information, portions of those low-level systems of Camps 1 and 2 are playing a role, along with the brain-stem jukebox. They push our conscious mind to act in ways to keep our body alive.

In theory, nowadays, there is no threat to our body from being alone anymore. In our modern societies, we have heating that keeps us warm, there are no lions around that may attack us, we can work and buy the food we need. We don't need to rely on a group of spiky porcupines. However, remember that these low-level brain structures, that brain-stem jukebox that worries about our body, was made by evolution in times of trouble, back in a very dangerous prehistoric world. These systems have an in-built need for human connection, full stop. Loneliness makes our body-orchestra chime out the stress symphony, making us vulnerable to viruses; and the pink elephants in our mind will make us feel depressed, lonely and anxious; they will be up there, alert, stealing our sleep at night.

Hugs, Smiles and Caresses: The Power and Importance of Human Contact

When I arrived in London for my first postdoctoral position, I was new in town, had only a few acquaintances, and I was starting a new role in one of the highest-level research institutes for movement neuroscience in the world, the famous Institute for Cognitive Neuroscience (ICN) of University College London. This was all a bit scary, and very unfamiliar.

I'm sure there are people that shrug off the discomfort of the unfamiliar in a split second and throw themselves out there. I just haven't met anyone like that yet.

So it was on one of those days that I was pondering my new existence in the impersonal city of London, that one of my new colleagues convinced me to join her for a talk. Amazing scientific talks are organised on a weekly basis in the research institutions of the Bloomsbury area of London, where the ICN is located too. They are organised by scientists for scientists, to give a platform for knowledge exchange. The title of the day's talk sounded interesting, given my situation as a newbie: 'Affective Touch and the Brain'. I wondered what affective touch could have to do with the brain, and what was 'affective' touch anyway?

What an exciting new world would open up before my eyes that afternoon.

The speaker of the day was Professor Francis McGlone from the Liverpool John Moores University, and he told us that we have special receptors in the skin, the CT cells that fire, ta ta ta ta, when stroked at a specific speed. Those receptors only exist on sensitive parts of our body, where we have glabrous skin,[6] like the inside of our forearm, not on hairy skin.[7] And when those receptors fire, they funnel that information via long ganglia, up through the spinal cord and into the structures of our social brain. Those brain structures are, interestingly, also implied in reward and in the maintenance of homeostasis and the regulation of our immune system. They matter for our health and wellbeing.

After World War 2, many a horrific news story hit the headlines, revealing what had been going on during the years of darkness. One of these accounts was about Romanian orphans. Deprived of human social contact, of smiles, touches and cuddles, they had developed terrible autoimmune diseases like eczema. They constantly had infections, and some died of health complications. The lack of social contact had depleted their immune systems.

Inspired by those harrowing findings, Professor Harry Harlow undertook a series of experiments in the 1950s; unethical by today's standards.[8] Harlow selected three groups of new-born monkeys. One group was allowed to stay with their mums and receive all the cuddles and hugs and kisses that they wanted. Another group was put in cages alone but with a 'surrogate' teddy-mother made of fur, which also contained enough food and drink for the new-borns to survive. Another group of little monkeys was put in a cage with no surrogate mother, they simply had enough food and drink in a corner of the cage – enough to sate their physical needs, in theory. But this was not enough to *survive*, as would soon become evident.

The little monkeys that had spent time in isolation and were then re-introduced to others in a group were socially odd, self-injured and were generally loners, staying away from others. Many died, either because they refused to eat, or because of health complications.

Building on what we already know about the Romanian orphans and Harlow's studies, McGlone was about to show us just how great an impact affective touch has on all of us in our everyday lives, not only during our formative years. During his talk he showed us a video of a person sitting in something like a dentist chair. They had one arm locked in some sort of vice that kept the arm immobile in a slightly awkward position, palm facing upwards, exposing the inner side of the forearm. Where usually the dentist's lamp reaches towards the patient's mouth, via its multi-joint arm, the researchers had instead mounted something that looked like a wheel the size of a large tea cup. It was oriented vertically, spinning slowly in mid-air, getting nowhere. Three paintbrushes had been mounted on the wheel in the direction of travel, and from time to time, the researchers would lower the metallic arm towards the forearm of the participant in the chair, and the paintbrushes would, slowly and carefully, almost tenderly, stroke the participant's inner forearm. Whenever they did so, a rattling sound was heard; ta ta ta ta . . . and this was a neuron firing.

On the same arm, a small distance above the place where the paintbrushes were stroking the participant's skin, the researchers had attached a tiny electrode in the receptive field of a receptor in the skin. Receptors are the docking stations for information coming into our bodies, in this case for touch information, and we have them all over our skin. Different types of receptors in our skin tell us about hot and cold, about sharp and soft, about stretch and compression . . . and about whether we're being 'affectively touched'.

The researchers had attached an amplifier to the signal from the receptor that transmitted the information to its neuron – and made it fire. And that was making the sound, whenever the receptor was stimulated. This strange construction of paintbrushes circling on a wheel was in fact stimulating the participant's social brain structures indirectly, via the skin!

McGlone showed us how 'affective' touch is when someone caresses us at about 3 cm per second – the teacup wheel on the video was spinning slowly, at the speed of a caress – and the neuron was firing, ta ta ta ta . . . sending off all those good messages to the social brain. If the movement on the skin was too fast, like 18 cm per second – the teacup wheel was spinning quick rounds – this was perceived as uncomfortable, and the neuron wouldn't fire – there was silence.[9,10]

He said that these special skin-brain connections are in fact super important for the maintenance of bodily health and wellbeing. Put very simply: if you caress your loved one, you're in fact regulating their immune system, and making them healthier.[11]

In an impersonal city like London you certainly wouldn't touch, let alone *affectively* touch other people just like that. Yet, a loneliness pandemic has been raging in London's skyscraper jungle for decades.[12–15] I saw more than one of my fellow researchers sneaking a passing glance down at their inner forearm, the place on our body where there are many of those special receptors.[9,10]

→

This is the important nugget of information on our pathway to flow: social connection is important for the wellbeing of our physical body. When we don't have these connections, pink elephants populate our mind, stirred up by the threat. If we have no social connections, no hugs and caresses, no smiles, this is a threat to the system.

Why?

Think back to the time when these low-level systems of our brain were sculpted by evolutionary pressures. Individuals that could live together in groups had a larger chance of surviving than a lone wolf individual. Hence, lack of social contact (which whispers into our conscious mind as the feeling of loneliness) is a threat to the system, and if we're alone or excluded from our group (imagined or real), depressed and scared pink elephants will enter our mind via these basic survival mechanisms.

To show you how basic, and somewhat 'simple' those systems are, working largely outside of our awareness,[16] consider these two experiments. In 2008, researchers from Yale University played a trick on their research participants' social brain. They gave two groups of participants a drink to hold, while they asked them questions about another person. Those participants who held a steaming brew in their hand found their experiment buddy more caring and generous than those who jarred their sense of touch with an iced drink. In a second experiment, participants were asked to hold a warm or a cold therapeutic pad – and now, those holding the warm pad became more generous; they were more likely to buy a present for a friend than for themselves.[17] Low-level information about the body's homeostasis, like its temperature and social information, like 'trust', are both represented in the insula (the brain systems that we're here loosely referring to as Camp 2), and we can see how easily they are biased.

A Japanese research team also played a trick on their research participants' social brain. They came up with what they called 'a huggable communication device'. For fifteen minutes each, the researchers had one group of participants texting with loved ones abroad on a smartphone, while another group texted, holding a hugging device, like a huge teddy. The results showed that the group holding the hugging device while texting had less stress hormones circling in their blood.[18]

Do you see the power of what we expose our senses to – in this case, the tactile sense? Even if we consciously know that it's just a fluffy toy, the information funnelled to our Camps 1 and 2 due to the impressions on our touch receptors from the teddy tell the stress mechanisms of our brain to relax and get rid of the stress hormone, fight and flight is over.

Rental Health

In February 2023, 58-year-old medical secretary Sheila Seleoane was discovered dead in her flat in the Lord's Court housing estate in Peckham, London. The expiry date of the food in her refrigerator suggested that she had been dead for over two years.[19] Without anyone noticing. Neighbours described her as friendly but distant, someone who greeted others on the staircase, but who didn't seek contact. According to the UK Office for National Statistics about 7 per cent of British adults say that they always feel lonely, or often do, and 25 per cent feel lonely at least some of the time.

Often this type of self-imposed exile is due to some kind of trauma, of bad experiences, the break-up of relationships. But the feeling of loneliness reinforces their pink elephants and lonely people become convinced that other people are impossible to be around and will bring them only harm. That's the porcupine dilemma.

The outrage at Sheila Seleoane's late discovery was heard all over the large news outlets. But she wasn't the first case. In 2006, Joyce Vincent was discovered, the expiry dates of the food in her fridge suggesting she had been dead for three years without anyone noticing. The beautiful 38-year-old had withdrawn from everyone in the years before her death, so no one was surprised about her being missing. She had previously lived in a shelter for domestic abuse victims, and was known as someone who would withdraw if there were conflicts: changing jobs, houses, her circle of friends.[20] We don't know much about the case, but you can make an educated guess about what was going on here.

The reason for her death, just like in the case of Sheila, was impossible to determine, but it is thought that she died of complications from a recent peptic ulcer (an autoimmune disease related to stress to the system) that she had been treated for, or due to asthma from which she suffered. Remember the health complications that occurred in the loneliness studies mentioned above, with non-human mammals?

In winter 2022/23, BBC radio 4 started a series called 'Rental Health', trying to start a conversation about the housing nightmares that exist in the UK. The programme is about landlords and tenants and their common problems. It could well also include the social layer of our brain in the conversation. Because, just as mould is dangerous for our health,[21] social isolation is 'unfit for human life' too.

A Special Tether: The Vagus Nerve

In medieval Europe, doctors were forbidden by the church to dissect dead bodies, even if this was in the service of science. However, luckily for the progress of science, scientists did not conform to those rules imposed by the church and made important discoveries for all of us. When those medieval doctors dissected dead bodies in secret to investigate the mysteries of human health and disease, over and again their notebooks contained allusions to a very special nerve. Whichever part of the body they studied, this nerve would be present. It seemed to come from the brain, run through the spinal cord to the heart, to the lungs, to different organs of the gut, and its ramifications would even reach different muscles in the body. When exploring the head, the doctors were able to follow the meanderings of this nerve all the way up into our facial muscles. The nerve was connected to the muscles that we need for our facial expressions, to the muscles that modulate our vocal prosody (meaning whether we speak with a high pitch or a soft pitch) and to those muscles that are responsible for our head movements and the nerves in our ears that enable us to listen.

Imagine: the muscles that we use to smile and frown, to speak and to listen, and those that we use to nod and shrug – they are actually connected with our heart, our lungs, our spleen, our gut and many more parts of our internal milieu. The popular notion that suggests that smiling makes you feel better, even when you have nothing to smile at, makes a lot of sense if we think about that connection.

The medieval doctors called the nerve the *vagus* nerve, to honour its vagabonding nature.

Research led by Professor Stephen Porges from the University of North Carolina has in the past decades revealed that the vagus nerve is even more important than medieval scientists ever imagined: the vagus nerve is actually an incredibly important aspect of our health and of disease. His team is particularly eager to raise awareness about the face–heart connection[22–26] because it showcases just how central the importance of our social environment is for our wellbeing.

When the facial expressions of the people around us and our own facial expressions express safety and wellbeing, studies have shown that this is a direct signal to our heart and extended body.[27] Positive facial moves activate a specific restorative state in the body.

As a result, our body relaxes.[26,28] Safe surroundings make our heart slow down, get rid of the stress hormone cortisol and reduce inflammatory processes in the body by acting on cytokines (important agents of our immune system[29]). Porges and his colleagues call this orchestration the *Social Engagement System* of our brain. When things are safe, our body goes into restorative mode and becomes healthier as a result. This is how people around us can contribute to our physical health and wellbeing, simply by being there, signalling safety and comfort. And we can do the same for them of course. If someone looks frightened or lonely, smile and speak with a low-pitch voice. The vagus nerve is indeed very special.

→

In 1938, Harvard University started the longest happiness study in the world.[30,31] A young John F. Kennedy, who was a student at the university at the time, was among the first cohort of people whose life was mapped and measured in all possible ways.

The study started small, just a few hundred participants. But since then, it has grown. And its research question revolves around the conundrum: how to live a happy and healthy life, how to live longer? Might the secret to a long, happy and healthy life be hidden in money? In a good education? In a good job?

No, the very simple answer to this research question, after all these years of measuring people's lives, seems to be this: the ingredients of a long and happy life are wrapped up in the *relationships* with other people that we forge throughout our lives.

Having strong trusting relationships with others decreases risk for heart disease, for getting ill, and so on. As we've seen in the previous sections, the reason is simply that being with others switches off the fight and flight mode in us. Inside the bodies of lonely people, as I was in those first London months, the fight and flight symphony is playing at full blast, the stress hormones ringing in their veins, increasing inflammation in their bodies, making them ill. But people who have the opportunity to share a hug, chat with a trusted person about nothing in particular, have a good laugh and friendly eye contact, release the relaxation symphony into their body, making it healthy and ready to rumble again.[27]

The neurohormone oxytocin is the main marker of attachment,[11] and the social brain has many receptors for this messenger substance. When it's around, we feel 'home', safe, secure. We get it from healthy social interactions.[32–34] Some scientists say that we need eight hugs a day to stay healthy!

Trust in others is one of the keys to success. Yet – as we all know, life in human societies is anything but ideal. Those spines are not easy to live with . . .

Rejection: A Cyber Ball Game

It's a beautiful, dreamy summer's day. You're on the lawn with friends, playing a ball game. You toss the ball back and forth through the air between you. Giggles and cheers fill the air. But during the last few tosses, your friends have somehow stopped tossing the ball in your direction. They keep it between them, laughing at the funny ways they catch the ball in turn, and then make it fly back through the air. Between them. You wave your arms, signalling you're ready to take the ball. They don't even look in your direction any more. Why not?

It is as if you don't exist.

You get a sinking feeling in your belly, and a tingling cold sensation on your skin.[35] The chill of the shade is taking over.

These sensations that you perceive consciously are accompanied by many processes in your body that you are unaware of. These are processes that evolution crafted so they can keep you safe – because social rejection is a threat to the system. Because that's what's currently happening: social rejection.

You feel terrible and your mind space gets narrowed down to one objective: be part of the group again.

The situation that I describe above is part of an experiment that psychologists designed in the 1990s to test in the lab the effects of rejection on our body-orchestra. Sitting at a computer, you're asked to play the 'cyberball game',[36] a ball-tossing game, with co-players over the internet. What the experimenters don't tell you is that the virtual players are, at some point, going to stop tossing the ball in your direction. While you play the game, the psychologists are monitoring things like your heart rate, your perspiration and your breathing rate via little electrodes attached to your body. They may also take a saliva sample before and after the game to determine how much stress hormone is out and about in your system.

Even in such a controlled lab situation, playing a virtual ball-tossing game with a computer, with virtual agents who are not your friends at all, who are, in fact, just programmed bits and bytes, the moment that they start excluding you from the game is marked by your heart rate, sweat rate and general stress hormone levels skyrocketing.

Rejection impacts our physiology. You know by now what arousal in the body can mean: activation of congruent negative, sad, angry or otherwise negative memories, that burst open the floodgates for the pink elephants. In the 'cyberball questionnaire' that experimenters give to their participants after the experiment, most participants share that they feel sad, frustrated or angry. The scientists of the study conclude that 'the experience of distress associated with being ostracised is innate'.[37] If the virtual version of ostracism can bring chaos into the system,[36,38] imagine what happens in your body when this happens with real friends in a real situation.

The cues of social rejection are hard-coded in our brain to set off alarm bells and compel us to seek social contact. Yet, if social contact is linked to trauma caused by other people, the very medicine that would make us feel better makes us stay away: other people.

The Imprint of Trauma on the Brain

While I don't want to suggest that the arts could be a sole therapy for trauma, the science of trauma helps us understand how we can use the arts to overcome difficult situations.

One important point that the science of trauma has revealed is: what our brain is good at depends on genes, but also, importantly, on our life experience.[39] The brain changes in a *use-dependent way*, says the American psychiatrist, Bruce Perry.[40] We have neuroplasticity and we never lose the ability to learn.[41] Thus, if our brain *learns* that the world is a dangerous place, with many threats, and that we can't trust anyone – then that's what it will be good at: detecting threats.[42] Therefore, after trauma, the world is experienced with a different nervous system, that has an altered perception of risk and safety, according to expert trauma psychiatrist Bessel van der Kolk.[43]

Strange Behaviour

There are very few dance movies and shows that I can bear watching. Most directors seem to think that professional dancing is about nothing more than getting *that* role, and about anorexia. The characters are usually quite flat. There is one exception, however, and its central narrative shows how trauma can affect our behaviour.

In the 2021 French series *L'Opéra* with Ariane Labed, we join the life of a party girl, Zoé, drinking, not sleeping much, and having loads of casual sex. Oh, and then she's an Étoile at the Opéra de Paris too, one of the highest possible echelons a ballet dancer can reach. But she's a falling star, a ballerina in trouble. As the story unfolds, we learn that the glamour is unreal, that her behaviour, in fact, is what trauma psychologists refer to as 'self-aggression'. Some people cut, hit or otherwise injure themselves in a process of self-loathing, which is all too common in people who have suffered trauma. Zoé drinks, parties, takes drugs. And this self-destructive behaviour has driven many people away from her. As spectators of Zoé's battle to try to regain others' trust and her job, we're torn between feeling sorry for her and finding her behaviour a little 'off'. Seeing the world through her eyes, however, we understand that she is a survivor of some dark stuff. In passing, we learn that she had a miscarriage, that she had a terrible injury that left her unable to dance, scared and traumatised, and alone . . . 'I lost my body, my baby *and you* . . .' she shouts at the handsome Sasha when he enters the story, and we find out that he left her after *all that*, and that he went off to the Bolshoi ballet to become a star there. Bastard.

The Brain Changes in a Use-dependent Way

When you hear about the awful things that have happened to people in an abusive relationship, or who have survived great losses like Zoé, you may at times rest your head in your hands, overwhelmed by the cruelty of what they've endured. Now, still with your head in your hands, visualise that inside your skull, you have all these interconnected neural systems, with neurons firing along beautiful pearl strings. Then there is the low-level brain-stem jukebox playing life-saving discs, depending on the buttons we push on the jukebox with our behaviour, and Camps 1 and 2 taking care of reward, meaning-making, pleasure, learning and a great deal of our social relations.

One very important change in the brain brought about by trauma is a hyper*activated* Camp 1. A traumatised person's Camp 1 is now like David Hasselhoff's *Knight Rider* car, scanning the surroundings for threats related to their trauma. These threats can be real or imagined. The bottom line is, many cues are easily and sometimes irrationally interpreted as a threat to the system. This hypervigilance of traumatised people is truly excruciating, for themselves, and for others around them. They become very defensive.

In one scene, Zoé shouts at a colleague after a lift in which he supposedly touched her in the wrong way during a partnering situation. He had agreed to partner her in a pas-de-deux, to help her, but she explodes at him and hisses, 'If you ever hurt me like this again, you'll see what happens!' Zoé gives the impression of using other people to her advantage, while never giving much in return.

Zoé's vampirish behaviour is common in victims of trauma. Their nervous system is changed. It is possibly still in fight and flight mode, grasping anything they can, as an act of self-defence. 'A drowning person cannot rescue another from drowning,' they tell you in therapy education courses, to prepare future therapists for trauma victims. It may be difficult to understand whether or not someone who is partying, laughing and being gorgeous is a trauma victim. The exuberance and arrogance are, in cases of trauma, a mechanism of self-defence, a self-protection to overcome a nagging internal feeling of inadequacy and self-loathing. Zoé sabotages all relationships because she hates herself on a very subconscious level. If you'd ask her, she'd deny it. The trauma literature refers to this as the re-enactment of trauma, that maintains it, in one huge vicious cycle.[44]

Generational Trauma

While I was studying in Spain, news about boats with refugees arriving on the beaches was regularly in the papers – but it wasn't really news. From my friends in Mallorca, I heard that this has been happening for decades. One lady once told me how she had met a nicely dressed gentleman with a light backpack on one of the southern beaches of the island. He had kindly asked her in broken Spanish, 'Excuse me, could you point me in the direction of Valencia?' (which is on mainland Spain and not on this island).

I met Aamos in Spain during my PhD. His parents had come over the water before he was born and obtained asylum as political refugees. His is a story about how children of traumatised adults can come to carry the trauma of their parents. There are some indicators that trauma can persist three generations down, and that this is due to different reasons.[45] One of them may be genetic.

Some research suggests that the cues of trauma may get coded into our genetic material as a way to react to cues in the environment. It's still early days to make firm conclusions about this, but there are studies with rodents that present interesting findings. Their mammal brains are very similar to ours, so we can tentatively use this evidence to understand more about our human brain too.[46] Researchers have been able to show genetic transmission of fear of a smell related to a parental traumatic experience to the next generation. The scientists created traumatic experiences in a group of mice (they gave them mild but uncomfortable electric shocks to their feet), and each time, they also gave them the smell of aceto-phenone which is a smell like oranges. We know that this smell activates a specific odorant receptor called Olfr151. In the trauma-tised mouse parents' pups, the scientists found that the genetic information relating to the Olfr151 pathway was enhanced – as if this information had been signalled with a highlighter so the indi-vidual would be able to have a particularly good ability to detect this smell. And what was even more striking was that if genetic material from a traumatised mouse was taken and used to fertilise in vitro another non-traumatised mouse, the highlighted Olfr151 pathway was still transmitted to the next generation. This was the fear of the smell of oranges – transmitted transgenerationally![47]

Why is this relevant? Because sometimes the trauma we are carrying is not ours. The trauma and all possible solutions to the problem are of the previous generation.

Besides the genetic transmission that may happen, behaviours, anxiety-led choices, scared looks, are transmitted to the next gen-eration via the associative learning mechanisms that we've spoken about. Little ones sit at the morning table with their families, observe them, and do what our species has done since the dawn of civilisation: they learn by imitation. The mirroring mechanisms of our brain kick in as soon as we see something that's relevant for survival. And something that is potentially dangerous is definitely relevant to survival. If Mum, Dad or Granny makes a scared face at a loud sound, like the doorbell ringing, because it could be the secret police, rather than just a courier with a package calling, then the little brain sitting at the morning table may develop an aversion to the doorbell too – and not even know why. It's a *learned* fear. For the rest of their life, they may startle and have an uncomfortable feeling when the doorbell rings.[48]

Many of us have parents or grandparents who have been touched by war or crisis in some way or another. My grandmother kept her clothes stacked in a very particular order next to her bed all her life – the blouse, the skirt and then the tights on top, in the order she'd put them on – in case she had to dress quickly if there was an air raid siren in the middle of the night. She'd always have her shoes lined up, her key ready to go, and there would never be anything obstructing the way to the door. I notice in myself that I stack my clothes in the order I will put them on, that I always know where my keys are, the way to the door is never blocked. Why? Well, likely because I learned it from a very important person to me. I saw her slightly uneasy looks when I didn't comply with these rules. She was never angry, just looked so concerned that I would choose to do as she preferred, just to see her smiling face again. With time, these behaviours became learned, and now I myself feel very uncomfortable if I don't have these things under control.

Children of refugees may be haunted, rushed, driven to keep going their whole lives, running away from something, or towards something, without actually knowing what that something *is*. If their parents came over the sea, their children may be irrationally scared of the sound of waves and get nauseous at the smell of the sea – even if they were not yet born at the time of the boat trip. This was the case for Aamos. He despised the sea and he lived in the centre of the island, Sineu, that is the farthest possible distance on all sides from all beaches.

We, the next generation, have the trauma, but not the key to solve it. Hence, this is a perfect ruminative loop that will never cease. Unless we find a different solution to it, like expressing all these unspoken questions, the sensations, the images and sounds that trouble us, through some means other than the spoken word. For example, through writing, drawing, dancing or singing, and so on.

Maybe you want to take a moment to think about which of your own behaviours may be a left-over trauma from a generation before you? And what are the cues that trigger them? Are there behaviours of yours that are illogical, that others ask you, 'Why do you do that?' or look surprised when you do them? Maybe they are not caused by anything that matters to you, but by something that mattered to family members of yours before you were born? Those are good existential questions to ask your creative brain about and, then, to express through a creative activity and find flow. You may find a strong feeling of relief afterwards. Always ask yourself – what are the cues that set my mind spinning? Then grab them, and express yourself.

→

Robin Williams once said, 'Everyone you meet is fighting a battle you know nothing about. Be kind. Always.' The multiple-Oscar-winning actor, known for his warmth and quick wit, secretly struggled with addiction and bipolar disorder. The characters we've spoken about here (the dancer Zoé and the second-generation refugee, Aamos) have in common that they, for different reasons, have a hyper-activated Camp 1 of their brain. Their brains detect threats, real and imagined, everywhere. These act as cues that send their pink elephants spinning in one huge ruminative habit loop. It always starts with a cue related to the trauma, and off spin their minds, flashbacks rain down on them, activating their bodies' defence mechanisms, and this arousal sends even more pink elephants into their minds. That's why it's important to know your 'trauma' cues. Even if we're not trauma victims ourselves, we all have cues that overstep our boundaries. What are they for you?

Identify Your Cues

Try to zoom out and look around in your mind. Be a sniffer dog for a moment, and let him zoom around inside your mind, to detect *that* cue, thought or feeling that sets off the domino-chain reaction of ruminative loops in *your* mind. Is it a feeling of anger, sadness, fear, loneliness, unfairness, betrayal, humiliation, hatred, love, attraction . . . or the neon lights of an unfinished task that makes you feel small? It is generally something that overwhelms you. Grab it, and here is the first remedy you can turn to right here and now. It was recommended to me by Aamos many years ago, and now I have found the science that explains why it works.

Download it Onto the Page

'First of all, I'm not here to sell you a codified, copyrighted system. Experiment, and see what works best for you. Set aside three or four days, find ten or fifteen minutes, and just sit down and write. The only rule I have is to write continuously, don't worry about grammar, or sentence structure, or spelling. And, in fact, plan to throw it away afterwards.' This is Professor James Pennebaker from the University of Texas, speaking on Michael Mosley's BBC Radio 4 programme, *Just One Thing*. He is speaking about what he has spent the past thirty years studying: expressive writing.[49,50]

The first important study in the 1980s about expressive writing showed that expressive writing about a stressful experience improves biomarkers of physical health. Researchers asked two groups of people to write for fifteen minutes on four consecutive evenings. One group was asked to write about a personally traumatic event, the other group was asked to just write about trivial happenings in life. Six months after these writing episodes, the scientists collected the surprising findings: the group that had written about the traumatic event had significantly reduced their number of visits to the doctor! Writing honestly about the emotional impact of a personally traumatic happening seemed to reduce the effect on health of such traumas simmering in the background.[51]

'It's so surprising, how honest and authentic you suddenly feel when you just write,' Aamos once told me. 'I always try to pretend that I'm all right when I'm in public and on my job. I put on a mask. But that mask just makes me feel miserable. When I write, I'm back to myself, and it's like taking a breath again, finally.'

→

The list of astounding benefits of doing this three to four times per week is long: expressive writing has been shown to have a positive impact on sleep quality, asthma[52,53] and arthritis.[54,55] It improves wellbeing in patients with irritable bowel syndrome,[56] in patients with Parkinson's,[57] and chronic pain,[55,58] and it has been found to lower blood pressure.[59] Pennebaker's recommendation to write twenty minutes a day for three or four consecutive days improves cancer patients' wellbeing,[60,61] their quality of life,[62] and reduces the negative impact of the experience, as regular expressive writing has been shown to decrease stress hormone reactivity after trauma other than a cancer diagnosis.[63,64] It has also been shown to reduce post-traumatic stress syndrome symptoms,[63] lower stress hormones in blood after a stressful episode,[65] and enhance brain power.[66] One meta-analysis showed that expressive writing especially improves physical health variables,[67] and serves as a buffer against anxious and depressive rumination.[68,69] Another scientific intervention showed that expressive writing about stress related to their sexuality improved gay men's psychosocial functioning, as compared to a group that just wrote about a neutral topic.[70]

In one double-blind randomised controlled trial (the best type of study),[53] 146 adults with asthma were divided into two groups. One group was asked to practise twenty minutes of expressive writing for three consecutive days in a week over a twelve-month period, the other group was asked to practise non-emotional writing for the same time. Results showed that the included patients' lung function improved by 14 per cent with regular expressive writing.

A research group from New Zealand asked a group of medical students to write about a personal traumatic event the day before they were vaccinated. Six months later, the group that had done expressive writing had a stronger immune response, and so many more antibodies than the control group, who had only had the vaccine.[71] The important part is that you should do the expressive writing *before* whatever happens to you. If you do that, other studies show that you'll have improved and faster wound healing.[72] Researchers generally use what they call a punch biopsy, where they give participants a small painless punch in the skin and then look at the wound healing.[73–75] Results have been replicated with patients after surgery.[74,76] If you write it out, you heal better.

A Chinese research team trained a large group of children, who had been exposed to the Sichuan earthquake in 2008, in calligraphy, for one hour a day over thirty days. Another group didn't get any training. Before and after the course, the researchers measured several aspects of trauma, like the level of arousal, fear, and the levels of cortisol in the children's blood. After the thirty sessions, the group that had received the calligraphy lessons had much lower arousal and cortisol in their blood.[77]

Struggling to fall asleep? Well, bed-time writing has been shown to be a neat antidote against bed-time worrying. Download it onto the page and leave it there as you drift off into sleep.[78]

→

The classic expressive writing paradigm prescribes that you should write three to four times a week for twenty minutes over a two-week period.[79] The topic of what you write should be something that worries you, stresses you or has in some way traumatised you – the cues that haunt you. Download it all to the page. Just like that? Yes, sit down and write.[80]

If, after a while, you want to go a step further, there are different types of bibliotherapy and scriptotherapy:[81] interactive journaling, focused writing, narrative therapy and song-writing.[66] You could also go on a creative writing course, or read some books about fiction writing.

For example, throughout this book, I'm using some fiction-writing techniques: I've been writing about different people. Not all of them really exist. They are combinations of cases of people I know, mixed with situations that I may have experienced myself, or that have been told to me. This way of fictionalising knowledge or situations into characters is as old as storytelling itself. And it's a technique that modern therapeutic approaches use too. Write what happened to you into fictitious characters and make them interact. Express what you feel through them. This is a way to reach a reappraisal of a situation. One randomised controlled trial, with people who had recently experienced a traumatic life event, showed that writing in the third person yielded the most important health benefits, and people experienced less intrusive thoughts than those trauma patients who had written in the first person.[82,83]

For the simplest form of expressive writing, and to get started, Professor Pennebaker recommends that what you write should focus on the emotional impact of what has happened to you, more than on a factual account of the events as they happened.[51,84,85] (If you want to expand your practice from there, he provides a full guide on how to go about expressive writing in his book.[86]) And I repeat: importantly, write it, planning to throw it away afterwards. If you write while thinking about someone reading it you risk falling prey to mind hooks that distract you and cause you to become self-critical, analysing and adjusting what you write instead of writing freely.

This goes for any artistic expression: dance it out, purr it into the piano, draw a line. Do it all as a form of free and fleeting momentary expression, 'as if no one's watching'.

The Power of the Arts to Appease Our Social Brain

To recapitulate: if you're under the effects of 1) social isolation or 2) porcupine spines, you will have a very unsteady mind (for the reasons outlined earlier) and find it difficult to find flow. Expressive writing can help you deal with some of that, as we saw above. In addition, a series of other arts can offer you opportunities to find that missing ingredient for your pathway to flow – healthy social connection.

You can get all your hugs a day, eye contact, smiles and giggles from the community around your artistic practice, and unwind your lonely and tormented mind.

Three Powerful Ways the Arts Make us Connect and Feel Less Lonely

Physical contact, sharing a laugh, dancing, singing and making music together causes benevolent bonding hormones to be let loose in our bloodstream. As a result of these unruly little messenger substances, our brain attaches 'like' stickers to those people we've shared these moments with, and we feel a little closer to them and a little less lonely.

The second mechanism by which shared creative activities give us a feeling of belonging is *synchrony*. Moving in synchrony with others not only releases bonding hormones like oxytocin; if you are practising one of the 'synchronicity arts', where we synchronise our movements with those of others, like dancing, singing or playing an instrument, our physiology synchronises along with the movements that we do.[87–103] Besides, a funny process called 'co-representation' happens in our brain when we move in synchrony.[104] Normally, there are distinct neural mechanisms that tell us who's moving, me or you. However, if we use our brain's ability to imitate each other and we move in sync, well then, our brain gets confused. The neural activation for me and you starts to overlap. Moving in synchrony tricks our low-level brain systems into thinking we're one. While research is still ongoing about these strange synchrony effects, co-representation may be one of the reasons why people are more empathic with those people they have moved in synchrony with.

The third mechanism by which we may quickly feel very bonded with the people of our arts community (apart from sharing an important interest, namely *that artistic practice*), is genetic. When we practise an art, especially if it involves movement, we may sweat a little, and get closer to each other than we normally would to people. There are many biochemical messenger substances that bustle around in the space between us, signalling to other people everything from genetic compatibility[105] to how scared we are.[106] So, as surprising as this may sound, if we like being around someone, it may be because our brain – outside of our awareness – has detected that we are genetically compatible.

For a decade or so, there have been attempts to tackle the loneliness epidemic in the UK with 'social prescribing'. This means that people are being prescribed dancing classes or bingo club attendance, as a way to get this crucial social contact into their biological systems. And that's a great development. However, you know by now that the science shows that 'just do art' is not a good enough instruction. As we saw in Chapter 3, the arts can create rumination or a behavioural addiction, and in Chapter 2 we saw that being a professional artist is not a secure pathway to flow either, because of the stress hormones that competitiveness causes us to have in our blood. The social layer of our brain also holds some risks to a healthy artistic practice which we should be aware of.

Good to Know

This is something that friends from different arts communities have begged me to include in this book. Creative practices offer many opportunities for human connection, to combat loneliness and the health hazards that it entails. And we should make abundant use of these opportunities. But here is the *but*.

Due to the special elements of creative practices, like shared creation and problem-solving, synchronicity and co-representation, and due to the automatic exchange of genetic compatibility information that may happen between bodies that are close, we may *very* quickly feel *very* close and connected to someone. After one night of dancing, you may *feel* closer to a person than after one year of conversations over coffee. But, please remember that you really *know* the person much less after one night than after one year of conversations. Similarly, when we connect with a person's art, dance or music, we can find ourselves transferring that connection to the person behind the art, but that connection isn't automatically reciprocated, nor is it necessarily healthy.[107–110] This applies to art forms that don't include physical contact too. Experiencing beauty in a painting or a piece of music can lead you to see beauty in the creator of that work as well, and in doing so you might not immediately see other parts of their personality or you may start to feel like you know them more than you do.[111] This may seem obvious, but the truth is that while these mechanisms ensured survival of a group in the wild, they can and do occasionally cause havoc in modern arts communities.[112] In the arts, we also see this manifest in cults of personality that arise around really talented or well-known individuals and teachers. When people open themselves up to these individuals to get closer to their art or to learn from them, they can become more vulnerable to manipulation or abuse, especially if that individual has more social privilege or authority within the relationship. This doesn't only happen with celebrities; it can also arise on a smaller scale within a smaller creative community.

Based on the science, my recommendation is this: whenever you feel you've met a 'soul mate', be happy, be appreciative. But then take to the *verbal* communication channels to find out whether attitudes, values and life goals are aligned too. And really, only time (spent together at that coffee table) can tell.

A second disclaimer regards the arts institutions we may practise in. The 2010s and '20s (finally!) saw an increase in reported cases of former and current students of professional artistic careers, gymnastics and sports calling out the toxic culture at some professional dance schools and other professional institutions, culminating ultimately in the #MeToo movement. Even when a situation doesn't escalate to abuse, sometimes the relationships we have with other creatives can cause us to start feeling competitive or self-conscious about our creative work because of what they may think or say, or how other people might compare you to them. Arts institutions are not holy places and porcupines exist there also; they can become pink-elephant generators if not managed well.

To sum it up, to unwind your mind and build your pathway to flow, you may have to adjust *who* you spend time with, because of how they, or you, behave. The next chapter is about how to creatively and elegantly set these boundaries and grow, both in your neural networks, and in your *self* – with the arts!

5.   How and When to Set Boundaries

For portions of your day, suck your soul into yourself, and set boundaries for your senses, your work and your people. This chapter is about how we can use the arts – either in the act of creating, or as a consumer of others' art – to help our mind to focus, by easing away from cues that send our pink elephants spinning. And, importantly, in the process, give our mind something meaningful and rewarding to do *instead*.

This Is Not a Film is a movie that was shot illegally in an apartment in Tehran. Filmed on a simple mobile camera, it shows a day in the life of Iranian filmmaker Jafar Panahi. For one day, while waiting to hear whether his appeal was granted, Panahi shares how he eased his mind away from fear, and found flow in creation. It kept him sane while he waited. The appeal wasn't granted, but the movie was smuggled out of the country on a USB stick hidden inside a cake. Panahi has won three awards at the Cannes Film Festival, among them, one Camera D'Or. He expresses himself; he shows Iran how he sees it, with all its good and bad sides. But for porcupines in a totalitarian regime, showing bad sides is a no-go. Due to a travel ban imposed on Panahi by the regime, the organisers of the Cannes Film Festival have kept an empty chair with his name at the event.

Panahi was arrested again during the protests that started in 2022 and imprisoned to serve a six-year prison term. At the start of 2023, he was freed temporarily for health reasons. Regardless of where he is right now and what challenges he is facing, let's all hope that this wonderful, creative mind is regularly in the zone, setting boundaries for the porcupines, creating the next film script, to stay sane, no matter what happens next in his life. For sure, we'd all love to see him as a juror in Cannes one day!

Thankfully, for most of us, our bothersome everyday cues are nothing close to a totalitarian state out to get us, but we all encounter porcupine spikes that can inhibit our flow, if we let them. In order to embark on our pathway to flow, we need to shield ourselves from them, at least temporarily, and boundaries are the key.

Common Mistreatments

Experimental psychologists have carried out systematic experiments about the most common mistreatments that we people do to each other, either on purpose, or just because we are how we are. There is a series of traumas that we often just invalidate because they are so common, but that doesn't make them less likely to generate awful thought loops in our minds that last decades of our life. Some of these 'common' traumas involve other people, others don't. Traumas include neglect, infidelity, bullying, infertility, loneliness, experiencing oppression, witnessing violence, betrayal by friends or family, caring responsibilities, undiagnosed learning disability, divorce, abuse from authority figures, poverty, immigration, chronic pain, unemployment, loss, having a partner with addiction, and the list continues.

How do you set boundaries for this *exactly*?

I could say that you need to set 'emotional' or 'mental' boundaries. But these words are abstract concepts, and telling you to set boundaries for 'emotions' would leave you none the wiser. Besides, if you've read Chapters 1 and 3, you'll know that the 'emotions' and the 'mental things' would jump over the fence and assault your mind effortlessly like the white polar bear did for Dostoyevsky's brother. You cannot stop mental phenomena at will.

Instead, now, before you read the next sections, I'd like you to briefly identify your eight senses: sight, hearing, smell, taste, touch, interoception (the sense of your body from within), proprioception (your limb and movement sense) and exteroception (the sense of where you are in space). Second, identify the people who are regularly around you. Third, identify what your work is, or your education, or daily chores that you could group as 'your work'. Ready?

When creating our pathway to flow, these are the three domains that I recommend setting boundaries for from time to time. If you prevent the cues from entering your senses (and thus, your brain), you prevent them from starting off the pink elephant ballet in the first place. And with practice, your mental behaviours will become steadier, and your mind will have *learned* to stay focused, even when those cues are around you.

Boundaries for Your Senses

How often do you get distracted? Psychologists use what they call 'distractor tasks', where they set a person a task, and then distract them with new information that is somehow emotionally salient, to load their working memory. And boom – their attention goes. It's a test for executive function (e.g. how resistant you are to distractions). Many office spaces today feel like one big distractor task in a psychologist's experiment.

There are many different network tools today that are designed in ways that keep our attention hooked to generate revenue for multinational companies. Our eyes do their little micro saccades propelled by our brain's body-protection mechanisms. Over and again, our eyes jump over the visual field like a confused rabbit, never collecting any information of value. Switching between tasks during multi-tasking costs us up to 40 per cent of our processing time.[1] And some research suggests that after just twenty minutes of multi-tasking, our stress and frustration levels skyrocket[2] while productivity dwindles.[1,3,4] Our brain processes horizontal movement before form, in milliseconds, long before we become aware. Our attention is immediately caught by it. This is likely because, in a prehistoric world, processing horizontal movements was important for survival – see the enemy move before they see you. Yet, when the horizontal movements are not enemies, but notification icons, this survival mechanism for the wild isn't very useful for staying focused. There are workplaces where all employees are connected via chat apps *without any breaks*, and receive chiming, pinging, zipping and visually moving notifications *constantly*. There is an understanding that people should be available all the time, respond to emails immediately, always pick up the phone, be okay with someone knocking on the door with a question or for a chat. This is a proper training in fragmented attention. And if you have ADHD it is particularly torturous.

Similarly, if the temperature is high, it is difficult to concentrate. Researchers have analysed the relation between crime data and heat in the United States in the years 1950–1995. A high temperature induces a state of alert in the body. Their analyses showed that during days with temperature of over 90 degrees Fahrenheit, there was a higher number of serious and deadly assaults than on days with more moderate temperatures.[5] Affective aggression usually comes out of annoyance – or, as you know now, out of the arousal misattribution that we saw in Chapter 2. Affective aggression is what you do when your thoughts are clouded by annoyed pink elephants and you can't pinpoint why, so you may misattribute your negative feelings to the person in front of you. That's your arousal misattribution right there. Office spaces where you can't open a window and it gets hot in summer are conducive to pink elephants, just due to the temperature alone. This adds to what we saw in Chapters 1 and 2: that sitting too much, the wrong diet, tiredness, etc, will allow cues to rise to your awareness *via your interoception*, the sense of your body from within, making you edgy and terribly unfocused. You are unlikely to be able to find flow when you are in such a state.

In preparation for building a pathway to flow, for portions of your day, make sure you are in conditions where your senses don't perceive constant distractions and are not affected by uncertainty. Train your attention to last.

Boundaries for Your Work

In experimental psychology, there is a task called 'mood induction'. We use mood induction when we want to study the influence of negative emotions (like annoyance or frustration[6–8]), for example, on productivity or problem-solving. For this, you as a researcher set up a task, usually a computer task (painstakingly evaluated and approved by an ethical board), where you give the participant clear instructions about how to do the task and how to achieve bonuses if they, for example, manage to press the button that is indicated faster than in two seconds. The task starts and the participant is motivated to get the bonus. However, you, evil experimenter, have programmed the task in a way that it is, in fact, impossible to get the bonus. Even if the participant hits the button in under two seconds, there is an unpleasant bzzt-sound and the word 'wrong!' is splashed over the screen.

At first, this makes people even more motivated to 'get it'. But then, at some point, it tips. People get increasingly frustrated. I've seen people punch the table, yell at the computer, and at the experimenter. And this is only the beginning of it all. Afterwards, we give them a second task to test how being in that mood affects their attention, memory, decision-making or productivity. In a different condition, then, we'd use a 'joy' mood induction paradigm, for example, or a 'neutral' mood induction, to compare the performance to the condition where people were frustrated. The frustrated group always has the worst productivity and does worst at problem solving.

Frustration, Uncertainty and Learned Helplessness

Have you ever tried and tried something, at work, or in your life, failed repeatedly, and at some point, just given up and felt totally useless and frustrated?[9–11] In the mid-twentieth century, in a series of experiments[12–15] that would be considered unethical today, investigators put dogs (and other mammals) through a very terrible plight. They gave them strong electric shocks from when they were very young pups.

They divided the dogs into two groups. One group only received the shocks when they were in a specific corner of the cage they lived in. These dogs quickly learned that to live a pain-free life, they just had to stay out of that corner. They grew up to be strong and self-confident, with shiny fur and a deep, healthy voice for a good bark.

The other group of dogs, however, received shocks at random intervals. No matter where they put themselves, a shock would hit them when they least expected it. There was no logic to the shocks, when or where they would strike. The dogs were completely out of control of their own wellbeing. This is what is known in psychology as 'contingencies'. Perfect contingencies are when you know exactly what will happen if you do something.[16,17] The first group of dogs learned after a little while that if they went to that one corner, they would receive a shock. So they stopped going there. They were in control.

The dogs of the second group also tried to control what happened to their bodies. But each time they thought they had understood the pattern with which the shocks occurred, they were shocked randomly again. These dogs, at some point, capitulated, along with their immune system. They just laid down, receiving the shocks with a whine, and stopped trying to do anything about it.

They suffered eczema, caught bacterial and viral infections and did not even react when they got a reward. This effect has come to be known as 'learned helplessness'. The dogs' brains had learned, that means that they had made the neural connections, that they could not change anything about their lives. They were out of control.

Can you 'learn' to be helpless? Yes. Learning is a process by which connections are made between neurons. Hence, if you repeat a contingency, it will be learned. Remember from chapter 4 – our brain changes in a use-dependent way.[18–21]

You can see that this is the opposite side of the coin to what Rat Barnaby experienced. He received rewards at variable ratio. The dogs from these experiments received punishments at variable ratio. And this is another cue for doomsday pink elephants for our brain.

Taking advantage of the fact that we humans share basic brain structures with dogs and mice, we can learn from research with other mammals that 'contingencies' are important for our wellbeing, whether we are a dog or a human.[22] And we humans develop spinning pink elephants as a result.[23]

This is why it is so important that you, or your children, or your pets, live a life where most of the things that happen follow some clear contingencies, so you know what happens to you. Meritocracies, with clear contingencies, foster healthy minds and bodies, at work and in life.[24] Random ratio contingencies, on the other hand, both for good and for bad things, send pink spinning elephants to your mind that you cannot escape. Variable ratio *rewards* hook you as we saw in Chapter 3, variable ratio punishments, for example at work, make you learn to be helpless and can ultimately make you spin into depression or anxiety.[25–28]

Bureaucratic jungles and too many processes in a workplace can teach your brain to feel helpless.[29–31] The hours of your project-based contract tick away, while you're not getting your work done, because you are having to click through a maze of boxes, never knowing when, or whether, you'll find your way out of that maze (= uncertainty) – that's a psychologist's mood-induction task for frustration right there.

The comedian Daniel Ryan-Spaulding takes the mickey out of Germans in his sketch 'Germans Aren't Efficient', but having lived in different countries, including Denmark, Germany, France, Spain, Italy and the UK, I can assure you that it seems to me that every country has their own bureaucratic processes that leave us all fuming.[32] Especially, if you're a foreigner used to a different way of 'solving' problems, wading through bureaucratic nightmares in your new country of residence can be trying. The French say 'compteur de haricots', the English say 'bean counter', the Spanish say 'contador de fijoles' to refer to the person in private and public sector companies that cares more about the processes, rules and regulations at the expense of the overall aims of the company, obstructing both progress and profit.[33–35] They input pink elephants into the minds of colleagues, teaching them to be helpless. 'Death by a Thousand 10-Minute Tasks' is the title of one paper in this field of research.[36]

Therefore, for hours in your day, to get work done and to ensure your health and wellbeing, create boundaries for the processes of your work, and prevent yourself from learning to be helpless.[37]

Boundaries for Your People

Have you ever sat there, plagued by many a pink elephant spinning in your mind, because of other people? Either because they have misbehaved (in your view), or maybe because you care so much about them that you worry constantly what would be best for them?

Psychology categorises this problem under the name of 'personality' – we all have different personalities.[38–40] In Chapter 2 we saw that we all differ in terms of how much need for sensation-seeking we have. That we're different is a fact of life and a perfect cue for rumination.

Twenty Birds

Once upon a time, there were twenty birds. They were all annoyed with their rulers who were a quite incompetent and power-hungry bunch. The twenty birds didn't much like each other either, but at least they were united in their frustration against the rulers. So, one fine day, while the rulers were having one of their lavish feasts, decadently celebrating themselves and themselves all over again, the twenty birds flew off. Just think of all the taxpayers' money the rulers were spending for their feasts! In a loudly twittering general assembly, the twenty birds had decided to create a new, much better, even perfect state in the clouds, Cloud Cuckoo Land.

At first, everything was much better. The birds congratulated each other and celebrated their success, for being so daring, starting something new. What a clever move they had made! They were all quite pleased. Especially with themselves.

But as nature is capricious at times, each bird had its own personality; each had its own beak, perch and imperfections. They certainly also all had some good characteristics too, they could agree on that. Yet, their negatives started to shine more in the light of day, than any of their much-praised good attributes.

This made Cloud Cuckoo Land anything but perfect.

Soon, there were some bossy birds who wanted to take the lead, and some cowardly birds, too, who were glad that they 'didn't have to do it'. There were also some anxious birds who were as afraid of the new authority as they had been of the old rulers, so they 'preferred to remain neutral'. Then there were the underdogs, well, underbirds, who chirped their discontentment behind flustered feathers, and kept a little flock of followers in opposition.

As always, there were also some individuals that had absolutely no integrity and flew as the wind blew – which generated quite some tension too. The family birds just wanted to 'get on with life and make a nest for some good eggs'. They often wondered loudly, 'when people would grow up', hoping the others would listen. At the same time, they generally excused their little ones' antisocial behaviour with the explanation that they were, well, 'just children', and reassuring everyone that 'they would grow out of it for sure'.

A well-mixed bag this was. When would this ideal society finally materialise?

It wouldn't. Cloud Cuckoo Land never became anything other than an illusion. Things spun out of control. One day, one final big bang dispersed all the birds, furiously squeaking or fearfully tweeting, to the four winds, and they were never heard of again.

The story about the twenty birds is my own free-style version of the play *The Birds* by the Greek playwright Aristophanes, performed for the first time in Athens around 414 BC. The moral of the story? People are different. And it's precisely these differences, our characteristics, that *make* the societies we live in. Over and again, for the past 2,500 years, and likely, for many millennia before that, since *Homo sapiens* started to walk the earth about 300,000 years ago; their bodies *needed* to be in a group to stay sane, while groups are also one of the greatest generators of pink elephants. *We* have *created* the societies and power structures the way they are, *because of how we are*. Each one of us.

What is more, each one of us also carries a Cloud Cuckoo Land in our mind, a fantasy about how our society, friendship group, politics, family, really *should* be, ideally. And we get disappointed, sad, angry and tormented by herds of pink elephants grinding in our mind, when our expectations are not met and people don't behave in the way we expected them to and that we believe would be *the right way*. If only people would *listen*, right?

Here's the secret knowledge nugget: they won't. They are waiting for *you* to listen.

➜

There is no solution to the personality problem of human existence, other than taking yourself out of the situation from time to time. Like the filmmaker Jafar Panahi did, while under house arrest awaiting his verdict. He eased away and took a break from it all, by immersing his senses into a new sensory landscape, and leaving the totalitarian porcupines at the door while he fictionalised and expressed himself with the simple means of a mobile camera. On the occasion of the 2023 Booker Prize ceremony, Nazanin Zaghari-Radcliffe spoke about the healing power of enjoying others' art as a way to set boundaries. She kept a copy of *The Handmaid's Tale* in her secret prison library. After five months of solitary confinement, she received her books. 'Books helped me to take refuge in the world of others when I was incapable of making one of my own. They salvaged me by being one of the very few tools I had, together with imagination, to escape the Evin walls without physically moving.'[41]

In the remainder of this chapter, let's have a look at how we can use the arts to spin boundaries around us from time to time and step into a cocoon of bliss, to give our senses and our minds a creative break. By enjoying our own art, or maybe that of others.

Step Into a Cocoon of Bliss

Back in France, when I was still a ballet student, the onslaught of critique and overpowering authorities would sometimes threaten to suffocate me and my mind would be spinning. When that happened, I'd buy a ticket and disappear.

There is a square in the city where I used to live that contained a portal into a secret world. Let's call the square Gramsci Square – or '*Place Gramsci*' in French – in honour of the political theorist who criticised the totalitarian ruler Benito Mussolini and his fascism, and spent the rest of his life in prison for that. To stay sane, Gramsci disappeared into his notebooks for hours on end. We know that, because he thankfully left us *The Prison Notebooks*. His namesake, Place Gramsci, offered me a mental escape of my own.

In the southern corner of Place Gramsci there was a tiny cinema, tucked away under some neo-classic-style arcades. Some of its cinema 'halls' didn't have more than twenty seats. Yet, in there was a world that was 'larger than life, and better than real'.[42] The cinema at Place Gramsci screened all the classics. Whenever I wanted, I went into this cocoon of bliss, disappeared and felt my mind stretched and awed, expanded into different dimensions[43] – and found flow by enjoying the art made by other people.

In 2020,[44] a study at University College London (UCL) looked at what happens in our brain when we disappear into a film in a movie theatre. For starters, there is the perfect opportunity to put ourselves and our hypervigilant senses into a pocket. The cinema is a cocoon in itself. As we glide into the hall, there are all these cues that are so different from the everyday, all looking a bit old school. That's novel to our brain, and novelty stirs up the Camp 1 philosophers, the hedonists, foraging the surroundings for pleasure opportunities and treats alike. We're alert. The red carpets, the golden decorations, the thick curtains muffling everything. And when the movie starts, it's dark and we're removed from the world.[45,46] And there is a proper cocoon etiquette. We don't speak, phones are on silent, no phone screens allowed. Psychologists call that 'cutting off distractions'. Trying to do that at home – no talking, no phones, no other screens, nothing else to do but focus only on one thing – we often find hard, but in the cinema it is easy.

The sweet and salty allure of popcorn tangles our senses – the tongue, the nose, the fingers and the ears. Those are cues that belong with the cinema experience. The huge screen and the much too loud all-around sound system immerse us into that other world, and absorb our senses. If this cocoon of bliss is visited regularly, those cues become habit cues that reliably send our mind off into flow. The moment you enter the cinema, your mind starts flowing and all worries are forgotten.

Besides, just the fact that we're watching a story on a large screen and not a small one makes a difference for our brain,[47] says UCL's Professor Joseph T. Devlin. A larger area of the part of our brain that is responsible for 'seeing' is engaged, so more sensory experiences need to be processed. Research shows that watching something on larger screens makes us more alert, makes the content more memorable, and we feel more absorbed.[48]

Going to the cinema is also a social experience; it can appease the social layer of our brain. As we marvel and wonder at the story that unfolds before our eyes, feeling the thrills and the chills, our heart rate syncs with those around us. This makes the emotions that we feel stronger, both the good and the bad ones – which explains why you might find the same movie disappointing if you watch it alone at home. And remember what we said in Chapter 4 about synchronisation; we bond with those we synchronise with, and we stop feeling lonely.[49] Tom Hanks once said, 'Everybody has something that chews them up and, for me, that thing was always loneliness. The cinema has the power to make you not feel lonely, even when you are.' Pedro Almodóvar, the great cinéaste, has a similar philosophy, saying, 'Cinema can fill in the empty spaces of your life and your loneliness.' And, bonus, more science shows that cinema audiences can, in fact, reach a heart rate of light aerobic exercise – so who knows, going to the movies could actually be good for your heart health.[50]

Of course, movie watching can make us feel good – or bad. It's all about how we use the behaviour. At the Gramsci cinema I once watched a horror movie and it did me absolutely no good. Which movies appeal to us, and which send our mind spinning off into fearful or otherwise unpleasant loops, depends on who we are, and what cues are inside the movie. You may find something entertaining that I find terrifying. Some people love to fear those key moments in *Doctor Who*. They hide in the corner of the sofa, cushion at the ready for when fear strikes. Others can't stand this type of suspense.

Yet, it seems that our human brain reacts to high levels of suspense and terror in the same way. These situations, even if on screen, act on those low-level circuits of our brain that we cannot control. Professor Jonathan Williams, and his colleagues from the Max Planck Institute for Chemistry in Mainz, analysed the chemical compounds contained in the air condition filters of cinema halls after suspense and comedy movies. We humans exhale chemical compounds all the time, and the mix depends on how we are. If we're stressed, our breath tells a tale of stress hormones. If we're giggling in delight, the tale is all endorphins. Guess which compounds were found after suspense and horror movies? Stress-related compounds.[51] So – depending on what you're looking for, choose your movie well!

Audiobooks

Some people get flow out of reading,[52] but some of us are often just too tired to let our eyes flow over a page, or we struggle with ADHD which makes this hard.[53] Headphones in ear, stories unfolding before my inner eye, I've solved many an issue of my overwhelmed brain – with audiobooks. One study by Professor Devlin and his colleagues showed that listening to an audiobook catches our physiology.[54] 'Listening to an audiobook is a far more active process than watching a video. The listener co-creates the author's contents, picturing the scene, inventing the characters, and simulating the experience as if they lived it themselves. This is what makes the story so engaging.'[55]

Whenever I arrived somewhere new in my life, my audiobooks travelled with me. First night in a new bed, and I'd plug in my brain to one of those familiar stories that I'd listened to a thousand times, and my mind would flow away from all the stressful uncertainty and into the story I knew so well. I'm not surprised that clinicians have successfully started to use audiobooks for children in the waiting room before they have to undergo surgery, to ease their anxiety.[56] Professor Devlin and colleagues are still the one of the few groups researching those astounding effects in adults – hopefully more research is to come in the next few years. Meanwhile, however, if you're still spinning your cocoon around yourself with your favourite audiobooks, it is probably a very clever thing to be doing. Just remember the wanting-liking principle from Chapter 3. A new and exciting story will make you *want* to hear the happy ending, activating your craving dopamine pathways. Rather, re-listen to that favourite story, watch that box set for the *n*th time, and make your mind ease along those meanderings that you know you *like*.

Special Spaces and Impressive Buildings

Several research teams are reporting that people who go to the cinema, to museums, exhibitions or concerts tend to have better health and live longer.[57–59]

Some of the success of special spaces and impressive buildings is probably due to the fact that they spin boundaries around us, literally. Jeffrey K. Smith calls this *The Museum Effect*.[60] Being in creative spaces gives our senses a break, and instils in us a restorative feeling of 'out-of-this-world'. Such special spaces can be architectural wonders like la Sagrada Família or the Hospital San Pau in Barcelona. They make the 'self' feel small and surrounded by beauty.[61,62] This may stimulate the reconstruction of body and mind after deconstruction during pain and disease[63,64] – lacing thoughts and memories with beauty, or 'food for thought', and self-growth. Some architecture engages our social brain layer, for example, when we become aware of the historical significance of a building.[65]

The Grand Factory is a disco on an industrial site in the port area of Beirut.[66] As you walk through the rough exterior; nothing suggests the presence of a dance floor. You take the cargo lift up, and as the doors slide open, behind a black wall, you're sucked into a world of rhythm and flashing lights. The Grand Factory was rebuilt after the terrible explosion that tore through the fabric of the port area in August 2020 and is re-emerging from the ashes, offering a space to escape it all. Beirutians seek this space, night after night, to forget, to escape, even if just for some hours, from the political and economic crises of Lebanon, as they groove the night away.[67] Of course, any club environment can also be a generator of pink elephants if drug use is around,[68–70] so for finding flow in a club, as always, it's about how you use the behaviour.

Awe

Big spaces make our brain feel a little uneasy – of course, since our brain is a cave-brain and large spaces were difficult to stay safe in.[71] But when we *know* we're safe, for example in some nature spaces[72–74] or in a concert hall, this is usually pleasant.[75] This feeling of being a bit uneasy, but also feeling impressed and liking it, could be summarised as awe.[76]

Research shows that people who make sure to have regular experiences of awe[77] have higher life satisfaction and health.[78,79] And not only that, they even have lower levels of arousal in the body when exposed to daily stressors – fewer pink elephants![80]

Besides, while situations that engender a competitive mindset, like a basketball game, promote antisocial emotions and behaviours,[81,82] this feeling, awe, of being small in the view of something big, seems to have interesting social effects.[83–85] In one study, groups of elderly people were sent out on nature walks. One group was sent on paths where they were likely to experience awe, the other group just did a normal walk with no awe-inspiring possibilities. The awe walk made participants feel small. The researchers had pulled a funny stunt on the participants; they encouraged them to take selfies during the walk. The awe-walk group took selfies in which they looked increasingly small. They hadn't been instructed to do this, but their photos reflected how they felt. Both groups felt good after the walk, but the awe group had much stronger prosocial emotions towards other people and smiled more – suggesting that having regular experiences of awe, of feeling a bit smaller than we really are, makes us nicer people to be around.[86]

This wellbeing-enhancing shrinking of the 'ego' through experiences of awe during aesthetic episodes is something that stands in stark contrast to some of the recently described effects of 'mindfulness' meditation and yogic practices – something to be aware of.

Yoga Studios

I practise yoga myself and I like it very much, but our story here would not be complete if I didn't share some research I've recently discovered about this internationally much-loved practice. Remember that we are building a pathway to flow, and with it comes a knowledge tool-box that enables us to make informed decisions about our actions. So here we go: I'm not discouraging yogic practices, just, again, saying *it depends on how we use that behaviour.*

Psychological research has long demonstrated that the practice of any skill in which the self is central runs the risk of breeding a self-enhancement bias.[87] It happens sometimes that everyone gets so focused on 'the most important thing in this world – you', that they forget basic courtesies like a smile, holding the door for others, respecting cues, or saying 'thank you'. Professor Thomas Joiner from Florida State University says that the original teachings of yoga have shifted into 'a self-focused, self-glorification mechanism'[88] in some yoga studios. This folding in of the self *on* the self contributes to an expansion of the ego. One study showed that breathing-focused mindfulness meditation made people less likely to feel guilty if they had caused harm and made them less likely to seek to repair the damage via apologies and other prosocial behaviours.[89] And recently, the methodologies used in studies showing 'positive effects' of mindfulness practice have been called into question.[90,91]

Dr Michael Poulin, in fact, was able to show that whether or not meditative and yogic practices make you selfish is likely linked to where you're from.[92] The results of his study echo Carl Jung's warning against Westerners practising yoga: 'Europeans would be starting from a completely different mindset and on a different set of assumptions [. . .] and yoga will therefore likely produce a worsening of their neurosis,'[93] and modern research has shown that mindfulness meditation can worsen anxiety and depression – with at least 25 per cent of practitioners experiencing adverse effects.[94] In other words, according to Poulin, Jung and modern science, in the West, we have a very individualistic mindset, and it seems that having such pre-conceived beliefs in our mind can make mindfulness meditation an 'ego enhancer'.

Conversely, if you're from a collectivist culture, like some Eastern cultures, mindfulness meditation may have a different effect on you.[91] The way forward is probably a middle way, although such a way still needs to be thoroughly investigated.[95]

In principle, moving yourself into a yoga studio could spin a cocoon of bliss around you. The repetitive movement sequences and the special sense-scape of yoga studios hold all the potentials for being healthy for our mind and helping with building a pathway to flow. Yet, many of these classes are competitive, and people chase after the reward of striking that perfect pose and posting themselves on Insta. The risk-taking mind hook also lurks around, as many of these teachers keep using teaching methods like shaming to push you.[96]

A yoga teacher, in a studio where I once practised, said that those people who couldn't bind in complicated twisting poses were inflexible, in their bodies and minds, and were generally very unempathic. So I, with my back injury that makes me unable to do strong rotations of the upper body, had to patiently listen to her shaming of us 'inflexible' people. Later, we were asked to stand on one leg and close our eyes. This is a difficult exercise that we practised a lot during my dance education, to develop a good interoception and proprioception, an awareness of our body from within and from the outside. Today, due to hip issues after my injuries, standing for long sometimes hurts me like knives in my lower back and hip. So, I wasn't very stable during the two-minute-eyes-closed-on-one-leg exercise. According to the enlightened teacher, for those of us that were unstable on our legs – that was our too-big ego to blame.

Science tells a somewhat different story to that tale. In fact, it has long been known that a hyper bendy body is linked to higher risk of developing anxiety disorders.[97–100] Similarly, there is no research that has compared the 'size' of the ego and the difficulty of standing on one leg. It is a skill you can develop via training by a good teacher who patiently works on your limb alignment with you. Meditative practices aren't bad regardless, of course. But as you choose your teacher,[101] just make sure to remember Mahatma Gandhi's words, 'I will not let anyone walk through my mind with their dirty feet.'

Remember – I'm not here to deter you from seeking boundaries for your senses in a yoga or other meditation class. It's all about *how* we use a behaviour, and I'm here to tell you the scientific evidence of the consequences of some behaviours, if not managed in a balanced way.

And obviously, anything that gives *you* awe, but is dangerous and deadly for other people, should be avoided – otherwise it turns you into a spiky psychopath porcupine for others. The Nazis surely felt awe while listening to the music of Wagner, whose art they used to justify their totalitarian beliefs. Many totalitarian states like China or Russia use awe-inducing dance performances to spin people's minds into patriotic followers of 'the Greater Good', which usually involves oppression, war and death for the non-conforming. Professor Anthony Shay from Pomona College refers to this nationalistic use of the art form dance, for example, as *Choreographic Politics*.

It's all about how we use a behaviour.

So, on our pathway to flow, let's agree to seek *life-affirming* awe.

Choose Well

Do you remember that I mentioned 'pleasure-plus' behaviours in Chapters 2 and 3? That's those wonderful behaviours that both give us pleasure and link to higher-order neural structures, to those eudemonist philosophers in Camp 2 of our brain, and contribute to us having a meaningful life. We embrace the power of creative pleasure-plus behaviours to heal our mind when we internalize the wanting-liking principle. We stop chasing after wanting something and simply *enjoy* that we're doing something that we *like* while we're doing it.

→

Wherever people come together, the porcupines are out and about. 'In this world, the bad guys can win,'[42] says the villain in the movie *The Last Action Hero*, as he passes into our world. And that's true. In our reality, there is rarely a happy ending, and we need to learn to live with that and, from time to time, to set boundaries for the madness. Spin a cocoon of bliss around you with your art – be it submerging yourself into a beautiful building, concert, cinema, dance, movie, book, or while creating something yourself, so afterwards you can remerge refreshed like a phoenix from the ashes. Choose pleasure-plus behaviours and spaces for a healthy self on your pathway to flow.

PART II

BREAKING THE LOOP

*Brain-based solutions to the restless
mind problem — with the arts*

6.   Mind Expansions – Create how you feel by what you *do*

You now know a lot more about what can cause arousal in your body, and what cues can send your mind off into a ruminative loop. We've also strolled through the science that shows that it's impossible to control these processes at will; we need to be smarter. Creative behaviours, either as a maker or as a consumer of art, are a way to catch our mind and spin it in a different direction.

We humans are uniquely equipped to create our conscious experience. In principle, we have freedom of choice,★ thanks to the neural systems behind our forehead: the prefrontal cortex. However, of course I've just told you how we're influenced by what happens around us, which may compel us to do things we didn't plan to. So are we *free* to choose after all? Yes we are. How? By choosing – beforehand – what we expose our senses to we can influence our cave-brain's response and our wider brain's broader meaning-making systems too. The ability to plan ahead what we expose ourselves to is a fairly unique skill in the animal kingdom.[1] We can use the arts in times of trouble, to stay sane and, even, to thrive. We'll now talk about *how* exactly to do that; how to *create* good experiences, feelings and flow.

In this chapter, we'll stroll through the science of how emotions are made. Those strange sensations that bubble up in our chest and give rise to thoughts in our mind; sometimes as a result of cues entering our eight senses, and at other times due to cues that are already spinning in our mind. This is important science because once you've understood more about how emotions are made,

★ Whether or not we humans have free will or not is a hotly debated topic in the academic realm, but this discussion lies outside of the scope of this book.

you'll be uniquely equipped to *create* the emotions you want – with the arts and other creative behaviours.

In Chapter 7, I will explain the six golden mind liberators: specific strategies to unwind your mind. Actually, these are what clinical psychology has called *Emotion Regulation Strategies* for decades – but we'll look at them through the lens of our pathway to flow, and this will make them very easily applicable to our life. Based on the science from previous chapters, we'll unpack which of these strategies works *when,* and which strategies we'd better stay clear of sometimes, and *why.* What does that have to do with the arts? Well, we can apply those six strategies to our life *via* the arts and creative behaviours! In this way, you don't need to wait for life to present a situation where you can apply the strategies. Instead, you can take an active role and create moments with your art and creative activity. You'll learn to apply those strategies and teach your mind healthy habits that you can rely on, in good and bad times. Because the next cue to send your mind off into ruminative loops awaits you just around the corner. After reading Chapter 7, you'll know what to do. Depending on the situation, you'll pick one of the six, and your mind will already be trained to flow with the cues that inhabit it.

I'd like the six strategies to simmer in the back of your mind while you read this chapter, so here is a little spoiler before we start with the science. These are the six Emotional Regulation Strategies:

1. Situation selection and modification (avoidance, escapism, setting boundaries)
2. Attention deployment strategies (distraction, 'prayers', rumination)
3. Problem-solving (incubation, inspiration, social support)
4. Cognitive change (reappraisal, acceptance, the emperor's new clothes)
5. Response modulation (mood induction, expressive suppression)
6. Cognitive restructuring (creative expression, self-growth)

As with all behaviours, it's how we use these strategies that determines whether or not they are good for us. Chapter 7 will give us the tools we need to make informed decisions.

How Emotions are Made

The word 'emotion' is very abstract. What are they *actually,* these *emotions*? Let's spin them into something tangible that we can act on.

Scientific and clinical psychology, and Western educational methods, have in past decades tried to teach us to label sensations that surface in our conscious mind as 'happy', 'sad, 'annoyed', and so on, and we're taught to call these sensations 'emotions'. It would indeed be a very practical system for our peaceful co-existence in porcupine societies, if only we were all able to consistently label what's going on inside us, and communicate it to others. This labelling, however, is anything but easy to learn – just think of the arousal misattribution examples we've looked at in past chapters.

The convoluted nature of emotions is illustrated in the Pixar movie *Inside Out*. Inside the heads of the people in the movie, there is a command centre governed by five characters. A grumpy red character, *Anger*, a fairy-like yellow dancer, *Joy*, a downcast blue shadow, *Sadness*, a purple worrier, *Fear*, and a capricious green soul, *Disgust*. We zoom in and out of people's heads and we observe their behaviour on the 'outside', which is sometimes in stark contrast to what it looks like on their 'inside'.

These emotion characters receive information from the world through the senses: sight, hearing, taste, smell, touch, interoception (the sense from within), proprioception (movement sense) and exteroception (spatial sense). The information about what is going on is funnelled to the command centre and visualised on control panels. Depending on what is happening outside, either one or the other character – emotion – takes over, and compels the body to react in the way they deem fit.

For example, Joy is nowhere to be seen inside the protagonist, pre-teen Riley's brain. Riley and her family have moved to a new place, and she misses her friends. When people speak to her, she sometimes lashes out. But not out of anger. In her command centre we see Sadness at the controls. Riley just wants to be left alone to review her happy memories in a loop (aka ruminate). We learn that Joy has got lost in the 'memory systems'. And we briefly follow the yellow fairy dancer Joy wandering about lost and broken, emanating a sad blue hue, in something that looks like a forest of huge filing cabinets – the memory systems. As we know from earlier, in the trauma literature this inability to experience pleasure and positive feelings is referred to as 'anhedonia'.[2,3] Being alone in a new place can be traumatic. You miss your social contacts that made you feel happy and safe; they are now gone and lost with them in your memory systems is your ability to let Joy take over the controls in your brain's command centre.

One day, Riley's dad, his own emotion characters engrossed in meanderings about a recent football game, misinterprets Riley's behaviour at the dinner table. He only sees her downcast face, defensive answers and refusal to do 'as told'. Red Anger takes over his command centre, fuming at the behaviour of the daughter. Anger compels Dad's body to 'put his foot down'. Dad sends Riley to her room, making her feel even more awful than before. As a spectator, we see how wrong Dad's reaction was in view of what was going on 'inside' Riley's mind, but we know he couldn't see what we saw.

Inside Out is endearing – if only it were really that simple: that inside our 'command centre' live some basic emotions that we all have and understand: joy, anger, fear, disgust, sadness, disgust, surprise. Unfortunately, it isn't that simple at all. How can we possibly turn the 'inside out' – to understand each other, but, especially, *ourselves* better? And once we've understood, how can we then change how we feel?

We can *create* how we feel with the arts, but we're still some science away from the explanation of how to do that.

How Did we Come to 'Label' Emotions?

Charles Darwin was one of the first to speak about 'emotions' in scientific terms in his book *The Expression of the Emotions in Man and*

Animals in 1882. Initially, the idea had been to just write one chapter about emotions in his book *The Descent of Man*. However, there was so much material that 'emotions' required a whole book in itself.[4]

In the mid-twentieth century, the emotion psychologist professor Paul Ekman and his colleagues travelled the world, to remote villages like those of the Fore tribespeople in Papua New Guinea. With complicated constructions of cameras out of angle, the researchers filmed and photographed people when they felt unobserved, so as to get genuine 'emotional' expressions in different situations on tape. The researchers realised that people everywhere in the world get happy, sad, angry, fearful and surprised. And they do look quite similar when they do. This means that we *express* our 'emotions' in very similar ways.

The idea that there should be distinct, clearly recognisable 'basic emotions' – like those depicted in the movie *Inside Out* – in all people, all over the world, is based on Paul Ekman and his colleagues' work from the 1960s and '70s.[5] I love the movie. It provides a wonderful tool to start speaking about emotions with children. The creators and scientific advisors of the movie know that it doesn't tell the whole story about how emotions are made and how many there are, but it gets us started in a wonderfully entertaining way.

Since Ekman's initial research, scientific efforts to systematise have taken over, and when reading the literature, you get a sense that maybe some researchers have forgotten that what we call 'emotions' come from the body, and from mechanisms in our brain that ensure survival of our body in the wild.[6]

Let's take *fear* as an example, but similar things could be said for other emotions.[7]

In Chapter 1, we spoke about the Fear Symphony. It prepares the body to run away from danger. Yet, the total of the sensations that make up something that we're scared of is very varied and not easily grouped into a category that could be described with *one* word, fear.

Neuroscience professor Joseph Ledoux from New York University is a serious man. If you google him, you'll find many pictures of him with a very serious look on his face. Fair enough: His area of research is *fear and the brain*. Thanks to Professor Ledoux, the world has gained important insights into what the amygdala does, how fear works and what happens in our mind when we're scared and stressed.

Now that you know what the amygdala is – do you want to venture a guess what the 'Amygdaloids' might be?

Another fancy brain structure . . . ?

No!

It's a rock band! Neuroscience meets rock 'n' roll, to be exact.

And guess who's the lead singer and guitarist? Professor Ledoux.

The lyrics of the song 'Fearing' explain how fear works, and 'Piece of My Mind' recounts a brain's eccentric perspective on what happens when a relationship breaks up. So, we may feel 'fear' at the sight of a lion, other people screaming in terror, the smell of fire, our bank account overdrawn, a relationship break-up, etc.

Other animal species have similar mechanisms, and have specific ways of reacting to threats. Evolutionary scientists would refer to these 'ways of reacting to threats' as 'adaptive behaviours'; it's something that we do to adapt to a scary situation (e.g. something scares us and we run away, or otherwise solve the situation). In other words, the function of these adaptive behaviours is to keep us safe and help us survive. Education teaches us to refer to these 'adaptive behaviours' as 'emotions'. This means that fear has many, many different ways to manifest itself, depending on the situation that causes it and what adaptive behaviour is needed to overcome the threat (e.g. a lion, a relationship break up, an exam, etc). Therefore, if you ask two people to label whether a person looks scared or surprised or excited, they may fail at this task, especially if they don't know in which context the fear occurs. Just like Riley's dad misinterpreted her silence at the dinner table, and wrongly 'put his foot down'. Learning how to choose the right adaptive behaviours based on how we feel is a very important ability to hone throughout our life. It is not enough to learn how to label what it is that we feel. That's only the first step. The second step is to know what to do about it.

An Imperfect Instruction

No other animal species spends as much time educating their young as we do; we're uniquely obsessed with education.[8,9] And that's a very good thing. Yet, sometimes, these educational methods simplify to a point that they distance us from our own body, making it harder to understand it, rather than easier.

One of the things we're taught during education is that we're expected to learn to regulate our emotions. We're not allowed to act in 'hot anger', for example. As a first step towards *regulating* emotions, we educate our young to label what it is they're feeling. And this, as you saw above in the many faces of fear, is in itself an imperfect instruction.[10]

With the improvement of measurement techniques in the past decade, scientists have found out that there are no 'clear' signals in the body, nor in the brain, for anger, fear, joy and so on.[11] It depends very much on the *context*, and on previous life experience, how you interpret the signals from your body.[12] Your belly may contract and feel weird. You may be hungry because you haven't eaten in a while. Or, if you're watching a scary movie, it may be because you just startled. Or, it may be because your lover has just walked into the room. Or, if they've just walked out on you, like in Ledoux's song 'Piece of My Mind', you'll feel weird in your belly too. So, label that: the same sensation from the body, different contexts — and we'd probably 'label' these as different 'emotions', even if the physical sensation is the same.

As we grow up, we develop the ability to use language.[13–15] We learn to group abstract concepts into one category, concepts that don't look the same in the world.[16,17] Think of the word 'home'. Throughout your life, probably what you referred to as 'home' looked and felt rather different, and *was* different places. Likewise, you don't expect other people to be living in your home if they say 'I will go home now' — what they are referring to when they say 'home' is different to what you mean. The same is true with emotions. Depending on context and who we are, we learn to label sensations as fear, anger, joy, etc.[18,19] But that doesn't mean that there is any 'hard-coding' of emotions in the brain.[20] Labelling emotions is a useful, yet imperfect instruction.

Professor Lisa Feldman Barrett explains in her many scientific articles, and recently also to the general public in her great book *How Emotions Are Made*, that 'emotions' are just this unspecific arousal in the body that we've spoken about all along. Sensations that we don't understand, and that compel us to act in different ways (remember – they are part of our body's survival mechanisms!). Looking for 'emotional fingerprints', in the body or brain, is like searching for ghosts.[21] They don't exist.[22,23] This neuroscientific evidence also explains why there is not just one adaptive behaviour for each emotion. What the right reaction to a given situation is depends on that situation and how it makes you feel.

→

People who spend time with children know that they don't automatically know what they are feeling, nor how they should react to how they are feeling.[24] Children start shouting or crying at times that may seem totally unreasonable. They may do it when they're hungry, or when they're tired, when someone wrongs them, or when they're confused. They can't tell the difference. Even as adults, we know the feeling of being 'hangry', lashing out at loved ones because of a difficult-to-define bad feeling in the stomach.[25–28]

You may think, 'ah, that's just children'. But that's not the whole story.

We spoke about arousal misattribution in Chapter 2; of adult football fans whose team has lost, and who become violent against their partners, and of people who, on a scary bridge, find a stranger more attractive than if they meet the same person on stable ground. Those feelings and sensations from our body cause us to see the world through those tinted glasses, be they rose or otherwise. Even if we're supposedly responsible adults. One study found that what the judge had for breakfast made a difference to whether parole was granted or not.[29] Judges' general parole approval rate was about 65 per cent just after having a break, while before the next break, when their blood sugar levels had plummeted and they were hungry – approval rates dropped to near 0 per cent.

This phenomenon – that we inadvertently use how we feel in our body as a way to guide our decisions and behaviours – has been termed *affective realism* by scientists.[30,31] It means that we take the affect that we're feeling 'for real' – and are probably wrong in most of the cases. We are biased by how our body feels, and we're not even aware of it.[32–34]

It is true that trying to classify and systematise those sensations would be a good idea. Yet, it remains an imperfect instruction. As we continue our journey of creating our pathway to flow, remember that our *interoception*, our sense of the body from within, brings sensations from the body up into our mind.[35] That's an imperfect process, and we vary in terms of how aware we are of those sensations,[36–38] and how well we can label them.[39–41] Yet they influence our choices and behaviours, be we aware of them or not.

To see how imperfect the process is, how malleable, and how dependent on experience, let's see what happens with another sense: vision.

Invisible to the Eye

'What is essential, is invisible to the eye,' says the narrator in the book *The Little Prince* by Antoine de Saint-Exupéry.[42] He wonders why people are not scared of his drawing. It shows a huge lump with some narrow horizontal lines on both sides. 'It's a hat,' says everyone. But no, according to the narrator, the drawing shows a boa constrictor that has just swallowed an elephant.

Once you *know* this, the basic sensory information (a lump with two horizontal lines to the sides) that your Camp 1 is receiving from the senses (your *eyes* in this case) and which your Camp 1 is probably disregarding as boring, now receives a whole new meaning.[43–48] This meaning attribution comes from your Camp 2 systems, which have connections with memory and language systems of your brain. These know what a boa constrictor is, and how big an elephant is. When you realise that the strange lump with two horizontal lines is a boa constrictor eating an elephant, your mind goes, 'Ahaaaa!' This 'aha! moment' is golden for our brain. The neural pathways that link your Camp 1 and Camp 2 are exchanging information, and Camp 2 is also exchanging information with wider structures in your brain.

Camp 2 makes the link, but Camp 1 is responsible for the rewarding feeling that you're now getting.[49-51] The neuroscience of insight shows that these moments ping the reward system and cause a release of messenger substances into our wider body – that butterfly ballet that we feel when our mind goes 'aha!'[52] They are also a learning signal for your brain (dopamine shower!), so aha moments are good to create habit loops!

For your pathway to flow, you want to choose art that makes *your* brain go 'aha!' a lot. This is also part of what makes *your* art intrinsically rewarding.

Neuroscientific research shows that during insight, sensory information is inhibited, and we turn inward.[53,54] So, quite literally: we don't 'see'. Our senses and Camp 1 will not be able to reveal what is really essential to a meaningful life and long-term prosperity; it can only contribute to it, in collaboration with Camp 2. What is essential is invisible to the eye. Our brain *creates* it, thanks to the meaning-making systems of our brain. Any t-shirt with that quote 'Ceci n'est pas un chapeau' [This is not a hat] will now forever remind you of Camp 1 and Camp 2 and their neural pathways. And the reason for this is the intrinsic reward that you felt when your mind went 'aha'; this is a juicy *learning signal* for our brain, and it feels so good.

A sensation coming from your eyes – coming to your mind via your vision – can have different meanings for you, depending on the context and what you know about it. A huge lump with some narrow horizontal lines on both sides could be a hat or a boa constrictor swallowing an elephant. The 'deeper meaning' is something your brain creates on the basis of this low-level perceptual stimulation, with Camp 2 and wider brain structures, depending on who you are.

Constructed Emotion

As the scientific evidence about our body's physiology started to become more solid in the 2010s, Professor Lisa Feldman Barrett developed the *Theory of Constructed Emotion*.[21] With this theory we move away from the view that emotions are necessarily distinct categories (like Ekman and many others proposed, and which has served as an invaluable starting point for the study of emotions).

Instead, new evidence suggests emotions are something we construct, based on old survival circuits, but they are also very dependent on our lived experience, on what we already carry in our brain's memory systems. If something happens to us, our reaction to it is a result of integrating previous experiences and the way we feel in our body. We may call this happy or sad or angry. But for the brain, this is nothing but a convention that we've learned as we grew up; other people with different experiences logged in their memory systems may classify their sensations slightly differently, *and,* importantly, have slightly different meanings associated with them.

If this is true, and let's for a moment assume it is, this is a huge chance for us: if emotions are something that we *construct* by means of the low-level circuits together with *learned* predictions about the world, then we 'just' need to expose this brain of ours to different experiences, so it can create a better feeling than the one we have right now.[55,56]

This sounds a little bit like we're hallucinating our world, depending on what's already inside our brain's memory systems, but of course we're not. There are objective facts in our world, too. However, this *amazing*, adaptive ability of the brain – the predictive coding mechanism – is very important,[57–60] as it allows us, to a certain extent, to *create* a different experience in our mind, by choosing what we expose our senses to *over time*. So our brain can make us 'hallucinate' a different reality, that is, predict good stuff, and make us feel good as a result. Now briefly cast your mind back to the six strategies that I revealed at the beginning of this chapter. We're only a dash more of science away from them.

Construct How You Feel by What You Do

Learning to express through an art is a little like learning a new language. You've probably heard the metaphor 'the arts are the language of the soul'. But what does that actually mean?

When we learn a new language, at first, we learn only individual words, then we start creating sentences. It takes some time before we can really express ourselves in a new language, beyond mere communication of needs, like 'I'd like a beer'.

As we learn the steps of a dance, the notes of music, songs, painting styles and so on, a similar process is underway. We first learn the words – the steps and positions – then we learn the grammar – the rules of when to do what move, and how to combine arms and legs – and finally, using imagery, we create sentences and poetry – we express complicated feelings through our movements – be they a song, a piece of music, a painting or . . .

The place in which I lived for my dance education has an important night-life district in the old city. It's not particularly safe there, but with a hoodie and flat shoes, you get along. And, one night, bruised by words and workouts, disappearing into a cocoon of bliss was all I wanted. I wanted to blend into a grooving crowd in a disco, in wide clothes that didn't show my body, in flat shoes that kept my feet close to the ground, and to music that was not classical.

It was night, and it felt forbidden, as I snuck out of the flat that I shared, to meet up with some other people from school. It's not like professional dance school directors would appreciate their students tiring their bones on a disco dance floor. But that was the plan. Our bodies aching, but senses hyped, we threw ourselves out there, into the thumping techno beats, the fizzes and the hisses – and all those lights that lit up nothing at all, but spun a wonderful cocoon around us on the dance floor. And there, in the very unlikely place for professional dance students to be practising their moves, in the belly of some old building, our intuitive minds suddenly took over and made the last missing connections in our brains. You may call what we did 'improv', but what it felt like was this: we became rhythm and with that, our bodies spoke ballet.

I can imagine the sight this would have been. Ballet students going crazy on the techno dance floor with their weird body language. But the good thing was, no one cared. Here, no one judged us; there were no stern looks, no exams. We just were. And suddenly, we didn't only use ballet movements. It was a bit like Esperanto of the body. We used all the 'words', or movements, that we knew, to express whatever we wanted through our bodies, without any word spoken by our mouths.

This passing of the boundary, between 'doing steps' and really dancing, using a dance language to express, is truly exhilarating. I've experienced it many times after that first time; in techno discos, and later after milonga nights. Like a friend of mine who recently telegrammed me from an Argentine tango marathon, 'It is as if my feet are dancing on the screen as I'm writing you.' This merging of perception and action of the whole body, when any expressivity becomes *one,* that is *it*. We don't have to be professional dancers to achieve this. You can get into trance by just grooving along to a beat. Learning a dance vocabulary just expands your experience, and possibilities for expression on the dance floor, says my friend Dr Anna Lambrechts, who is both a neuroscientist and a professional swing dancer. She and her husband Simon Selmon lead SwingDanceUK. Simon also cares deeply about that expressivity. He says you can be fabulous at doing the steps, yet it creates a shell. It's empty. Only when you truly express yourself, you dance.

Draw a Line

In previous chapters, we've spoken much about how cues can be the gunshot that sets off pink elephants in our mind. From addiction science that we spoke about in Chapter 3, we know of the importance of cues. Developing an artistic practice that we can use to confront them is what I recommend – by *expressing those cues* inside the safe space of your hobby art. Bonus: you don't need to become a professional in the technique before this works for you!

I discovered drawing by chance during my PhD, as a way to confront the cues that sent my mind spinning.

For me, the trail of events would usually go something like this: something or someone would remind me of ballet (cue). I'd start thinking about dancing, about how it feels in my body to do certain movements. Then, my mind would spin off into daydreams (ruminations) about different choreographies that I might do. If music was playing, especially classical music, it would be even worse; my mind would be all ballet. Scientists call this 'music-induced imagery' – and in my case it was ballet choreographies. I especially liked to imagine what had been my favourite movements; *attitude* and *arabesque* movements. I used to do them as a portal to myself. When I was a dance student and I'd be somewhere new, I'd do ballet barre training in my room, and then do those much-loved movements on repeat at the end. I'd have the familiar feeling of *me* when I moved like that; even if I was somewhere totally foreign, they were bringing me back to myself. It was like having a portable 'me' with me at all times and available to be enacted, no matter where and how I was.

You may say that doesn't sound like a bad daydream. No, ballet is not a bad rumination to have. The *problem* was that soon, triggered by the ballet cues in my mind, shadow-cues from the past would start to mingle with this imagery and with the movement sensations that I knew so well, and that brought me back in time. Clinical psychologists call these backwards travels 'flashbacks' and they are a particularly grinding type of pink elephant.

As a result, I'd done what I shouldn't do, as you well know now: I had slammed the door shut to anything ballet, inclusive of music, and hoped this would delete these memories too. I suppressed and avoided. I didn't listen to music for years, refused all invitations to join friends for a night at the ballet. But while doing a PhD on dance, this was difficult to uphold. Like a ping pong ball, and Dostoyevsky's little brother's white polar bear, the cues kept resurfacing before my mind's eye.

→

When I ventured back into the arts, I had one major advantage. I still remembered the feeling of making. Whether it was a dance, a piece of music, a painting or a beautiful garment; I remembered how the process itself took me away from the here and now, transported me into a different reality, soothed my thoughts and calmed my mind into one single inviting trail of thought, simultaneously relaxing and making me productive, as time zipped by.

At university, I'd learned that this is what the Hungarian scientist Mihaly Csíkszentmihályi refers to as 'flow'. As I mentioned in the introduction to this book, flow is the much-cherished state of recovery and relaxation for our body, both physical and mental, that activates the brain in a very special way. Many people experience it when reading,[61,62] submerging themselves into the zone of a story,[62,63] or when listening to or making music,[64,65] dancing,[66] and so on. There is evidence to suggest that regularly experiencing flow may be related to good health outcomes,[67] and may protect against burnout and depressive symptoms in the work context.[68,69] And learning this showed me that the feeling I got from dance, that I was mourning and ruminating over, was something that could be accessed in different ways.

That's when I rediscovered this blissful flow-state, finally, years after my last experience of flow in ballet. It came to me again one lazy Mallorcan Friday afternoon in September in our dusty university office. We needed some illustrations of dancers for an article that we were writing. However, we didn't have the money to pay for the copyright of the images that I wanted to use. But we really wanted the illustrations.

I had an idea: What if I just copied the images with a pencil? I had taken some drawing classes as a child, though no special talent had been discovered during these dreary drawing-technique classes at the academy, but it couldn't hurt to try. Note that, compared to the dreary technique classes, where the sole goal had been to improve technique, I now had a completely different motivation to try out drawing. I wanted something very specific: specific body positions that expressed a very specific thing. However, I was doing something *that meant something to me*, I was visualising the dance, feeling how it would feel to do these positions. I was suddenly intrinsically motivated. For some reason, the result ceased to matter.

What does intrinsic motivation feel like? I can only agree with what the father of flow research, Professor Mihaly Csíkszentmihályi said in the 1970s about play and intrinsic rewards: we all need to remember back to what it felt like to be in that state of hour-long contented play, when we were children.[70] Intrinsic motivation comes when the reward for the action is wrapped up in the joy of doing the behaviour. This is when we *like* what we're doing, instead of doing something because we *want* to get something out of it at the end. It's the liking-wanting principle that we spoke about in Chapter 3. Drawing had become a pleasure-plus behaviour for me.

But we're not children anymore, and as 'reasonable' adults, intrinsic motivation is sometimes difficult to come by. It sometimes comes to us as if out of the blue, such as my drawing experience. But how do we make intrinsic motivation a reliable source of energy to keep us going? We can let findings from the psychology of motivation inspire us. Influential theories of motivation suggest that we all have some need for achievement; for some it's more, for others it's less.[71,72] However, we must remember that 'competence' is a very important building block for developing intrinsic motivation about something.[73,74] This means that 'just feel it' is not enough for fostering intrinsic motivation and finding flow. Building competence, that is, in our case, the skill of our art, is an important element on our pathway to flow.[75] Only then, as a next step, our ability to submerge ourselves into the waters of contented flow hinges on our ability to let go of our conscious mind, those prefrontal brain systems of rules and reason, and dive into the implicit memory systems, where our art is a language that we can use to express and to understand. And we can only do that when our skill level is high enough so we don't need to *think* about how to draw the line, make that shadow to suggest movement, and so on, when we can let our inner visualisations guide us.

And that's when Csíkszentmihályi says we'll also be beyond boredom (too easy) and anxiety (too difficult), and feel that we 'concentrate [our] attention on a limited stimulus field [our attention is inside a cocoon of bliss, see Chapter 5], forget personal problems, lose [our] sense of time and of [ourselves], feel competent and in control, and have a sense of harmony and union with our surroundings'.[76] He writes that it is only when we 'cease to worry about whether the activity will be productive or whether it will be rewarded' that we enter a state of flow. So make sure you get those practice hours under your belt, because for flow, task difficulty and your skill need to be in balance.[77] We will speak about how to hone that skill in Chapter 8.

While I was drawing, I felt in tune with my body, which was strange, because I was just sitting almost entirely still, for hours. Sometimes I'd get up to trace something against the window, or to get some utensils or more paper from somewhere in the room. I felt entirely free. I was breathing deeply, all the way down to the bottom of my lungs 'where stale air and toxins so easily accumulate during a day of work' – as yoga teachers like to say. But the good thing was, I didn't have to *think* about it, I didn't need a yoga teacher to remind me to breathe *deeply*. The same thing was true for my laser-point focus on the task I was doing. My attention held and held . . . without any effort at all.

The sense of creating something gave me sugar-sweet feelings of achievement. But it wasn't *just* pleasure I felt. There was a delicious feeling of meaning. I had managed to express feelings and ideas in the drawings; seeing them materialise on paper was like a present from me to myself. And the feeling kept coming. It was like surfing an eternal, enticing wave. For our brains it makes a big difference if we do something only pleasurable and only focused on achievement, or if what we're doing is also somehow meaningful to us. It's the good old hedonism-eudemonism debate, a fight between pleasure-seeking and meaning-seeking, going on right there in the tender folds of our brain. I was firmly connecting Camps 1 and 2 in this experience. And here is one very important aspect that I recall when I think about this episode today: It didn't matter what the dancers looked like or whether we'd be able to use them for what I initially set out to do, as illustrations for the article. During all this time, I wasn't thinking about the *outcome* at all – just like Pennebaker recommends for expressive writing (see Chapter 5). What mattered in that moment was entirely the moment itself and me in it. I think that this was the first time in a very long time that I had managed to 'activate' my brain in this special kind of way that gets rid of pink elephants.

What had happened there? A number of researchers have in past years measured people's experience after sessions of creating art – like the one that I experienced after my unexpected six-hour (six!) drawing session. People without any arts training at all, from all over the world, report feelings of sublime self-expansion, elevation and being part of a greater whole[78] as the result of engaging with the arts. Be it as a spectator or as a maker of art.[79–85] We feel like better people afterwards; we feel better about ourselves, about the world and what we do in it. If we're lucky, such art experiences can even make us rethink our lives, help us induce positive changes in our everyday, long after the arts experience is over.[86–88] At other times, the art-effect, this elation and intoxicating feeling of connectedness with the universe only lasts for some minutes. It doesn't matter. Sometimes having flow experiences with the arts is exactly that: just a break during which time all the biological systems of our body and brain can get busy with relaxing. Feel good.

I've been drawing ever since that night in our university office, and surprise – I was even allowed to make some drawings for our book *Dancing is the Best Medicine*.

Still today, when I see ballet, I feel bad. It's a cue that sets my mind spinning into loops about the life not lived. But since I discovered drawing, things have changed. I can now express that cue, through a different language than dance – through drawing.

→

Let me finish with how that drawing flow sparked something that has stayed with me. That moment started off my interest in flow research all those years ago and continues to shape my life to this day. When I finished drawing that night, I went outside to my car. The University of the Balearic Islands on Mallorca is in the middle of the countryside, at the feet of the Tramontana mountains. At night it's pitch black out there, except for some rare street lights that make a couple of metres' radius around the lamps look like sapphire-filtered photographs from a different time. I was experiencing some weird wowing-effect of my senses. My entire brain was hyped from the hours-long drawing session, and the aesthetics of this night-sight of our campus became like the sweet icing on the cake. There was the smell of humidity, pine trees and a little bit from the green leaves of the cottonwood trees. And meowing cats. The whole campus is full of cats. They hide during the day. At night they take over the place. Now they followed me to my car. I was loving the whole scene, no, the whole world. It was so beautiful . . .

The dancers on the other side of the paper-portal to the world of my imagination had made my brain and body connect in a strangely exhilarating way, and that made me incredibly happy.

I know I must sound like a drug addict – 'Uh, you really need to try *this*'. But that's the whole magic about it. Those altered states of consciousness we get from art act on the exact same neural circuitries that would give us a hit if we were to take drugs. The difference is that they don't limit their action to our brain-stem jukebox and Camp 1. They're not just candy – if we happen to choose an art that works for us – they reach us *within*.

Creating a Different Experience

The two examples of me hiding on a techno dance floor as a professional ballet student and discovering drawing by chance as a PhD student were situations during which I was in distress. The tough reality of a dance student was imprinting on me and I felt terrible. Similarly, during my PhD – ruminative pink elephant thoughts were tormenting me, because I was sitting too much, because a life in science is tough and unpredictable, and because I kept feeding them with my past cues of distress.

Later I discovered the science for why what I *did* in these two situations worked and *made* me feel better, great even. That's emotion regulation.

Say we're in a *situation* and our *attention* is directed at whatever happens there. Our senses perceive – our external senses (vision, touch, etc), but also the internal (interoception, etc). Based on our prior life experience, stored in our memory systems, and many variables that psychology and neuroscience are still in the process of investigating (like our personality make-up, temperament, genes,[89] and so on), our brain appraises the situation in a positive or a negative way, depending on our momentary goals and general life goals. As a result of this, we *respond*, that is, our physiology may react in a certain way as a part of that response (for example, our heart pounds) and we *behave* in a certain way (that is, we choose certain behaviours).

We start to create a different experience of 'what's coming' or 'what's going on', at five points along the emotion generation process, by using the specific *regulation strategies* which I mentioned on page 136, and will go into further in the next chapter. We can use the arts as such regulation strategies, as we will see.

Put simply, we can use the arts at six different points of the emotion generation process to change the conditions that are affecting our emotional state:

1. select the situation before we're in it (this is called situation selection), or once in the situation, we can change something in it, and with that the emotions that we feel as a result of the situation (situation modification);
2. choose to direct our attention either towards something else, or away from whatever there is in a situation, like when you distract yourself (attentional deployment);
3. engage in active problem-solving, creatively creating solutions to a problem at hand (problem-solving);
4. change how we think about what is going on in the situation and with that change our emotional reaction to it (cognitive change);
5. choose what we do about the emotional response that wants to be expressed (response modulation);
6. we can restructure our emotions and grow – by engaging in creative expression (cognitive restructuring).

Of course, the emotion generation process is not that linear[90,91] – that's precisely the point of the theory of the predictive brain,[92-96] and what Lisa Feldman Barrett proposes with her theory of constructed emotion.[97] The stages of 'emotion' generation interact with and influence each other – depending on the priors that we already have stored in our memory systems as a result of our life experience.[98,99] Similarly, the strategies to regulate emotions interact,[100,101] and they generally happen outside our awareness as we've seen above.

However, teasing these different points apart, allowing us to influence the experience that we create from a given situation, can help us choose these strategies more consciously. For example, next time we must face one of the situations that I outlined in Chapter 4 about porcupines, or pick up our phone to start doom scrolling through the news or our social media feed, as we touched on in Chapter 3.

Express the Tree That Grows Inside You

So how is it that the arts and other creative behaviours can help us with this emotion regulation? We find hints that it works from a surprising source. Sometimes, studies show that people who practise creative behaviours like music, dancing, singing or painting seem to have a *higher* risk of clinical levels of anxiety disorders, depression, bipolar disorder or schizophrenia. How is that possible? Well, again, it's all about how we use the behaviour, and in this case, very specifically, how we use creative behaviours as a self-help if we're already struggling.

I suspect you may have heard of the assumption that there may be a link between creativity and 'madness'. People with ADHD and ADD also know well the fine line between chaos and high levels of creativity. And it is also known from art history that, for example, Vincent van Gogh and many other musicians, painters and artists have suffered from bipolar disorder. Because we're talking about emotions here, and I'm suggesting that you use the arts to create a better feeling for yourself, let's briefly revise this myth. Can creative behaviours cause ill mental health? The long of the short is, no, creative activities don't cause 'madness' (unless you use them too competitively, hedonically or riskily maybe – see Chapter 2). Instead, they can help regulate difficult emotions which can make them particularly important to people who are already struggling. So 'mad' people use the arts – because they help them. How?

By finding a way to put what is tormenting them inside, *out*, into the outside world; recreating what it feels like inside, into a medium that can be touched, heard or looked at, like a piece of paper, a song, a dance. We may again call this *expression*.

When he was interviewed by Susan Chenery for *The Guardian*, the children's book author, composer and painter Matt Ottley describes what he calls 'a visceral experience of psychosis'. Psychosis can be part of bipolar disorder, and in this interview, Ottley reveals why he spent three years painting bipolar disorder.[102]

One day, says Ottley, he had the feeling that something was growing inside him. A tree? A flower? He grabbed the cue in his mind and painted it out into the world, onto a canvas. The cue had come to him, via his interoception, from somewhere inside him, in the beginning of a psychotic episode. Besides a painting, the cue became the basis for his new book *The Tree of Ecstasy and Unbearable Sadness*. The story 'grew' out of him, Ottley says, and it describes the different stages of psychosis. It is a story about a boy who is hypersensitive to the beauty and the horrors of the world. The images accompanying the story, painted by Ottley, show the boy travelling through a bizarre world. What is really happening is that the boy is travelling through the stages of a psychotic episode. The bizarreness of that journey is shown in the imagery in the book, of awe-inducing natural scenes; mountains to climb, waterfalls so big you seemingly cannot overcome them, and animals that don't exist in real life, but seem so real you cannot take your eyes off them, like a cow with wings. Ottley has also composed a soundtrack to go with the book, that expresses the aural aspects of the journey the boy is on, who, of course, has some specific similarities with Ottley himself. Adult Ottley takes child Ottley by the hand and travels through the 'stages of fragility', and thankfully emerges on the other side.

Ottley is adamant about the fact that if you suspect you suffer from this disease, you need to get your diagnosis and receive your treatment. He knows the condition won't go away, 'but life goes on and you can find peace'. And he uses the arts very efficiently for that, to channel the sensations inside him, out.

When asked about the high peaks of creativity that you get while inside the psychotic state, he says, 'If you could have access to a magic button that would turn this illness off, most people would say no because of the creativity. But I would say yes.'

So does creativity cause madness? No, it is the hyperconnected-ness of neural systems that can happen during psychosis that can make people seemingly more creative during those episodes. In this book we are speaking about creating such wonderful intercon-nected pathways in a healthy way, via practice.

What some new analyses with large population-based samples show is that it is not the artistic or creative practice that *makes* people have mental health problems, nor that they cure them, but rather, some people have a predisposition to mental health issues. This may make them more prone to take up a creative practice like music-making, specifically *because* of what they are experiencing, as a coping mechanism.[103,104] Because it helps them; it is a relief from the pain. Like writing, painting and composing for Ottley.

Using the arts as a way to express or to otherwise deal with your reality, to heal, and to emerge stronger than before, is a clever way to cope with your reality, whichever it may be, and to *create* a new one.

Healthy Expression

In the next chapter, we will speak about the six specific Emotion Regulation Strategies that you can use to create how you feel, and with that, your pathway to flow. For all of these, there are some points to be aware of, for healthy expression.

Don't Fall Into the Trap of Toxic Emotional Discharge

I'm sure you know someone who says they easily 'get rid' of their negative feelings, often anger, by letting it all out. Maybe you are one of these people that raise their voice, punch a ball or directly explode in a rant and let everyone around you know how you're feeling.

Some people want to convince me that tantrums are a matter of cultural differences. However, this is not aligned with the science. Toxic emotional outbursts are something that happens in people in any culture, and it is generally associated with lower emotional intelligence.[105] By a process that isn't entirely conscious, most tantrum-prone people have *learned* early on that they can coerce people into giving them what they want by expressing their negative emotions loudly and demanding that the problem be solved the way they want it. It's basic reinforcement learning, like Rat Barnaby with his lever. It all started with that tantrum at the supermarket checkout we spoke about in Chapter 3, to get that sweet, when Dad couldn't resist and bought it, just to avoid the embarrassment – it has worked so often that now it feels 'genetic'.

The ugly nature of tantrums aside – do they actually work as 'emotional discharge'?

No. Research shows that expressing anger or disagreement carelessly does not extinguish the flame.[106] Heart rate remains high, sweat bursts on your front, and all that arousal just enflames you and everyone around you even more. Thus, unsurprisingly, it makes you actually feel worse off than before, often riddled with guilt. This guilt then sets off cognitive dissonance that we spoke about in Chapter 3, making you self-justify your foolish act, probably reaching the conclusion that the other 'had it coming', in turn sparking a vicious circle which will have you ruminating angrily, and then having another tantrum when the anger and frustration bubble over.

Thankfully, there is a method for preventing an angry rumination cycle when we blow up: Science shows that an apology decreases heart rate and arousal in the body, both in yours and in the person you've wronged.[107–111] And for the rest: healthy disclosure via a creative expressive writing,[112] as we discussed in Chapter 4, or dance, or sing it out.

The Risks of Disclosure

The human drive to share, to express and to disclose is very strong, and it will help you overcome complicated situations.[113] Clinicians like Professor Anke Ehlers and her colleagues from the Institute of Psychiatry in London show reliably that disclosure of the traumatic event, re-experiencing it by verbalisation, sometimes over and again, is a crucial step on the path to getting rid of the intrusive thoughts and getting what happened integrated into one's life's narrative.[114–116] What we can learn from trauma psychiatry, even if we don't have any trauma, is that our mind – and that of other people – works the way it works. We all want to disclose, and doing so helps.[117,118]

However, there are some risks to disclosure which it's better to be aware of, so it doesn't backfire. Remember – it's all about how you use a behaviour,[119–122] and disclosure through the arts is a behaviour.

Disclosure isn't automatically good and won't always help you. In his paper 'Theory of Emotional Inhibition',[123] Professor Pennebaker, the scientist who dedicated his career to investigating the effects of expressive writing, cautions against disclosure to the wrong people – it may make us feel ashamed, ridiculed or rejected.[124]

People may judge your art as not very good, laugh at it. And there you are, having exposed your vulnerable self.

And if what you're disclosing involves other people, the risks of disclosure are particularly expensive. People may not believe you, say you're an impostor. Or, they may put a label on you, 'the troublemaker'. The brave individuals of the #MeToo movement have my utmost respect for daring to speak up against authority. Science has its own version of the artworld's bullying colleagues,[125,126] and also here, well done you who have dared to speak up against humiliations, manipulation, bullying and abuse of power. In the US, it is estimated that workplace bullying costs $180 million a year in production days.[127–130] So on many levels, it should make sense to call out all of the above – maybe in a public creative writing piece.

But here is the risk: it's not like the bullies (who, by the way, may be trauma victims themselves!) will immediately give in and confess to having wronged you, once you dare to speak up, maybe by writing a poem or choreographing a dance piece that exposes them. Institutions are tightly knit structures of favours and counter favours, and the webs are maintained by 'cronyism' and 'schmoozing'. If you pull one string, several puppets in the web will be affected and they don't like that.[131] More likely than not, they will collectively turn against you; diminish, ridicule and gaslight you,[132–134] while they reward the yes-people.[135] Self-justification will kick in on their side, and before you know it, *you* are the troublemaker. Similarly, victims of abusive partners know too well that the perpetrator won't immediately hang their head in shame just because you call them out in public in an artwork or, say, in a novel. On the contrary, they will use their manipulative skill against you once more, and before you know it, again, it's you that is the problem – but this time it's in public.[136]

What is the worst, for you, that can happen from public disclosure through an artwork? The answer from trauma psychology is clear: retraumatisation.[137,138] You will be retraumatised. Disclosing to the wrong people, or via the wrong means, re-opens the scar. So, the well-meaning advice, 'it will help you to speak about it', is in principle correct, but *only* if your counterpart is a trained professional or someone you can trust.

The comedian Daniel Ryan-Spaulding cautions, 'I don't think that comedy is a safe space. It's a dangerous zone! I can't control how other people perceive me and what they might get offended by.'[139] In the comedy-drama *The Marvelous Mrs. Maisel*, another problem with disclosure is revealed: 'bombing' – which is when a comic on stage exposes their most vulnerable selves, and no one laughs. They feel awful afterwards. Similarly, in his *Ten on Ten* series on YouTube, Indian comedian Vir Das starts his video with a warning that the video may be taken down due to his humorous take on his country's problems and controversies. And for the Iranian filmmaker Jafar Panahi who we spoke about in Chapter 5 – his filmmaking is only a safe space until he has the movie smuggled out of the country in a cake, winning international awards for showing Iran as he sees it.

And those are professional artists speaking.

For your pathway to flow, take this intel with you: express what bugs you, but beware *how* you disclose it and *who* you disclose it to. My advice is not to disclose your trauma to social media, to work colleagues, journalists, etc, unless you are also being accompanied by a therapist and this speaking out serves a very clear function in your healing process. Otherwise, it could retraumatise you over and over again and there will be no resolution to it.

For finding flow and a meaningful life, your art must be your safe space, a pocket into which you can submerge yourself to express your emotions when you need it; to be authentically *you*.

The Advantages of Anonymity

Throughout time, some artists have wanted to remain anonymous for different reasons, sometimes to protect themselves, or the identities of the people or groups featured in their art, be it in books or paintings. Elena Ferrante is the nom-de-plume of a novelist who guards her anonymity ferociously. In her opinion, her art should stand alone, once published, to appeal to people, or not, and not be connected to her as a person at all. The rock band Daft Punk who sang 'Get Lucky', for example, have a similar philosophy. Faces concealed with helmets at any public appearance, they express what's on their mind through their art, with no concerns of exposing their vulnerable selves. Because their 'selves' are hidden, any criticism or shaming will not reach them personally.

→

There are many reasons for creating without concern for producing anything that will please anyone. We spoke about the risks of succumbing to the three mind hooks in our artistic practice in Chapter 2, which will prevent us from finding flow. In this section, we've heard what clinicians call the 'risks of disclosure': when we express what is on our chest, we are vulnerable, and we must think of the recipients of our delicate truth. Professional artists worry about this, and so should you. Your art may simply and importantly be for one person only, and that's *you*.

7.   Mind Liberators – Six strategies to unwind your mind

Emotion regulation is a creative process, where we reshape the way we feel and react in situations, either before, while, or after we're in them.[1]

Professor Daisy Fancourt, a seasoned pianist, as well as a scientist at University College London, has been linking research from the past decades about emotion regulation from the field of clinical psychology, to how we use *the arts* as Emotion Regulation Strategies.[2]

For example, you can use the arts to distract yourself. That may be a good way to get your mind off a chore; however, if you routinely use your art to procrastinate or to flee your reality, this is not linked to positive health outcomes in the long run – just think of my friend Hamish who developed a behavioural addiction to Argentine tango in Chapter 3. Or, if you've watched the 2020 Pixar movie *Soul*, you've seen another example of someone (mis)using 'the zone' as a flight from a reality that isn't aligned with their dreams, wasting their precious life-time. A life-threatening accident brings this realisation to Jazz musician Joe Gardner. As a result, as soon as he manages to navigate his 'soul' back from the Great Before and back into his body, he sets out to use that very body and the behaviours he can do with it in the real world, to change his life for the better. So, let's unpack those Emotion Regulation Strategies mentioned in the last chapter – through the lens of creative behaviours. All the strategies that I will reveal in the next sections are art-able.

Strategy 1. 'Cook it Like you Want it': Situation Selection and Modification

Avoidance, escapism, setting boundaries.

The textbook example of Strategy 1 is this: the night before your driving test, instead of staying at home and letting your anxious thoughts plague you, you go and see a friend who always makes you laugh (situation selection). And, if that friend then asks you anything regarding your upcoming test, you may ask them if you could possibly speak about something else (situation modification).[3–5]

I myself used situation modification – with the arts – when I felt so lonely in my first London months and went dancing Argentine tango. I was still lonely in London, but I had modified that situation in a way that I didn't feel as lonely anymore as I flowed on the Argentine tango tunes, embraced with other lonely people in wonderful eternal milonga nights, showering my brain in oxytocin and dopamine, as I created moves with the partners I danced with. With this, I appeased my social brain's cravings for human proximity and expressed my desire for connection; as a result, my lonely pink elephants receded back into their own cages and let me live.

The examples about setting boundaries for your senses, your people and your work in Chapter 5 can help you implement Strategy 1 with the arts. You can set boundaries for cues *before they happen*. Or, once you're in that complicated situation, you can *do* something creative instead. Like Princess Sisi did, who arrived on Corfu and vanished behind the high walls of Villa Vralia, setting boundaries between her senses and the world – literal walls, in her case, so the toxic court life couldn't generate more pink elephants in her mind. But she didn't just hide there. And that's an important point: once behind the walls, she started *to create*, with the arts.

Maybe you struggle with falling asleep? You can let the situation continue to chew you up or you can let a good book, a movie or an audiobook catch your thoughts and spin them into one cohesive trail of creative thought, letting them flow along the unexpected and rewarding meanderings of a story you love. This strategy is all about using the arts to create a situation that triggers a different, more desirable emotion inside you.

Let's now look at another beautiful art that works wonders if you want to 'cook it like you want it': enjoy the art of cooking during the evening to unwind.

The Art of Cooking

'An exquisite pleasure had invaded my senses, something isolated, detached, with no suggestion of its origin,' Marcel Proust famously wrote about the 'Little Madeleine', in his novel, *In Search of Lost Time*.[6] Our senses of smell and taste are rooted in the most ancient parts of our brain that we share with many other animals, deep down in our brain-stem jukebox. They are also the senses that mature earliest during our life, due to their importance for keeping us safe. Therefore, our first memories will be linked to experiences with these senses, reliably transporting us back to our youngest self.[7-10] Proust is transported back to his childhood, one morning when he eats the little seashell cake with tea. Without needing effortful attempts at mind control, tastes and smells absorb our attention in fascinating ways. This makes cooking a reliable sense-catcher for starters.

Cooking also involves repetitive and clearly purposeful movements, it's very kinetic (catching our proprioception). Then, there are familiar sounds during the preparation of foods (hearing), and we're surrounded by colours (sight), different textures (touch). Literally all our senses are caught in the act of cooking. Absorbed, we flow away from the everyday and into the colourful *zone* of the culinary arts. The trick is to purposefully exploit this survival mechanism of our brain, building, by association, a pathway back in time to where we feel safe, satiated and powerful. If we have different cues that can take us into this pocket from time to time, for example by having the right cues in plain view in our kitchen, we're rich.

Bestselling author Jamie Oliver speaks openly about his dyslexia, and about how he finds flow in cooking which helps him avoid, for some portions of his day, the situations that hurt. In cooking, he creates moments of self-realisation. In a conversation on the BBC radio 4 *Today* programme on 27 December 2022, with musician Loyle Carner – who has ADHD – they share how to use cooking for more than food preparation. 'Food was always a space for my neurodiversity to exist, right? It didn't get in the way. It was actually kind of helpful in the kitchen,' Loyle shares. Jamie recalls a situation where his dad gave him a pat on the back for cooking a great dinner, and how he remembers the hairs on the back of his neck going up, because the usual interactions with his dad were about school and it not going very well. 'Food saved me,' he says, 'because it gave me a purpose,' and Loyle adds, 'Cooking is like meditation for me, and for sure some of the space where I got some positive reinforcement.' Loyle hopes to help other neurodiverse individuals find their sense of purpose with cooking in his new cookery school.

If you are neurodiverse, you may benefit particularly from little pockets of time away, where you avoid 'the world' because it otherwise overstimulates you in a bad way. Instead of persevering with stuff that makes you feel small, find and create situations that make you grow, *cook it like you want it*, and your mind will flow. Find how to put your skills, which you sure have, to good use – could it be cooking?

The New York-based filmmaker David Freid uses the art of cooking in a different way to give his senses a short break from a stressful work life. He doesn't cook it, he films food. How?

David directed a corporate video clip I was part of in Germany. At the same time, however, he was working on a personal project of his, a food show, focused on Black food history in America (with cookery writer C.R. Williams). What we were working on together was a commercial film. 'This is what puts food on my table,' he explained to me in the evening, when he headed off instead of staying for dinner with the crew. He preferred to create a different situation for his senses in the evening, instead of hearing more of the same, also over dinner, about the stressful work context. Instead, 'the food show is what brings food to my soul,' he said. When he spoke about it his eyes came to life in a way I hadn't seen during the whole day of shooting. In the couple of minutes while I got a summary of the food show, I met the real David – a glowing enthusiast, kind, passionate and with an immense curiosity for what his project might reveal next. And off he flowed, into the night, back into himself to tirelessly create, until the early morning hours, this soul-food of his, called 'Hungry for Answers'.

Take Flight, but Don't Flee

A final cautionary note about Strategy 1. If you always 'cook it like you want it' – you can end up in avoidance behaviours. Remember Daniel Wegner and colleagues' research on white polar bears from Chapter 1?

The trap is that we may choose to do art when we know we should be doing something else; when *avoidance* becomes a way of life. There is also the social aspect of avoidance. If the issue that you are putting up boundaries for involves difficult interpersonal situations in family, social life or with work colleagues, and the problems never get solved because you avoid the conversation, this will not be healthy for you in the long run. This is beautifully and sadly illustrated in the movie *Soul*, where Joe Gardner uses his music to escape the reality that his life has actually completely derailed. Instead of working on fixing that, he keeps tuning out into the zone. I once knew a manager who kept on avoiding situations he didn't like: hoping they'd go away, he'd just leave the room. They didn't, they kept brooding, until one day it all blew up in his face.

Similarly, it can be tempting for someone who is shy to avoid social situations. This gives them a short relief, but at the expense of the long-term benefits of socialising.[11] Life with other people is unpredictable, and pink elephants are ready to rumble into our mind at the slightest cue. Staying home, however, binge-watching soap operas (that are basically 'ready meals' with loads of artificial rewards!) gives us a sense of having social contacts, supposed friends, even family.[12] The situations are highly predictable, soothing our prediction brain; however, they are not real.

Since the mid-noughties it has been known that soap opera binge-watching isn't good for us. It can become a behavioural addiction,[13] with all its elements (salience, mood modification, tolerance, withdrawal, conflict and relapse).[14] Soap opera watching has been linked to body dissatisfaction,[15,16] anxiety and feelings of loneliness,[17,18] making us feel terrible.[19,20] One study even showed that having a bad soap opera habit was related to poorer cognition – it makes your neurons sleep. The line between good and bad avoidance is fine; it's up to you to navigate yours very wisely.

Strategy 2. 'Expecto Patronum!': Attention Deployment Strategies

Distraction, 'prayers', rumination.

The textbook example of Strategy 2 is: you are witnessing an accident and to distract yourself from the gore, you focus on some beautiful flowers on the side of the road for a moment.[21] The beauty of a scene can help our mind escape from what would otherwise overwhelm it. By focusing very strongly on something you love doing instead of letting the situation imprint on you, you deploy your attention elsewhere.[22]

Harry Potter doesn't remember the death of his mother. However, when 'dementors' come his way (dark beings that suck all joy out of you), he suffers from flashbacks. When specific cues converge, Harry hears his mother's screams and he passes out. Trauma victims know this seemingly inexplicable fainting behaviour very well. It is, in fact, caused by the brain's fight and flight mechanism. When the memory is too painful to fathom, this threat triggers the vagus nerve to tell our muscles to 'freeze', and we may faint.[23] Clinicians refer to this symptom of trauma as 'vasovagal syncope'. Even if it doesn't feel good, and I know the feeling, it's good to know that this is just our brain trying to keep our body safe: in the face of unfathomable threat – in the wild, this would have been a tiger, for example – it makes our body pretend it's 'dead', so the predator may lose interest and go away.

After one such fainting experience, Remus Lupin, Harry's Defence Against The Dark Arts teacher, gives Harry a piece of chocolate to chew, as an antidote to the effects of the dementors. This great twist of the story (amazing – a teacher gives you chocolate as a medicine!) could in fact also have some science in it. For one, our senses of taste and smell are reliably caught by chocolate as we've established above, directing our thoughts in 'sweet' directions.

For two, chocolate beans are the best natural source for *flavonoids*,[24] a metabolite produced by some plants. And it is probiotic – improving our mood, removing the dementors, via the gut-brain axis.[25] So maybe, practising 'the art of *chocolât*' from time to time could be a good attention deployment strategy.[26,27]

Now – I obviously don't want you to binge on chocolate. So, besides this first-aid against dementors, let's discover less caloric attention deployment options. In the magical world of Harry Potter, the spell against dementors *while* they attack you (so, attention deployment – away from the gore) is 'Expecto patronum'. You have to grasp one happy thought in your mind, focus your attention on it with all you have, and express *that*. This expression happens through the wand in the fantasy novels of J.K. Rowling – and through the arts in real life. And that's exactly what the filmmaker Panahi did when, in the most terrible vortex of worries, he grasped on to a happy thought and expressed it, through his art, film. That's attention deployment right there.[28] Similarly, remember the filmmaker Susana from Chapter 3. She cannot escape the fact that she is short-sighted, however, when she removes her contacts, she deploys her attention away from the bad feelings it causes in her, with her art.

Pray it

Let's find another inspiration for how to create an attention deployment strategy from a maybe unexpected source: religious practice. Even if you're not religious, you know what a prayer is. Since ancient times, people have been using prayers at specific times in their day, or carried, in their pockets, tools like prayer beads, Drishti stones, candles, etc, *to direct their attention away from the world around them for portions of their day.*

Prayers are a clever invention for two reasons.

One: prayers and religious practices are what scientists call 'multi-modal'. That means, they stimulate several senses at once – they appeal to many 'modalities' and absorb them: the visual, auditory, tactile, proprioception (body movement), interoception (sensations from within), exteroception (where we are in space), and sometimes even also appealing to our sense of smell (like when we use incense), or taste (like when the practice includes eating or drinking something, oblates, for example). They use our brain's love for cues and its ability to associate cues with specific feelings as a way, with practice, to send our mind into a meditative space. People who pray regularly can enter a state of meditative focus easily, as soon as they perceive the cues of their religion.

Two: in their basic elements, prayers are a combination of behaviours that are repeated, on cue. They consist of many habit loops. Specific prayers or mantras are recited expressing a specific intention, sometimes chanted, using specific movements, even choreographies (get up, sit down, bend your knees, look to the left, the right, down, etc). They are practised at specific times of the day, initiated by auditory sounds like bells, the *adhan*, or other cues that send our mind into the space of our prayer. Sometimes prayers are done in specific directions or locations of our body in space, like within a specific space of a room, towards an improvised altar or towards something as simple as a Drishti, a small prayer stone that can be put anywhere we need it so we can focus on it for the prayer with our gaze. Or we may have prayer beads in our hands that help us maintain focus, via the sense of touch.

The meditative state that we reach with this combination of behaviours is good for us. But what people forget is that we can use the arts very much in the same way to regularly reach this meditative state, without needing any religious intention at all. This could mean running scales on your instrument at a set time every day or sitting down to draw something on a sticky note during your lunch break every day.

To implement Strategy 2, 'Expecto patronum!', with the arts, I propose that we all reserve pockets of time in our day where we deploy our attention to our art. Not as a flight, a distraction or a suppression of what is currently happening. But, as something you plan to have in your daily life, to give your senses (and with that, your brain), a break from chaos and spinning worries, like you'd do with a prayer, and with this, train your attention for your pathway to flow too. For example, pull out your needle pouch regularly.

The Needle Pouch

Needle-loop-stitch, needle-loop-stitch, needle-loop-stitch is a repetitive rocking behaviour with creative twists *par excellence*. It absorbs our attention greatly.

Nazanin Zaghari-Radcliffe is an Iranian-British dual national who was arbitrarily imprisoned in Iran for five years, accused of spying. She speaks about her and her family's ordeal in her memoir, *A Yard of Sky*. After her release in early 2022, she was guest editor on the BBC Radio 4 *Today* programme in December 2022, and told the world how she'd knit to keep her mind away from the fear and uncertainty of prison life, and from the unfair accusations. It kept her hands busy, and it filled the time.

Research shows that pulling out the needle arts pouch from time to time activates the body's relaxation response and gets rid of excess stress hormones that might be in our blood due to our continuous fight against the pink elephants and the other bad thoughts that they come with. Knitting, crochet and company have been found to successfully combat insomnia, irritability and build self-esteem. As a radio guest editor, Zaghari-Radcliffe introduced the work by the British charity Fine Cell Work which teaches needlework in prison, sells the finished items, and helps people rebuild their lives. An inmate called Louis explained the transformational experience of having a pocket of time with his needlework, his pouch with his stuff always at hand. He found Fine Cell Work when he was still in prison.

'It was a different kind of addiction for me, it was very therapeutic. You see, when you actually pick up that needle and thread, for me, it is actually very, very addictive. You pick it up and you can spend hours and hours sewing without even realising.' Remember from Chapter 3, that 'addiction' is made by the same neural circuitries that are also involved in learning a new skill. Louis was creating a new habit there, repurposing his cues.

'Any time I feel I'm getting a little stressed or a little worried, or getting a bit uncertain about, you know, just general things in life . . . I just pick up my needle and thread . . . it's like a hidden talent that I never saw coming.'

The workshop manager of the Hub at Battersea explains, 'Stitching can be so powerful. If you're alone in your cell, and you've got multiple worries in the world, you can really transport yourself. You're surrounded by colour, you're learning a new skill, and you're connecting to the outside world.'

Just like a prayer takes a person out of the here and now, as they chant or recite a poem, or make specific movements with intention to express adoration of a God, the practice of an art can do the same, as you grab a happy thought in your mind and express *that* – expecto patronum!

Pray It, But Don't Purge It

There are moments when using the arts as a targeted distraction is the right thing to do, to stay sane, as long as we're clear that this is what we're doing. When our surroundings are complicated, we in fact *should* use the arts as a distraction (not as avoidance or suppression though). As long as we're aware that this is what we're doing.

Someone living in an abusive relationship or suffering from other porcupine spines, can use 'expecto patronum' with the arts as a way to get away from the cues for a little while. With time, this may help them start to think straighter and formulate the decision to leave for good. However, the artistic practice cannot become a flight that is complicit in remaining in that abusive relationship, for example.

One final note of caution about attention deployment: Rumination is an Emotion Regulation Strategy that many of us choose intuitively, even if, as we've seen in Chapter 3, it is not a good idea. My friend Hamish used tango addictively. Similarly, you can use expressive writing to ruminate over your worries instead of expressing them. *Rumination* is also an attention deployment strategy, just not a very healthy one. So, pray it, but don't purge it.

Strategy 3. 'Spin it': Problem-Solving

Incubation, inspiration, social support.

There are three ways to use the arts for problem solving, to 'spin it'.

The first is what scientists call *incubation times*,[29] little time windows that we set between the time we become aware of a problem and when we try to solve it.[30] Instead of sternly persevering, we ease off for five to ten minutes maximum, do our art, and let the problem simmer in the back of our mind. Then we come back to it. We may find that we suddenly come up with creative ways to solve the problem because we've given our mood a boost,[31–33] for instance, by listening to our favourite music,[34,35] or because we've left our unconscious mind free to spin it.[36–38] We're basically using the polar bear to our advantage. As we focus away onto our art, our mind throws the problem in and out of our awareness (remember the Zeigarnik effect from Chapter 1), and we may suddenly find ourselves 'inspired by distraction'.[29] I played this trick on your mind in Chapter 6, when I told you about the six strategies that we would speak about in this chapter, before actually explaining them. While you were reading the science in Chapter 6, your mind was already nibbling away at the six strategies, possibly increasing your creativity for using them later.

The second way of using the arts for problem solving is what I've been doing throughout the previous chapters; literally using the arts to find a solution.[39] For example, in Chapter 4, we strolled through science about the social brain by using examples of storytelling from movies and novels,[40] and so on. Many artworks are full of knowledge about how previous generations have dealt with this conundrum that human life is; spun into a good story and hidden in a book, a movie, a beautiful poem, or in a witty gag – for you to find, spin and apply to your own life.[39]

Besides, art that connects the feelings of pleasure that we get from a good story with deeper meaning, connects very different parts of our brain with each other and makes them jam in sync.

This is what pleasure-plus behaviours give us. While we stand in wonder before the castles of our mind, built by a story we're reading, both the low-level reward systems and the high-level meaning-making systems of our brain are active, forging pathways, and sending us off into flow. When we connect with that meaning hidden inside an artwork, this is gold for the pearl strings linking our brain systems. You can find that inside a book or inside a museum as you contemplate artworks that appeal to *you*.

The third way in which the arts can help with problem solving is by relying on the people in our arts community, simply by being with them, or by directly asking them for advice. We know from the largest happiness study in the world[41,42] that the people who were able to rely on a social network to share life's ups *and downs* with, were those who were happiest. And we know from Chapter 4 that our body needs human connection for our mind to spin out of the loops of loneliness. So, if you're part of an arts community, you're rich! You can ask for advice that you wouldn't have access to, if it weren't for that arts practice that you've started.

Leave Space for the Benefit of the Doubt

Research about the usefulness of incubation times to bring our creativity up to speed is still mixed.[43] But when in times of trouble, instead of firing off that email in despair or anger, why not pull out that needle pouch and stitch a patch? Give incubation times the benefit of the doubt and find out what works for you.

Turning to other's advice can also spark a solution to a problem; just remember the section 'good to know' about porcupine prickles from Chapter 4 (page 89), when you ask for advice.

Strategy 4. 'Look for the Silver Lining': Cognitive Change

Reappraisal, acceptance, the emperor's new clothes.

The textbook example of this group of strategies goes like this: when facing a difficult exam, you say to yourself, 'Well, it's just a test, I can retake it if I fail.'[3] Reappraisal and acceptance consist in us doing something (with our art, in our case), and that makes us change the way we think and feel about what's happening to us or has happened to us in the past.[44-47]

I'm personally still in the process of reappraising positively my past and the injuries I took from it. Here's one: if I hadn't been injured, I would probably not have studied psychology and neuroscience, and wouldn't have made dance the topic of my research. I wouldn't have written a bestselling book with Dong-Seon about dance. And considering all the wonderful messages that I'm still receiving five years after publication, from people who feel that finally their art is being recognised and tell me how it helps them in their life, this was a good thing. Looking for the silver lining inserts all the positive emotions that I could possibly hope for.[48]

Technically, there are two types of reappraisal: detached and positive reappraisal, and when you use them, this shows in the brain.[49,50]

Detached reappraisal means that you look at what is happening as if from the outside, like watching it unfold through a window, for example. Or you use your imagination to make it look something like a black and white movie, where you can switch channel or turn down the volume as you see fit.[51-53] Doing this recruits regulatory brain networks of the right hemisphere (prefronto-parietal) and downregulates the scared Camp 1 system (amygdala). All this contributes to reducing the felt emotional intensity of negative stuff that is happening.

Positive reappraisal instead changes the emotional impact to the positive; you're looking for the silver lining in it all. It doesn't have the same soothing effect on Camp 1 activity. Instead, it recruits the left prefronto-parietal regulation network in the brain.[50,54,55] For example, some studies on emotion regulation in HIV patients and their caregivers have found that some individuals would purposefully look for the 'silver lining' of the situation. Silver-lining patients and caregivers would say that probably, without going through the experience of the illness together, they wouldn't have been able to develop the level of trust and intimacy that they had.[56]

Those individuals who used this positive reappraisal also generally felt much better. One metanalysis confirmed these findings in 2009. AIDS patients who used positive reappraisal had generally better wellbeing levels and better physical health outcomes.[57] A finding that has also been found in people with diabetes – positive appraisal is associated with lower mortality.[58]

Outside the clinical realm, looking for the silver lining has shown to be extremely helpful for everyday worries too. A group of researchers asked college students to tell them how they had reacted to the worst situation of the day.[59] Those that had spontaneously used positive reappraisal had generally felt better. It's just really good for us if we practise seeing the bright side of things with all these little everyday hassles too.[60-62] This is something we can learn from people that clinicians would call 'resilient'. These individuals intuitively use positive emotions to bounce back from negative emotional experiences.[63]

An Art Gallery Visit

Maybe you are a campaigner, overwhelmed by the cruelty of wars that keep exploding throughout the world, and ask *when will we ever learn*. A resilient person would maybe use the arts to help deal with that sting of reality. We can see ourselves and our opinions reflected in artworks – giving the righteous pink elephants spinning in our mind a break.

Pablo Picasso rendered the air strike by the German Condor Legion that destroyed the village Guernica in 1937 in cubist style. As you stand before the 3.5 × 7.8 m canvas and the black and grey shapes intrude on your senses, the suffering of the civilians imprints on your senses. Maybe it sets off some reappraisal about who you decide to spend time with, who you vote for, and so on. But that's all you can do. Don't lose yourself.

And for the rest, remember that a single being cannot change this cyclical nature of history. New movies, series and books keep telling the same coming of age stories for each generation anew, just set in different times. New babies are born, they make the same mistakes as generations before them, because culture and knowledge are not genetically transmitted. They must be learned, and experiences *constructed*. We start at square one with each baby.

Children don't 'grow out' of bad behaviour unless you educate them.

Research from past decades suggests that all the small changes for the better that we have seen in human societies – the Universal Declaration of Human Rights is one change for the better (even though it is not yet perfectly implemented) – occur through a phenomenon that scientists refer to as 'cumulative culture'. Professor Celia Heyes from Oxford University describes the process in her research.[64,65] If change is possible, it will be through cumulative culture.[66,67] Through the coordinated action of societies together, using the accumulated knowledge residing inside multiple cultures (for example, in the libraries and art galleries . . .) about human errors over past millennia.

To reappraise, accept and grow with the arts, it may be helpful to revisit 'the layers of meaning' in artworks that you surely learned about in school, so that you can use them in your own self-expression.

Layers of Meaning

Depending on which country you grew up in, you will have read the grand novels of your culture in school. And your teacher will have walked you through the symbols and metaphors of those novels. And likely you've been like, 'What?!' But with time, you started to see patterns. These symbols and metaphors lay hidden in many texts, paintings and dances around you. Suddenly they were everywhere! They unlocked the arts for you, like a key opens the lock to a closed door. We *learn* the symbols of our culture – in the West a cross is holy, and a swastika is evil. We're not born with that knowledge, and depending on where we've grown up, they will mean, *symbolise*, different things to our predictive coding brain when we see them. The same goes for the arts.[68]

For example, in Danish literature, often 'a beautiful garden' in a story symbolises childhood. If you read Danish stories with that in mind, suddenly an additional layer of meaning pops out of the pages. Your brain goes 'aha!' as you understand the double meaning, and happily activates both those high-level structures of reason and deliberation, but also those low-level reward systems of Camp 1 – and of course, this will connect with your feeling of 'me'.

Looking below the sugar coating of glossy artworks opens up a whole toolbox of symbols that you can then use as pleasure-plus, on your own pathway to flow.

In summer 2023, the British Film Institute curated a summer of movies and events with the objective of examining the portrayal of women in the movies of Howard Hawks (he directed *Scarface* – most people know that one). The curator of the Hawks movie series, Ruby McGuigan, wanted to look *below* the glossy surface of some pretty glamorous movies.

Marilyn Monroe stars in several of his movies. She was stylised as a sex symbol, a blonde bombshell character, and killed herself aged thirty-six. What remains hidden to some people, however, is that Howard Hawks has woven heavy social critiques into his movies, about how society sees and treats attractive women. Much of it is still topical today.

With every sparkle of the diamonds, every come-hither look . . . Monroe is despising the world that brought her so much pain. She does that by singing 'Diamonds Are a Girl's Best Friend' full throttle, and matter-of-factly justifying marriage for money, because 'Men grow cold as girls grow old'. She is mocking the viewer who sings along and nods in agreement. And at the end of the movie Monroe innocently convinces the father of her husband-to-be that she 'is intelligent' because, she explains, 'if you had a daughter wouldn't you also want her to be well off?' It is a parody, an absurdity; a statement with which Hawks invites us to think. As we giggle in delight, these movies help us reappraise and accept that the world simply is like that.

And then, as part of the acceptance process, we can cherish the hope that the type of movies that have more than one simple layer of candy offer possibilities to grow for everyone. They may, with time, contribute to changing the society we live in. As Danish filmmaker, Lars van Trier, puts it – a movie should be like a stone in your shoe: annoying, impossible to find, but also impossible to ignore. This goes for any art that we can use as a pathway to flow, movies, paintings, dances, music . . .

Symbolic Thought, Metaphors, Intentions

To understand the 'second layers of meaning' of artworks, we need the ability to infer intentions from other people's actions. This ability needs to mature in our brain. We're born with the predisposition in place, but the skill needs to develop during childhood.[69] And we can nourish it, throughout our life, through learning. Scientists refer to this skill as 'theory of mind': we develop an understanding that others have thoughts, wishes and minds of their own and that they may be different from ours.[70]

Think of yourself when you were little. As soon as the hurdle of the first two to three years was overcome, the games of 'as if' started.[71–73] The living room was a castle and the walnuts in the bowl, the crown jewels. And it went on; the dolls and teddy bears came to life. They ate, felt, got happy and, sometimes, upset.[74–76] And you learned that 'to really understand other folks, you need to put on their shoes and walk around in them'. That's the advice that Atticus Finch gives his daughter Scout, when she asks why people behave the way they do in *To Kill a Mockingbird*.

Choose Art That Makes You Feel Strong, Not Art That Makes You Feel Inadequate

Maybe you're neurodiverse and struggling with how people see you?

I've always enjoyed sitting in cafés to write out my cues. One day, while writing away in a small café in London, I noticed a lady reading a book with a title that caught my eye. *The Curious Incident of the Dog in the Night-time*.[77] Something was off. My research focuses on body language, be that dance or everyday gestures. And to my eyes, the lady's expression was conflicted; it didn't match the cover that looked as comical as the title sounded. As far as I knew, the book was a famous instance of a novel about an autistic boy. The twist of the book is that it is never mentioned that the main character Christopher is autistic. We follow him from never leaving his street alone and insisting on routines and patterns, to having a transformational experience when he embarks on a quest for the murderer of a dog.

In a 2016 article, Sara Barrett, herself on the spectrum, and a journalist for the *Guardian*, explained how distressing books like *The Curious Incident* can be for people on the spectrum.[78] Many of these books tell the story of how the family crumbles *because* the child has autism. It's all their *fault*. Christopher's mother had left the family because she couldn't deal with it. Similarly, TV series like *Big Bang Theory* and *The Imitation Game* show how autistic individuals disrupt the lives of others and how they struggle to maintain friendships.

I remember reading this and thinking how sad I'd be, if I was made to feel responsible for my family not working – how guilty I'd feel. Sara Barrett likes the books of *The Night School* series by C. J. Daugherty. People in those books love being around the protagonist Zoey, often *because* of her autism.

If you are autistic or have a child with autism, your path is more difficult than the path of other people, and you have to create and look for silver linings wherever possible.

The arts can help us reappraise how we and others feel and behave, by listening to their realities, explained, for example, in books, songs, movies, paintings, etc. They may help you reappraise behaviours and not be offended by them. Maybe check out the movie rendering of the life of Professor Temple Grandin. The movie, *Temple Grandin*, tells the story of a young lady becoming an expert in cattle rearing. Many of her inventions are today implemented on farms worldwide. You stay glued to the screen as Claire Danes plays a young Temple, who has a special gift to see links and mechanisms where no one else does. We witness her being ridiculed for that. People have a tremendous lack of imagination and vision sometimes – not so Temple. She slowly finds a way to prove her points. She does not give up, nor do her parents. Temple kept creating – and today she inspires millions.

Oh – and she is autistic.

The Emperor's New Clothes?

There is a rather arrogant assumption that 'you must *understand* art to fully appreciate it, otherwise there is something wrong with you'. This type of unwritten social rule leads many of us to shy away from the arts. Apologetic, we say, 'I don't know much about art,' and we close the door to a world of possibilities to find flow, just to prevent embarrassment. It's that social brain layer again, that we spoke about in Chapter 4. We want to fit in, and avoid being the weird one that 'doesn't get it'.

So, in the service of our pathway to flow, let's explore that. Why might you not 'get it'?:

1. The art you're watching may be a case of The Emperor's New Clothes; it could just be a fraud.
2. A specific piece may simply not jam with you and your sense of self, your past, your *you. And that's fine too.*

Many 'contemporary', 'modern' and 'abstract' arts have populated all parts of the world at any point in time, and people have struggled to 'understand' them if they didn't happen to have grown up inside the social group that the art emerged from. It helps to remember that 'modern' art, throughout history, has always emerged from the work of highly creative individuals who wished to 'break out' of conventional ways of art-making, or of society altogether, because they, in some way, felt that it limited them. Just think of William Turner – certainly not as accepted in his time as he is today. 'Modern' artists express a reality that most other people may not (yet) know so much about. Therefore, understanding the multiple layers of 'modern' arts is like trying to understand a foreign language without having studied it. Today, it's all about seemingly incomprehensible dashes and splashes of colour, squeaking saxophone sounds, 'ugly' dance moves and movies without any apparent plot or expressivity. How to understand *that*?

What we can do if we don't 'understand' a piece of art is to use our brain's neuroplasticity, its ability to learn new skills, and we'll speak more about that in Chapter 8. Briefly, you may set out to practise the skill, learn the symbolism and the metaphors, learn how to express, and how to understand the expressivity of others through that art. For example, ballet dancers are taught a very narrow corset of movements from childhood on. They are constrained in every movement they do, always. Imagine that – like you're in a plaster cast your whole life. Wouldn't you, at some point, want to 'break out' of that cast? Take that knowledge nugget with you next time you see a 'modern' dance performance – do you understand the 'strange' movements better now? As a simple start to understanding paintings you've never seen before, for example, next time you speak to your Iranian friends, or consult a book on Iranian art, try to find out a bit about the symbolism of Negargari paintings. I'm sure you'll be pleasantly surprised about the many layers of meaning of some of these paintings! Some even contain the entire symbolism of poems by the philosopher Hafez. Learning about the symbolism, history and creation of a piece helps you create new connections in your mind, and, yes, then, to 'get it'.

As a final note, I'd also like to invite you to give the arts the benefit of the doubt and let your brain nibble at things it doesn't understand – suddenly you may get one of these golden 'aha' moments. An artwork may, suddenly, unexpectedly, make you feel something. For your pathway to flow with enjoying others' art, here's what could happen to you too. In our book *Dancing is the Best Medicine*, my co-author Dong-Seon shares how he once watched the dance piece 'Echad Mi Yodea' by Ohad Naharin, performed by Batsheva dance company. With no education in contemporary dance, the movements at first seemed incomprehensible to him. However, then, as the individual dancers were 'breaking out' of the circle of the other dancers, only to be forcefully reabsorbed into the circle, something suddenly resonated with him. He was reminded, by those expressive body movements, of his own past of being forced to conform to a group-norm that he didn't believe in. In this case, the artwork resonated with Dong-Seon's memory systems, his sense of self.

Beware of Rumination and Suppression

We just need to remember that reappraisal, or the process of trying to reappraise, can lead to rumination too.[79,80] You have to practise this, it won't just work regardless.[79,81] You need to take yourself with you on the way,[82] meaning that you need to practise until you can successfully implement the strategy without it making your mind spin off into pink elephant ballets. And of course, it's easy to tell yourself that you've accepted something when in reality you're actually *suppressing* it. This is where therapeutic help can be very important, and 'just interacting with art' can be a slippery slope, especially if you have no experience with the arts yet.

Strategy 5. 'Do the Chameleon Move!': Response Modulation

Mood induction, expressive suppression.

The textbook example of Strategy 5 is: 'you have been wronged, but instead of expressing the anger verbally and in your facial expressions (frowns, etc), you inhibit the outward signs of anger. We know from the field of clinical psychology[83] that people with social phobias may be particularly prone to seek to suppress, out of fear of rejection or to avoid further confrontation. Even without suffering from social phobia, many of us may resonate with those sentiments. Yet, while suppression may in some cases be necessary, we know from Chapter 1 that the fire in the chest will not be extinguished by suppression.

What we can do, instead, is kind of *the opposite* – express a *different* feeling through our body, and with that, change our mood. In Chapter 5, we spoke about how psychologists use 'mood induction' to frustrate research participants with the objective of studying cognitive processes, for example how frustration impacts memory and attention. Now let's use the same function of our brain to make ourselves feel better. In mood induction we use our brain's adaptability, become a chameleon, and change the way we feel, by changing what we express.

You can watch a movie, dance a dance, sing a song (or listen to one!). The list of options for using the arts to express and lighten our mood (instead of pulling it down) is endless. Let's look at one example.

During the final weeks of the Covid lockdowns, while many of us were in a rather sombre lethargic mood, my student Eva-Madeleine Schmidt approached me. For her upcoming master's thesis, she wanted to empower people to change their mood. And because she had a background in both dance and psychology, she wanted to change people's mood with simple dance moves that everyone can do. For dancers it's obvious that you can change your mood by dancing. But as scientists, we needed to test this systematically, and so we did.[84]

The Emotion Regulation Strategy 'Response Modulation' is emotion regulation after the fact. You change how you feel about something by inhibiting the behaviour that would go with whatever is happening to you. For example, if something bad happens, but you don't frown, cry, or *do* the *behaviour* that expresses the emotion, you suppress it and prevent yourself from feeling it in the moment. This is suppression, which we saw in Chapters 1 and 2 as a behaviour that doesn't help us access flow. The good version of this strategy is mood induction: deliberately *doing* a behaviour that expresses a different mood.

For her master's thesis, Eva asked a large group of people to come to the lab, and one by one, seated alone in a room, they first learnt a series of simple dance moves by imitating a dancer model on the computer screen. These were just simple dance moves with the arms, so you could even do them seated. Once learned, she then asked participants to repeat these moves, but this time, expressing happiness or sadness, again by following the dancer model on the screen, who was now, also, expressing happiness or sadness.

Results showed that with this very simple task, participants' mood changed for the better. And not only that. We had also asked participants their work-related motivation before and after the 'dance-break'. The more positive mood change they experienced from the dance-break, the higher was their work motivation after the dance break.

Comparing Suppression With Reappraisal – What Happens in the Brain?

Many experiments show that compared to reappraisal (part of Strategy 4), suppression leaves high levels of arousal in people's bodies. The crude recommendation from clinicians is: don't suppress it (it will rebound) and don't think of it over and again – that's rumination, and ruminating will just strengthen the nerve connections of the traumatic memory[85] and blow up the pink elephant beyond all proportion.

Imaging studies show that when people reappraise a negative stimulus or event, there is an increase in activity in the prefrontal cortex, specifically the ventral lateral and dorsolateral portions. These regions are all about cognitive control of our behaviour, and are 'non-emotional'.[45,86,87] At the same time, during reappraisal there is *less* activation in limbic structures of our brain, that is, the most emotional parts (amygdala and insula).[52,86,88,89]

Suppression, on the other hand, looks different in the brain. We also have the heightened prefrontal cortex activation. But we *don't* have the much-appreciated decrease in limbic system activation.[52] It means that the high arousal remains in the system. The arousal doesn't return to normal levels when we use suppression, although we may *look* calm from the outside.[90,91]

There are also studies that show the opposite.[55] However, my hunch about these different results is that *it depends*. It may depend on who you are, and what the problem is, which strategy will work best as your *chameleon move*.

Strategy 6. 'Lace it with Gold': Cognitive Restructuring

Creative expression, self-growth.

The textbook example of what happens when *not* applying cognitive restructuring is: 'I didn't get the job. I'm worthless. As a result, I've stopped applying for jobs, I overeat and am just sad.'[92]

The beautiful element of this strategy, which is based on decades of positive psychology work, is about changing what happens inside our mind and brain (often outside of our awareness), *before* our reaction to a cue. When applying cognitive restructuring, we attack our dysfunctional **beliefs** ('I'm worthless' in the above example), about cues that are happening to us ('didn't get the job'), and *with that*, we change how we *feel* and *act* as a consequence ('I've stopped applying for jobs, I overeat and am just sad,' is the unhealthy **consequence**). The idea of cognitive restructuring relies on theories from the clinical realm that propose that external events don't cause emotions, it's the **beliefs** that do.[93–96] As the cues of an event enter our senses, they collide with our 'beliefs' (stuff that's in our memory systems), and that's where things can go either way.[95,97,98] Remember the defensive ballerina Zoé in Chapter 4? The bad experiences from the past have made her feel very small and insignificant. In the present, she hates herself for that (**belief**). Any slightest cue signalling aggression (to her mind) is met with abusive, defensive and self-destructive behaviour. It's a complete loop of self-sabotage, when you attack the people who are trying to help you.

You may notice that this is just another take on what we've been saying all along. Our brain changes in a use-dependent way, and if it has been 'used' for bad experiences, our brain is like the *Knight Rider* car – woop, woop, scanning the environment for possible threats. For our hyperactivated Camp 1, the 'incentive value' (Chapters 3 and 4) of the cue 'I didn't get the job' is a huge pink elephant in our mind, and it will be preparing us for defence (aggression or withdrawal) in no time. As a result, our reaction to the same cue ('I didn't get the job') will be very different than the reaction of a person who didn't have this bad experience in the past. This, of course, also links to what we spoke about in Chapter 6: our predictive coding brain constructs the emotions we feel and how we see what happens to us, *based on past knowledge and experiences,* our priors. And these priors condition how we react. Our brain is a prediction engine.

How to attack those beliefs, if we're not even aware of them, self-sabotaging ourselves? If you have experienced any of the 'invalidated traumas' that I listed in Chapter 4, or worse, you are likely to have more or less unhealthy **beliefs** about yourself and the world, no matter how much you pretend that you don't. And that, according to positive psychology professionals since the 1990s, and many scientists since then, is a problem for cues that enter your senses, because of how you react to them. Here is the mantra: **ABC**.

A(ntecedent) → **B**(elief) → **C**(onsequences)

'Antecedent' is what we've been calling 'cue'. How do you react and feel as a result of that cue? If Zoé's self-worth hadn't been so low, she would have met the attempts at helping her with joy and a much more constructive development would have ensued. But it's never that easy, and that's why, at times, we need to lace the thoughts about ourselves with gold. Meaning, what we need is to change that dysfunctional belief that we have about ourself. And the arts offer this opportunity. Remember Jamie Oliver and Loyle Carner earlier in this chapter speaking about neurodiversity? Their lives were a string of failed attempts, until they discovered the art of cooking.

Other examples of unhealthy **B**s that life may have 'taught' us are feelings of *not being enough* (and therefore your **C**s may be 'helpaholic' or we are profoundly jealous of others), *being a bad person* (as **C**s we act as people pleasers, trying to impress others by overworking, or being overly sweet), *having all responsibility on our shoulders* (your interactions with others may be marred with **C**s of you trying to take the lead to the detriment of everyone else), or *being an impostor* (our **C**s will be anxiety riddled). One study with over 2,400 students showed that low self-esteem biases our social interactions profoundly; we persistently predict that others won't like us and that conditions our interactions.[99]

What to do about it? For one, we should stop persevering at things that keep us feeling small and inadequate – as Jamie and Loyle taught us. Instead, collect successes! Remember that the little dopamine showers in our brain when something works out are *learning signals*, helping our brain make new connections. How to collect those successes? Well, with our art. Little daily successes with our art give us a string of little boosts of self-esteem that will help us (re)construct that self-worth, and grow. Besides, reliable successes give us moments of being in control, appeasing our predictive coding brain; as we saw in Chapter 5, uncertainty is a killer of minds and of our self-confidence. Chapter 5 also provided examples of how awe and beautiful spaces can help you (re)construct that self-worth. With time, our creative practice will contribute to slowly change our dysfunctional beliefs about ourselves, and with that, we'll develop healthier ways to react to cues, no matter what they are, because *I* am intact.

Use Your Art (or that of others!) to Boost That Self-esteem

Midge Maisel, the protagonist in *The Marvelous Mrs. Maisel*, suffers what clinicians would call a nervous breakdown because she has been cheated on; and she happens to be a stand-up comedian performing on stage as it happens. On stage, after her husband leaves her for his secretary, the stupid 'Penny Pan', Midge transforms her traumatic experience into jokes. On the spot, she jams, and tells the audience how her perfect world came crashing down on her because her now ex-husband thought that after he failed at a performance in a club, she (Midge) would 'never be able to look at him the same anymore'. The only solution that occurred to him was to take his bruised self-esteem to Penny Pan for confirmation of his manhood; a lady so dumb that even his parents tell him, 'This is not a girl that you introduce to your parents.' Midge, as the creator of these punchlines, receives an enormous amount of self-validation from that gig, and by turning her experience into a joke and recasting herself as the storyteller rather than the victim, she demonstrates how we can use our art to boost our self-esteem.

But we don't all need to go on stage and become comedians. We can enjoy shows like these, and feel a sense of self-validation through the comical renderings of porcupine problems, as we understand that we're not the only ones feeling the way we do. This helps reconstruct our self-worth too. Studies have shown that even consuming art that presents alternatives to your internalised beliefs can help you restructure your thoughts. For example, several episodes of this comedy show express the topic of how many very proud men feel threatened by self-sufficient, smart and powerful women. These men hurt their wives and partners, and themselves terribly and unnecessarily because of that. In several highly comical twists, the viewers become aware that all the women in the show are perfectly aware that men are not the strongest sex, but love them nonetheless – if only the men would realise! *The Marvelous Mrs. Maisel* is one big cognitive restructuring of the dilemmas of the genders.

Trauma memories are sometimes disorganised and growl under the surface of our consciousness, and they insert their venom into our feelings of self-worth and the beliefs we have about the world and ourselves.

We need to work on *restructuring* the traumatic memories with the arts and creative behaviours. Think of lacing the memory with beauty and a different meaning, creating a new memory with the colours of your art. Instead of thinking that you need to 'mend' yourself, think *Kintsugi*, the Japanese art of creating something new and beautiful out of broken pottery, joining the edges with lacquer laced with gold. Lace your thoughts and actions with beauty and precious, creative energy, and with that success and surrounded by that beauty, you grow. Because this is so important, let me give you two more examples.

My friend Miguel Azorin loves making other people laugh by just telling stories from his life. If there is a mishap to be had, Miguel will have had it. Is there a word to be misunderstood, mispronounced or used to scandalous effect? Miguel will accidentally say it. He could be someone without any self-esteem at all. But – not so. Quite the opposite.

For him, bad situations are just stuff that will later become the anecdotes you tell to your friends, all sitting around a table, laughing. He's actively lacing his memories with the golden glow of laughter, all those endorphins, mingling into the memories, making them pleasant and not threatening at all.

Torsten Sträter is a German comedian, TV presenter and writer, and he is the patron of the German Depression League because, well, he struggles with depression himself. His creed – 'You need to keep fighting until the depression starts suffering from you instead of you from *it*.' For him, people with depression are the strongest and bravest people in the world because, for them, each day is a fight between life and death. He spins the madness of everyday life into puns. His new book contains precisely such stories about not taking it all too seriously,[100] and how to better spin it all into a punchline, to give you self-esteem that makes life worth living, despite it all.

Drawing, painting, knitting, story writing are all activities that we can purposefully use to restructure any memories and experiences we may have, and give our self-esteem a boost with all these little successes, hooked neatly up on a string, and then to change these beliefs. For example, reframe your thoughts, draw them on a canvas with loads of light, flowers and gold on them. The painter Jochen Maiwald's main motif is a beautiful golden fish that swims in a huge shimmering ocean, looking very happy. It's swimming against a swarm of very ugly, simple fish. His motto is *be different, be happy*. Go visit him in his gallery in Santanyí, Mallorca, to see his painted take on being different and lacing *that* with gold. There are many ways to restructure unhappy memories about who you are, and how much you're worth, with the arts. Find yours.

Mix and Match

You may have noticed that some of these Emotion Regulation Strategies and the examples I have given are very similar or intertwine somehow. As we are not speaking about this within a clinical context, it's completely safe to say that you can mix and match to your heart's content and find what works best for you. I don't mean you to slavishly choose *one* strategy and then sternly apply it. This list of six strategies gives you a toolbox to choose from as you experiment with your creative activity, building your pathway to flow. According to the theoretical background of these strategies, each of them is particularly suited for different moments of the 'emotion generation process'. However, as we saw in Chapter 6, more often than not, the emotion generation process is not that linear; cause and effect are not as easily established in real life as on paper. And often, which strategy will work best for you will also depend on who you are (your personality, goals, etc),[101] what emotion, memory or situation you are trying to regulate, and so on.[102] Therefore, try out what works best for you, with your art. And now, let's get closer to how to develop that skill we need in practice.

8. Process Over Progress – How we learn a new skill

And now, you wonder, how do you really get cracking with your creative practice and learn a skill that can become your pathway to flow? We've established that you don't need to be a master in an art to use it as a pathway to flow, but you do need enough basic skills in an art form so that you can catapult yourself off into flow.

How do we go about creating those 'Atomic Habits'[1] that become big and then change our life for the better? The first step is, well, the first *step*, literally. To help ourselves make that step, let's discover a little more about how our brain *makes* and *learns* movement.[2] Entire books have been written about how to learn and optimise skills, so in this chapter we'll focus on the basics.

We only have *one* brain, and it takes care of everything; from keeping us alive to learning the language of an art, both to express and to understand it. This is great news because it means that the same neural systems that we are already using for other behaviours will be the ones we'll tap into and take advantage of in our creative practice – so we won't be starting from zero. We just need to 'repurpose' those neural systems a little, strengthen some pathways between Camps 1 and 2, and with the wider brain, especially, with our movement and memory systems. The best thing about neuro-plasticity is that we can develop new connections in our brain throughout our lives and get back to creating and learning, no matter how old we are.

Neuron-Hugging Myelin

'What fires together, wires together,' said neuropsychologist Donald Hebb in the mid-twentieth century.[3] He was referring to the behaviour of neurons when they communicate. When you perform a behaviour that is meaningful, millions of neurons fire along the pathways that they are part of. The more frequently specific groups of neurons fire together, the more special cells called oligodendrocytes[4,5] are called into action to create stronger neural pathways by coating our nerve cells with myelin.[6,7] Myelin is a marvellous glittering layer around nerve cells, made of proteins and fatty stuff that insulates nerve cells and makes electrical impulses (information) travel faster and more efficiently along the neural connections.[8,9]

You may have noticed that I said 'meaningful' behaviour above. That's because it isn't enough to just passively repeat a behaviour: you also need a learning signal that may feel like a small 'aha moment' for a skill to stick,[10] a reliable feedback from the practice itself that tells you 'you're doing this right'. So, you have to celebrate the little successes for it all to stick. As incredible as this seems, to learn, you need to have *fun*.

For efforts that work out, we get rewards, or rather, our brain does.[11] These are learning signals for our brain,[12] and they make us feel a little sense of achievement each time. We can get an empty version of this self-fulfilling feeling by collecting rewards like 'mastering' a jump in a computer game. However, when our brain gets the reward through a real jump with our body, new connections are made that will make us better at real jumping, as myelin starts hugging neurons. You have literally become a little bigger, well, your neural web has. There is no other way to get that than by *doing*.

So, let's start with the beginning.

Baby Steps

Who helped you to start walking? As we saw in Chapter 6, learning is a high priority for us humans, to learn to fit in socially, for instance, by labelling how we feel with emotion words. But long before that, the first type of learning is much more about movement and physicality.

When you were little, you were profoundly rooted in your

body. At first, most of us were crawling, and then walking. A little unsteady still, but then, with large strides, we started running, and climbing stairs unaided. With experience, a fair share of giggles, and with the everlasting patience of our parents, we also got better at using tools, like cutlery to eat our favourite dishes and spades to dig all the holes we needed. These early lessons were learned physically, through trial and error, as well as through imitation, for example, when developing our speech skills by imitating the sounds we heard. As babies, we didn't overthink what we were learning and laughed easily when we made small mistakes. With all that movement and practice, we forged connections in our brain that made us able to do these things *skilfully* and *efficiently*. Then, we also started to develop language, the ability to think logically, and to defer gratification through the same process of practice, imitation, trial and error; forming all kinds of connections in our brain.

Everything, all that we know, seems profoundly rooted in the bodily experiences that we had as we grew up. But then, as we passed through our first years, something happens in our brains that allows us to imagine our way through a scenario without needing to enact it every time. We don't need to have jumped from the tenth floor to understand that it's dangerous. We jumped down from a haystack, and that hurt. That was enough. Likewise, abstract concepts like stock markets, or high-level maths – we don't need to have had bodily experiences of *all* of these to understand them. Our brain likely uses simpler experiences to build an understanding of these more abstract concepts.* However, as we dive deeper into the science about how our brain learns, remember the unconvoluted, very physical way of learning, by *repetition*, with *fun*, and with a little help from other people we can *imitate* or ask for a hand.[13,14] Even if our childhood is some decades away now, science

---

* This topic is part of a lively debate in the ivory tower, known, for example, as the embodiment debate. I may be ruffling some feathers here by not explaining more, as I anticipated in the disclaimer of this book. So let's briefly acknowledge that this is an ongoing debate.

suggests that our brain still learns best in the very same, unconvoluted, physical way.[15] We just need to let it.

Celebrating the Small Wins on the Way (just as our parents did, each time we succeeded at something)

Do you remember what it felt like to draw as a child? Many of us would have started drawing before our formal education began, getting lost in the colours, shapes and movements without there being any right or wrong way to do it, and our efforts would have been rewarded with delight and praise – perhaps even with a coveted place of honour for our work on the family fridge. When we enter formal education, however, our relationship with the arts starts to change. In Western cultures very often, drawing, art and other abilities like writing, language learning and maths are seen as separate things and taught to children separately.[16,17] We forget that we have only one brain and that brain takes care of *everything* we do, hence, functions overlap and can be optimised by using different behaviours that stimulate the same mechanisms in the brain. Yet, we're taught to separate the arts from everything else, as a separate category of behaviours, while in reality they are part of a continuum of stuff our human brain does. Teaching children that the arts are part of life and continuing to encourage their intuitive play, celebrating their ten-minute absorption in creative materials (and our respite), would not only build audiences for tomorrow for the cultural sector, but, more importantly, bring much-needed benefits for children's cognitive development.[18]

In China, a long-standing tradition has children copy drawings from adult models. However, in 2002, a new curriculum was implemented which added episodes of creative expression through painting, letting children draw what was on their minds.[19]

Initial research shows that drawing regularly has several positive effects on children's and adults' cognitive skills, like, for instance, on writing skills,[20] and on memory.[21] Children learning geometry via a dance class, where they make the angles and the circles with their hands and arms to music, score better than children who were taught the same material while sitting at their desk.[22–24] Children who sketch science concepts retain them better than children who summarise them in writing.[25] Using your body to learn helps you retain information better, improving memory for events and abstract concepts.[21] 'Drawing it out' also seems to improve socio-emotional skills in children and help them deal with emotionally challenging situations.[26–29]

As we know, the benefits of using creativity to focus our minds aren't just for children – they're important for all of us. Fortunately, there are ways to return to that intuitive movement-based approach to learning within the arts to help us get over the first step and our performance anxieties. And while you do, remember the liking-wanting principle from Chapter 3. Fuel you brain with endocannabinoids and endogenous opioids by enjoying the journey, more than *wanting* a specific outcome.

It Is Not Important What *You Draw, But* That *You Draw*

The Danish professional artist Kasper Købke reliably tricks our brain's motor system into overcoming obstacles to learning a new skill. His solution? Make it fun. I know – *fun* is an unusual approach to art! But not unheard of: you may remember the much-loved TV series *Art Attack* from the 1990s and 2000s, or Bob Ross's *The Joy of Painting*?

'It is not important WHAT you draw, but THAT you draw,' Kasper repeats enthusiastically on Danish morning TV, while he's monitoring a drawing game unfolding between two young girls and the TV host.[30] He has a stop watch, set to forty seconds, and each time the clock chimes, he shouts, 'Drawings up!' and the drawers obediently drop their pencils and raise their drawings into the air. The situation has a comical hint to it, and everyone's faces are all smiles and giggles. On Kasper's signal they pass it to the next person in the line. Then they draw again, now on top of each other's drawings. Kasper holds workshops for children and adults alike, gives talks and moves the masses to draw. The game he's playing in the TV studio is one of his ten drawing games for the whole family.

Kasper is a descendant of the Danish Golden Age painter Christen Købke (1810–48), who is known for perfect figurative paintings of seascapes. Kasper is very different – for him, drawing and painting is prioritising enjoyment over perfection. On his homepage, you can find 'the doodle game', 'let the pencil tell the story', 'copycat', 'draw ahead', and so on. These are all games you can play at a table with sheets of paper, lots of colours and your favourite people. The doodle game consists of making a huge messy doodle on a sheet of paper with one pencil line, and then starting to explore the cracks and creases between the lines – adding an eye here, another one there and, after a while, under the strokes of colourful pens, extraordinary creatures start emerging. It really is *fun*.

Kasper's process-over-progress drawing practice has had tens of thousands of us Danes drawing in delight so far. The giggles, smiles and good times that he prescribes make dopamine rain down on our little neural connections, calling the oligodendrocytes into action to create myelin that hugs our neurons, building stronger neural pathways.

Every art has a set of core movements that build up to form an expressive toolbox. Don't be too stern and stressed about learning your skill.[31] For skill learning, humour (and a little bit of self-irony) is your super power.

It's up to us which experiences we give our brain to forge new pathways, and to *create* the life we want to live. This is easier said than done, for example, if you are battling with issues genuinely out of your control, like illness or caring responsibilities. But I'd like you to take that idea with you, of *creating* the life you want to live, as we dive in deeper – even if it's just for brief moments in your day. I'll be talking a lot more about *movement* from now on. I want to get you to *move*. You may feel that my 'everything is movement' mantra becomes a little repetitive after a while. However, I promise, it will make sense in the end. So, please stay with me.

Pathway Prompts

I would like to share with you what I call Pathway Prompts. My friends and colleagues in the ivory tower will find this simplistic.

However, on the other hand, a lot of what we do in academia needs translation and interpretation before it will ever become useful to anyone. I'm aware of that, so here we go.

Most of the time, we're caught in habit loops and that's why we keep doing what we do.[32–34] It's the same with thoughts; we usually circle around in the same thought habits. As my clinical psychology professor Miquel Tortella always said, 'The best predictor of future behaviour is past behaviour.'

For example, for a middle-aged scientist with an expanding waistline, the *habitual* action in the evening is to bend the knees, stretch out one hand and then lower the bum down onto the sofa. There it stays for the rest of the evening. During that time, the hands also do specific actions on repeat, zapping on the remote, swiping the phone, moving food and drink from the table to the mouth. For these actions to happen, like reaching for and grabbing a doughnut from the table, a quite long chain of events has to happen in the brain and body first, and continue, while the hand moves the doughnut towards the mouth. The type of reach-and-grab movements that we need to grab a doughnut are encoded in our motor system as 'motor plans', depending on the object we want to grasp. Our brain has plans for all the movements we do. Particularly well designed are the plans for movements that we've practised a lot, like grasping doughnuts. Motor plans are made up of many 'motor commands', which are basically all those small electrical impulses that travel between neurons as part of the neural communication between them. Our hand automatically makes a different shape when we grasp a hazelnut, as compared to when grasping a doughnut. That's because our brain makes sure that the motor commands of the grasping motor plan are executed in the right order, reach the long motor neurons of our brain stem and travel down into our body, to the muscles – in this case, the muscles of our arm, hands and fingers to grasp the doughnut.

There is also communication between body and brain via similar channels,[2] to update how this movement is going, as the doughnut travels towards the mouth, and whether we need to adjust strength, lest it falls on the floor! All this happens with each movement we do, within fractions of a second and outside of our awareness. My typing on the keyboard right now, your eyes moving over the page as you read, all these are movements. Even if you are listening to the audio version of this book; there are little hairs in your ear, and as the sound waves of the voice reading this to you move over them, these hairs are *moved*. This in turn stimulates the roots of the hairs, and that sends off little cascades of electrical signals that transport the information, via neural transmission, to the systems of your brain responsible for hearing. All of these are neural processes that happen because of . . . *movement*. Everything is movement.[35]

What sets off these habitual movements? As we saw in Chapter 3, *cues* are what make the habit loop go round. The *cues* that set off all the actions of the middle-aged scientist with an expanding waistline are, for example, the sight of the sofa (promising relief), the feeling of the remote in the hand (promising excitement on the other side of the flickering screen), the sight and smell of the doughnut (promising pleasure). These habit loops happen throughout the evening, and throughout all the evenings of the scientist with an expanding waistline's life.

If they don't interrupt this circle, for instance, by initiating the habit loop of an artistic practice instead.

To break vicious (habit) loops, we need to move. Specifically, we need to do *new* actions, setting ourselves on a new path. And that's the most difficult part. Self-evidently, I can't do this first action that changes everything for you. It really *has to be you* that does the first move.

The best way to initiate actions is with a prompt – with (new!) cues. While I can't move for you, I *can* give you ideas for Pathway Prompts that you can design yourself, and implement, to suit your needs with your art.

We modern humans already have many cues around us in our everyday. The alarm clock in the morning makes us initiate the actions of getting onto our feet. The sight of the sink and the toothbrush prompts some of us to initiate the action of grabbing the toothbrush and so on. Church bells or the *adhan* from the mosque call for prayers. Timers on our phones prompt us to act; call a friend, go to the doctor, congratulate a birthday person. To create new habits, structure the occurrence of Pathway Prompts to guide you in a new direction at times you'd otherwise fall into bad habit loops. This can as simple as pulling your hoover out of the closet so that it is within your line of sight, prompting you to initiate an action (hoovering just one room). Start simple. A Pathway Prompt should be the most basic type of cue that you can think of that could start you off with your art. This will help you make yourself an 'Interest-Driven Creator' instead of an 'Exam-Driven Learner'![36]

The Interest-Driven Creator

The 'Interest-Driven Creator' model is a new educational framework being implemented in Asia.[37] It is a way of thinking about what is motivating us to learn and shifting that motivation away from external rewards (grades on an exam) towards internal rewards (the satisfaction of pursuing your interests and creating something new). Remember the liking-wanting principle; work on *liking* what you do while you do it. Let's take this idea with us in this chapter and see how it can be extended beyond the classroom into our everyday lives. For example, designing a 'cueing' environment is one of the framework's main action points. The cues we plant in our environment can act as habit triggers, helping us direct our behaviour towards the habit pathways we'd like to strengthen.

Now be a detective in the service of your new arts habit, and hide cues in plain sight that prompt you to initiate the actions of your art. Have an 'altar' of your art somewhere in your room, office or kitchen that prompts a specific action with your art. The artist Kasper Købke has a whole atelier with canvases, colours and charcoal. You don't need that. Simple is more. Have a special pencil pouch, needle pouch or tango pouch containing your essential supplies that you keep close to you as you practise, so that this cue is reliably woven into your memory systems with your good feelings of flow. With time and repetition, this cue will become the Pathway Prompt that sets off all the habit loops of your art and brings this big change in your life. For over a decade I have painted my little fingernail red. It's a Pathway Prompt. For what action, I won't reveal; that's personal. But what I can reveal is that this tiny cue has since tsunamied through my life and changed it for the better. It has been a journey of trial and error, and will always be. But the good thing is, it's always there, reminding me, prompting me.

I mentioned another Pathway Prompt of mine in Chapter 3; the glittering Argentine tango shoes in the red satin pouch. I'd keep them in my work purse during the day, on the floor, next to my legs, under the table. Whenever my mind would go stale, I'd peek down where I'd left the bag open a crease, so the glitter and red would remind my brain. An immediate boost of motivation was the result, and then, at night, this Pathway Prompt of mine pulled me out into the freezing winter London night and made me dance it all away.

But, how did I *learn* the moves of Argentine tango; how did I build the skill?

Everything is Movement

Have you ever wondered how we remember movements? What I learned when I studied psychology and neuroscience was surprising for me as a dancer. Movements are planned and ultimately *made* by our brain. All movements. As a dancer, my assumption had always been that movements are somehow made by our muscles, and that the muscles have, well, a memory. A muscle memory. That's how we learn ballet choreographies like *Swan Lake* and *Giselle*, right? Turns out, no. 'Muscle memory' is something that happens in our brain, stored as motor plans, consisting of many motor commands that are nothing more, but also nothing less, than many electrical signals; memory for movements is not in the muscles. And it has everything to do with the motor cortex.

'A sea squirt is like a professor,' jokes neuroscientist Daniel Wolpert in his 2011 TED talk. 'When it's found its fixed position, it doesn't need to move anymore, and it eats its own brain.' According to Wolpert, and many movement neuroscientists, the real reason for brains is *to move*, to make adaptive movements, movements that help our body survive. The only thing that doesn't require movement is secretion, like sweating. Everything else happens via the contraction of our muscles, by motor plans made by our brain. Not all organisms have a brain. And those that don't, don't move. A smile is a movement. Looking at something coming toward us is a movement, of our eyes. Eating – is movement. And so on. Systems of homeostasis, of our sense of self and of survival – are all intertwined with the movement systems. Our emotions are movements too; someone's smile, frown and wrinkled nose are movements that our brain perceives. Likewise, our own emotional expression is *movement* of our body. With everything in our life so intensely linked to *movement* in our brain, this is incredibly important also for our artistic practice. Why? Because of a special kind of magic that our brain does when we repeat movements meaningfully.

From Explicit to Implicit Memory Systems

Have you ever wondered what it really means when we say that a skill is our 'second nature'? *Explicit* memory systems are in use when you consciously have to *think* about what you're doing. *Implicit* memory systems are humming away benevolently when you don't have to think about it anymore, the skill has become our second nature. In fact, this is an energy-saving mechanism of our brain. When we repeat a movement, our brain assumes that this is an important skill that we need. However, effortfully, consciously having to remember how to enact the skill is too costly for our brain. Remember that our brain already uses a lot of energy. Hence, it switches on energy-saving mode for often-repeated movements. They pass from *explicit* to *implicit* memory systems. This goes for all often-repeated movements: walking, turning the pages of a book, doing a ballet pirouette – and unfortunately also for grasping doughnuts. Simplifying a little, for the brain, learned movements are nothing but habits; nothing but many repetitions of loops of cue → action → reward.

That's where we want to get with our artistic skill, because *then* we can focus on expression – use the movements of our body to *express*. You're already able to write, hence this is a movement-skill you already have under your belt as your second nature, as it is anchored inside your implicit memory systems.[38] That's why, if you want, you can already today, *now*, start with the art of expressive writing that we spoke about in Chapter 4.

You may not remember how you learned to write, or any other skills, so let's retrace the process of learning a movement skill with the example of learning to drive a car.

If we perform an *action* over and again in response to specific *cues* (e.g. shifting gears each time we hear our car howl too loud), and we get a *reward* for that action (the car sounds pleasant again), our brain will recognise this. Our brain will assume this action is important for us and will memorise the *cue* that came just before it (e.g. the sound of the howling motor). But it will also want to save energy.[39–42] As we said above, performing actions consciously each time is too effortful for our brain in the long run. Therefore, our brain shifts the knowledge of how to do this action into the implicit memory system.[43–45] This frees up energy resources for our brain to focus on something else *while* using that skill (much like driving a car and talking at the same time). That's an advantage if the skill we're learning is driving a car, or doing a tango move; it's a disadvantage if it's the skill of eating doughnuts each night. Because as it gets implicit, it's a habit that is harder to break. Bad for hedonic eating, good for an art.

Think about it – in the first driving lesson it all seemed very complicated, you had to be focused on only that. But today you can probably navigate the heavy morning traffic while listening to music, eating a croissant and speaking to your friend. Your implicit procedural memory systems take care of 'the rest'. That's our brain's special magic that we want to use also for our art. Remember we have just one brain and it takes care of everything. It doesn't have different systems for everyday movements and for artistic movements. It's all one.

Say your art of choice is knitting. As for all arts, needle arts will need brain regions responsible for planning, paying attention and for keeping a mindful focus during the activity. We integrate sensory and visual information, store information in memory, coordinate and time the movement of our hands in a very precise way, to the rhythm of the clicking needles. This shapes nerve connections between brain systems, and the practice keeps them lubricated, happily working away, and importantly, *connected*. When a movement works out, a hook catches on the wool as intended, we get a little blossoming feeling in our chest, and the dopamine learning signal in our brain. The habit loop is starting to form.

In the new Asian educational framework that we spoke about above, of the Interest-Driven Creator,[37] this blossoming feeling in our chest that happens when we have those little successes, where we feel satisfied and relieved that it worked out, is wonderfully referred to as our moment of 'harmony'.[36] This very private feeling will then link us to the activity that gave it to us, and, with that, create this hard-to-grasp *intrinsic* motivation inside our memory systems, that will continuously pull us towards the activity again. We will be *interest*-driven, not *outcome*-driven.

A study among over 3,000 knitters from an online knitting community showed that frequent knitters felt calmer and happier in life, and rated higher on a concentration scale than people in the community that knitted less frequently.[46] Research shows that while happily knitting, stitching and crocheting away, practitioners develop a sense of fulfilment, identity and personal connection.[47] Intrinsic motivation is created, step by step, hook by hook. And, as you know from the practice of Kasper Købke, all those good times make the endorphins rain on our neurons, call the oligodentrytes into action, and myelin starts hugging our neurons for the benefit of our skill learning. And bonus: in interviews, needle arts practitioners share surprising cognitive effects and improvements, and one longitudinal study in France showed that among a series of hobbies, regular knitting was associated with a lower risk for dementia and cognitive decline in a sample of 2,000 people.[48] A similar finding was reported for several needle arts including knitting, quilting and crocheting in the US in 2011.[49]

The Pathway to Flow

Be *the Movement, Instead of* Making *the Movement*

In the cognitive science of movement, let's simplify for a moment and say that there are two main factions of scientists. One faction believes that *thinking* is enough to learn a skill. That's the cognitivists.[50,51] The other faction thinks that you need to *do,* to learn a skill.[52–55] For the latter faction, you need to *move* with your body, you must *embody* the skill, to learn it.

When I read texts from the most extreme version of the cognitivist perspective, I'm always reminded of the eighteenth-century German Enlightenment philosopher Immanuel Kant. 'Thinkers' like Kant thought that humans can *think* themselves to everything without any need for a body at all. Our brain just floats around being marvellous, while the body is full of strange pulsations, secretions, orifices and incomprehensible drives that we should better suppress!

Scientific findings from the past decades have by now rather firmly established that the extreme cognitivists are wrong. There is simply too much research showing how states of the body influence our brain and vice-versa. What is likely to be true, at least for learning, from a scientific point of view, is that some degree of 'embodiment' will help you learn – and that's what the Asian educational framework of the Interest-Driven Creator[36,37] is picking up on. It's all about how a behaviour that we actually *do* will change how we feel and who we are. Remember, everything is movement; what makes you *you,* is your movement – your gestures, your smiles and all your moves with your art. For sure, the cognitivist-embodiment debate continues and more research might yet shed more light on the matter and help us better understand both cognitive learning and embodied learning better.[56–58] But for now, as a former dancer, let me recommend that when it comes to developing your artistic skill, make sure you use your brain's ability to optimise itself through *actual* movement.[59]

Embody it – Meaning, 'Put it into your body'

To be able to express yourself through your art, you need to learn the technique of your art. It's a bit like learning the words and sentence structures of a new language. Unfortunately, many Western educational systems are still, today, based on the cognitivist idea that we don't need to move to learn; there's too much theory. The way to learn anything, including also an art form, is through systematised knowledge transmission. You're asked to learn things by heart, you're taught abstract concepts and rules. All of these are behaviours that engage our prefrontal brain systems. These are brain systems for reasoning and logical problem solving.

So, maybe by introducing extra energy into this logical brain system, making it even *more* active with transcranial magnetic stimulation (TMS), artists could get even better at improvising? Turns out, no. When scientists used TMS to apply electrical currents to the prefrontal (logical) brain structures, expert jazz musicians got worse at improvising.[60] Introducing extra energy into the prefrontal cortex made the professionals worse at expressing with their art; it was pulling them away from their deep implicit memory connections, their 'second nature'. Jazz music beginners, instead, had a slight advantage when TMS was applied to their prefrontal systems. This could mean that novices were still using a lot of rules for playing, so introducing extra energy into that logical system via TMS seemed helpful to them, while experts were likely already using other neural networks.[61,62] The novices had not yet internalised their art, much like a driving student is still relying entirely on explicit memory systems. The language of jazz hadn't yet passed into their implicit, deep memory systems. More experienced practitioners, instead, 'let go' of controlling everything.[63] This 'letting go' in neural terms is visible as an attenuation of those prefrontal control networks in the brain, and that seems helpful for catapulting us off into flow.[62]

I learned to dance ballet using a rules-based framework. We were taught individual movements over and again, just the movements, learned to do them perfectly, and only later would we put them together into a dance. With hindsight, I compare this type of learning to learning only the words of a new language until you can say them all correctly but never say a sentence with a meaning.

The opposite way to learn an art is via our intuitive expression and imitation. There was no ballet syllabus 300,000 years ago, people just danced. So the most unconvoluted way to learn an art, for our brain, is how children do it.

I experimented with this different, more intuitive way into an art form for the first time when I started to practise Argentine tango.

The classes were scheduled to take place in the vault of a church near Farringdon in London. They were in the evenings and the first time I approached the church along deserted residential streets, I could hear an unfamiliar type of old-school music getting louder and louder. As I walked down the steps it was like passing into a different world – new cues everywhere! The light was dimmed, red and golden, people were dressed in beautiful clothes and wore shiny shoes. I guess this was when my red and gold glitter shoes got firmly anchored into my memory systems as my tango Pathway Prompt, and I became an Interest-Driven Creator.[37]

First, Copy!

The teacher, Racquel Greenberg, instructed us to follow her. She just walked on the beat of the music and we followed. She didn't talk much at first. We just imitated her body movements to the sound of this unknown music. It was mesmerising. You don't know where you're going, you just do your best to follow along, you have a thousand questions popping up in your mind, but you can't ask them. That's your prefrontal cortex right there demanding to understand it all rationally. Let go of that for a moment, *just copy, imitate*. And at some point, you realise you *actually* don't need to *know* the answer to all these questions *right now*. The initial embarrassment and fear of making a mistake subside a little. There is a lot to keep up with, the beat, the steps, the hips, the arms.

If you feel self-conscious about starting to learn your skill by imitating and copying others, please think again. Imitation is the most basic human form of learning, and a very precious one. It emerges early in our life, taken care of by low level circuits in Camp 1. Children, a few days old, imitate the movements of caregivers' facial expressions, like smiles and frowns, without knowing what they're really doing. We're born with this imitation mechanism, thankfully. As babies, we went on for hours and hours, imitating the facial expressions of those around us, then starting to imitate movements like waving. Then we started to imitate sounds: first, pretending we're dad on the phone, 'bababaieblabla', saying nothing in particular, and everything at once. Once a toddler does that, developmental psychologists are very happy, because any ability to learn and develop more complex skills than that hinge on this basic, seemingly so simple, ability, willingness and intrinsic enjoyment *to imitate others*.[15]

Talking, walking, eating, and anything that comes after that, are all based on much trial and error, observation and learning from what and who we've imitated. This is the basic principle of how the human brain learns.[64–70]

After almost thirty minutes of us just imitating our tango teacher's movements, as in trance, like a movement meditation, she paused a little and gave some explanations for each step that we'd done, then we practised again. The interactions that followed between us and Racquel were completely movement-based, hardly any words were spoken.

This Argentine tango class was my first contact with a teaching system that wasn't first and foremost about rules and structure, but about feeling and intuition. Talking about tango today, therefore, feels like my soul is being sucked out and I'm looking at myself from the outside. I also despise mirrors in the room when we dance in a milonga, because it pulls our attention to the outside, and makes us reliant on the external image, more than on how harmonic the movement *feels*. You can use a mirror to correct yourself occasionally, but not when you want to dance to connect with yourself and to express. Remember the study that showed that professional jazz musicians got worse at their craft when their prefrontal cortex was stimulated? It impeded them from sinking deep down into the submersion, into themselves, and going with the pulsating flow inside them.

So, do not feel bad about imitating intuitively. In fact, do loads and loads of it! Just remember how, back in the day, you learned the moves to 'Macarena', 'Nossa – Ai Se Eu Te Pego!' 'YMCA', 'Gangnam Style' – or, why not, the classic 'Agadoo' from 1984.[71] Very simple movements were imitated to an earworm song that everyone loved. And when the DJ threw it in the mix, everyone would join in, doing the very same, super simple moves, but expressing themselves delightfully with every move. There wouldn't be two dancers looking the same. So simple, and so effective. Did you know that many famous artists copied and traced their paintings before painting them? Van Gogh copied *The Good Samaritan* by Eugène Delacroix – and Vincent van Gogh's version is mirrored, likely due to the way he copied it, from a print.[72] While Delacroix's version is held in classical painting style with the colour scheme we know from Renaissance paintings (dark reds, greens, browns, black, etc), van Gogh's rendering of the same motif is held in the Dutch painter's signature style; he expressed himself in sunflower and hay colours, blues, whites and light reds.

Of course, it is very important that we do not stick to the copy-cat level. Imitation of what we like is the act that can get us started, and it works very well for our brain. At some point, however, your brain will want to move on, explore new words and meanings, stretch the boundaries. So why not combine the two ways of learning? Rule-based and the intuitive body-based ways?

Follow along, while making sure to stay clear of mind hooks: don't start dreaming about your success, stay away from judgemental people with your art, and also, don't get obsessed with technique only – because all of those things shift you into a competitive mode of creation.

'You have to be a little bit obsessed'

Say you feel a natural pull toward pencils, paint and the paintbrush. But whenever you venture onto a canvas or a piece of paper, it looks like anything but a Monet. What you produce has similarities to what a child would produce. You feel Dalí-*esque*, but despite your vivid dreams, no clocks gracefully drape themselves over edges of shelves at the stroke of your paintbrush.

Neuroscience professor Vince Walsh and his team study sleep, brain stimulation and creativity. The evidence that they have gathered over the last decades is clear: to be creative and find flow with your art, you have to put in the hours to learn your skill. Otherwise, it won't work. 'You have to be a little bit obsessed.' And 'obsession' is just your brain's ability to make pink elephants spin in your mind, but the other way around – to your advantage. Remember from Chapter 3 that addiction, rumination and obsessions are habit loops in our brain? Now repurpose this ability of our brain to create habit loops, and get obsessed, instead, with your art. But take care: *'Todo lo que necesitas son horas y horas de pista,'* said my other Argentine tango teacher Ricardo, when I once did start to get a little too obsessed with technique alone. *All you need are hours and hours of dancefloor*, meaning, practise *meaningfully*, not blindly with your eyes on the trophy. It's all about being an Interest-Driven Creator again, not an Exam-Driven Learner.

Throughout history, there have been accounts of people who came up with creative insights and artworks that changed how we see the world. What is often not told is that, to make these inventions, these individuals had put in hours and hours, honing their skill. There is a legend about the cubist and surrealist painter, Pablo Picasso (1881–1973). On a sunny day in a Parisian café, he was approached by a fan who asked him for an autograph on a napkin – that was all the person had in that moment. Picasso scribbled his name and drew a little surrealist face next to it. Next, he asked the fan for quite a large sum of money. The fan was outraged, stating that this was just a napkin with some scribbles. Picasso smiled to himself and stuck the napkin in his pocket. To the fan he mumbled that it took him a lifetime to learn to make those 'scribbles' that very way.[73]

During my time working at UCL, there was a special exhibition at the National Gallery, just a few tube stops from Russell Square station, about the famous artist William Turner (1775–1851). A rebel, an early impressionist, who shocked the establishment with unruly seascapes, alluring colours and stormy messages underneath the varnish. In one of the exhibition rooms, several little notebooks were laid out behind thick glass, showing scribbles and little drawings. Next to them, it said that Turner had started every day with an 11a.m. technical Life Drawing class, to train his drawing habit with the first-year students at the Royal Academy. For the rest of the day, he used his art to express and to flow. Just like a ballet dancer goes through the moves at the barre every morning, *plié, tendu, degagé,* the musician practises her scales, and the actor verbalises and does breathing exercises, for a lifetime, each morning anew. These movements become a part of their sense of self. For me, it's the movements of ballet that bring me back to myself, repeated so many times, over years and feelings. They are *me*.

We're nothing but a heap of habits, said the father of psychology, William James. We must practise, obsessively, to become who we want to be. Maybe we want to be someone who draws to find flow. Well then, *practise*! And make sure you *like* it while you do.

These are stories of celebrating process over progress. It is in this way, with hours of intentional expressive practice, that the artist emerges from the brain, and those changes can be traced at neural level too.[74,75] This is all about habit loops again, and about those actions being encoded in our implicit memory systems and become our second nature.

Of course, apart from practice, it is also important to take a break – to have an incubation time during which your brain can make those implicit connections; something that the father of flow research, Csíkszentmihályi, also underscored repeatedly.[76,77] It is also important to sleep well.[78–80] Very slow brain waves during sleep are conducive to being a little more creative.[81] But above all, as Professor Walsh says in his TEDx talk: practise for hours on end.[82]

Use the Imagination to Learn Your Skill

'*Sit up straight!*' is a bad instruction. You'll pull your shoulders back, tilt your hips unnaturally, pull your chin backwards, jamming your neck vertebrae. Your whole body will be in tension and you'll probably hold your breath to make your back look straight. If I say, 'Imagine that I'm pulling you gently upwards by your hair,' your spine will ease upwards, respecting its natural curvature, your shoulder blades will slide down and back intuitively. Like little wings they will majestically fold in on your back. You'll breathe in, and finally reach an upright position that feels right: ca-ching: reward! The reason why this works is that your brain already owns all the information about how it feels when someone pulls you gently up by your hair. You don't need to effortfully assemble all the motor plans to make that movement happen.[83,84]

In recent decades, awareness about the usefulness of using imagery when teaching in physical practices,[85] be they sports or arts, is rising.[86–89] Neuroscience is discovering what artists have probably known forever: when the mind flows along a mental image of a move we are trying to do, we learn better.

In Chapter 3, I shared how I discovered drawing by chance and how copying and tracing helped me start off on this skill. I was a little bit obsessed and I soon realised that I wanted to modify things in the drawings; copying, fun as it was, wasn't enough. I suppose my Interest-Driven-Creator brain had now had its little successes, was feeling 'harmony', and now wanted to increase the self-relevance and meaning of the activity *for me*, through me expressing myself.

I put the paper down on my table and started working on the lines that became dancers, and dancers that became movements on paper, as though by magic. All the while, imagery of how I wanted the dancers to look hovered before my inner eye – my imagination was firing up the motor plans of my brain in advance of all the strokes I made. Pencil, rubber, pencil. More pencil. I kept drawing until midnight, just me, my desk lamp and the white paper that ceased being paper but a portal into a three-dimensional world of dancers, dance classes, movements of joy, sadness, anger, surprise, fear and joy again . . . Can you *draw* emotions? Apparently, you can. I knew that I could *dance* emotions, but drawing them was new for me. I suddenly remembered emotions and memories of myself that I had entirely forgotten. It was as if I was finding the feeling of 'me' again in these drawings. Of a past and very happy *me* that was very much in tune with my*self* and my surroundings.

Storytelling (visualising personal meaning, feelings and the imagination) while practising and expressing with our art is not just intrinsically rewarding for our brains, it is physically rewarding too. Loads of endorphins raining about, making myelin hug neurons, creating a positive physical signal within our bodies, so we keep at it. This storytelling also connects with neural systems deep down that improve movement via automatic processes, like habit loops that we've forged long ago.

Obviously, it's not that easy, and science is still in the process of investigating how this all works. Yet, the evidence so far shows that when you express through language, dance, music etc, *what you feel* and what is personally relevant for you, you tap into neural mechanisms that somehow seem to link the motor commands in surprisingly efficient ways.

A Surprising Ingredient in Skill Learning: Perception-Action Links

Artistic practices, especially the performative ones like music making, dancing and singing, are highly multisensory.[90–93] That means that many senses are involved when we do them. This absorption of all senses that we find in artistic practices is an important pathway to flow. When you can't think of anything else, because all your senses are busy in the present action, your mind frees up space to flow. Besides, this connection between sensing and doing offers loads of opportunities for different systems throughout our brain to jam together with the movement systems of our brain, thanks to what neuroscientists refer to as the perception-action links in the brain.[94–98]

For example, for humans there is a curious link between the systems of our brain that we use to speak and the systems that allow us to express ourselves through movements and muscles other than our mouth and larynx, with our gestures and *body*-language.[99] Modern neuroscientists like Professor Eric Jarvis[99] have collaborated with evolutionary scientists to understand why some species use their body movements to express through song, dance and complex aesthetic displays – while other species do not.[100,101] Surprisingly, today's humans, a handful of other mammals (bats, dolphins, whales, seals, sea lions), and songbirds are among the only creatures that do. Why? These two very different species had a common ancestor about 300 million years ago, one that likely did not sing, make music or dance, nor did it look anything like today's songbirds or humans. Nevertheless, for some reason a neural pathway in the brains of the species that resulted in songbirds and humans duplicated. Specifically, the one that controls complex vocal movements of the larynx. And it turns out that songbirds and humans use precisely that neural pathway now when they express through the whole body, in song, music and dance. This ability to imitate sounds, facial expressions and gestures is also intertwined with those pathways that allow us to sync our movements to beats – and to the movements of other people.[99,102]

Another fascinating perception-action linking example, is the wiring of the brains of singers. In neuroimaging research looking at the brains of professional singers, for example, we can see that a pathway between auditory and motor regions – a pathway known as the 'arcuate fasciculus' – is much stronger in the singers, there are more connections! In relation to trauma in Chapter 4, we saw that the brain changes in a use-dependent way. The good news is that it also does that if what we use it for is, for example, singing.[103,104] Children train these pathways when they sing spontaneously, instead of speaking. People who have or work with children know very well this behaviour of singing along sentences all the time, something that scientists call 'intermediate vocalisations',[105] and children love doing it. They intuitively embrace the liking-wanting principle in their singing-play. Hence, we should just let kids keep at it and they will forge important pathways that may come in handy later in their life, to express themselves freely.

And it seems that *rhythm* is a facilitator of that effect.

Fluency

After very few seconds of listening to the song of contestant number 9 in the second season of the TV talent show *The Voice of Australia*, vocal coach and juror, Seal, hits the buzzer. His chair spins around to face the singer. Clearly impressed, Seal observes eighteen-year-old Harrison Craig's powerful voice knocking every one off their feet. All four jurors end up hitting their buzzers before the end of the song.

'Voices like yours make guys like me want to teach!' exclaims Seal. 'What's your name?' he asks.

Silence.

Then, a shy voice replies, 'Harrison Cccraing.'

'Your name is what, sorry?' asks Seal.

Harrison Craig repeats: 'Harrisssson Craig.' Then he adds, 'My apologies, I have a stutter.'

Sheer bewilderment.

Harrison can sing any line of words without difficulty. But if he tries to say the very same line without linking the words into a song, the stutter kicks in.

It has been known for some decades now that singing makes people with a stutter 'say' sentences without any stutter at all, while the very same sentence spoken without singing riddles the sentence with stops.[106–109] In the German comedy movie *Jailbirds* from 1996, love has struck the dangerous prison inmate Hammer-Gerd. He sets out to turn his life around and to become the artistic manager of his queen of hearts, Maren. She's a girl with a stutter who, when she sings, doesn't stutter at all. What an act!

Yet – it's not an act at all. Something seems to happen when our actions are expressive. We grow out of ourselves, expand, and are able to do things we otherwise couldn't. And this effect is not unique to singing.[110]

Twenty-one-year-old Andrew starred in the 2019 UK talent show, *The Greatest Dancer*. His mother introduced Andrew in a little video message to the audience before his dance, also talking about his Down's Syndrome. Affectionately, she shared her nickname ('the plodder') for Andrew with the audience. People with Down's Syndrome are known to have some movement difficulties and often describe themselves as a bit clumsy. 'But when the music comes on, it's all gone,' she says, just before Andrew's stage show starts.

His freestyle dance to Timberlake's 'Can't Stop the Feeling', literally *moves* his audience and the jurors to tears. That man can dance! No clumsiness anywhere to be seen, just one fluid movement, very expressive and very stunning.

The reason why it works seems to be the incredibly strong coupling between perception and action *via rhythm*.

Rhythm Is It

I was introduced to the science about the power of rhythm to interconnect brain and body by Professor Antoni Rodríguez-Fornells, a Catalan neuroscientist at the University of Barcelona. At one of my first scientific conferences, the Music, Mind and Brain conference in 2011, in Edinburgh,[111] professor Rodríguez-Fornells gave an example of his team's research with stroke survivors.[112] One of the big problems after stroke is movement disability, and rhythm seems to help bring it back!

Rodríguez-Fornells showed us videos of stroke survivors who were given an electronic piano and electronic drum pads to play on. They were taught specific simple rhythmic patterns, and told to repeat these daily. The rehabilitation effects after some weeks with this music-supported therapy for stroke survivors was astounding. Together with the stronger pathways in the brain, the function of the hand that had been affected by the stroke, returned.

Why is music so helpful for recovery of motor skills? It seems it's all down to the rhythm.

Our brain looks for regularities in its surroundings. If we have a regular beat bubbling along in some loudspeakers next to us, our brain's auditory systems will simulate that beat. If the beat suddenly stops, our brain's electrical waves will keep *simulating* the beat for a little while. New-born babies' brains already do this for a few hours after birth – hence this is an ability that we're born with.[113,114] The prediction engine between our ears simulates the next beat and that somehow has a gating effect on our motor systems, calling them to action. And this ability has everything to do with the research by Eric Jarvis and others that I mentioned earlier in this chapter about expressivity. Comparative psychologists have tried to find those couplings in non-human primates – but they simply don't have the long ganglia (nerve cells) linking ears and legs![115–119] It's only us humans, and a handful of other mammals, plus very few species of non-mammals, including songbirds, parrots and hummingbirds, that have the neural pathways that make this coupling possible. All other species' brains are 'blind' to rhythm.

The way a rhythm connects our whole body's movements into one fluid movement is via those perception-action links. Our sensory systems are connected with the motor systems, and those with our wider body, with the big muscles. That's how we can nod along to a beat, stamp our foot, or clap on the beat.[115–119]

The patients in the trials of Professor Rodríguez-Fornells and colleagues did exactly that – what so few other species can do: they synchronised their movements to an external beat, without thinking much about it, thanks to the audio-motor coupling in their brain. And that, slowly, reconnected the neural connections and they could regain some functionality of the limbs.

If you start to think too much about how to move your prefrontal cortex, your reasoning systems get in the way. Linking your movements to the music you love brings you back to an intuitive interaction with the beat,[120] like that of a child.

In the 2010s, Professor Rodríguez-Fornells' research group[121] and others[122,123] expanded the research programmes that show considerable rehabilitation for stroke survivors in terms of their movement abilities.[124] Even just listening to music on a daily basis after a stroke has been shown to improve different markers of recovery, including both cognitive effects like verbal memory, and also mood.[125] So, if in doubt, put on some music, especially when you're creating with your arts. Be your art dance, singing, drawing or knitting. Rhythm helps you with learning all these. You can use a simple metronome to pace yourself into action, or you can let words trick your brain into a pleasant rhythm, and your mind will follow . . .

→

If you read the poem 'From a Railway Carriage' by Robert Louis Stevenson out loud, you'll find the words make your voice match the rhythm of an old steam train. Poets use different tricks to catch our mind with their words,[126] like reduplication[127] (using words like 'chiffchaff'), or parallelistic patterns.[128,129] For example, they may put rhymes at the end of each line (like in Stevenson's poem, where he rhymes 'witches' and 'ditches'). Or choose specific words with a mix of unstressed and stressed syllabi (like '*da DUM da DUM da DUM*') which make each sentence have a specific meter ('*iambic* meter' in this case). Now your voice quickly falls into the rhythm of a steam engine as you read each line. And this rhythm may even help your brain learn it by heart.[130] And now, you, the hobby actor, can put all your expressivity into it, mimicking the train, becoming *it*. Why not recite some poems as you cycle to work through the morning traffic, instead of ruminating about the idiotic car drivers? Everything you focus your mind on grows. What do you want to grow in your mind – annoyance or a beautiful poem? Many research labs have studied the curious effects that poets' parallelistic word choices have on our brain. It just loves it![129,131]

Similarly, children with language delay, stutter,[132] autism,[133] Down's Syndrome,[134] ADHD, Tourette's,[135] and also troubled children, be they neglected or abused – will benefit from rhythm bobbing along next to them so they can hook their predictive brain on to it. Rhythm is *it* – said Sir Simon Rattle in the documentary movie about troubled youths by the same name. Shepherded by the choreographer Royston Maldoom, the kids were taught meaningful movement, and to express what was on their mind, to the beat of the Berliner Philharmonic orchestra. 'This is not a luxury,' Rattle says about rhythm, 'it is a necessity. People need it, like the air they breathe and the water they drink.'

More research shows that people with other neurological movement disorders benefit from music-supported therapy, dancing and singing.[110,136] These include also Parkinson's,[137] and aphasia.[138,139] Perception-action-led learning opportunities remap the brain![140] The temporal arts offer the opportunities to rehearse the neural pathways that otherwise lie dormant or underactive. And it's all thanks to these essentially human *perception–action links*.

Confront the Hurdles to Progress

A roadblock to flow, no matter how good you are at a skill, can be performance anxiety. Research shows: when under stress, be that competitive stress or the stress of our own expectations, we fail.[141] Such anxieties can literally freeze us (remember from Chapter 5 that the fear research by guitar-playing Professor Ledoux shows that fear may send signals to our muscles, to freeze). This makes progress impossible. This is obviously linked to doing your art in public, but many people actually worry about failing, even if they are just creating on their own.[142] We can learn from professional artists, like musicians or singers, dancers, actors how to deal with it – for our hobby practice.

The sports psychologist and acclaimed mentor of high-performance athletes and artists, Dr Don Green, gives four important pieces of advice for soothing that attention away from the fear.[143]

1. **Set boundaries.** In Chapter 5, I recommended you set boundaries for your senses, your work and your people. This is to ensure that your senses are exposed to the right cues, at the right time. With practice, you will be able to create this bubble around you, *as you practise your art*. The rhythmic repetitiveness of the movements that you know so well will come to your aid. Green calls this 'Presence of Focus'. Professional musicians sometimes play themselves firmly into that bubble by practising scales and parts of a piece, just before they go on stage. They won't talk or interact with anyone while inside that bubble. Allowed

inside the bubble are only the sensations of the instrument against their skin, it's coolness or warmth, the strings or the keys, the sensations on the skin when a tone appears, how it sounds, and the movements, always the movements, and the rhythm that gives this all-encompassing fluency.

2. **Pace yourself.** Remember to remain an Interest-Driven Creator, focusing on an intention *that matters to you* in your practice. Don't be an Exam-Driven Learner. Always return to your intention. Why are you doing this? What and why are you expressing? Don't get ahead of yourself, maybe even literally, *pace* yourself. Musicians sometimes use a metronome and dancers have counts for their movements too. If you draw, you could use some external pace maker like music, or drum solos; something that goes with what you're creating. For flow, skill and demand have to be in balance. Green calls this 'Intensity of Focus'; don't over- or underdo it.

3. **Practise practising with distractions.** In Chapter 5, we spoke about how some work places can become one big 'distractor task' in a psychologist's experiment due to all the notifications and interruptions that are part of many work places today. To train our focus, let's use this knowledge about work-place distractions to our advantage. You know what distracts you most: a TV, a radio, people talking, music, people around you, your phone, etc. Practise while these distractions are around. This will train your laser-point focus for other moments. Green calls this 'Duration of Focus'.

4. **Be courageous and take a break from time to time.** Remember incubation times from Chapter 7, and what Professor Vince Walsh has said about creativity and sleep in Chapter 8. You can get alpha-wave activity from a walk in nature, which has restorative effects on our brain. And if you take a break, just thinking of nothing or maybe enjoying the art of others, you've got your default mode network gearing up for housekeeping,

cleaning out the debris that you don't need anymore – as we discussed in Chapter 1. Having such meaningful breaks regularly will help with focus more generally. Green calls this 'Mental Quiet'. I find this the hardest instruction. We've all experienced the difficulty of being 'mentally quiet'. We need to experiment with what does it for us. It may be the practice itself, or, if we have a very sedentary art, like drawing or knitting, we may need to give our body some exercise, like dancing, tai-chi, yoga or similar to get that movement junkie brain of ours calmed down for regular times of 'mental quiet'. Also, honing the awareness that being different is okay, is another way to practise mental quiet, and to confront your performance anxiety.

→

The wonderful thing is that we can find inspiration for how to immerse ourselves into our art . . . from ourselves! Let's look back at the past 300,000 years of *Homo sapiens'* life. There, in the centre of any prehistoric human society, we find *the arts*.

Now follow me, as you meet humanity's oldest tool of self-regulation.

9.   Modern Problems, Ancient Solutions?

'When you're being creative, there is no such thing as making a mistake,' says John Cleese in his *Short and Cheerful Guide to Creativity*.[1] Historians and archaeologists theorise that many artefacts that we today refer to as art were not created with the intention to be art at all. They likely were the result of rituals, acts of worship, *expressions* of desire or celebration. Today we admire and protect these treasures as valuable works of art – we put them on a pedestal, but perhaps what really mattered for those who created them was the *process*, the (self-)expression, not the outcome. Some spiritual practices even went so far as to prescribe burning or otherwise destroying the object that was being created so as not to become attached to it. It seems like there were also James Pennebakers back then, telling us to not show our art to anyone, cherish the process of creating, and plan to throw it away!

We can find our way back to this intuitive inspiration to create without worrying about the aesthetic (or commercial) appeal of what we produce – by focusing back on the expressive opportunities that the arts offer. Seen in this way, artistic practices demonstrate astonishing parallels with spiritual practices like rituals, religious worship and/or yoga meditation. There is an *intention*, *thought* or *wish* in our mind – for instance, worship, admiration, love – which we then *express*. This expression goes via poetry, chanting, dancing, drawing or music making. We already briefly spoke about the usefulness of 'praying' our art regularly in Chapter 7 in relation to Strategy 2, Attention Deployment. There is no limit to what we can express through our art. We may wear an amulet around our neck that is both decorative but also has an expressive meaning, for instance, the hand of Fatima, or the blue eye for protection against the evil eye. And so on. Considering the evolutionary origins of artistic behaviours can help us find inspiration for our own arts practice, and enjoy the unexpected positive effects on our cave-brain.

→

In the late 1930s, in the Republic of Karelia in Russia, about 200km from the Finnish border, there was an archaeological rescue operation.[2] Archaeologists had found a burial site of about 177 individuals that lived around 8000 years BC. Archaeologists are still today combing through the evidence, disentangling knots and riddles, step by step.

Along with the dead bodies in the burial site, the archaeologists found important artefacts, like tools and garments. These give us important insights into how the people lived, all these many years ago, in uninhabitable circumstances from today's point of view. With the cold and imminent danger constantly lurking around them, those ancestors of ours managed to survive and keep a clear mind, and that allowed them to lay the foundations of our modern civilisations.

Several times throughout these pages, I've suggested that the arts are the oldest tool for self-regulation that we humans have.

What fascinated the archaeologist Dr Riitta Rainio and her Finnish–Russian team of colleagues about the neat rows of teeth that had been unearthed,[3] as if on a string, woven across the garments of some of the individuals that had been buried at the Yuzhniy Oleniy Ostrov burial site, was that they showed very strange signs of use-wear. 'Use-wear' is a term that archaeologists use when they do 'traceology' analyses on tools that they find, searching for, well, *traces* on them.[4]

The elk teeth found at Yuzhniy Oleniy Ostrov had traces. But the traces couldn't be explained by general wear. How did these strange pits and jabs on the perimeters of the crowns get onto *all* the teeth, and so regularly? It is rather firmly established today that people in prehistoric societies were dancing quite extensively during ritual practices. The archaeologists, therefore, wondered; might the traces come from scraping, grooving, grinding and retouching *while dancing*?

And that is how Riitta came to dance in a literally very old-fashioned kind of attire, beautifully accessorised with elk teeth. It was a mesmerising performance that had been conjured up in collaboration with the artist Juha Valkeapää and can be admired on YouTube. The traces that Riitta generated on the elk teeth in her rendering of the prehistoric dance confirmed the hypothesis: the traces on the modern elk teeth looked exactly like those 10,000-year-old ones. The only difference was that the traces on the old teeth were much deeper, suggesting that the prehistoric humans had grooved along with those stone-age rattles for much longer than Riitta had.

The soundscape that emerged from Riitta's dancing was surprising for the archaeologists. They had just been looking to check for the traces on the teeth after dancing, but after the performances, Riitta said that the sounds of the stone-age rattles made 'it easier to immerse yourself in the soundscape, eventually letting the sound and rhythm take control of your movements. It is as if the dancer is led in the dance by someone.' So the archaeologists hadn't only got a step closer to what stone-age dances looked like, but also what they *sounded* like. The oneness with the rhythm and feelings of connectedness that came just from dancing suggest that the sound and movement were both part of the creative expression that made the marks on the teeth.

→

The dance-inducing elk teeth from Yuzhniy Oleniy Ostrov are about 10,000 years old, but if we want to identify the birth of creativity, we'll have to go even further back than that. Our species, *Homo sapiens*, is about 300,000 years old in our current form. Unfortunately, we only have relatively systematic historical writings from all over the world from about AD 300–500, and even those are only fragmented and leave us to make inferences about people's activities at the time. Luckily, we can dig even deeper into the past with archaeological excavations to find signs of human creative expression that predate human record-keeping.

Some archaeologists believe that around 35,000 to 45,000 years

ago, some 'cognitive revolution' happened that changed our cognitive systems and enabled a cultural revolution of a sort.[5] The main
reason for this assumption is that the archaeological record explodes
in size after this time in terms of tools and artistic artefacts, for
example, what are possibly the first bone flutes[6] dated around 35,000
BC. But we cannot know for sure whether something happened
then that made our species particularly good at producing art and
tools after that time.[7] It may simply be that we have not yet found
more artefacts, or the samples have been destroyed. Or, we did what
we humans do so well, we learned from each other,[8,9] how to express
through art, and not every generation had to reinvent the wheel (or
paintbrushes).

In the Blombos Cave, in South Africa, there is evidence of the
world's first abstract 'painting'.

This prehistoric 'doodle'[10] from 73,000 years ago shows us our
ancestors used colours to decorate[11,12] and express themselves long
before Kandinsky's painting 'Picture With A Circle' launched the
contemporary abstract art movement in 1911.

Stepping back even further in time, in a cave close to Taforalt,
Morocco, archaeologists found 82,000-year-old sea shells.[13] They
look like little beads. Modern archaeological traceology analyses
again show more than the bare eye can see: the beads are perforated
and have residues of colour on them. Might they have been painted
red? Or were they worn like ornaments on a string, and rubbed
against materials that were coloured, like animal skin or fabric?
This may be one of the oldest proofs that we humans have enjoyed
what archaeologists call 'body ornamentation' and what we today
call jewellery.[11]

With ever more sophisticated technologies, archaeologists are
unearthing still more hidden treasures of civilisations before us.
Apart from shedding light on tools, diet, and the dwellings that our
ancestors lived in all those tens of thousands of years ago, one
important 'class' of objects that archaeologists keep finding throughout the record are artistic artefacts. I put the word 'class' in quotation
marks because I want us to keep an open mind about what consti-
tutes 'art'. The boundaries are fuzzy. Attempts to define what is art

and what isn't, regularly leave artists, academics and everyone else, really, fuming in frustration. Thus, long books have been written about archaeological findings. When is something 'just' a tool, and when is it art, and is there a difference? And what about it when a weapon (= a tool) has artistic engravings; then it's both a tool and art – and where is the boundary to the spiritual then? Do the stick figure drawings on a vase show a war scene, or are they raising arms as part of a dance?[14–16] For sure, prehistoric engagement with what we today call 'art' was different from present-day engagement with the arts, but the archaeological record shows us that for as far back as we can see, humans have always engaged in creative expression.

First Signs of Symbolic Thought

Some of these ancient art objects show us that alongside creative expression, we've used art to express abstract ideas. In Israel, at Skhul Cave on Mount Carmel, just south of the city we today call Haifa, there is one of the oldest-known pieces of evidence of 'symbolic burials' among humans. It's 132,000 years old.[17,18] One of the bodies buried here seems to have some sort of amulet clasped between its crossed arms, a piece of a boar jawbone, similar to another body found in a neighbouring cave, Qafzeh, where an adolescent was buried clasping deer antlers. These findings indicate that our ancestors cared for what happened to their dead, they didn't just dispose of the bodies, but possibly had symbolic rituals to mark their passage.

Symbolic thought is important for our artistic practice today. It is the basis for a neural predisposition that allows us to use writing systems and artistic systems to communicate with ourselves, others and, for some of us, with what we understand as God, or Creation in our religious practice. Symbolic thought is what allows us to attribute and decode meaning from artworks, as well as encode them in our own creations – as we spoke about in Chapter 7.

Many of the artistic artefacts that have been found around the world suggest that they were created within the boundaries of religious or ritual practice, as amulets (beads in different colours against the evil eye, for example), as offerings to gods or other spiritual beings, as ways of worship (zig-zag scrapings, drawings and stencils on walls and pottery, and later on metals), as modes to connect with something bigger than the self (drawing, calligraphy, poems or 'prayers'), reaching trance-like states during these practices (dancing, drumming, fluting, praying, saying mantras, singing). This is strong evidence that we have always been embarking on a pathway to flow in order to access the clarity, communion, focus, awe and inspiration that we unlock through the flow state. It seems that we have always recognised flow as a special and desirable state of being.

Prohibiting the Arts

We don't enjoy, nor do we create, art in a vacuum. We're surrounded by a society and by a culture that we conform to. And, as we saw previously, those prior experiences that we have as we grow up create our experience of how we perceive our world.

In our 'modern' times, the arts have often been forbidden for political or social reasons. The arts are dangerous in some people's eyes, depending on what they express through their deeper layers of meaning. While purely decorative or superficial art is usually okay because it keeps the masses entertained and distracted, art that speaks to our Camp 2 philosophers can be dangerous – maybe because it questions authority, or because it supposedly arouses people and endangers 'social order'. For example, the 1984 musical movie *Footloose*, directed by Herbert Ross, tells the story of an American town in the 1950s, where dancing is forbidden because it 'leads young people to behave in indecent ways'. The film is based loosely on a true story about an American town that upheld dance bans until the 1980s, Elmore City in Oklahoma. One reverend from that town, F.R. Johnson, is quoted as saying,[19] 'No good has ever come from a dance. If you have a dance somebody will crash it and they'll be looking for only two things – women and booze. When boys and girls hold each other, they get sexually aroused.

You can believe what you want, but one thing leads to another.' These sorts of bans are common whenever people panic about cultural shifts happening around them.

Freedom of expression through the arts is enshrined in article 27 of the Universal Declaration of Human Rights. So instead of forbidding expression, I propose that we start using the evidence we have from the sciences to help us humans make informed choices about our behaviours. That's what cumulative culture is about; educating the next generations using the knowledge gathered by previous generations. In this case, we can help the next generations to understand their biology and the consequences that may occur if we let biology take over and we blindly follow the call of mind hooks that lead us towards impulsive risky behaviour, competitiveness and short-term pleasure-seeking. Then we can educate them about what arousal misattribution and affective realism are, as discussed in Chapter 2, and about issues of the social brain that are 'good to know' as we saw in Chapter 4. The Declaration of Human Rights also sets out that this freedom for all comes with the same level of responsibility over our actions – for all. To be able to make *informed* decisions about our behaviour, and to be worthy of the freedom that we are given, we need to educate ourselves and every new human being that is born after us. Knowledge doesn't transmit genetically; it must be taught. We don't 'grow out' of problematic behaviours, unless we're taught to change them, nor are we likely to 'grow into' healthy behaviours, unless we learn them. Our cave-brain will be a pleasure-seeker, sensation-seeker and a competition junkie if we let it – because we have a body that needed to survive in a prehistoric world. Finding a way to live with that – that's what cumulative culture is for.

No Sax Before Marriage

Religious prescriptions and rules are one way that societies have tried to control unruly people enthralled in making and consuming art. Spiritual leaders simply rule out some art forms as 'sinful' or 'haram', end of story. Another way that has been practised by

Western cultures since the Middle Ages to control the masses and their drive to the arts, was by making some art forms 'classical', which heightens them.

Around the sixteenth century, kings at several courts in the Western world started to elevate some arts above others, beginning to refer to them as 'classical' arts. For example, classical music, classical ballet, or classical painting styles. Michael Church explains, in his book, *The Other Classical Musics*, that for music to be 'classical', it should usually have been practised at court and powerful people would have raised it to the level of something special. Like the King of France, Louis XIV, known as 'le Roi Soleil', did for classical ballet. There would have been masters of the art form, a notation system and a canon of practised pieces. One of the reasons for elevating 'classical arts' seems to have been, precisely, to create a frame within which the arts could be consumed 'safely', instead of forbidding them.[20]

If you've ever been to a classical music concert in the West, or seen a classical ballet, you will be aware that there are specific rules about how to behave. Everyone sits very still, enjoys the art in silence with a detached kind of allure. Even coughing is restricted only to the breaks in between pieces! And – no spontaneous applause please, if you can avoid it. It's against the rules. Basically: don't *show* any pleasure. Expressive suppression is the order of the day.

But, clearly, this is not how a child reacts to music. As soon as the groove kicks in, they're up there on their feet, bouncing, and wriggling their hips. Between that intuitive hip-wriggling and the very still hips in a classical concert, firmly rooted in the seat, lies a long process of 'enculturation' – meaning the process by which a culture teaches their young how they're to behave as part of a particular society.[21] Their predictive brains have been exposed to loads of sitting and restraining the body in the face of music – to the point that sometimes we Westerners have lost the ability to dance altogether.[22] Our predictive brain is overwriting a natural impulse to groove along to a rhythm.

In other societies, the proscenium stage, the separation of performer and audience, and the immobile sitting, is a very artificial concept. Many non-Western cultures, to this day, combine it all into one – such as the genuine Flamenco jam sessions that happen in the back rooms, far away from the touristy, Westernised versions of the art form. For these cultures, the idea of systematising, creating a 'canon' and a notation system is perceived as an imposition that inhibits the natural development of the art form. You can feel some of this natural interaction between performer and audience if you go to a pantomime, as here, audience and performer *share* the experience. The audience interacts with the actors, who respond and incorporate improvisation into their act. 'The art of panto', much loved by the late Queen Elizabeth II,[23] is also an amazing segue into the world of theatre for children, says theatre producer Gyles Brandreth.[24]

Our species has a history of prohibiting arts that have the power to tear at our heart strings and make us do silly things. The body is part of our life on earth, but we're taught to suppress, ignore or avoid anything to do with it, distract ourselves from it, as best we can. Webs of social and cultural conventions were put in place to safeguard the young, especially, against the malicious arts that would 'corrupt' their minds, which is why the arts have often been forbidden, looked down on, or forced to be 'classical'.

I believe that thanks to the scientific advances in the past decades that have allowed us to understand our body better, and how it's intertwined with our brain and behaviour, we're more than ready for a new way of understanding and engaging with the arts.

Dancing Queen

In lavatories used by politicians in the government buildings of several European countries, including Whitehall in the UK,[25] the Bundestag in Germany,[26,27] and even in the European Parliament in Brussels,[28] police have in the past reportedly found traces of cocaine on surfaces. Whenever the news about yet another politician with a nose for things other than politics hits the headlines, people are outraged. And rightly so. That outrage, however, is nothing compared to what happened when Finnish Prime Minister, Sanna Marin, chose to blow off some steam in summer 2022.

'Finnish Prime Minister caught *dancing*!', announced more than one news outlet. And social media flowed over with controversy.

Caught dancing? As in, she was doing something forbidden?

The Islamic Republic of Iran and Afghanistan are countries that currently heavily restrict dancing for cultural reasons, especially for girls and women in public. According to historical sources, however, dance bans were abolished in most Western nations at the beginning of the twentieth century and awareness about the potent health effects of recreational dancing is spreading like wildfire. Dance bans only persist during festivities like Easter, for example, in Germany. Prime Minister Sanna Marin was dancing on a summer night, with friends, in Finland. Voices were fast to rectify their initial condemnations. It was not *that* she danced, it was *how* and *where* she danced, the *specific movements* she used, and how she was *dressed*. And then, the archetypical misunderstandings about dancing hit the news outlets: because she was dancing, she had likely also taken drugs and was unfaithful to her husband. Women who dance are 'light'. Otherwise, why else would she dance like *that*?

Like *what* exactly? Prime Minister Sanna Marin has great moves and a nice expressivity. In these videos, you see a powerful woman taking control of the dance floor.

Clever, admirable and responsible Sanna Marin rolled her wise eyes and, of course, swiftly made sure to take a drug test to shut up the critics. Her husband joined the eye-rolling and released a statement that he didn't feel cheated on. And Sanna generously and fully participated in the inquiry that followed. Had she left the country in danger and 'unattended' *while she was dancing*? Obviously not. And she was finally acquitted of any wrong-doing in November 2022. End of story.

There are many misunderstandings about the arts. For some art forms like dancing it's particularly bad. These misunderstandings are often due to puritanical concerns about the body as something 'bad'. Yet, paradoxically, 'getting back into your body' is what we need for a healthy mind, as we have established in the previous chapters. And dancing, like Sanna Marin did, is one of the most natural behaviours of the human species.

There's a term in psychology called the 'aesthetic experience', which refers, basically, to the feeling triggered by a piece of art. For a long time, however, people believed that a profound aesthetic experience was something you could only have for certain 'art', but not for others. This was totally classist. Kant-inspired thinkers drew artificial boundaries to what constituted 'art', and which form was therefore 'good' and 'healthy' and 'pure' – these were, of course, those artificially classified arts called 'classical'. We now have evidence that this is a complete social construct that has *nothing* to do with how our brain processes things from our surroundings. Our brain *does* understand categories; however, whether or not a category like 'classical art' is understood by an individual brain depends on whether it has grown up with that category or not (remember predictive coding from Chapter 6?). There is, however, no division in the brain for processing 'art' and 'non-art', as our brain doesn't have a way to draw a clear boundary between what is art and what isn't. Rather, there is something like a continuum between what is art and what isn't art to our brain. And we're starting to see scientific evidence that suggests that where you put these artificial boundaries is very dependent on who you are.

➡

The takeaway here is that despite there being a long history telling you otherwise, there is no scientific reason to discriminate between different arts – you can safely and successfully embark on a pathway to flow using any kind of expressive art form, from knitting to music to doodling to dancing, in every style you can think of. While you do, remember what John Cleese said at the start of this chapter: while you're being creative, there is no such thing as making a mistake.

10. Getting Started – And off you go, *flow*

One of the great sources of psychological pain in our modern world is feeling disconnected from what makes life meaningful. Through our education and enculturation we learn a lot about how to be professionally successful, but we don't necessarily learn how to make ourselves happy.[1] The road of life is paved with good, but misguided, intentions about what makes life fulfilling.

For sure, this meaning-of-life is unlikely to knock at our door one day all by itself. Instead, we need to create it, step by step exposing our predictive coding brain to the right experiences, as we saw in Chapters 6 and 7. But there is a secret and very important ingredient to make this work: while we create, we must remain life-affirmingly *true to ourselves*.[2–7] Otherwise, our predictive coding brain will create an illusion, an 'image', that is far from who we really are. That can never be the meaning of *my* life. It's not *me*.

Growing Up to Fit In

As we grow up, around the age of twelve to twenty-four months, we start walking on our feet. We don't yet know the conventions of the society we grow up in. We make 'faux pas' – wrong steps – more than once; both literally and metaphorically speaking. With time, we learn to conform to the conventions that surround us – in fact, conforming makes the reward systems in our brain relish in delight.[8–10] That's a learning signal, and we do it again. On our way to conformism, there is a lot of trial and error, but with the rewarding feeling that comes with conforming, we quickly learn the rules of the game.

Around twelve months, we crawl and pull ourselves up to stand on uneasy feet, and about the same time, we look around and start to imitate others and play imitation games with them (peekaboo!).[11,12]

Around twelve to nineteen months, while our feet slowly become able to climb stairs with assistance, we start to imitate other people's actions.[13] Around eighteen months, we run and kick, climb stairs on our own and 'talk on the phone' like Mum. Between two and three years, we start to understand others' minds, something that psychologists refer to as us having a 'theory of mind'.[14] It involves understanding that others have independent minds from ours. We console someone who is sad, share things with others that we think they may like. As we efficiently pedal around on a tricycle around the age of three, our ability to play elaborate 'pretend-plays' and 'role plays' matures.[15,16]

So, in parallel to the process by which our motor skills get better and better, our ability to imitate others' actions and intentions matures. And that's also when 'socialisation' kicks in: one big pretend-play that we make our children play, as we add layers and layers of social coating on to their authentic 'me'. This teaches them when to smile, and when not to, and everything else they need to get along with others in our society. It's a curse and a blessing at the same time.[4,7,17,18]

'Conforming' to some social norms is good for the group and for the individual too – it protects us from our own porcupine spines and those of others, if we all agree a little bit on how we want to behave and treat each other. It's also good for the group because it ensures cohesion and fewer conflicts – it makes the group stronger. Regardless of what your personal beliefs are about conformity, your brain likes it, and rewards you when you do it. It's a low-level basic survival mechanism that gave our group an advantage in the wild.

However, at the same time, this conforming to an image, to a standard that may not naturally be ours, comes with drawbacks. As we get further and further away from ourselves, we simply feel unwell, and as we strive towards the image, the more difficult it becomes to find flow.[19] The arts and creative activities offer a space, where you can finally be yourself, find flow and experience all its beneficial effects. When you find self-relevance in what you do, you flow.

The Eight Principles of Flow

The father of flow research, Mihály Csíkszentmihályi, proposes that being in flow feels a specific way that can be summarised in eight elements.[20–23] When you're in flow, you:

1. are completely concentrated and absorbed in the activity;
2. have clarity about what you are trying to achieve (goals) and you are able to get reliable feedback on whether you are doing it right (you have clear learning signals pinging your reward system);
3. feel a transformation of time (it zips by or slows down);
4. do it for intrinsic rewards;
5. feel effortlessness in what you're doing;
6. are in perfect balance between your skill and the demands of the activity – not too easy or too difficult;
7. experience a fusion of your actions and your awareness and you lose the ruminative thought loops;
8. feel in control and escape the unpredictability of life.

This is a perfect description of what it *feels* like to be in flow. But, for those of us who have tried, we all know, we can't just decide that this is how we want to feel while doing something. Therefore, we will now use the science we've reviewed in this book to 'reverse engineer' the feeling of flow, meaning what *you* need to *do* to flow. We've built the pathway, now let's revisit each milestone on that path.

You know that to be able to focus and concentrate, you must stay clear of mind hooks at certain times in your day (Chapters 1–3), avoid uncertainty, and occasionally set boundaries to your senses, the people around you and your work (Chapters 4–5). That will train your attention to last on any activity. To foster those intrinsic rewards that will make you carry on, you know that the activity you'll be choosing needs to be appealing to the hedonist Camp 1 philosophers, as much as to the meaning-making structures of your brain, where the Camp 2 philosophers reside. For this, remember the liking-wanting principle from Chapter 3: the creative activity that you choose for yourself should be one that you enjoy doing *while* you do it, rather than something that makes you strive toward an ultimate goal that you *want*. You also know that you have the power to create the experience and feelings you need for this, by taking advantage of your predictive coding brain (Chapter 6), and by using specific Emotion Regulation Strategies to cope with your everyday, maybe even using cognitive restructuring, to change those dysfunctional beliefs about yourself that impede you from reaching your full potential (Chapter 7).

You also know that your goal has to be to have *fun* while you copy, imitate, use your imagination and practise your skill over and again in order to generate dopamine-laden learning signals and aha-moments within your brain (Chapter 8) while you learn. This will create habit loops in your brain because myelin will be hugging your neurons thanks to all the repetition, and the skill will pass from explicit memory systems to implicit memory systems, making it feel effortless. This will make your art your second nature, a language that you can use to express yourself. You also know that you should focus on emotional expression, on both the superficial and the deeper meaning of the art that you create or consume, so that the art becomes intrinsically motivating for you, as it connects with your sense of self and activates your default mode network and your body's relaxation response. Your imagination can help with that (also Chapter 8).

This may all sound a little technical at first. Therefore, I've developed a practical navigation aid, of seven behaviours that I believe help us reliably to find flow if we include them in the creative practice that we choose. Most of this book has been about how to prepare our brain and body to be able to find flow. Now, let's look closer at flow itself. If we make sure to collect all seven stars with our practice, we're golden.

Seven Stars on the Pathway to Flow

Throughout human history, star clusters in the sky above us have been used by sailors and wanderers as guides to navigate murky waters and foggy paths. The seven-star cluster called *The Pleiades* is one such ancient navigation guide. It was immortalised on the Nebra Sky Disk, which is the oldest-known concrete depiction of the cosmos from anywhere in the world. It was discovered in Germany in 1999, and is probably almost 4,000 years old. Very likely, the boat that Princess Sisi travelled to Corfu on was being guided by sailors who knew to follow the stars for direction to arrive safely at destination.

The stars have inspired stories as far back as human memory goes. For example, the fairy tale 'Snow White and the Seven Dwarfs' and the story of the 'Seven Nymphs' in Greek mythology (daughters of the titan Atlas and the sea-nymph Pleione), are based on the seven sparkling Pleiades stars' mystical existence in the sky above us.

Why not, once again, use our brain's love for stories? Just as there are seven stars in the Pleiades, there are seven 'active principles' to be aware of for our pathway to flow. We've already touched on all seven in the past chapters; let's now draw them all together.

In Denmark, we have a saying, *'for lidt og for meget'*. It means 'too little and too much'. This expression means we should find and do everything in good measure. As you look out for these seven 'active principles' in your artistic practice, make sure that you don't have too much or too little of each in your life.

Star 1 – Have a Routine

Avoid the fear of fear that comes from uncertainty in life with small routines that also help create the right habit loops – within stable boundaries, your mind will reach new levels of creativity, and flow.

Pink elephants feed on uncertainty. Whether that uncertainty is about good or bad stuff, uncertainty is a killer. And that's because of those binary low-level survival mechanisms of ours that whisper into our awareness (Chapter 1), setting off the pink elephant ballet. Remember Chapter 6; our brain is a prediction engine; if stuff is predictable, it likes it. If it is not, our brain gets edgy and so do we.

We started out, in Chapter 2, by learning about how indulging our Camp 1 philosophers too much is not a good idea. If we randomly chase after any opportunity that presents itself to indulge in the three mind hooks (competition, pleasure-seeking, and risk- and sensation-seeking), this teaches us to have a very unsteady mind. And in Chapter 3 we saw, with the example of Rat Barnaby, how this random ratio reward that we get from the mind-hook behaviours can make us spiral into a behavioural addiction, like the Argentine tango dancer Hamish.

Psychological research has shown that nagging fear – whose source we are often unable to quite name – comes from uncertainty and uncontrollability in life, like learned helplessness that we saw in Chapter 5. When we cannot control what happens to us (random ratio contingencies), when we feel that we don't have agency over our lives, a strange creepy fear starts making pink elephants spin in our minds. Many people caught in the hands of the bean counters in the immigration system, or in any of the other bureaucratic jungles that surround us for that matter, know this feeling very well.

Unwind that

Avoid things that teach you to be a hedonist or to feel helpless because of random ratio contingencies. You can do this by taking advantage of how our predictive brain likes regularities (Chapter 6). It uses them to create our experiences, and our self-esteem. So, instead of being a victim of uncertainty *all the time*, we can help our predictive brain with our artistic practice, to give it *some* certainty, at least, *some of the time*. Regularly give it movements and routines *that it knows*.

'Repetitive movements are washing machines for minds!' says Simon Baker, alias Patrick Jane in *The Mentalist*, as he and his team are observing a golf practice range, and a large group of people hitting balls on repeat. Spiritual practices have prescribed repetitive move- ments for millennia, for the soothing effect that they have on us, like during prayer as we saw in Chapters 7 and 9. Repetition gives our brain a sense of safety. Make an altar, and from time to time, step into a cocoon of bliss (see Chapter 5), where the uncertainty doesn't exist.

And of course: rhythm is *it*. Make sure to have actual rhythm in your life for all the enhancing and soothing effects that it brings (Chapter 8).

Disclaimer: Remember, with all of these stars it is about having each in moderation. Don't rigidly adhere to routines, rules and regulations to the detriment of your overall wellbeing. Sidestep perfectionism with your routine or you will be spinning off on another merry-go-round with your pink elephants, hurting yourself and those you love most. Go with what Professor Walsh said in Chapter 8: we need to be *a little bit obsessed*, but not too much. Plus, we need to leave space for sleep and for breaks, so-called incubation times (Chapter 7).

Star 2 – Practise Skill and Technique

Master technique; not as a goal, but as an end itself – you're learning the vocabulary of your art, like the words of a language, to express yourself, so keep your eyes on the meaning.

We need skill and technique practice, to develop an art into our flow tool. That can feel like a massive hurdle at first. That's your expectations sabotaging you. They can be overcome, by starting *with the first move*.

'It is not important *what* you draw, but *that* you draw.' In Chapter 8, we learned how the brain makes movement, that it needs fun to learn, and that we learn best *through our body*. It's a process that we can help along by starting with *the first move*, by designing our personal *Pathway Prompts*. This will help our brain create those habit loops, so our skill can pass from explicit to implicit memory systems and it becomes our second nature.

Remember to start by copying, imitating, *then* expand. Remember how a child learns? And did I say it already? Remember *to have fun,* like the painter Kasper Købke.

Unwind that

Sometimes, you may experience beginner's luck. You start and you immediately get two pirouettes done. And then, you suddenly freeze and you can't do it anymore and you freak out, you're about to quit. Before you do, let's listen to the science.

There are two main reasons for this:

The first is that you're starting to think about it. That's your conscious prefrontal neural systems at work. Remember that the expert jazz musicians got really bad at improvising with their instruments, as soon as electrical impulses were applied to their prefrontal cortex. Maybe yesterday you went about it more intuitively?

The second reason is motor variability. Our sensorimotor system isn't very accurate. Not all body parts are represented with the same amount of precision in our brain. Our body has about 206 bones, 360 joints and 900 ligaments. That's a lot of degrees of freedom when we move, a lot to coordinate if the movement is new, and not over-rehearsed like walking, driving a car or eating with cutlery. With our body we're controlling a multi-dimensional system, and movement is known to be a complex computational problem. It is unlikely that you will easily and deliberately make the same exact movement over and over again perfectly, at least not without extensive practice.

There are three instructions about how to deal with this beginner's luck and learning the skill of an art:

1. **Get back into your body, and out of your head.** You may have started to use external sensory information instead of internal. Processing external information to update movements as they happen is some milliseconds too slow for movements like dancing, running, skiing, etc. So you need to get back into your body, meaning you should be using internal or more intuitive info because that intention accesses the motor planner directly.

2. **Use your imagination.** Your body is a multi-dimensional system; the only way to 'string it all together' is by linking it via your brain's ability to optimise movement through the imagination – as you let your mind move along an imaginary, visualised, meaningful movement – the real movement improves. We spoke about it in Chapter 8. Sportspeople also call this visualisation or mental training. You can google examples of 'visualisation aid' for any sport. As you

visualise the movement you need to imagine what the movements will feel like *from the inside.*

3. **Practise with intention.** 'Just feel it'! How to implement that instruction? First of all, don't. Because it is unlikely to be useful until you've internalised some vocabulary of your art, and your brain has made habits out of it all and passed it on to your implicit memory systems. So, patience with this one and start with the most basic skills!

Disclaimer: As we're learning, we again need to watch out for mind hooks connected with perfectionism. The competitive drive to improve quickly is lying in wait. Then our pink elephants return, now with whips in their trunks. They use them to lash out at us, to the rhythm of the perfectionism symphony. The adrenal gland drizzles enormous quantities of stress hormone into our blood stream. This is thinning the walls of our blood vessels and putting our heart in danger because the little sinus node on top of our heart is getting completely confused about all these additional beats dictated by the stress hormones. Rather than feeling recharged by your practice, unhealthy practice focused on technique alone will turn your creative escape into another source of stress, so be ready to take a break if you start to feel mind hooks digging into you.

Star 3 – Create a Community

Combat loneliness, prompting neurobiological mechanisms of bonding and health by sharing your practice with others – the human social brain needs others to stay sane and healthy; the arts are a channel for communication and connection, beyond words.

When we feel a sense of community, our anterior pituitary gland is one of the important organs that play the notes of the bonding hormones like prolactin into our blood. This makes us feel we belong.

As we saw in Chapter 4 with Sheila and Joyce, social isolation is an extreme stress situation for our health. Without the social connection, our immune system and metabolism become deregulated, and pink elephants take off in our minds.

Unwind that

Arts communities offer abundant possibilities for socialisation and connection. As we saw in Chapter 4, hugs and touches, synchronicity and the little chemical messenger substances conspire to bond us together in a group. Besides, as oxytocin and other bonding hormones rain down on our neural connections, we feel intrinsically motivated to keep at it. And as we enjoy the joys of a good laugh together, our creative actions together become even more meaningful, as Camps 1 and 2 of our brain forge new pathways. As we saw in Chapter 7, the arts can also offer us a community, where we can ask for help and advice, and where we can practise problem solving.

Disclaimer: the section 'Good to Know' in Chapter 4 reminds us of the porcupine spines. And we saw in Chapter 5 that sometimes, we need to set boundaries and step into a creative cocoon of bliss to give our senses (and brain) a break. We saw earlier in this chapter that the conformism that is so common in human societies, even necessary for our peaceful co-existence, can derail us from our authentic self and make us feel terrible. Reserve time and space in your creative practice for expression that is just for you and that's plenty.

Star 4 – Aim for Connectedness and Aesthetic Feelings

Avoid empty thrills by seeking activities that provoke genuine feelings of awe and self-relevance – the arts move you, and connect you with your sense of self.

Connect Camps 1 and 2 by choosing creative behaviours or arts that connect these two layers of your reward system as they reach, through your senses, within your brain to those deeper meaning-making systems in your brain. Star 4 very much links to the liking-wanting principle from Chapter 3 – do things that make you have aesthetic emotions – these will make you like what you're doing!

Since the start of the noughties researchers of a new discipline, called neuroaesthetics, have been studying how the human brain, psyche and body react to special objects and experiences such as the arts. Paintings, dances, movies . . . let us stand in awe, make us feel small and out of our depth, catch us again, puzzle and confuse us, and force us to re-think . . . and to re-*feel*. 'Aesthetic emotions' are emotions that we may feel both in our everyday life, and as a response to the arts; including awe, being moved, curious, thrilled, and so on. Those are definitely emotions that will make you *like* your art. In Chapter 5 we saw how different spaces can make us feel awe and moved. And in Chapters 6 and 7 we found ideas about how to creatively create how we feel, and *like* what we're creating, by applying different Emotion Regulation Strategies.

Unwind that

The emotional impact of artworks, a dance, a song, a piece of music . . . can be life-changing. They are strong emotions and can have transformative power, maybe even strong enough to change dysfunctional beliefs about ourselves and the world, as we discussed in Chapter 7. In several experiments in live settings like concerts[24,25] and museums,[26,27] participants are asked to spontaneously say what they feel. Engaging with something that can get these feelings into our neurobiological system makes us connect back to our authentic self, melting through the coating like a hot stone through a frozen lake.

Disclaimer: Even the most beautiful and awe-inspiring can bore us after a while and our mind goes off into apathy, or just flips back into ruminating about whatever is bothering us. Chasing after aesthetic emotions, if that's all we do, is deprived of meaning for our brain.

Also, when you connect with yourself, beware of ego inflation; being 'authentically you' can be painful for others. In Chapter 7 we learned about the benefits of building a stronger belief about ourselves, so we can foster more healthy reactions to cues in our surroundings (and have fewer pink elephants in our mind as a result). A creative practice, or sport, can be such a way to (re)build that self-esteem. However, if we fall into the trap of the competitive mind hook that wants us to be better than everyone else, this *inflated* self-belief will now also condition how we react to cues.

For example, we pass through a door and see another person arrive (cue or **A**ntecedent), but *the most important thing in this world – me –* is above this other person of course (**B**elief), so *I* don't smile or hold open the door for that person (our reaction, or **C**onsequence). Likely, next time when the roles are reversed, that other person will do the same to us and with that, we're back to the porcupine prickles in Chapter 4, setting off our pink elephant ballet.

Remember **ABC**. We should foster healthy beliefs about ourselves and the world (**B**s), so our reactions (**C**s) to events and cues (**A**s) are as healthy as possible. This will make our mind and our interactions healthier, and contribute to create *our* pathway to flow.

Star 5 – Use Your Imagination

Use your imagination to trigger new neural connections, so your creative habit can spill into other areas of your life and your thought patterns – the human brain learns best when the learning process is powered by the imagination and woven into a story that guides the process.

Place your hands on your head so your fingers spread out over your head. About half a centimetre under your hands is the 'associative cortex' and that's an important part of the brain for letting creativity and imagination happen. During imagination, the associative cortex connects in plentiful ways with brain structures in deeper levels of our brain, including our memory systems where our recollections of previous sensory impressions are stored. That's why we can imagine *anything*. Dragons doing space travel, our maths teacher as a prima ballerina on pointe shoes, or dancing pink elephants on parade. Our imagination is unlimited and it is based in the brain; it's portable, and we can always rely on it to bring us solace. We also touched on the power of the imagination to optimise movement in Chapter 8, and to aid 'mental training' in Star 2.

Unwind that

Think of all the times you've fallen asleep on the sofa, following a story in a movie, a book or an audiobook that magically eased your mind away from your personal pink elephant craziness. Or think about how easily a child falls asleep when her parent tells her a bedtime story. Humans have sat around the fireplace telling each other stories for millennia, before the invention of the modern skyscrapers of loneliness. Studies show that during the dark winters at the borders of the polar circle, the Icelandic Sagas keep people's minds shielded from the pink elephants of depression, and for children affected by conflict and war in the Gaza Strip, story-telling has been found to ameliorate the symptoms of fear and trauma. When you immerse yourself in your creative practice and let your mind flow, part of what we are doing, in our mind and through our movements, is telling a story. We tell ourselves the stories of our recent experiences, recontextualising our lives (for more on this, flip back to Chapters 6 and 7), and we create entirely new worlds and events that help us process what we know about the world. Our imagination can help us discover new forms of expression within our creative practice as we allow ourselves to experiment with the ideas that drift into our mind. And we use our imagination when we apply Emotion Regulation Strategy 6 and lace our thoughts with gold as we imagine what we fear most as something ridiculous that makes us laugh. Using the imagination is definitely also a behaviour that will make us *like* what we're doing, while we're doing it (see the liking-wanting principle, Chapter 3).

Disclaimer: The castles of our mind have a caveat. You can use them to escape into your imagination, to avoid. Fleeing into the imagination when we avoid, suppress or distract ourselves from negative emotions uses the wrong emotion regulation tools as we saw in Chapters 1 and 7, and will not bring us peace of mind in the long run. In fact, using the imagination to flee is a sure route to rumination. Use the imagination as a guide to learn your skill and expand *your lived experience*.

Star 6 – Practise Movement and Expression

Snap out of stagnation and conformity; express yourself with the movements of your body for health and wellbeing – live as your authentic self within the safe space of the arts and collect intrinsic rewards to generate healthy habit loops.

In Chapters 1 and 8, we learned that our body and brain were made to move, and when we keep them still for too long, uncomfortable pink elephant ballets in our mind are the result.[28] To guard ourselves from that, we need *to move* regularly. Around 150 to 180 minutes of aerobic exercise[29–32] – that means your heart rate should be over 140 beats per minute – per week is the sweet number. If you do a movement art like dancing, you'll probably have these 180 minutes under your belt quite easily. However, if you choose any of the more sedentary arts, you need to factor in enough movement that you can get somewhere outside of your art. Maybe you could briefly go to Chapter 8 and revisit using Pathway Prompts to get started at that.

Unwind that

Movement makes the world go round and keeps your body and mind healthy as we saw in Chapter 1. 'Create how you *feel* by what you *do*' was the mantra of Chapters 6 and 7, and as you use your movements to *express* with your art, this is when Camps 1 and 2 of your brain connect, and become your pathway to flow.

Disclaimer: Focusing on the competitive aspects, pleasure and risk in movement practice (Chapter 2) will bring you nowhere, but into a ruminative hell of pink elephants spinning in your mind.

Star 7 – Cultivate Purpose and Intention

Circumvent fixation on competition by developing goals with meaning and cultivating intrinsic rewards – train the neural pathways that connect basic and complex rewards (Camps 1 and 2) with the arts.

Since Chapter 2, you've heard me speak a lot about us having a *choice* in what behaviours we engage. We have a say in what we expose ourselves to, in terms of healthy cues (for example, by stepping into a cocoon of bliss like in Chapter 5), activities, or unhealthy ones as we saw in Chapters 5 and 6. We can choose to be informed about the consequences of our actions, and choose to do *otherwise*. Thanks to the knowledge that you have gathered throughout this book, you now know what can spin you off-track. Identify the cues of your bad habits and *plan* your actions so you don't keep falling into the same habit traps.

Unwind that

Setting a clear intention for your creative practice can help you protect that time from mind hooks, and prevent your mind from spiralling off into sour rumination. Especially if you also practise your art in ways such as when an artist warms up with loose life drawing sketches like Turner, and Købke, who we met in Chapter 8, that are deliberately imperfect and not meant to be shared – similar to Pennebaker's expressive writing practice, where your writing is entirely focussed on 'what you feel' (Chapter 4). Keeping a clear purpose for your creative practice that intentionally sets it aside from flow time for practice for practice's sake, for reflection and self-expression, will help protect your pathway to flow.

Disclaimer: On the other hand, be careful with setting too rigid an intention. If we chase after an intention, getting obsessed with finding it and expressing it can become exhausting, and it can be our pathway to rumination, as discussed in Chapters 3 and 7. While you can set yourself the goals of learning specific compositions or choreographies to practise and develop your skills (those are extrinsic motivations!), try to escape the purpose dictatorship by sometimes simply creating freely, focussing on what it *feels* like, practising your skills repetitively, or having a break from it as recommended by Professor Walsh in Chapter 8.

Back to Planet Earth

Together, these behaviours become a beautiful ballet, making all our body's systems tune in to the body's relaxation response, boosting our health while doing what we love. When we make sure to collect all seven stars in our creative practice, it's more than the sum of the quantity of its parts. Altogether these experiences make us healthy, in mind and body.

If we notice we're a little low on one of these behaviours, just *knowing* about the seven will help us aim our behaviour at the missing star.

Embracing Beginnings

When you move to a new place, your senses are immersed in everything new. There are new cues everywhere that funnel information to our brain, imprinting it with new impressions — it's an opportunity to create new habit loops in your brain! New cues offer opportunities to take action, and with that, to create new habit loops. You may not have the opportunity to move to a new place, to forge new habit loops. But what you can do is enter into a new world, in the very city you live in . . . into a new artistic practice and community. Here, you'll find plenty of new cues you can use to design Pathway Prompts, for you to attach actions to. The key is to find new cues to immerse yourself into *that you like*, and feel intrinsically motivated by, and then take action. This final chapter is to assist you in finding, starting and practising your art as a creator and practitioner. Plus, remember from the embodiment debate in Chapter 8 that any artistic skill that you practise also expands your experience of that art when you consume it.

→

'You are a scientist?' the taxi driver asked, surprised, studying me in the back mirror.

I was dressed in a sparkling dress, wearing a fair amount of makeup, and my hair was looking quite glamorous. It was a Friday evening and I was on my way to the first milonga of the year 2016 in London.

'Yes,' I answered.

'And you work with the brain,' the taxi driver wanted to know, 'and what it does with art?'

I can't remember how we got to speak about the arts and the brain, but as our conversation unfolded we connected over his Iranian background and my work with Iranian artists and scientists. He told me that he was thinking about taking up calligraphy as a way of getting closer to God, and at the next red light, he pulled out his mobile and showed me examples of wood carvings and calligraphy expressive of adoration and faith. I told him about the evidence that we have that much art in earlier times happened within a ritual context and that they were acts of worship. Some drawings in holy books, etc, many dances we enact today, have ritual origins, and so on. He listened attentively and as we glided across the bridge over the Thames, he reflected on all the materials and space he'd need to get started, but I shared the science with him that the best way to start is to start simple; without the three mind hooks, with the most basic equipment. When we embark on a new artistic process, making things too complicated and buying a bunch of expensive equipment can make it harder for ourselves because it sets expectations too high. The best way to try something new and stick with it long enough to learn the basics is to remove as many obstacles to practising as possible by starting with the basics so that you don't feel overwhelmed or afraid of making mistakes – like John Cleese cautioned at the beginning of this chapter. The taxi driver and I shared a meaningful silence, each of us engrossed in our own thoughts about our arts. Sometimes he'd excitedly emerge from a thought and ask a question about the arts and the brain and then think some more. When the journey was over, he joked, 'See you soon – in the *zone!*'

Getting Started

But what if, unlike our taxi driver, we don't know which art to choose? We don't feel a calling yet, to any one art form? How do we choose a creative activity that will bring us flow?

Well – that depends very much on who you are and what you need, which pink elephants dance about in your mind, what your cues are, what your personality is, your genetics, what surrounds you on a daily basis, what your life experience is, and so on. And it needs to be something that you feel *intrinsically* motivated to practise for hours on end, reaching contented flow, sometimes, by mere repetition of 'your' movements.

Your Art

If you're struggling to decide which art to choose, I've compiled seven steps that can help you identify the art form for you. Know that once you get into the mode of creating, you may start realising that the boundaries between different arts are not as clear-cut as our cultures want to make us believe. And you may choose different arts for different Emotion Regulation Strategies, and so on. It's up to you to mix and match to your heart's content.

Write down some answers to the questions below to identify the arts that may work for you:

1. **Take a trip back to childhood**: What were the activities that you enjoyed most, in school, at home? Are there any stories about you, told by your parents, of activities that you'd engage in for hours on end?

2. **Do a time travel**: What were you doing that day when hours just flew by? Do you remember some good times when time just zipped by and afterwards you felt so happy, free, elated and self-confident?

3. **Inform yourself of the options**: For instance, read about different arts options in books and magazines, or google 'art forms', list them and then give them ratings from one to five stars depending on how much they resonate with you as you read. You may also want to get a feel for the kind of people that you'll find in the community. Which options have the highest ratings for you?

4. **Time yourself**: Browse shops which provide tools for each of the different options: in which shops do you stay longest? Read online resources about the different options: on which pages do you stay longest?

5. **List your strengths and what you love**: List all the things you like doing, your favourite subjects in school, your favourite TV programmes, etc. List them all and *include* those things you always wanted to learn, or

admired others that did them . . . but you never dared to *explore* yourself. Which are they?

6. **Ask your friends**: You might find your soul mate activity in what they do. If they're your friends, chances are they might be doing something that you like too. They might even be able to help you get started.

7. **Try out several hobbies**: Enrol in (and commit to) different short courses of activities that could work for you over a longer period of time. Which one sticks? Which one do you feel excited about, waiting for the next class to come up? At the end of which class are you happy it's over and when are you disappointed that time is up? Start to practise listening to yourself . . .

Now Take Three Steps

We know by now that it's not just about *what* you're doing, but *how* you approach it that matters. I propose a three-step process for developing a practice that's right for you:

1. Know thyself

Know your *intrinsic* motivators.

You may wish to be able to draw like Picasso or dance like John Travolta, but we have to disentangle the dreams we aspire to – which are important in their own way – from what is going to help us find that all-important flow. Which art contains those actions that you'll come to love and do for hours on end? These three suggestions may help you identify that.

Set your intention. Set a clear intention for what you want to feel and express through your practice; don't focus on what you want to produce. Close your eyes and feel into the centre of your chest for a moment. What do you feel? Express *that*. This will allow you to focus on the process and banish outcome-based thoughts. Which art will allow you to best express *that*?

Find your why. Scientific evidence shows that health benefits are obtained specifically when we practise our art for recreational purposes, where we can be our own authentic selves. So get clear on genuine enjoyment versus external obligation. Make sure that you don't just go for the art that you feel you 'should' enjoy, that fits with the image other people have of you. Also identify which Emotion Regulation Strategy you are planning to use your art for. Escapism? Acceptance and reappraisal? Cognitive restructuring? Problem-solving?

Trust your taste. This one is particularly important for you as a consumer of others' art. Practising an art may 'unlock' deeper meanings that are otherwise invisible to the eye. Art is 'right', when it feels right to *you*. And, what feels right to your friends might not feel right to you, and that's okay. The people around you might not see what you see in your art. This is where you'll dig into what you love, what you're drawn to, what allows you to express yourself as you truly are, and what makes you lose track of time. Remember the artificial boundaries that we've set for different art forms: try to ease away and look at the world from the outside – which art appeals to you, regardless of its social 'category' as classical art or not?

For our brain, 'the arts' are just another mode of expression. The artificial divisions between them are culture-made. Undo those wirings in your brain and reinvent yourself.

Your art *may* be belly dancing, even if your religion forbids it . . .

2. *Nothing in Excess*

Create habits that *make* the life you want to live. Work on identifying *your* cues.

Use the previous chapters to educate yourself in spotting which aspects of an activity have flow potential and which have mind-hooking qualities that send your mind into ruminative loops. Even the healthiest behaviour can become a bad habit if we let the mind hooks take over, so learn how to stay clear of the pull, get to know your warning signs.

Prepare yourself to face the mind hook of competitiveness. When you start a new creative practice there must be no performance pressure, no competitiveness. You're doing this activity to find a pathway to flow, not to become a professional artist.

It's more than ever *the journey* that matters – remember *process over progress*. Do you sneak a look at your neighbour in class to *compare* your moves? No. Only look at them *to observe, imitate* their skill or to *improve*. Do you worry about sharing your work and the praise you will or won't get, while you're still creating it? Just don't do it. Give yourself the gift of privacy and keep your new fledgling practice to yourself. Focus on expressing yourself instead and ask yourself *what* you need to learn to express what you want. Nothing else matters. Making this about the process of creating and not about the final product is key. Use your imagination and download it onto the page, the dance, the keyboard – and leave it there.

Prepare yourself to resist the mind hook of risk-taking behaviours. On your pathway to flow, less is more. Start with the basics. When it comes to physical art forms, such as dance or gymnastics, don't attempt advanced movements until you are ready because going too quickly and skipping over the warm-ups and conditioning that you get from practice can result in serious injury. And consider this: community can be an amazing asset in finding peace and calm, but judgement before we're ready can throw us off course. This is a risk too. Remember the porcupine dilemma – accept and reappraise it. Besides, the people closest to us sometimes have a particular image of us and starting something new (that may not neatly fit that image) can sometimes trigger feedback we'd be better off without. Be courageous, dare to be wrong and follow the four steps (in Chapter 8) to combat performance anxiety that freezes your muscles. Whether you keep your hobby to yourself for a while or connect with a new community and exchange your thoughts with people learning alongside you, making this a personal practice is crucial.

Prepare yourself to resist the superficial rewards of pleasure-seeking mind hooks. Start with the most rudimentary of tools. Remember: it's about collecting intrinsic rewards. Don't get caught up with kitting yourself out with all new equipment before you begin. If you want to draw, all you need is a pencil. For knitting, it's one pair of needles and one ball of wool. For dancing, sports clothes and a dance school, a YouTube clip, an app. For flow, simple is plenty. Also keep in mind that you won't know which materials and equipment will be right for you until after you get to know your art better, so save your money for when you're ready to take your skills to the next level.

3. Certainty Brings Insanity

Don't let your art become your new dogma. Don't cling to rules; instead, master uncertainty by celebrating the little successes that are more about how you feel and less about what you've created. Our brain loves to learn in manageable chunks. Experience how satisfying it is when small intermittent goals work out. Pay attention to the little 'Aha! I did it!' feelings. And remember that it takes time to strengthen neural pathways. Patience with yourself is key.

Pray with your art. Make time and routines in your day for your arts practice. Think regular, repetitive movements for your predictive coding brain. Establishing a routine for the arts practice gives your brain enough certainty to deal with the uncertainty outside your practice. The regularity sets free mental energy for your brain to find new creative ways to solve problems. Regular practice is also the safest way to forge the neural pathways that will make your art your 'language', when the skill passes from explicit prefrontal brain systems to your implicit procedural memory systems.

Make an 'altar' for your arts practice. Select a place in your home, office, working space that is reserved for your art. The visual, auditory, olfactory, etc, stimuli of the 'altar' will become what psychologists call 'conditioned stimuli' with time, helping you to slip into the zone more easily. Have you ever smelled something or heard a song that sent you immediately back to a time and place? That's the power of *associative learning*: impressions on our senses attach to memories about the situations and cues that triggered these impressions. The same impressions on the senses (smells, sounds, movements) now become *conditioned stimuli* – and as a result trigger the memories all over again. We want to create many cues that you can use to trigger the memories of your blissful arts practice, forming part of a healthy habit loop and becoming your reliable pathway to flow.

Use the power of the imagination. It is possible to mentally return to your art even when you are unable to physically practise. You can compose a poem, paint a picture, dance a choreography – all in your mind's eye. Adopting the practice of 'mental rehearsal' used by professional dancers, musicians, painters and sculptors has many benefits. For one, you continue to build a reliable pathway to flow by training your neurons to fire along the right pathways and build motor plans. And, two, using your artistic practice as a reliable guide for thoughts, away from everyday stress, you can access peace of mind when *you* want it, even if you can't take out your paintbrushes right in that moment.

Ideally, you'll find an art that can help you meet your psychological needs through the behaviour that you invite to direct your body-orchestra.

The Phoenix Circle

I have a final little trick for you, as you start out with your art. I call it the Phoenix Circle. It has three parts and will help you keep moving and evolving through your practice. Let's take the needle arts as an example.

Copy – Expand – Express

If you were to take up knitting, you might get started because you spotted a scarf pattern that you really liked, so you gather the materials and instructions to get started, gradually knitting away until you successfully recreate the scarf you saw, only to discover, once you're done, that you could, with only a few changes, or a slightly more advanced technique, alter the pattern to enjoy the process more, making it even more *you*. So, inspired, you embark on the next project, taking what you've learned to help create again.

This is the Phoenix Circle of your arts practice never ending: you're never done. It's cyclical on purpose, it keeps rolling and rolling, like a washing machine for minds:

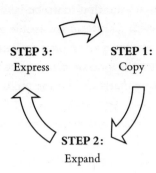

STEP 3:
Express

STEP 1:
Copy

STEP 2:
Expand

Step 1: Copy

Start by copying 'words' and simple 'sentences' of your art. In the case of the needle arts, this is about finding the most basic stitch that you can, and practising it. Over and over again. In the different needle arts, the stitches have names, so find out the name of the stitch that others in these art forms have started with, and then do the same. Do it as often as you need to, until it's automatic. It works best if you have chosen an object to make already. Something simple, something that you have the chance to actually finish, even as a beginner. A shop attendant or a more experienced practitioner can tell you what that might be. A scarf, a flower, a bookmark, etc. Something that doesn't take ages to finish, and that you can make using just ONE type of stitch.

Step 2: Expand

You will need to expand your knowledge of the grammar and culture of this art form. Once you master this one type of stitch, try to find out more about it. What is it used for, what's the history of it (e.g. when did people start using it and what is it used for?). Try varying with different colours. Try to understand more about the technique behind the stitch, how to optimise it.

Step 3: Express

Now you can express yourself with 'this art form'. There will be a moment when you start wanting to go beyond the pure copying, and you get adventurous. Go step-by-step also for that. It can very easily discourage you if you start setting goals which are too ambitious. Remember that the goal here is the practice itself, not the final product. Anything that feels like a struggle: ease off. Simple is better, simple is plenty.

Once you've reached Step 3 for one type of stitch or skill within the needle arts, you can rise from the Phoenix's ashes again, from scratch, with a new type of stitch or skill, pattern, or 'thing' that you create. Some of these skill acquisitions can go in parallel of course, once you start getting the hang of it. And you may already be expressing yourself within one domain, while sitting down, like a humble beginner next to Turner in the National Gallery's beginners' course, to practise your stitches from scratch in another art form.

→

For former US First Lady, Michelle Obama, knitting is a survival strategy in an uncertain world. For her, there is 'something in that tiny and precise motion on repeat, the gentle rhythm of those clicking needles, that moves my brain in a new direction.' It's the same for dancing, sewing, drawing, making music, and so on. Do *that* movement, whichever works for you, on repeat, with the right intention, and with *your* expressivity.

As you do, the systems of your brain and body connect, setting your mind free to fly . . . and off you go, *flow*.

Conclusion: Art Matters

Behaviours influence our biology a little like medical drugs. They take advantage of messengers and receptors that are already in the body just as drugs do. In this way, creative behaviours can also potentially act like medicines, producing good or bad effects inside us.

Different medicines have different active principles that work on different specific symptoms or problems. A patient may be prescribed naratriptan to help with a migraine because the active principle is what clinicians call a 'selective serotonin receptor agonist'. Triptans dock on specific receptors on blood vessels, causing them to *narrow* the blood vessels. This action makes them help people with migraines: the pain dissipates. You wouldn't prescribe triptans to someone with a heart condition, like high blood pressure. These patients rather need 'calcium channel blockers', meaning medicines with an active principle that reduces the blood pressure by *widening* their blood vessels, like amlodipine or diltiazem.

Something similar may go for the arts – they may have 'active principles' too. One study showed that a dance session increased participants' pain threshold[1] and another that chronic pain patients' pain levels decreased with dance lessons,[2] while a longitudinal study showed that people who regularly dance have a lower probability of developing heart disease at all.[3] However, here's the catch: we don't yet really know why, which means that we can't use the arts in the same targeted way that we use medical drugs.

'Active Principles' of the Arts

Science is really only starting to provide the first answers about how different arts may have different 'active principles';[4-7] how some arts may be better for us than others – for our physical and mental health and to find flow. The pioneering research by Professor Daisy

Fancourt shows that 'social prescribing' with creative activities doesn't work regardless. For example, it doesn't work if we use our artistic community to flee and procrastinate real life, commitments and responsibilities – that's unlikely to bring us health and well-being in the long run. In Chapter 7, we saw that learning to apply the six Emotion Regulation Strategies via our creative activity may be our key to success.

Some 'active principles' like the 'Seven Stars' I proposed in Chapter 9, may be shared among all arts, but within different arts there is considerable variation, for example, with regards to how they engage our 'social brain'.

Let's continue to use dancing as an example.

Dancing has an important social principle. However, 'solo dancing' less so (like belly dancing or ballet), whilst some partner dances require the participants to be at arm's length (swing, salsa), others closely embraced (traditional Argentine tango). So, the social touch opportunities are different between these dances, as will be their effects on our brain and body. If what your looping thoughts need to unwind themselves is the social principle, some dance styles will work better for you than others.

However, if you are a trauma victim, and the cues that set your mind spinning are linked to intimacy, then maybe don't go dancing Argentine tango. Choose a solo dance, or choose an art where people won't come close to you until you feel ready for that.

Someone with Parkinson's, in turn, may benefit from Argentine tango, but not as much from the waltz, because of the 'active principles' of these dance styles.[8-10] Among the symptoms of Parkinson's are difficulties with initiating gait and keeping the balance. The characteristics of Argentine tango are many stop-and-go moments, and steps, where one dancer carefully touches the other person's foot with their own foot and steps over it. Translated to the Parkinsonian symptomatology, practising start and stop and having prompts (e.g. touches) to initiate gait are golden, as are the balance exercises of standing briefly on one leg. When dancing Argentine tango, you have all these exercises woven into one fluid movement, aided by a fine rhythm, while you are listening to good music and having a great time.

Waltzing around and around, you'll also have a great time, but waltz turns and turns without the stop-and-go and balance exercises.

What are the symptoms of *your* pink elephants? This is about the dosage and treatment range of the art that you choose. Science is not yet ready with a differential diagnostic for what is 'best'. So it's up to you to find your art.

Can the Arts Be Studies Scientifically?

Yes they can. But this is not common knowledge yet. Let me give you an example from the front line of this science. During a public outreach event in London in 2019, one audience member pointedly asked, 'So, that dance that you are showing on the screen, would the dancer be able to redo exactly the same movements, and if not, is what you are doing science at all?' I sighed to myself – there is always at least one person who asks that sort of question.

The dancers in the auditorium started giggling and winking at me from the audience ranks. Their eyes were like little suns shining into the darkness of that question which is so omnipresent in my area of research – *is what you do science at all?* Of course, for the dancers among the spectators, it was obvious that the dancer in the video that I was showing could easily recreate the same movements; it's called choreography. Even an improvised dance can be recreated by a dancer, and we can study that with scientific methods.[11–16] But this question, posed to me many times before and since, sets the stage for a much bigger problem that we researchers in empirical aesthetics, neuroaesthetics and health science of the arts face daily. By the way this spectator had been asking questions throughout my talk, it was safe to assume that he was a professor of a related science. So, he was a colleague.

I smiled briefly at the dancers and took their warmth with me as I faced the whole audience. To break the frozen silence, I first joked, saying that it's always great fun when I'm speaking to a general audience using a vocabulary full of metaphors and catchphrases to make science accessible for everyone, to be probed by a scientist who is expecting a completely different vocabulary. Most people in the audience, especially the dancers, laughed.

The attitude of that professor is what we scientists studying the arts with scientific methods are up against. They sow doubts about our scientific credibility and the soundness of our research designs, both in peer review and in grant peer review. As a result, we don't get the funding we need for the large research projects that we would need to move this field of study forward. In the disclaimer at the start of this book I pointed out that this area of research is still very much in its infancy – many more experiments are still needed to confirm the exciting results that we're starting to see. I hope that with this book, I've been able to show that the arts *could* be such an important tool for health-bringing activities if supported more: with long-term funding for the research – and with funding for everyone in our society, regardless of their socio-economic background, to be able to engage with and learn the languages of the arts. Yet too many 'seasoned' professors keep blocking access to funding, likely due to their inability to understand what the arts are and how you can conduct science in the field of creative activities. Their stance is understandable, given that we're all a product of the societies we grow up in. And in most Western societies 'the arts' are conceptualised by many as a strangely special class of fringe activities that no one really understands and that are, if anything, only for 'professionals'. In Chapter 9, I gave an overview of why I think this is a problem and what we could do about it – to move the arts back to where they belong, in the centre of every society.

The type of research that we need to change these conceptions and move the field forward is a heavily interdisciplinary enterprise – which means that it isn't enough to have scientists on board. We need professional artists and humanities scholars on board just as much for such research to be successful. This ensures that the research is meaningful and that taxpayers' money – which is what pays us mostly – is spent wisely.

I took a breath and turned to the doubtful professor in the audience and explained what he surely knew with regard to his own research, but what he had doubts about when it came to ours:

when we do research, we must follow the process accurately, and operationalise our 'research questions'.

For example, our research question could be, 'When do we get health effects from dancing?' We scientists 'operationalise' by observing a phenomenon, for example, dancing, music-making, football, or any other hobby, and then isolating all the different 'variables' that make this behaviour *it*. Then we keep studying the phenomenon in the lab until we understand, after much repetition, which of the variables, and their interactions, contribute most decisively to the output, for example, health effects. In the example of our dance research question, we could look at cortisol in blood (= outcome variable) on competition days and on non-competition days (the study variable is = competition). You may recognise this from Chapter 2 where, indeed, one research group looked at the variable 'competitiveness' in the context of dancing.

Another research question could be about the variable 'music': 'When do we have best health outcomes – when we dance with music or without music?'[17] Or, 'Are there specific dance styles or dance movements that are particularly helpful for a specific outcome or health effect?'[18–20]

Whatever our research question, when we have done our experiment once, we next try to replicate the effects we find: in different situations, in the lab, maybe in different labs, and by different researchers, to be sure that the effect is genuine. This is called 'replication'. As a next step, we may take the phenomenon back into the real world again, and continue to study it systematically there. That's what scientists refer to as 'ecologically valid' research – it is not easy to do, but it is possible.[21,22]

The arts and other creative behaviours are what scientists call 'multivariate' phenomena. This means that there are many 'variables' at play here. In this book, we've studied some of those variables that may be part of a creative activity like dancing, music-making, cooking or film-making. The seven stars are variables that are part of most creative activities. But there are many more variables, like, 'Does the activity involve competitiveness, pleasure and risk?' – Chapter 2 – and so on. These variables may be aspects of our hobby to a larger or lesser extent, and contribute to the 'output' – how we feel and how healthy we are. As scientists, we study these systematically, step by step, and this may take decades, and much trust from funders and colleagues. I hope that the years to come will see many, many more research projects flourish that do exactly that: investigate the arts *systematically* with the best-practice scientific methods, and conducting peer-reviewed, pre-registered studies and randomised controlled trials.

For now, while this research will – hopefully – convince the doubters and gain force in the next decades, we can all, human beings as we are and equipped with this knowledge about 'variables', take these variables and experiment with them in our everyday lives. Be a scientist in the service of your own health and wellbeing and, by mixing and matching to your heart's content, find out which variables in *your* creative practice contribute most decisively to the outcome – of *you* feeling good.

I wish you a safe and exciting journey on *your* pathway to flow. Looking forward to meeting you in the zone!

Acknowledgements

I did not travel the pathway that led to this book on my own and I am profoundly grateful to a number of wonderful people who have been my loyal and trusted companions on this journey.

My most heartfelt thank you goes to my parents to whom I also dedicate this book. Thank you for making creative activities such an integral part of our life. And thank *you*, my sister-friend Nadine for always being there. I'd also like to express special thanks to some friends because of their inspiration and support in making this book happen. Isa with her art of bijouterie, and her husband (woho!) Pep Lluís with his art of sailing. And, of course, Miguel, who we met on page 188 who spins life's strange turns into comedy. And thank you, Dong-Seon Chang – dear colleague and friend, for your invaluable guidance. I hope, one day, we will go Swing Dancing. To my *compi* Lluís of many years, thank you, for all our wonderfully geeky science discussions over coffee and *ensaïmada* – thank you, also, for unlocking the art of miniature figure painting to me.

My passion for the art of chocolate, clothing, shopping and Japanese art has certainly taken off since I met my trusted friend and mentor, Professor Shelley Channon. My interest in the art of maths has since been spurred by her husband, Professor David Hand, who is a professor of maths, loves the art of magic, and in his free time finds flow by writing books that take a wonderful glance at maths, like *Amy's Luck*. I thank you both very much. And I am grateful to you, Professor Toni Gomila for all your support and for sharing your passion for singing in a choir each Christmas.

A book like this one is not the product of a single person. I have benefited from the teachings, wise guidance and creative inspiration of the best in their field – I couldn't have done this without you: Kate Evans, my absolutely brilliant agent with her miraculous ability to understand how my mind works and to ask the right questions to spin knowledge in the best possible way. Huge thanks to the magical, kind and immensely supportive PFD London team: to Rebecca Wearmouth and Lucy Barry and to everyone from the international rights team – you rock! And a special thanks to Tessa David and Tim Binding who were the first, years ago, to see promise in the idea that became this book. I also wish to express my joy and enormous gratitude to the teams at the publishing houses who will be the first to publish this book: exceptionally creative, kind and supportive Marianne Tatepo (loved our chats about the arts of cooking and guitar playing!) and her incredibly thoughtful and inspirational team from Square Peg, Vintage, including Emily Martin (fellow dancing queen!), Rhiannon Roy (who finds flow climbing the mountains of her home away from home, Eryri), Fiona Brown (Christmas, New Year's & Freya's Iceland – a most memorable time!) and many more. And my cordial thanks to you, Daniel Örtel and to the magnificently efficient team from ULLSTEIN Buchverlage. Thank you all for your trust in this project and for your patience when my scientist mind needed to double check each sentence for the nth time. And thanks to the two exceptional German translators of *The Pathway to Flow*, Anna Flückiger and Sebastian Vogel. I read your translation into German of *Immune* by Philipp Dettmer, loved it, and I was thrilled to hear you were onboard for *PTF* (thanks also, for making this happen, Daniel!). I would also like to thank the wonderful teams from the publishing houses Garzanti SRL (Italy), Alfabet Uitgevers (the Netherlands), and Huazhang (China) (China Machine Press) who are also soon to publish this book in their respective languages – and who trusted *The Pathway To Flow* from the proposal stage!

In a way, the most important people to thank here are the many scientists whose work I've consulted to be able to write this book. The book has over 800 references and there are many more that I couldn't include due to space considerations. Thank you all, for the amazing research that you do. The seed for this book was planted in my mind at the Warburg Institute London, years ago. I am particularly grateful for the discussions with Professors Guido Giglioni and Manos Tsakiris. Together, we wrote a piece about the intricate ways that the arts can make our mind take flight and increase our health and wellbeing – 'Let Your Soul Dangle: How mind-wandering spurs creativity', published by AEON in 2017, and beautifully edited by Sally Davies. Thank you all.

My scientific research on dance is currently funded by the Max Planck Society and I am very grateful to the directors at the Max Planck Institute for Empirical Aesthetics, Frankfurt/Main, Professors Fredrik Ullén, Melanie Wald-Fuhrmann and, previously, Winfried Menninghaus. Dance remains a niche subject even within empirical aesthetics – thank you for giving dance a chance. And thank you all my dear colleagues at the MPIEA and all the wonderful international research teams I have the honour to work with! A special thanks goes also to dance neuroscientist Professor Emily S. Cross for her kind support throughout the years from various parts of the world, boosting research on dance, despite all adversity. And thank you, Professor Joseph T. Devlin from UCL and Applied Consumer Neuroscience Labs, for our inspirational conversations on neuromarketing, the arts and the brain, for your kind and supportive advice always and for the fair share of banter through the years – *and* for being my 'critical friend', proofreading this book! I'm also massively grateful to you, Professor Vince Walsh from UCL. You have been one of my most constructive critics through my London years, making me stretch and reach in new directions. Thank you so very much. Thank you also for taking me to visit the Arsenal stadium in Highbury, and for sharing insights about the amazing sensation of being part of a football crowd during a game.

More people have inspired me with their wisdom and mantras and you may have read them in this book. Especially Mansur Nazarli who loves the imagery of the pink elephants and who gave me the wonderful idea to refer to the three mind hooks as three Greek Gods (competitiveness – goddess of the competition, *Nike*; pleasure-seeking – god of pleasure and wine – *Dionysius*; risk-taking – goddess of fortune, *Tyche*). The three gods didn't make it into the final version of the book, but thinking along those lines for years was incredibly helpful, especially for getting Chapter 2 right. Thank you, M.! And Lucciana Perreira, who repeats in yoga class, 'I cannot get into your head and do it for you. There's only you in there, who can take the decision to *change that movement*.' Lili Ribeiro, whose mantra in yoga class is, 'Stop looking into the mirror to see what it *looks* like, start feeling what it *feels* like, and progress will come.' Thank you, Christian Mayer from the *Sueddeutsche Zeitung* who mentioned the movie *The Social Dilemma* in conversation, which I happily referred to in Chapter 2; Michael Davelis, who showed me the archaeological article about the newly discovered elk teeth that we spoke about in Chapter 8; Matthias Blattmann from Gutmann Events who wrote the wonderful book *You're Now Leaving Your Comfort Zone* – thanks for your and your team's invaluable support in sharing our dance research so widely within the dance communities through the years.

And, of course, thank you for your support, and all the laughs – to everyone from la Pandilla del Pastel Danés, and to you, Tango Science Gang! And thanks to *you,* you many wonderful Argentine tango dancers who have beautified the nights for me, by dancing – you know who you are. I do practise yoga, and it is – besides writing, dancing and drawing – *hot yoga* that helps me with my chronic pain. I thank the hot yoga teachers at several studios including Palma, London, Kiel, Stockholm, Vienna, Hamburg and Berlin. And thank you Martje Schubert for your wisdom in composing Vinyassa and Hatha flow sequences that empower people.

Very importantly: I wrote this book almost exclusively in cafés all over Europe – yes, I enjoy the art of coffee too. I particularly thank the wonderful staff from Ca'n Joan de s'Aigo in Palma for letting me write for hours on end at the table in the corner next to the grandfather clock, bringing me that special *café con leche* with a hint of chocolate. The lovely staff at Café Wacker in Frankfurt/ Main sweetened the early mornings, as did the coffees and cakes of Café Guldægget and Lagkagehuset – somewhere in Denmark. And finally, thank you all, dear family, friends and colleagues, for your understanding and patience when I couldn't meet up for coffees, excursions, parties, chats, dinners, etc because I needed to go and write this book. Thank you, for still being there.

And thank *you*, for reading.

References

Introduction: The New Science of Why we Can't Stop Thinking

1 Csíkszentmihályi, M. *Flow* (Harper Perrenial, 1990).
2 Massimini, F. *et al* in *Optimal experience: Psychological studies of flow in consciousness*. 60–81 (Cambridge University Press, 1988).
3 Thissen, B. A. K. *et al.* 'The pleasures of reading fiction explained by flow, presence, identification, suspense, and cognitive involvement'. *Psychology of Aesthetics, Creativity, and the Arts* **15**, 710–24 (2021).
4 Thissen, B. A. K. *et al.* 'Measuring Optimal Reading Experiences: The Reading Flow Short Scale'. *Front Psychol* **9**, 2542 (2018).
5 de Manzano, O. *et al.* 'The psychophysiology of flow during piano playing'. *Emotion* **10**, 301–11 (2010).
6 Biasutti, M. & Philippe, R. A. 'Editorial: I got flow! The flow state in music and artistic sport contexts'. *Front Psychol* **14**, 1138638 (2023).
7 Bernardi, N. F. *et al.* 'Dancing to "groovy" music enhances the experience of flow'. *Ann N Y Acad Sci* (2018).

1. Mind-full-*ness*

1 Damasio, A. R. *Descartes' error: emotion, reason, and the human brain* (Nature Publishing Group, 1994).
2 Critchley, H. D. 'Neural mechanisims of autonomic, affective and cognitive integration'. *The Journal of comparative neurology* **493**, 154–66 (2005).
3 Critchley, H. D. 'Psychophysiology of neural, cognitive and affective integration: fMRI and autonomic indicants'. *Int J Psychophysiol* **73**, 88–94 (2009).

4 Critchley, H. D. *et al.* 'Interaction between cognition,emotion, and the autonomic nervous system'. *Handbook of Clinical Neurology* **117**, 59–77 (2013).

5 Damasio, A. & Carvalho, G. B. 'The nature of feelings: evolutionary and neurobiological origins'. *Nat Rev Neurosci* **14**, 143–52 (2013).

6 Damasio, A. R. *et al.* 'Subcortical and cortical brain activity during the feeling of self-generated emotions'. *Nat Neurosci* **3**, 1049–56 (2000).

7 Niedenthal, P. M. 'Embodying Emotion'. *Science* **316**, 1002–5 (2007).

8 Nisbett, R. E. & Wilson, T. D. 'Telling more than we can know: Verbal reports on mental processes'. *Psychological Review* **84**, 231–59 (1977).

9 Carver, C. S. & Harmon-Jones, E. 'Anger is an approach-related affect: evidence and implications'. *Psychol Bull* **135**, 183–204 (2009).

10 Bechara, A. 'The role of emotion in decision-making: evidence from neurological patients with orbitofrontal damage'. *Brain Cogn* **55**, 30–40 (2004).

11 Birbaumer, N. & Flor, H. in *Comprehensive Clinical Psychology* (eds Alan S. Bellack & Michel Hersen) 115–72 (Pergamon, 1998).

12 Dantzer, R. in *Encyclopedia of Behavioral Neuroscience* (eds George F. Koob, Michel Le Moal, & Richard F. Thompson) 126–31 (Academic Press, 2010).

13 Pévet, P. 'Melatonin'. *Dialogues Clin Neurosci* **4**, 57–72 (2002).

14 Hardeland, R. *et al.* 'Melatonin'. *Int J Biochem Cell Biol* **38**, 313–16 (2006).

15 Sequeira, H. *et al.* 'Electrical autonomic correlates of emotion'. *Int J Psychophysiol* **71**, 50–56 (2009).

16 Bechara, A. & Naqvi, N. 'Listening to your heart: interoceptive awareness as a gateway to feeling'. *Nat Neurosci* **7**, 102–3 (2004).

17 Jackman, S. L. & Regehr, W. G. 'The Mechanisms and Functions of Synaptic Facilitation'. *Neuron* **94**, 447–64 (2017).

18 Sheffler, Z. M. *et al.* in *StatPearls* (StatPearls Publishing Copyright © 2023).

19 Suszkiw, J. B. in *Cell Physiology Source Book* (Fourth Edition) (ed. Nicholas Sperelakis) 563–78 (Academic Press, 2012).

20 Tähkämö, L. *et al.* 'Systematic review of light exposure impact on human circadian rhythm'. *Chronobiol Int* **36**, 151–70 (2019).

21 Basta, M. *et al.* 'Chronic insomnia and stress system'. *Sleep Med Clin* **2**, 279–91 (2007).

22 Scher, A. *et al*. 'Sleep quality, cortisol levels, and behavioral regulation in toddlers'. *Dev Psychobiol* **52**, 44–53 (2010).

23 Eşer, I. *et al*. 'The effect of different body positions on blood pressure'. *Journal of Clinical Nursing* **16**, 137–40 (2007).

24 Barone Gibbs, B. *et al*. 'Effect of alternating standing and sitting on blood pressure and pulse wave velocity during a simulated workday in adults with overweight/obesity'. *J Hypertens* **35**, 2411–18 (2017).

25 Zeigler, Z. S. *et al*. 'Effects of Standing and Light-Intensity Activity on Ambulatory Blood Pressure'. *Med Sci Sports Exerc* **48**, 175–81 (2016).

26 Sundquist, K. *et al*. 'The long-term effect of physical activity on incidence of coronary heart disease: a 12-year follow-up study'. *Prev Med* **41**, 219–25 (2005).

27 Siebers, M. *et al*. 'Do Endocannabinoids Cause the Runner's High? Evidence and Open Questions'. *Neuroscientist* **29**, 352–69 (2023).

28 Sotolongo, J. 'Chasing that elusive "runner's high"? Seattle-area experts talk about their experiences'. *The Seattle Times* (9 February 2022).

29 Carlson, N. R. *Physiology of Behavior*. 8th edn (Pearson, 2004).

30 Craig, A. D. 'Interoception: the sense of the physiological condition of the body'. *Curr Opin Neurobiol* **13**, 500–05 (2003).

31 Craig, A. D. 'How do you feel – now? The anterior insula and human awareness'. *Nature Reviews Neuroscience* **10**, 59–70 (2009).

32 Raichle, M. E. *et al*. 'A default mode of brain function'. *Proceedings of the National Academy of Sciences of the United States of America* **98**, 676–82 (2001).

33 Raichle, M. E. & Snyder, A. Z. 'A default mode of brain function: A brief history of an evolving idea'. *Neuroimage* **37** (2007).

34 Vessel E. A., *et al*. 'The brain on art: intense aesthetic experience activates the default mode network'. *Front Hum Neurosci* **6**, 66 (2012).

35 Vessel E. A., *et al*. 'Art reaches within: aesthetic experience, the self and the default mode network'. *Front Neurosci* **7**, 258 (2013).

36 Vessel E. A., *et al*. 'The default-mode network represents aesthetic appeal that generalizes across visual domains'. *Proc Natl Acad Sci* **116**(38), 19155–64 (2019).

37 Du, F. *et al*. 'Tightly coupled brain activity and cerebral ATP metabolic rate'. *Proceedings of the National Academy of Sciences* (2008).

38 Wegner, D. M. 'Setting free the bears: escape from thought suppression'. *The American psychologist* **66**, 671–80 (2011).

39 Wegner, D. M. *et al.* 'Paradoxical effects of thought suppression'. *Journal of Personality and Social Psychology* **53**, 5–13 (1987).

40 Wenzlaff, R. M. & Wegner, D. M. 'Thought suppression'. *Annu Rev Psychol* **51**, 59–91 (2000).

41 Wegner, D. M. & Schneider, D. J. 'The White Bear Story'. *Psychological Inquiry* **14**, 326–29 (2003).

42 Dostoevsky, F. *Winter Notes on Summer Impressions* (1863).

43 *A Dynamic Theory of Personality* (ed. Lewin, K.) 300–14 (McGraw-Hill, 1938).

44 McKinney, F. 'Studies in the retention of interrupted learning activities'. *Journal of Comparative Psychology* **19**, 265–96 (1935).

45 Moot, S. A., 3rd *et al.* 'Fear of failure and the Zeigarnik effect'. *Psychol Rep* **63**, 459–64 (1988).

46 Hirsch, C. R. & Mathews, A. 'A cognitive model of pathological worry'. *Behav Res Ther* **50**, 636–46 (2012).

47 Watkins, E. R. 'Constructive and unconstructive repetitive thought'. *Psychol Bull* **134**, 163–206 (2008).

48 Syrek, C. J. *et al.* 'Zeigarnik's sleepless nights: How unfinished tasks at the end of the week impair employee sleep on the weekend through rumination'. *Journal of Occupational Health Psychology* **22**, 225–38 (2017).

49 Syrek, C. J. & Antoni, C. H. 'Unfinished tasks foster rumination and impair sleeping – particularly if leaders have high performance expectations'. *J Occup Health Psychol* **19**, 490–9 (2014).

2. Mind Hooks

1 Syrek, C. J. & Antoni, C. H. 'Unfinished tasks foster rumination and impair sleeping – particularly if leaders have high performance expectations'. *J Occup Health Psychol* **19**, 490–9 (2014).

2 Bechara, A. 'The role of emotion in decision-making: evidence from neurological patients with orbitofrontal damage'. *Brain Cogn* **55**, 30–40 (2004).

3 Bechara, A. *et al*. 'Emotion, decision making and the orbitofrontal cortex'. *Cereb Cortex* **10**, 295–307 (2000).

4 Bechara, A. & Naqvi, N. 'Listening to your heart: interoceptive awareness as a gateway to feeling'. *Nat Neurosci* **7**, 102–3 (2004).

5 Damasio, A. & Carvalho, G. B. 'The nature of feelings: evolutionary and neurobiological origins'. *Nat Rev Neurosci* **14**, 143–52 (2013).

6 Damasio, A. R. 'Investigating the biology of consciousness'. *Philosophical Transactions of the Royal Society of London Series B-Biological Sciences* **353**, 1879–82 (1998).

7 Berridge, K. C. & Kringelbach, M. L. 'Building a neuroscience of pleasure and well-being'. *Psychology of well-being* **1**, 1–3 (2011).

8 Kringelbach, M. L. & Berridge, K. C. 'Towards a functional neuroanatomy of pleasure and happiness'. *Trends Cogn Sci* **13**, 479–87 (2009).

9 Kringelbach, M. L. & Berridge, K. C. 'The Neuroscience of Happiness and Pleasure'. *Soc Res* (New York) **77**, 659–78 (2010).

10 Kamali, A. *et al*. 'Revealing the ventral amygdalofugal pathway of the human limbic system using high spatial resolution diffusion tensor tractography'. *Brain Structure and Function* (Springer, 2015).

11 Kamali, A. *et al*. 'Mapping the trajectory of the stria terminalis of the human limbic system using high spatial resolution diffusion tensor tractography'. *Neuroscience letters* **608**, 45–50 (2015).

12 Dong, H. W. *et al*. 'Topography of projections from amygdala to bed nuclei of the stria terminalis'. *Brain Research Reviews* **38**, 192–246 (2001).

13 Bechara, A. 'Decision making, impulse control and loss of willpower to resist drugs: a neurocognitive perspective'. *Nat Neurosci* **8**, 1458–63 (2005).

14 Rolls, E. T. 'Limbic systems for emotion and for memory, but no single limbic system'. *Cortex: A journal devoted to the study of the nervous system and behavior* **62**, 119–57 (2015).

15 Craig, A. D. *et al*. 'Thermosensory activation of insular cortex'. *Nat Neurosci* **3**, 184–90 (2000).

16 Mateos-Aparicio, P. & Rodríguez-Moreno, A. 'The Impact of Studying Brain Plasticity'. *Frontiers in Cellular Neuroscience* **13** (2019).

17 Craig, A. D. 'How do you feel – now? The anterior insula and human awareness'. *Nature Reviews Neuroscience* **10**, 59–70 (2009).

18 Critchley, H. D. 'Neural mechanisms of autonomic, affective, and cognitive integration'. *The Journal of Comparative Neurology* **493**, 154–66 (2005).

19 Critchley, H. D. *et al.* 'Interaction between cognition, emotion, and the autonomic nervous system'. *Handb Clin Neurol* **117**, 59–77 (2013).

20 Carver, C. S. & Harmon-Jones, E. 'Anger is an approach-related affect: evidence and implications'. *Psychol Bull* **135**, 183–204 (2009).

21 Frijda, N. H. 'Emotion, cognitive structure, and action tendency'. *Cognition and Emotion* **1**, 115–43 (1987).

22 Hietanen, J. K. *et al.* 'Seeing direct and averted gaze activates the approach-avoidance motivational brain systems'. *Neuropsychologia* **46**, 2423–30 (2008).

23 Whalen, P. J. *et al.* 'A functional MRI study of human amygdala responses to facial expressions of fear versus anger'. *Emotion* **1**, 70–83 (2001).

24 Craig, A. D. 'Interoception: the sense of the physiological condition of the body'. *Curr Opin Neurobiol* **13**, 500–5 (2003).

25 Critchley, H. D. 'Psychophysiology of neural, cognitive and affective integration: fMRI and autonomic indicants'. *Int J Psychophysiol* **73**, 88–94 (2009).

26 Seth, A. K. 'Interoceptive inference, emotion, and the embodied self'. *Trends Cogn Sci* **17**, 565–73 (2013).

27 Newson, M. *et al.* 'Devoted fans release more cortisol when watching live soccer matches'. *Stress and Health* **36**, 220–7 (2020).

28 Slimani, M. *et al.* 'Steroid hormones and psychological responses to soccer matches: Insights from a systematic review and meta-analysis'. *PLoS One* **12**, e0186100 (2017).

29 Segerstrom, S. C. & Miller, G. E. 'Psychological Stress and the Human Immune System: A Meta-Analytic Study of 30 Years of Inquiry'. *Psychological bulletin* **130**, 601–30 (2004).

30 Nes, L. S. & Segerstrom, S. C. in *Encyclopedia of Applied Psychology* (ed. Charles D. Spielberger) 191–5 (Elsevier, 2004).

31 Forsdike, K. *et al.* 'Major sports events and domestic violence: A systematic review'. *Health Soc Care Community* **30**, e3670–85 (2022).

32 Card, D. & Dahl, G. B. 'Family violence and football: the effect of unexpected emotional cues on violent behavior'. *Q J Econ* **126**, 103–43 (2011).

33 Piquero, A. R. *et al.* 'Do (sex) crimes increase during the United States Formula 1 Grand Prix?' *Journal of Experimental Criminology* **17**, 87–108 (2021).

34 Curci, A. *et al.* 'Negative emotional experiences arouse rumination and affect working memory capacity'. *Emotion* **13**, 867–80 (2013).

35 Moulds, M. L. *et al.* 'The impact of rumination on memory for self-referent material'. *Memory* **15**, 814–21 (2007).

36 Kuo, J. R. *et al.* 'Trait Rumination Is Associated with Enhanced Recollection of Negative Words'. *Cognit Ther Res* **36**, 722–30 (2012).

37 Christensen, J. F. & Chang, D. S. *Dancing is the Best Medicine [Tanzen ist die Beste Medizin, 2018]: The Science of How Moving To a Beat Is Good for Body, Brain, and Soul* (Rowohlt, 2021).

38 Rohleder, N. *et al.* 'Stress on the Dance Floor: The Cortisol Stress Response to Social-Evaluative Threat in Competitive Ballroom Dancers'. *Personality and Social Psychology Bulletin* **33**, 69–84 (2007).

39 Quested, E. *et al.* 'Basic psychological need satisfaction, stress-related appraisals, and dancers' cortisol and anxiety responses'. *Journal of Sport & Exercise Psychology* (2011).

40 Vrinceanu, T. *et al.* 'Dance your stress away: comparing the effect of dance/movement training to aerobic exercise training on the cortisol awakening response in healthy older adults'. *Stress* **22**, 687–95 (2019).

41 Skinner, B. F. 'A case history in scientific method'. *American Psychologist* **11**, 221–33 (1956).

42 Christensen, J. F. *et al.* 'Choice Hygiene for "Consumer Neuroscientists"? Ethical Considerations and Proposals for Future Endeavours'. *Frontiers in Neuroscience* **15** (2022).

43 Small, D. M. 'Individual differences in the neurophysiology of reward and the obesity epidemic'. *Int J Obes (Lond)* **33** Suppl **2**, S44–8 (2009).

44 Chentsova-Dutton, Y. & Hanley, K. 'The effects of anhedonia and depression on hedonic responses'. *Psychiatry Research* **179**, 176–80 (2010).

45 Singh, M. 'Mood, food, and obesity'. *Front Psychol* **5**, 925 (2014).

46 Mason, T. B. *et al.* 'Emotional disorder symptoms, anhedonia, and negative urgency as predictors of hedonic hunger in adolescents'. *Eating behaviors* **36**, 101343 (2020).

47 Bellis, M. A. *et al.* 'Ibiza uncovered: changes in substance use and sexual behaviour amongst young people visiting an international night-life resort'. *Int J Drug Policy* **11**, 235–44 (2000).

48 Bellis, M. A. *et al.* 'The role of an international nightlife resort in the proliferation of recreational drugs'. *Addiction* **98**, 1713–21 (2003).

49 Bellis, M. A. *et al.* 'Relative contributions of holiday location and nationality to changes in recreational drug taking behaviour: a natural experiment in the Balearic Islands'. *Eur Addict Res* **15**, 78–86 (2009).

50 Bellis, M. A. *et al.* 'Sexual behaviour of young people in international tourist resorts'. *Sex Transm Infect* **80**, 43–7 (2004).

51 Vivancos, R. *et al.* 'Foreign travel, casual sex, and sexually transmitted infections: systematic review and meta-analysis'. *Int J Infect Dis* **14**, e842–51 (2010).

52 Fernandes, D. M. *et al.* 'The spread of steppe and Iranian-related ancestry in the islands of the western Mediterranean'. *Nat Ecol Evol* **4**, 334–45 (2020).

53 Alcover, J. A. 'The First Mallorcans: Prehistoric Colonization in the Western Mediterranean'. *Journal of World Prehistory* **21**, 19–84 (2008).

54 He, Q. *et al.* 'Brain anatomy alterations associated with Social Networking Site (SNS) addiction'. *Sci Rep* **7**, 45064 (2017).

55 Ergün, N. *et al.* 'Social Media Addiction and Poor Mental Health: Examining the Mediating Roles of Internet Addiction and Phubbing'. *Psychol Rep*, 332941231166609 (2023).

56 Limone, P. *et al.* 'The epidemiology and effects of video game addiction: A systematic review and meta-analysis'. *Acta psychologica* **241**, 104047 (2023).

57 Lemmens, J. S. *et al.* 'The effects of pathological gaming on aggressive behavior'. *J Youth Adolesc* **40**, 38–47 (2011).

58 Leknes, S. & Tracey, I. 'A common neurobiology for pain and pleasure'. *Nat Rev Neurosci* **9**, 314–20 (2008).

59 Pattamadilok, C. *et al.* 'Automaticity of phonological and semantic processing during visual word recognition'. *Neuroimage* **149**, 244–55 (2017).

60 Johnston, W. M. & Davey, G. C. 'The psychological impact of negative TV news bulletins: the catastrophizing of personal worries'. *Br
J Psychol* **88** (Pt 1), 85–91 (1997).

61 Pfefferbaum, B. *et al.* 'Associations between News Media Coverage of
the 11 September Attacks and Depression in Employees of New York
City Area Businesses'. *Behavioral Sciences* (Basel, Switzerland) **11** (2021).

62 Pfefferbaum, B. *et al.* 'Disaster media coverage and psychological
outcomes: descriptive findings in the extant research'. *Curr Psychiatry
Rep* **16**, 464 (2014).

63 Szabo, A. & Hopkinson, K. L. 'Negative psychological effects of
watching the news in the television: relaxation or another intervention may be needed to buffer them!' *Int J Behav Med* **14**, 57–62 (2007).

64 Dutton, D. G. & Aron, A. P. 'Some evidence for heightened sexual
attraction under conditions of high anxiety'. *J Pers Soc Psychol* **30**,
510–17 (1974).

65 Jiang, X. *et al.* 'Effects of sensation seeking on habituation to novelty: An EEG study'. *Neuropsychologia* **129**, 133–40 (2019).

66 Dubois-Deruy, E. *et al.* 'Oxidative Stress in Cardiovascular Diseases'.
Antioxidants (Basel) **9** (2020).

67 D'Oria, R. *et al.* 'The Role of Oxidative Stress in Cardiac Disease:
From Physiological Response to Injury Factor'. *Oxid Med Cell
Longev* **2020**, 5732956 (2020).

68 Segura-Sampedro, J. J. *et al.* 'Balconing: An alcohol-induced craze
that injures tourists. Characterization of the phenomenon'. *Injury*
48, 1371–75 (2017).

3. Pink Elephant Ballet

1 Smith, J. M. & Alloy, L. B. 'A roadmap to rumination: a review of
the definition, assessment, and conceptualization of this multifaceted construct'. *Clinical Psychology Review* **29**, 116–28 (2009).

2 Hirsch, C. R. & Mathews, A. 'A cognitive model of pathological
worry'. *Behav Res Ther* **50**, 636–46 (2012).

3 Watkins, E. R. 'Constructive and unconstructive repetitive thought'.
Psychol Bull **134**, 163–206 (2008).

4 Kifer, Y. *et al.* 'The good life of the powerful: the experience of power and authenticity enhances subjective well-being'. *Psychol Sci* **24**, 280–8 (2013).

5 Kelley, A. E. & Berridge, K. C. 'The neuroscience of natural rewards: relevance to addictive drugs'. *The Journal of Neuroscience: the official journal of the Society for Neuroscience* **22**, 3306–11 (2002).

6 Shah, M. & Vella, A. 'Effects of GLP-1 on appetite and weight'. *Rev Endocr Metab Disord* **15**, 181–7 (2014).

7 Caron, A. *et al.* 'Leptin and brain-adipose crosstalks'. *Nat Rev Neurosci* **19**, 153–65 (2018).

8 Fruhwürth, S. *et al.* 'Novel Insights into How Overnutrition Disrupts the Hypothalamic Actions of Leptin'. *Front Endocrinol (Lausanne)* **9**, 89 (2018).

9 Berthoud, H. R. 'Interactions between the "cognitive" and "metabolic" brain in the control of food intake'. *Physiology & Behavior* **91**, 486–98 (2007).

10 Avena, N. *Hedonic Eating: How the pleasure of food affects our brains and behavior* (Oxford University Press, 2015).

11 Astrup, A. *et al.* 'The role of low-fat diets and fat substitutes in body weight management: what have we learned from clinical studies?' *Journal of the American Dietetic Association* **97**, S82–7 (1997).

12 Flood-Obbagy, J. E. & Rolls, B. J. 'The effect of fruit in different forms on energy intake and satiety at a meal'. *Appetite* **52**, 416–22 (2009).

13 Wojcicki, J. M. & Heyman, M. B. 'Reducing childhood obesity by eliminating 100% fruit juice'. *American Journal of Public Health* **102**, 1630–3 (2012).

14 Horton, T. J. *et al.* 'Fat and carbohydrate overfeeding in humans: different effects on energy storage'. *The American Journal of Clinical Nutrition* **62**, 19–29 (1995).

15 McDevitt, R. M. *et al.* 'Macronutrient disposal during controlled overfeeding with glucose, fructose, sucrose, or fat in lean and obese women'. *Am J Clin Nutr* **72**, 369–77 (2000).

16 Moss, M. 'The Extraordinary Science of Addictive Junk Food'. *New York Times* (20 February 2013).

17 Avena, N. M. *et al.* 'Evidence for sugar addiction: behavioral and neurochemical effects of intermittent, excessive sugar intake'. *Neurosci Biobehav Rev* **32**, 20–39 (2008).

18 Moss, M. *New York Times* (20 Feburary 2013).

19 Halford, J. C. & Harrold, J. A. 'Satiety-enhancing products for appetite control: science and regulation of functional foods for weight management'. *Proc Nutr Soc* **71**, 350–62 (2012).

20 Van Kleef, E. *et al.* 'Successful Development of Satiety Enhancing Food Products: Towards a Multidisciplinary Agenda of Research Challenges'. *Critical Reviews in Food Science and Nutrition* **52**, 611–28 (2012).

21 Van Kleef, E. *et al.* 'Successful Development of Satiety Enhancing Food Products: Towards a Multidisciplinary Agenda of Research Challenges'. *Crit Rev Food Sci Nutr* **52**, 611–28 (2012).

22 Gearhardt, A. N. *et al.* 'Can food be addictive? Public health and policy implications'. *Addiction* **106**, 1208–12 (2011).

23 Bechara, A. 'Decision making, impulse control and loss of willpower to resist drugs: a neurocognitive perspective'. *Nat Neurosci* **8**, 1458–63 (2005).

24 Kanoski, S. E. & Boutelle, K. N. 'Food cue reactivity: Neurobiological and behavioral underpinnings'. *Rev Endocr Metab Disord* **23**, 683–96 (2022).

25 Goldstein, R. Z. & Volkow, N. D. 'Dysfunction of the prefrontal cortex in addiction: neuroimaging findings and clinical implications'. *Nat Rev Neurosci* **12**, 652–69 (2011).

26 Noël, X. *et al.* 'The neurocognitive mechanisms of decision-making, impulse control and loss of willpower to resist drugs'. *Psychiatry* **3**, 30–41 (2006).

27 Bechara, A. 'Decision making, impulse control and loss of willpower to resist drugs: a neurocognitive perspective'. *Nat Neurosci* **8**, 1458–63 (2005).

28 Gupta, A. *et al.* 'Brain-gut-microbiome interactions in obesity and food addiction'. *Nat Rev Gastroenterol Hepatol* **17**, 655–72 (2020).

29 Goldstein, R. Z. & Volkow, N. D. 'Dysfunction of the prefrontal cortex in addiction: neuroimaging findings and clinical implications'. *Nature Reviews Neuroscience* **12**, 652–69 (2011).

30 Noël, X. *et al.* 'The neurocognitive mechanisms of decision-making, impulse control, and loss of willpower to resist drugs'. *Psychiatry (Edgmont)* **3**, 30–41 (2006).

31 Kalivas, P. W. & Volkow, N. D. 'The neural basis of addiction: a pathology of motivation and choice'. *The American journal of psychiatry* **162**, 1403–13 (2005).

32 Olsen, C. M. 'Natural Rewards, Neuroplasticity, and Non-Drug Addictions'. *Neuropharmacology* **61**, 1109–22 (2011).

33 Grant, J. E. *et al.* 'Introduction to Behavioral Addictions'. *The American Journal of Drug and Alcohol Abuse* **36**, 233–41 (2010).

34 Ryan, T. *et al.* 'The uses and abuses of Facebook: A review of Facebook addiction'. *Journal of behavioral addictions* **3**, 133–48 (2014).

35 Andreassen, C. S. & Pallesen, S. 'Social network site addiction – an overview'. *Current pharmaceutical design* **20**, 4053–61 (2014).

36 Kuss, D. J. & Griffiths, M. D. 'Online social networking and addiction – a review of the psychological literature'. *Int J Environ Res Public Health* **8**, 3528–52 (2011).

37 Boecker, H. *et al.* 'The Runner's High: Opioidergic Mechanisms in the Human Brain'. *Cerebral Cortex* **18**, 2523–31 (2008).

38 Berczik, K. *et al.* 'Exercise addiction: symptoms, diagnosis, epidemiology, and etiology'. *Substance use & misuse* **47**, 403–17 (2012).

39 Weinstein, A. & Weinstein, Y. 'Exercise addiction – diagnosis, biopsychological mechanisms and treatment issues'. *Current pharmaceutical design* **20**, 4062–69 (2014).

40 Freimuth, M. *et al.* 'Clarifying exercise addiction: differential diagnosis, co-occurring disorders, and phases of addiction'. *International Journal of Environmental Research and Public Health* **8**, 4069–81 (2011).

41 Kuss, D. J. *et al.* 'Internet addiction: a systematic review of epidemiological research for the last decade'. *Current pharmaceutical design* **20**, 4026–52 (2014).

42 Hickman, B. *et al.* 'Dance for Chronic Pain Conditions: A Systematic Review'. *Pain Med* **23**, 2022–41 (2022).

43 Tarr, B. *et al.* 'Synchrony and exertion during dance independently raise pain threshold and encourage social bonding'. *Biology Letters* **11** (2015).

44 Targhetta, R. *et al.* 'Argentine tango: Another behavioral addiction?' *Journal of behavioral addictions* **2**, 179–86 (2013).

45 Christensen, J. F. 'Pleasure junkies all around – why it matters and why "the arts" might be the answer'. *Proceedings of the Royal Society B-Biological Sciences* (2017).

46 Paulus, M. P. & Stewart, J. L. 'Interoception and Drug Addiction'. *Neuropharmacology* **76** (2014).

47 Alavi, S. S. *et al.* 'Behavioral Addiction versus Substance Addiction: Correspondence of Psychiatric and Psychological Views'. *International Journal of Preventive Medicine* **3**, 290–4 (2012).

48 Naqvi, N. H. *et al.* 'Damage to the insula disrupts addiction to cigarette smoking'. *Science* **315**, 531–4 (2007).

49 Duhigg, C. *The Power of Habit: Why We Do What We Do in Life and Business* (Penguin Random House, 2014).

50 Karsh, N. & Eitam, B. 'I control therefore I do: judgments of agency influence action selection'. *Cognition* **138**, 122–31 (2015).

51 Karsh, N. *et al.* 'Bootstrapping agency: How control-relevant information affects motivation'. *Journal of experimental psychology. General* **145**, 1333–50 (2016).

52 Haggard, P. 'Sense of agency in the human brain'. *Nat Rev Neurosci* **18**, 196–207 (2017).

53 Marshall, T. C. *et al.* 'The Big Five, self-esteem, and narcissism as predictors of the topics people write about in Facebook status updates'. *Personality and Individual Differences* **85**, 35–40 (2015).

54 Nadkarni, A. & Hofmann, S. G. 'Why Do People Use Facebook?' *Personality and Individual Differences* **52**, 243–9 (2012).

55 Evraire, L. E. & Dozois, D. J. 'An integrative model of excessive reassurance seeking and negative feedback seeking in the development and maintenance of depression'. *Clinical psychology review* **31**, 1291–1303 (2011).

56 Starr, L. R. & Davila, J. 'Excessive reassurance seeking, depression, and interpersonal rejection: a meta-analytic review'. *Journal of Abnormal Psychology* **117**, 762–75 (2008).

57 Orosz, G. *et al.* 'Elevated romantic love and jealousy if relationship status is declared on Facebook'. *Front Psychol* **6**, 214 (2015).

58 Muscanell, N. L. *et al.* 'Don't it make my brown eyes green? An analysis of Facebook use and romantic jealousy'. *Cyberpsychology, behavior and social networking* **16**, 237–42 (2013).

59 Elphinston, R. A. & Noller, P. 'Time to face it! Facebook intrusion and the implications for romantic jealousy and relationship satisfaction'. *Cyberpsychology, Behavior and Social Networking* **14**, 631–5 (2011).

60 Muise, A. *et al.* 'More information than you ever wanted: does Facebook bring out the green-eyed monster of jealousy?' *Cyberpsychology & behavior : the impact of the Internet, multimedia and virtual reality on behavior and society* **12**, 441–44 (2009).

61 Lup, K. *et al.* 'Instagram #instasad?: exploring associations among instagram use, depressive symptoms, negative social comparison, and strangers followed'. *Cyberpsychology, Behavior and Social Networking* **18**, 247–52 (2015).

62 Nesi, J. & Prinstein, M. J. 'Using Social Media for Social Comparison and Feedback-Seeking: Gender and Popularity Moderate Associations with Depressive Symptoms'. *Journal of Abnormal Child Psychology* **43**, 1427–38 (2015).

63 Hagerty, C. 'Silicon Valley parents banning tech for their kids'. *BBC NEWS* (5 June 2019).

64 Fleming, A. 'Screen time v play time: what tech leaders won't let their own kids do'. *The Guardian* (23 May 2015)

65 Bowles, N. 'Silicon Valley Nannies Are Phone Police for Kids'. *New York Times* (26 October 2018).

66 Huang, Z. 'ByteDance's New TikTok for Kids in China Limits Access to 40 Minutes a Day'. *Time* (20 September 2021).

67 Crone, E. A. & Konijn, E. A. 'Media use and brain development during adolescence'. *Nature Communications* **9**, 588 (2018).

68 Koob, G. F. & Volkow, N. D. 'Neurobiology of addiction: a neurocircuitry analysis'. *Lancet Psychiatry* **3**, 760–73 (2016).

69 Carmi, L. *et al.* 'A prospective clinical cohort-based study of the prevalence of OCD, obsessive compulsive and related disorders, and tics in families of patients with OCD'. *BMC Psychiatry* **22**, 190 (2022).

70 Benzina, N. *et al.* 'Cognitive Dysfunction in Obsessive-Compulsive Disorder'. *Curr Psychiatry Rep* **18**, 80 (2016).

71 Figee, M. *et al.* 'Dysfunctional reward circuitry in obsessive-compulsive disorder'. *Biological psychiatry* **69**, 867–74 (2011).

72 Alves-Pinto, A. *et al*. 'Altered reward-related effective connectivity in obsessive-compulsive disorder: an fMRI study'. *J Psychiatry Neurosci* **44**, 395–406 (2019).

73 Lagemann, T. *et al*. 'Early orbitofrontal hyperactivation in obsessive-compulsive disorder'. *Psychiatry research* **202**, 257–63 (2012).

74 Xie, C. *et al*. 'Imbalanced functional link between reward circuits and the cognitive control system in patients with obsessive-compulsive disorder'. *Brain Imaging Behav* **11**, 1099–1109 (2017).

75 Moriarity, D. P. *et al*. 'Reward Responsiveness and Ruminative Styles Interact to Predict Inflammation and Mood Symptomatology'. *Behav Ther* **51**, 829–42 (2020).

76 Sansone, R. A. & Sansone, L. A. 'Rumination: relationships with physical health'. *Innov Clin Neurosci* **9**, 29–34 (2012).

77 Smith, J. M. & Alloy, L. B. 'A roadmap to rumination: A review of the definition, assessment, and conceptualization of this multifaceted construct'. *Clinical Psychology Review* **29**, 116–28 (2009).

78 Lyubomirsky, S. *et al*. 'Thinking about rumination: the scholarly contributions and intellectual legacy of Susan Nolen-Hoeksema'. *Annu Rev Clin Psychol* **11**, 1–22 (2015).

79 Clark, D. A. *et al*. 'The Meta-Cognitive Beliefs Questionnaire: Development of a measure of obsessional beliefs'. *Behav Res Ther* **41**, 655–69 (2003).

80 Monroe, S. M. 'Modern approaches to conceptualizing and measuring human life stress'. *Annu Rev Clin Psychol* **4**, 33–52 (2008).

81 Nolen-Hoeksema, S. *et al*. 'Rethinking Rumination'. *Perspect Psychol Sci* **3**, 400–24 (2008).

82 Nolen-Hoeksema, S. & Morrow, J. 'A prospective study of depression and posttraumatic stress symptoms after a natural disaster: the 1989 Loma Prieta Earthquake'. *J Pers Soc Psychol* **61**, 115–21 (1991).

83 Segal, Z. V. & Ingram, R. E. 'Mood priming and construct activation in tests of cognitive vulnerability to unipolar depression'. *Clinical psychology review* **14**, 663–95 (1994).

84 Aldao, A. *et al*. 'Emotion-regulation strategies across psychopathology: A meta-analytic review'. *Clinical psychology review* **30**, 217–37 (2010).

85 Purdon, C. *et al.* 'Thought suppression and its effects on thought frequency, appraisal and mood state in individuals with obsessive-compulsive disorder'. *Behav Res Ther* **43**, 93–108 (2005).

86 Watkins, E. R. 'Depressive Rumination and Co-Morbidity: Evidence for Brooding as a Transdiagnostic Process'. *J Ration Emot Cogn Behav Ther* **27**, 160–75 (2009).

87 Raines, A. M. *et al.* 'Associations between rumination and obsessive-compulsive symptom dimensions'. *Personality and Individual Differences* **113**, 63–7 (2017).

88 Watkins, E. *et al.* 'Comparisons between rumination and worry in a non-clinical population'. *Behav Res Ther* **43**, 1577–85 (2005).

89 Ehring, T. 'Thinking too much: rumination and psychopathology'. *World Psychiatry* **20**, 441–2 (2021).

90 Szabo, Y. Z. *et al.* 'Understanding associations between rumination and inflammation: A scoping review'. *Neurosci Biobehav Rev* **135**, 104523 (2022).

91 Thomsen, D. K. *et al.* 'Negative thoughts and health: associations among rumination, immunity, and health care utilization in a young and elderly sample'. *Psychosomatic medicine* **66**, 363–71 (2004).

92 Burtscher, J. *et al.* 'The interplay of hypoxic and mental stress: Implications for anxiety and depressive disorders'. *Neuroscience & Biobehavioral Reviews* **138**, 104718 (2022).

93 Chiappelli, F. *et al.* in *Stress: Immunology and Inflammation* (ed. George Fink) 39–45 (Academic Press, 2024).

94 Hori, H. & Hakamata, Y. in *Stress: Immunology and Inflammation* (ed. George Fink) 65–75 (Academic Press, 2024).

95 Marshall, G. D. & Morris, M. C. in *Stress: Immunology and Inflammation* (ed. George Fink) 1–8 (Academic Press, 2024).

96 Yin, W. *et al.* in *Stress: Immunology and Inflammation* (ed. George Fink) 53–63 (Academic Press, 2024).

97 Tavris, C. & Aronson, E. *Mistakes Were Made (But Not by Me): Why We Justify Foolish Beliefs, Bad Decisions, and Hurtful Acts* (Mariner Books, 2008).

98 Harmon-Jones, E. & Mills, J. (eds) *Cognitive Dissonance: Progress on a pivotal theory in social psychology* (American Psychological Association, 1999).

99 Nisbett, R. E. & Wilson, T. D. 'Telling more than we can know: Verbal reports on mental processes'. *Psychological Review* **84**, 231–59 (1977).

100 Johansson, P. *et al.* 'Failure to detect mismatches between intention and outcome in a simple decision task'. *Science* **310**, 116–19 (2005).

101 Westen, D. *et al.* 'Neural bases of motivated reasoning: an fMRI study of emotional constraints on partisan political judgment in the 2004 U.S. Presidential election'. *J Cogn Neurosci* **18**, 1947–58 (2006).

102 Knutson, K. M. *et al.* 'Politics on the brain: an FMRI investigation'. *Soc Neurosci* **1**, 25–40 (2006).

103 Kringelbach, M. L. & Berridge, K. C. 'Towards a functional neuro-anatomy of pleasure and happiness'. *Trends Cogn Sci* 13, 479–87 (2009).

104 Pelowski, M. & Akiba, F. 'A model of art perception, evaluation and emotion in transformative aesthetic experience'. *New Ideas in Psychology* **29**, 80–97 (2011).

105 Pelowski, M. *et al.* 'Move me, astonish me . . . delight my eyes and brain: The Vienna Integrated Model of top-down and bottom-up processes in Art Perception (VIMAP) and corresponding affective, evaluative, and neurophysiological correlates'. *Phys Life Rev* **21**, 80–125 (2017).

106 Pelowski, M. 'Tears and transformation: feeling like crying as an indicator of insightful or "aesthetic" experience with art'. *Front Psychol* **6**, 1006 (2015).

4. The Porcupine Dilemma

1 Mar, R. A. & Oatley, K. 'The Function of Fiction is the Abstraction and Simulation of Social Experience'. *Perspect Psychol Sci* **3**, 173–92 (2008).

2 Oatley, K. 'Fiction: Simulation of Social Worlds'. *Trends Cogn Sci* **20**, 618–28 (2016).

3 Schopenhauer, A. & Janaway, C. *Parerga and Paralipomena* (Cambridge University Press, 1851/2015).

4 Lefevre, A. & Sirigu, A. in *Decision Neuroscience* (eds Jean-Claude Dreher & Léon Tremblay) 387–96 (Academic Press, 2017).

5 Noonan, M. *et al.* 'Organization of the Social Brain in Macaques and Humans'. *Decision Neuroscience* Vol. 15 (eds J.-C. Dreher & L. Tremblay) 189–98 (Elsevier, 2016).

6 Dominy, N. J. in *Encyclopedia of Neuroscience* (ed Larry R. Squire) 39–42 (Academic Press, 2009).

7 Crucianelli, L. *et al.* 'Modeling affective touch pleasantness across skin types at the individual level reveals a reliable and stable basic function'. *Journal of Neurophysiology* **128**, 1435–52 (2022).

8 Harlow, H. F. *et al.* 'Total social isolation in monkeys'. *Proceedings of the National Academy of Sciences of the United States of America* **54**, 90–7 (1965).

9 McGlone, F. & Spence, C. 'The cutaneous senses: Touch, temperature, pain/itch, and pleasure'. *Neuroscience & Biobehavioral Reviews* **34**, 145–7 (2010).

10 McGlone, F. *et al.* 'Discriminative and Affective Touch: Sensing and Feeling'. *Neuron* **82**, 737–55 (2014).

11 Walker, S. C. & McGlone, F. P. in *Neuropeptides in Mental Health and Behaviour* Vol. 47 379–93 (2013).

12 Cacioppo, S. *et al.* 'Loneliness: Clinical Import and Interventions'. *Perspectives on Psychological Science* **10**, 238–49 (2015).

13 Baarck, J. *et al.* 'Loneliness in Europe before and during the COVID-19 pandemic'. *Health Policy* **126**, 1124–29 (2022).

14 Christodoulou, P. 'This is how it feels to be lonely: A report on migrants and refugees' experiences with loneliness in London'. *The Forum* (1993).

15 Kirmayer, M. 'It's time to rethink what loneliness is'. *The Guardian* (22 July 2021).

16 Bargh, J. A. & Williams, E. L. 'The Automaticity of Social Life'. *Curr Dir Psychol Sci* **15**, 1–4 (2006).

17 Williams, L. E. & Bargh, J. A. 'Experiencing physical warmth promotes interpersonal warmth'. *Science* **322**, 606–7 (2008).

18 Sumioka, H. *et al.* 'Huggable communication medium decreases cortisol levels'. *Scientific Reports* **3**, 3034 (2013).

19 Farley, H. 'Why was my neighbour's body not found for two years?' *BBC Radio 4 Today* (3 April 2023).

20 Morley, C. 'Joyce Carol Vincent: How could this young woman lie dead and undiscovered for almost three years?' *The Guardian* (9 October 2011).

21 'Awaab Ishak: Guidance on mould to be reviewed after toddler's death'. *BBC NEWS* (14 January 2023).

22 Porges, S. W. 'Vagal tone: an autonomic mediator of affect.' *The Development of Emotion Regulation and Dysregulation* (eds J. Garber & K. A. Dodge) (CUP 1991).

23 Porges, S. W. 'Vagal tone: a physiologic marker of stress vulnerability'. *Pediatrics* **90**, 498–504 (1992).

24 Porges, S. W. 'Emotion: an evolutionary by-product of the neural regulation of the autonomic nervous system'. *Ann N Y Acad Sci* **807**, 62–77 (1997).

25 Porges, S. W. 'The Polyvagal Perspective'. *Biological psychology* **74**, 116–43 (2007).

26 Porges, S. W. 'The polyvagal theory: new insights into adaptive reactions of the autonomic nervous system'. *Cleveland Clinic journal of medicine* **76** Suppl **2**, S86–90 (2009).

27 Porges, S. W. *et al.* 'Vagal tone and the physiological regulation of emotion'. *Monographs of the Society for Research in Child Development* **59**, 167–86 (1994).

28 Porges, S. W. 'Orienting in a defensive world: mammalian modifications of our evolutionary heritage. A Polyvagal Theory'. *Psychophysiology* **32**, 301–18 (1995).

29 Nes, L. S. & Segerstrom, S. C. in *Encyclopedia of Applied Psychology* (ed. Charles D. Spielberger) 191–5 (Elsevier, 2004).

30 Helliwell, J. F. *et al.* *World Happiness Report 2022* (Sustainable Development Solutions Network, 2022).

31 Saner, E. 'Forget regret! How to have a happy life – according to the world's leading expert'. *The Guardian* (6 February 2023).

32 Bachner-Melman, R. & Ebstein, R. P. 'The role of oxytocin and vasopressin in emotional and social behaviors'. *Handb Clin Neurol* **124**, 53–68 (2014).

33 Carter, C. S. *et al.* 'Oxytocin, vasopressin and sociality'. *Progress in brain research* **170**, 331–6 (2008).

34 Meyer-Lindenberg, A. *et al.* 'Oxytocin and vasopressin in the human brain: social neuropeptides for translational medicine'. *Nat Rev Neurosci* **12**, 524–38 (2011).

35 Zhong, C. B. & Leonardelli, G. J. 'Cold and lonely: does social exclusion literally feel cold?' *Psychol Sci* **19**, 838–42 (2008).

36 Williams, K. D. *et al.* 'Cyberostracism: Effects of being ignored over the internet'. *Journal of Personality and Social Psychology* **79**, 748–62 (2000).

37 Kelly, M. *et al.* 'All alone with sweaty palms – physiological arousal and ostracism'. *Int J Psychophysiol* **83**, 309–14 (2012).

38 Zadro, L. *et al.* 'How low can you go? Ostracism by a computer is sufficient to lower self-reported levels of belonging, control, self-esteem, and meaningful existence'. *Journal of Experimental Social Psychology* **40**, 560–7 (2004).

39 LeDoux, J. E. *The Emotional Brain: The mysterious underpinnings of emotional life* (Simon & Schuster, 1996).

40 Carlowe, J. 'Back to the beginning'. *The Observer* (20 January 2002).

41 Fuchs, E. & Flügge, G. 'Adult Neuroplasticity: More Than 40 Years of Research'. *Neural Plasticity* **2014**, 541870 (2014).

42 Ehlers, A. & Clark, D. M. 'A cognitive model of posttraumatic stress disorder'. *Behaviour Research and Therapy* **38**, 319–45 (2000).

43 van der Kolk, B. A. *The Body Keeps the Score: Brain, Mind, and Body in the Healing of Trauma* (Penguin Publishing Group, 2015).

44 van der Kolk, B. A. 'The Compulsion to Repeat the Trauma: Re-enactment, Revictimization, and Masochism'. *Psychiatric Clinics of North America* **12**, 389–411 (1989).

45 Yehuda, R. & Lehrner, A. 'Intergenerational transmission of trauma effects: putative role of epigenetic mechanisms'. *World Psychiatry* **17**, 243–57 (2018).

46 Bhattacharya, S. *et al.* 'Stress Across Generations: DNA Methylation as a Potential Mechanism Underlying Intergenerational Effects of Stress in Both Post-traumatic Stress Disorder and Pre-clinical Predator Stress Rodent Models'. *Front Behav Neurosci* **13**, 113 (2019).

47 Dias, B. G. & Ressler, K. J. 'Parental olfactory experience influences behavior and neural structure in subsequent generations'. *Nat Neurosci* **17**, 89–96 (2014).

48 Debiec, J. & Sullivan, R. M. 'Intergenerational transmission of emotional trauma through amygdala-dependent mother-to-infant transfer of specific fear'. *Proceedings of the National Academy of Sciences of the United States of America* **111**, 12222–7 (2014).

49 Pennebaker, J. W. 'Traumatic experience and psychosomatic disease: Exploring the roles of behavioural inhibition, obsession, and confiding'. *Canadian Psychology/Psychologie canadienne* **26**, 82–95 (1985).

50 Pennebaker, J. W. 'Confession, Inhibition, and Disease'. *Advances in Experimental Social Psychology* **22**, 211–44 (1989).

51 Pennebaker, J. W. *et al.* 'Accelerating the coping process'. *Journal of Personality and Social Psychology* **58**, 528–37 (1990).

52 Smyth, J. M. *et al.* 'Effects of writing about stressful experiences on symptom reduction in patients with asthma or rheumatoid arthritis: A randomized trial'. *Jama* **281**, 1304–9 (1999).

53 Smith, H. E. *et al.* 'The effects of expressive writing on lung function, quality of life, medication use, and symptoms in adults with asthma: a randomized controlled trial'. *Psychosomatic medicine* **77**, 429–37 (2015).

54 Lumley, M. A. *et al.* 'Does emotional disclosure about stress improve health in rheumatoid arthritis? Randomized, controlled trials of written and spoken disclosure'. *Pain* **152**, 866–77 (2011).

55 Broderick, J. E. *et al.* 'Written emotional expression produces health benefits in fibromyalgia patients'. *Psychosomatic medicine* **67**, 326–34 (2005).

56 Halpert, A. *et al.* 'Expressive writing is a promising therapeutic modality for the management of IBS: a pilot study'. *Am J Gastroenterol* **105**, 2440–8 (2010).

57 Cash, T. V. & Lageman, S. K. 'Randomized controlled expressive writing pilot in individuals with Parkinson's disease and their caregivers'. *BMC Psychol* **3**, 44 (2015).

58 Graham, J. E. *et al.* 'Effects of written anger expression in chronic pain patients: making meaning from pain'. *J Behav Med* **31**, 201–12 (2008).

59 McGuire, K. M. *et al.* 'Autonomic effects of expressive writing in individuals with elevated blood pressure'. *Journal of health psychology* **10**, 197–209 (2005).

60 Rosenberg, H. J. *et al.* 'Expressive disclosure and health outcomes in a prostate cancer population'. *Int J Psychiatry Med* **32**, 37–53 (2002).

61 Zakowski, S. G. *et al.* 'Written emotional disclosure buffers the effects of social constraints on distress among cancer patients'. *Health Psychol* **23**, 555–63 (2004).

62 La Marca, L. *et al.* 'Efficacy of Pennebaker's expressive writing intervention in reducing psychiatric symptoms among patients with first-time cancer diagnosis: a randomized clinical trial'. *Supportive Care in Cancer* **27**, 1801–9 (2019).

63 Smyth, J. M. *et al.* 'Expressive writing and post-traumatic stress disorder: effects on trauma symptoms, mood states, and cortisol reactivity'. *Br J Health Psychol* **13**, 85–93 (2008).

64 Mogk, C. *et al.* 'Health effects of expressive writing on stressful or traumatic experiences – a meta-analysis'. *Psychosoc Med* **3**, Doc06 (2006).

65 DiMenichi, B. C. *et al.* 'Writing About Past Failures Attenuates Cortisol Responses and Sustained Attention Deficits Following Psychosocial Stress'. *Frontiers of Behavioral Neuroscience* **12** (2018).

66 Soul, M. & John, D. H. 'Writing therapy: a new tool for general practice?' *British Journal of General Practice* **62**, 661 (2012).

67 Frisina, P. G. *et al.* 'A meta-analysis of the effects of written emotional disclosure on the health outcomes of clinical populations'. *J Nerv Ment Dis* **192**, 629–34 (2004).

68 Sloan, D. M. *et al.* 'Expressive writing buffers against maladaptive rumination'. *Emotion* **8**, 302–6 (2008).

69 Baikie, K. A. *et al.* 'Expressive writing and positive writing for participants with mood disorders: an online randomized controlled trial'. *J Affect Disord* **136**, 310–19 (2012).

70 Pachankis, J. E. & Goldfried, M. R. 'Expressive writing for gay-related stress: psychosocial benefits and mechanisms underlying improvement'. *J Consult Clin Psychol* **78**, 98–110 (2010).

71 Petrie, K. J. *et al.* 'Disclosure of trauma and immune response to a hepatitis B vaccination program'. *J Consult Clin Psychol* **63**, 787–92 (1995).

72 Robinson, H. *et al.* 'The effects of expressive writing before or after punch biopsy on wound healing'. *Brain Behav Immun* **61**, 217–27 (2017).

73 Robinson, H. *et al.* 'The effect of expressive writing on wound healing: Immunohistochemistry analysis of skin tissue two weeks after punch biopsy wounding'. *Journal of psychosomatic research* **161**, 110987 (2022).

74 Koschwanez, H. *et al.* 'Randomized clinical trial of expressive writing on wound healing following bariatric surgery'. *Health Psychol* **36**, 630–40 (2017).

75 Koschwanez, H. E. *et al.* 'Expressive writing and wound healing in older adults: a randomized controlled trial'. *Psychosomatic medicine* **75**, 581–90 (2013).

76 Broadbent, E. *et al.* Abstract #1758 'The effects of expressive writing on wound healing in surgical patients'. *Brain, Behavior, and Immunity* **57**, e15 (2016).

77 Zhu, Z. *et al.* 'Effect of calligraphy training on hyperarousal symptoms for childhood survivors of the 2008 China earthquakes'. *Neuropsychiatr Dis Treat* **10**, 977–85 (2014).

78 Scullin, M. K. *et al.* 'The effects of bedtime writing on difficulty falling asleep: A polysomnographic study comparing to-do lists and completed activity lists'. *Journal of Experimental Psychology. General* **147**, 139–46 (2018).

79 Cash, T. V. & Lageman, S. K. 'Randomized controlled expressive writing pilot in individuals with Parkinson's disease and their caregivers'. *BMC Psychology* **3**, 44 (2015).

80 Pennebaker, J. W. 'Putting stress into words: health, linguistic, and therapeutic implications'. *Behav Res Ther* **31**, 539–48 (1993).

81 Moy, J. D. in *New Directions in Literature and Medicine Studies* (ed. Stephanie M. Hilger) 15–30 (Palgrave Macmillan UK, 2017).

82 Andersson, M. A. & Conley, C. S. 'Optimizing the perceived benefits and health outcomes of writing about traumatic life events'. *Stress Health* **29**, 40–49 (2013).

83 Ehlers, A. *et al.* 'Intrusive re-experiencing in post-traumatic stress disorder: phenomenology, theory, and therapy'. *Memory* **12**, 403–15 (2004).

84 Francis, M. E. & Pennebaker, J. W. 'Putting stress into words: the impact of writing on physiological, absentee, and self-reported emotional well-being measures'. *Am J Health Promot* **6**, 280–87 (1992).

85 Pennebaker, J. W. & Francis, M. E. 'Cognitive, Emotional, and Language Processes in Disclosure'. *Cognition and Emotion* **10**, 601–26 (1996).

86 Pennebaker, J. W. & Evans, J. F. *Expressive Writing: Words That Heal* (Idyll Arbor, 2014).

87 Wiltermuth, S. S. & Heath, C. 'Synchrony and cooperation'. *Psychol Sci* **20**, 1–5 (2009).

88 von Zimmermann, J. *et al.* 'The Choreography of Group Affiliation'. *Top Cogn Sci* **10**, 80–94 (2018).

89 Valdesolo, P. *et al.* 'The rhythm of joint action: Synchrony promotes cooperative ability'. *Journal of Experimental Social Psychology* **46**, 693–5 (2010).

90 Tschacher, W. *et al.* 'Audience synchronies in live concerts illustrate the embodiment of music experience'. *Scientific Reports* **13**, 14843 (2023).

91 Tarr, B. *et al.* 'Synchrony and exertion during dance independently raise pain threshold and encourage social bonding'. *Biol Lett* **11** (2015).

92 Schmidt, R. C. & Richardson, M. J. in *Coordination: Neural, Behavioral and Social Dynamics* (eds Armin Fuchs & Viktor K. Jirsa) 281–308 (Springer Berlin Heidelberg, 2008).

93 Reddish, P. *et al.* 'Let's dance together: synchrony, shared intentionality and cooperation'. *PLoS One* **8**, e71182 (2013).

94 Oullier, O. *et al.* 'Social coordination dynamics: measuring human bonding'. *Social neuroscience* **3**, 178–92 (2008).

95 Marsh, K. L. *et al.* 'Social connection through joint action and interpersonal coordination'. *Top Cogn Sci* **1**, 320–39 (2009).

96 Launay, J. *et al.* 'Synchrony as an Adaptive Mechanism for Large-Scale Human Social Bonding'. *Ethology* **122**, 779–89 (2016).

97 Launay, J. *et al.* 'Synchronising movements with the sounds of a virtual partner enhances partner likeability'. *Cogn Process* **15**, 491–501 (2014).

98 Lakens, D. & Stel, M. 'If they move in sync, they must feel in sync: Movement synchrony leads to attributions of rapport and entitativity'. *Social Cognition* **29**, 1–14 (2011).

99 Jackson, J. C. *et al.* 'Synchrony and Physiological Arousal Increase Cohesion and Cooperation in Large Naturalistic Groups'. *Scientific reports* **8**, 127 (2018).

100 Hove, M. J. & Risen, J. L. 'It's all in the timing: Interpersonal synchrony increases affiliation'. *Social Cognition* **27**, 949–61 (2009).

101 Fischer, R. *et al.* 'How do rituals affect cooperation? An experimental field study comparing nine ritual types'. *Hum Nat* **24**, 115–25 (2013).

102 Ellamil, M. *et al.* 'One in the Dance: Musical Correlates of Group Synchrony in a Real-World Club Environment'. *PloS one* **11**, e0164783 (2016).

103 Bhattacharya, J. & Petsche, H. 'Shadows of artistry: Cortical synchrony during perception and imagery of visual art'. *Cognitive Brain Research* **13**, 179–86 (2002).

104 Noy, L. *et al.* 'The mirror game as a paradigm for studying the dynamics of two people improvising motion together'. *Proceedings of the National Academy of Sciences of the United States of America* **108**, 20947–52 (2011).

105 Santos, P. S. *et al.* 'New evidence that the MHC influences odor perception in humans: a study with 58 Southern Brazilian students'. *Hormones and behavior* **47**, 384–8 (2005).

106 Ackerl, K. *et al.* 'The scent of fear'. *Neuro Endocrinol Lett* **23**, 79–84 (2002).

107 Daly, M. 'More dancers allege body-shaming and bullying at UK ballet schools'. *BBC News* (20 December 2023).

108 Winship, L. ' "You're very fat up here": was dance god George Balanchine a controlling monster?' *The Guardian* (1 May 2023).

109 Connolly, K. ' "Still in the stone age": movie world in shock as Germany's MeToo moment arrives'. *The Observer* (7 May 2023).

110 Chrisafis, A. 'Gérard Depardieu documentary shows "vile" footage of sexist behaviour'. *The Guardian* (8 December 2023).

111 Wallis, L. 'Picasso's twisted beauty – and the "trail of female carnage" he left behind'. *BBC News* (23 September 2023).

112 Reid, T. & Mckay, R. 'California shooting suspect was regular at Monterey Park dance studio'. *Reuters* (24 January 2023).

5. *How and When to Set Boundaries*

1 Rubinstein, J. S. *et al.* 'Executive control of cognitive processes in task switching'. *Journal of Experimental Psychology. Human perception and performance* **27**, 763–797 (2001).

2 Becker, L. *et al.* 'Biological stress responses to multitasking and work interruptions: A randomized controlled trial'. *Psychoneuroendocrinology* **156**, 106358 (2023).

3 Rogers, R. D. & Monsell, S. 'Costs of a predictable switch between simple cognitive tasks'. *Journal of Experimental Psychology: General* **124**, 207–31 (1995).

4 American Psychological Association. 'Multitasking: Switching costs' *American Psychological Association* (20 March 2006).

5 Anderson, C. A. *et al.* 'Hot years and serious and deadly assault: empirical tests of the heat hypothesis'. *J Pers Soc Psychol* **73**, 1213–23 (1997).

6 Buss, A. *Investigating Aggression in the Laboratory. The psychology of aggression.* 35–52 (John Wiley & Sons Inc, 1961).

7 Taylor, S. P. 'Aggressive behavior and physiological arousal as a function of provocation and the tendency to inhibit aggression'. *Journal of Personality* **35**, 297–310 (1967).

8 Blair, R. J. R. 'Considering anger from a cognitive neuroscience perspective'. *Wiley Interdisciplinary Reviews. Cognitive Science* **3**, 65–74 (2012).

9 Andrews, G. R. & Debus, R. L. 'Persistence and causal perception of failure: Modifying cognitive attributions'. *Journal of Educational Psychology* **70**, 154–66 (1978).

10 Adler, A. *The science of Living (Psychology Revivals).* (1st edn) (Routledge, 2013).

11 Whalen, Paul J. & Kelley, William M. 'To Apply Yourself Is Human, to Reapply Divine'. *Neuron* **83**, 1227–8 (2014).

12 Seligman, M. E. 'Learned helplessness'. *Annu Rev Med* **23**, 407–12 (1972).

13 Winefield, A. H. 'Frustration-instigated behavior and learned helplessness'. *The Journal of Psychology* **102**, 267–74 (1979).

14 Rosellini, R. A. & Seligman, M. E. 'Frustation and learned helpless-ness'. *J Exp Psychol Anim Behav Process* **1**, 149–57 (1975).

15 Wagner, H. R., 2nd *et al.* 'The applicability of inescapable shock as a source of animal depression'. *J Gen Psychol* **96**, 313–18 (1977).

16 Mineka, S. & Hendersen, R. W. 'Controllability and Predictability in Acquired Motivation'. *Annual Review of Psychology* **36**, 495–529 (1985).

17 Karsh, N. & Eitam, B. 'I control therefore I do: judgments of agency influence action selection'. *Cognition* **138**, 122–31 (2015).

18 Wang, K. S. & Delgado, M. R. 'The Protective Effects of Perceived Control During Repeated Exposure to Aversive Stimuli'. *Front Neurosci* **15**, 625816 (2021).

19 Leotti, L. A. & Delgado, M. R. 'The inherent reward of choice'. *Psychol Sci* **22**, 1310–18 (2011).

20 Leotti, L. A. & Delgado, M. R. 'The value of exercising control over monetary gains and losses'. *Psychol Sci* **25**, 596–604 (2014).

21 Tricomi, E. M. *et al.* 'Modulation of caudate activity by action con-tingency'. *Neuron* **41**, 281–92 (2004).

22 Skinner, B. F. *Science and Human Behavior* (Macmillan, 1953).

23 Boddez, Y. *et al.* 'Learned helplessness and its relevance for psycho-logical suffering: A new perspective illustrated with attachment problems, burn-out, and fatigue complaints'. *Cogn Emot* **36**, 1027–36 (2022).

24 Polastri, M. & Truisi, M. C. 'Meritocracy? Ask yourself'. *J Intensive Care Soc* **18**, 276–78 (2017).

25 Finkielsztein, M. & Wagner, I. 'The sense of meaninglessness in bureaucratized science'. *Soc Stud Sci* **53**, 271–86 (2023).

26 Tacconelli, E. *et al.* 'Science without meritocracy. Discrimination among European specialists in infectious diseases and clinical micro-biology: A questionnaire survey'. *BMJ Open* **2** (2012).

27 Marino, I. R. 'Working toward meritocracy in Italy'. *Science* **320**, 1289 (2008).

28 Marino, I. R. 'A step backward for Italy's meritocracy'. *Science* **336**, 541 (2012).

29 Snooks, H. *et al.* 'Is bureaucracy being busted in research ethics and governance for health services research in the UK? Experiences and

perspectives reported by stakeholders through an online survey'. *BMC Public Health* **23**, 1119 (2023).

30 Zaleznik, A. *et al.* 'Stress reactions in organizations: syndromes, causes and consequences'. *Behav Sci* **22**, 151–62 (1977).

31 Pascoe, K. M. *et al.* 'Social Workers' Experiences of Bureaucracy: A Systematic Synthesis of Qualitative Studies'. *The British Journal of Social Work* **53**, 513–33 (2022).

32 Charlton, B. G. 'The cancer of bureaucracy: how it will destroy science, medicine, education; and eventually everything else'. *Med Hypotheses* **74**, 961–65 (2010).

33 Keulemans, S. & van de Walle, S. 'Understanding street-level bureaucrats' attitude towards clients: Towards a measurement instrument'. *Public Policy and Administration* **35**, 84–113 (2020).

34 Wiley, K. & Berry, F. 'Compassionate Bureaucracy: Assuming the Administrative Burden of Policy Implementation'. *Nonprofit and Voluntary Sector Quarterly* **47**, 55–75S (2018).

35 Blom, J. D. *et al.* ['Red tape in psychiatry: on bureaucracy, bureaucratism, and our secret fondness for procedures']. *Tijdschr Psychiatr* **58**, 520–28 (2016).

36 Bozeman, B. *et al.* 'Death by a Thousand 10-Minute Tasks: Workarounds and Noncompliance in University Research Administration'. *Administration & Society* **53**, 527–68 (2021).

37 Hattke, F. *et al.* 'Emotional Responses to Bureaucratic Red Tape'. *Public Administration Review* **80**, 53–63 (2020).

38 Eysenck, H. J. *The Biological Basis of Personality* (Thomas, 1967).

39 Eysenck, H. J. *A Model for Personality* (Springer, 1981).

40 Mitchell, R. L. C. & Kumari, V. 'Hans Eysenck's interface between the brain and personality: Modern evidence on the cognitive neuroscience of personality'. *Personality and Individual Differences* **103**, 74–81 (2016).

41 Zaghari-Ratcliffe, N. ' "Escape to another world": Nazanin Zaghari-Ratcliffe on reading in prison'. *The Guardian* (27 November 2023).

42 McTiernan, J., Black, S. & Arnott, D. *Last Action Hero* (USA, 1993).

43 Shimamura, A. P. *Psychocinematic: Exploring Cognition at the Movies* (Oxford University Press, 2013).

44 Devlin, J. T. 'Why Watching a Movie Could Improve Wellbeing' (ed. UCL Division of Psychology and Language Sciences, 2020).

45 Cohen, A. L. *et al.* 'The Power of the Picture: How Narrative Film Captures Attention and Disrupts Goal Pursuit'. *PLoS One* **10**, e0144493 (2015).

46 Bower, I. *et al.* 'Impact of built environment design on emotion measured via neurophysiological correlates and subjective indicators: A systematic review'. *Journal of Environmental Psychology* **66**, 101344 (2019).

47 Budge, H. 'The Science Behind the Impact of Cinema'. *CJ NEWS* (4 August 2022).

48 Reeves, B. *et al.* 'The Effects of Screen Size and Message Content on Attention and Arousal'. *Media Psychology* **1**, 49–67 (1999).

49 Dunbar, R. I. *et al.* 'Emotional arousal when watching drama increases pain threshold and social bonding'. *R Soc Open Sci* **3**, 160288 (2016).

50 Richardson, D. (2023). The Psychological Consequences of Getting Lost in a Movie. White paper. Applied Consumer Neuroscience. https://www.acnlabs.co.uk/case-studies/getting-lost-in-a-movie

51 Williams, J. *et al.* 'Cinema audiences reproducibly vary the chemical composition of air during films, by broadcasting scene specific emissions on breath'. *Scientific Reports* **6**, 25464 (2016).

52 Gerrig, R. J. *Experiencing Narrative Worlds: On the psychological activities of reading* (Yale University Press, 1993).

53 Parks, K. M. A. *et al.* 'The Task Matters: A Scoping Review on Reading Comprehension Abilities in ADHD'. *J Atten Disord* **26**, 1304–24 (2022).

54 Richardson, D. C. *et al.* 'Engagement in video and audio narratives: Contrasting self-report and physiological measures'. *Sci Rep* **10**, 11298 (2020).

55 Devlin, J. T. & Richardson, D. C. 'The Physiology of Narrative'. ACN Labs (1 June 2018).

56 Stein Duker, L. I. *et al.* 'Use of Audiobooks as an Environmental Distractor to Decrease State Anxiety in Children Waiting in the Pediatric Emergency Department: A Pilot and Feasibility Study'. *Front Pediatr* **8**, 556805 (2020).

57 Konlaan, B. B. *et al.* 'Visiting the cinema, concerts, museums or art exhibitions as determinant of survival: a Swedish fourteen-year cohort follow-up'. *Scand J Public Health* **28**, 174–8 (2000).

58 Bygren, L. O. *et al.* 'Attendance at cultural events, reading books or periodicals, and making music or singing in a choir as determinants for survival: Swedish interview survey of living conditions'. *Bmj* **313**, 1577–80 (1996).

59 Ughrig, S. C. N. 'Cinema is good for you: The effects of cinema attendance on self reported anxiety or depression and "happiness"'. *ISER Working Paper* (Institute for Social and Economic Research, 2005–2014)

60 Smith, J. K. *The Museum Effect: How Museums, Libraries, and Cultural Institutions Educate and Civilize Society* (Rowman & Littlefield Publishers, 2014).

61 Higuera-Trujillo, J. L. *et al.* 'The Cognitive-Emotional Design and Study of Architectural Space: A Scoping Review of Neuroarchitecture and Its Precursor Approaches'. *Sensors (Basel)* **21** (2021).

62 Edelstein, E. A. & Macagno, E. in *Sustainable Environmental Design in Architecture* (eds S. Rassia & P.M. Pardalos) 27–41 (Springer, 2012).

63 Higuera-Trujillo, J. L. *et al.* 'Multisensory stress reduction: a neuro-architecture study of paediatric waiting rooms'. *Building Research & Information* **48**, 269–85 (2020).

64 Eftekhari, M. & Ghomeishi, M. 'Evaluation of Multisensory Interactions Between the Healing Built Environment and Nurses in Healthcare Nursing Stations: Case Study of Tehran Hospitals'. *HERD: Health Environments Research & Design Journal* **16**, 210–37 (2023).

65 van Leeuwen, J. E. P. *et al.* 'More Than Meets the Eye: Art Engages the Social Brain'. *Front Neurosci* **16**, 738865 (2022).

66 'The Grand Factory'. *Time Out* (1 April 2015).

67 McWeeny, F. The Documentary Podcast 'Global Dancefloor: Beirut' (BBC News World Service, 24 May 2023).

68 Beselia, A. *et al.* 'Nightlife and Drug Use in Tbilisi, Georgia: Results of an Exploratory Qualitative Study'. *J Psychoactive Drugs* **51**, 247–53 (2019).

69 Kurtz, S. P. *et al.* 'Benzodiazepine dependence among multidrug users in the club scene'. *Drug Alcohol Depend* **119**, 99–105 (2011).

70 Gripenberg-Abdon, J. *et al.* 'Measuring substance use in the club setting: a feasibility study using biochemical markers'. *Subst Abuse Treat Prev Policy* **7**, 7 (2012).

71 Tajadura-Jiménez, A. *et al.* 'When room size matters: acoustic influences on emotional responses to sounds'. *Emotion* **10**, 416–22 (2010).

72 Jimenez, M. P. *et al.* 'Associations between Nature Exposure and Health: A Review of the Evidence'. *Int J Environ Res Public Health* **18** (2021).

73 Gonçalves, G. *et al.* 'Restorative Effects of Biophilic Workplace and Nature Exposure during Working Time: A Systematic Review'. *Int J Environ Res Public Health* **20** (2023).

74 Adkins, F. & Latham, K. 'The surprising benefits of blue spaces'. *BBC Future* (9 November 2022).

75 Ke, J. & Yoon, J. 'Design for Breathtaking Experiences: An Exploration of Design Strategies to Evoke Awe in Human–Product Interactions'. *Multimodal Technologies and Interaction* **4**, 82 (2020).

76 Lucht, A. & van Schie, H. T. 'The Evolutionary Function of Awe: A Review and Integrated Model of Seven Theoretical Perspectives'. *Emotion Review* **0**, 17540739231197199

77 Keltner, D. *Awe: The New Science of Everyday Wonder and How It Can Transform Your Life* (Penguin Press, 2023).

78 Monroy, M. & Keltner, D. 'Awe as a Pathway to Mental and Physical Health'. *Perspect Psychol Sci* **18**, 309–20 (2023).

79 Anderson, C. L. *et al.* 'Awe in nature heals: Evidence from military veterans, at-risk youth, and college students'. *Emotion* **18**, 1195–1202 (2018).

80 Bai, Y. *et al.* 'Awe, daily stress, and elevated life satisfaction'. *J Pers Soc Psychol* **120**, 837–60 (2021).

81 van Kleef, G. A. & Lelieveld, G. J. 'Moving the self and others to do good: The emotional underpinnings of prosocial behavior'. *Current opinion in psychology* **44**, 80–88 (2022).

82 Al-Yaaribi, A. *et al.* 'The Effects of Prosocial and Antisocial Behaviors on Emotion, Attention, and Performance During a Competitive Basketball Task'. *J Sport Exerc Psychol* **40**, 303–11 (2018).

83 Piff, P. K. *et al.* 'Awe, the small self, and prosocial behavior'. *J Pers Soc Psychol* **108**, 883–99 (2015).

84 Bai, Y. *et al.* 'Awe, the diminished self, and collective engagement: Universals and cultural variations in the small self'. *J Pers Soc Psychol* **113**, 185–209 (2017).

85 Perlin, J. D. & Li, L. 'Why Does Awe Have Prosocial Effects? New Perspectives on Awe and the Small Self'. *Perspect Psychol Sci* **15**, 291–308 (2020).

86 Sturm, V. E. *et al.* 'Big smile, small self: Awe walks promote prosocial positive emotions in older adults'. *Emotion* **22**, 1044–58 (2022).

87 Gebauer, J. E. *et al.* 'Mind-Body Practices and the Self: Yoga and Meditation Do Not Quiet the Ego but Instead Boost Self-Enhancement'. *Psychol Sci* **29**, 1299–1308 (2018).

88 Robson, D. 'How mindfulness could make you selfish'. *BBC Worklife* (17 August 2021).

89 Hafenbrack, A. C. *et al.* 'Mindfulness meditation reduces guilt and prosocial reparation'. *J Pers Soc Psychol* **123**, 28–54 (2022).

90 van Dam, N. T. *et al.* 'Mind the Hype: A Critical Evaluation and Prescriptive Agenda for Research on Mindfulness and Meditation'. *Perspect Psychol Sci* **13**, 36–61 (2018).

91 van Dam, N. T. *et al.* 'Letter to the Editor: Miscommunicating Mindfulness'. *Perspectives on Psychological Science* **15**, 1289–90 (2020).

92 Poulin, M. J. *et al.* 'Minding Your Own Business? Mindfulness Decreases Prosocial Behavior for People With Independent Self-Construals'. *Psychol Sci* **32**, 1699–1708 (2021).

93 Jung, C. G. in *Psychology and the East* 77–86 (Princeton University Press, 1978).

94 Schlosser, M. *et al.* 'Unpleasant meditation-related experiences in regular meditators: Prevalence, predictors, and conceptual considerations'. *PLoS One* **14**, e0216643 (2019).

95 Britton, W. B. 'Can mindfulness be too much of a good thing? The value of a middle way'. *Current Opinion in Psychology* **28**, 159–65 (2019).

96 Trumbull, D. 'Shame: An Acute Stress Response to Interpersonal Traumatization'. *Psychiatry* **83**, 2–14 (2020).

97 Garcia-Campayo, J. *et al.* 'Joint hypermobility and anxiety: The state of the art'. *Curr Psychiatry Rep* **13**, 18–25 (2011).

98 Bulbena, A. *et al.* 'Anxiety disorders in the joint hypermobility syndrome'. *Psychiatry Research* **46**, 59–68 (1993).

99 Martín-Santos, R. *et al.* 'Association between joint hypermobility syndrome and panic disorder'. *The American Journal of Psychiatry* **155**, 1578–83 (1998).

100 Bulbena, A. *et al.* 'Joint hypermobility syndrome is a risk factor trait for anxiety disorders: A 15-year follow-up cohort study'. *Gen Hosp Psychiatry* **33**, 363–70 (2011).

101 Rice, A. (2024). 'The teacher cupped her crotch. She never went back': when yoga turns toxic. The Guardian. https://www.the guardian.com/lifeandstyle/2024/feb/10/the-teacher-cupped-her-crotch-she-never-went-back-when-yoga-turns-toxic

6. Mind Expansions – Create how you feel by what you do

1 Engelmann, J. M. *et al.* 'Chimpanzees consider alternative possibilities'. *Curr Biol* **31**, R1377–8 (2021).

2 van der Kolk, B. 'Posttraumatic stress disorder and the nature of trauma'. *Dialogues Clin Neurosci* **2**, 7–22 (2000).

3 Frewen, P. A. *et al.* 'Assessment of anhedonia in psychological trauma: psychometric and neuroimaging perspectives'. *Eur J Psychotraumatol* **3** (2012).

4 Ekman, P. 'Darwin's contributions to our understanding of emotional expressions'. *Philosophical transactions of the Royal Society of London. Series B, Biological sciences* **364**, 3449–51 (2009).

5 Levenson, R. W. 'The Autonomic Nervous System and Emotion'. *Emotion Review* **6**, 100–12 (2014).

6 Tooby, J. & Cosmides, L. in *Handbook of Emotions*, 3rd ed. 114–37 (The Guilford Press, 2008).

7 Gendron, M. *et al.* 'Universality Reconsidered: Diversity in Making Meaning of Facial Expressions'. *Curr Dir Psychol Sci* **27**, 211–19 (2018).

8 Heyes, C. 'Grist and mills: on the cultural origins of cultural learning'. *Philosophical Transactions of the Royal Society of London. Series B, Biological Sciences* **367**, 2181–91 (2012).

9 Heyes, C. 'What's social about social learning?' *J Comp Psychol* **126**, 193–202 (2012).

10 Barrett, L. F. 'Categories and Their Role in the Science of Emotion'. *Psychol Inq* **28**, 20–6 (2017).

11 Barrett, L. F. & Satpute, A. B. 'Historical pitfalls and new directions in the neuroscience of emotion'. *Neuroscience letters* **693**, 9–18 (2019).

12 Gendron, M. *et al.* 'Emotion Perception in Hadza Hunter-Gatherers'. *Sci Rep* **10**, 3867 (2020).

13 Huberty, S. *et al.* 'Neural mechanisms of language development in infancy'. *Infancy* **28**, 754–70 (2023).

14 Fibla, L. *et al.* 'Language Exposure and Brain Myelination in Early Development'. *The Journal of Neuroscience: The official journal of the Society for Neuroscience* **43**, 4279–90 (2023).

15 Sanchez-Alonso, S. & Aslin, R. N. 'Towards a model of language neurobiology in early development'. *Brain and Language* **224**, 105047 (2022).

16 Waxman, S. R. & Markow, D. B. 'Words as invitations to form categories: evidence from 12- to 13-month-old infants'. *Cogn Psychol* **29**, 257–302 (1995).

17 Gendron, M. & Barrett, L. F. 'Emotion Perception as Conceptual Synchrony'. *Emotion Review* **10**, 101–10 (2018).

18 Barrett, L. F. 'Solving the emotion paradox: categorization and the experience of emotion'. *Pers Soc Psychol Rev* **10**, 20–46 (2006).

19 Hoemann, K. *et al.* 'Context facilitates performance on a classic cross-cultural emotion perception task'. *Emotion* **19**, 1292–1313 (2019).

20 Schiller, D. *et al.* 'The Human Affectome'. *Neuroscience & Biobehavioral Reviews*, 105450 (2023).

21 Feldman Barrett, L. *How Emotions Are Made: The Secret Life of the Brain* (Mariner Books, 2017).

22 Lindquist, K. A. *et al.* 'The brain basis of emotion: a meta-analytic review'. *The Behavioral and brain sciences* **35**, 121–43 (2012).

23 Barrett, L. F. 'Are Emotions Natural Kinds?' *Perspectives on Psychological Science* **1**, 28–58 (2006).

24 Barrett, L. F. *et al.* 'The experience of emotion'. *Annu Rev Psychol* **58**, 373–403 (2007).

25 Benton, D. 'Carbohydrate ingestion, blood glucose and mood'. *Neurosci Biobehav Rev* **26**, 293–308 (2002).

26 Bushman, B. J. *et al.* 'Low glucose relates to greater aggression in married couples'. *Proceedings of the National Academy of Sciences of the United States of America* **111**, 6254–7 (2014).

27 Anderberg, R. H. *et al.* 'The Stomach-Derived Hormone Ghrelin Increases Impulsive Behavior'. *Neuropsychopharmacology* **41**, 1199–1209 (2016).

28 MacCormack, J. K. & Lindquist, K. A. 'Feeling hangry? When hunger is conceptualized as emotion'. *Emotion* **19**, 301–19 (2019).

29 Danziger, S. *et al.* 'Extraneous factors in judicial decisions'. *Proceedings of the National Academy of Sciences of the United States of America* **108**, 6889–92 (2011).

30 Feldman, M. J. *et al.* 'Affect and Social Judgment: The Roles of Physiological Reactivity and Interoceptive Sensitivity'. *Affect Sci* **3**, 464–79 (2022).

31 Wormwood, J. B. *et al.* 'You are what I feel: A test of the affective realism hypothesis'. *Emotion* **19**, 788–98 (2019).

32 Anderson, E. *et al.* 'Out of sight but not out of mind: unseen affective faces influence evaluations and social impressions'. *Emotion* **12**, 1210–21 (2012).

33 Barrett, L. F. & Bar, M. 'See it with feeling: affective predictions during object perception'. *Philosophical Transactions of the Royal Society B: Biological Sciences* **364**, 1325–34 (2009).

34 Garg, N. *et al.* 'The Influence of Incidental Affect on Consumers' Food Intake'. *Journal of Marketing* **71**, 194–206 (2007).

35 Quigley, K. S. *et al.* 'Functions of Interoception: From Energy Regulation to Experience of the Self'. *Trends in neurosciences* **44**, 29–38 (2021).

36 Brown, C. L. *et al.* 'Coherence Between Subjective Experience and Physiology in Emotion: Individual Differences and Implications for Well-Being'. *Emotion* (2019).

37 Côté, S. *et al.* 'The ability to regulate emotion is associated with greater well-being, income, and socioeconomic status'. *Emotion (Washington, D.C.)* **10**, 923–33 (2010).

38 Mauss, I. B. *et al.* 'The tie that binds? Coherence among emotional experience, behavior, and autonomic physiology'. *Emotion* **5**, 175–90 (2005).

39 Bagby, R. M. *et al.* 'The twenty-item Toronto Alexithymia Scale: I. Item selection and cross-validation of the factor structure'. *Journal of psychosomatic research* **38**, 23–32 (1994).

40 Taylor, G. J. *et al.* 'The twenty-item Toronto Alexithymia Scale: IV. Reliability and factorial validity in different languages and cultures'. *Journal of psychosomatic research* **55**, 277–83 (2003).

41 Vorst, H. C. M. & Bermond, B. 'Validity and reliability of the Bermond–Vorst Alexithymia Questionnaire'. *Personality and Individual Differences* **30**, 413–34 (2001).

42 de Saint-Exupéry, A. *The Little Prince* (Reynal & Hitchcock (1943)/ HarperCollins: Farshore (2017).

43 Bar, M. 'Visual objects in context'. *Nature Reviews Neuroscience* **5**, 617–29 (2004).

44 Bar, M. 'The proactive brain: using analogies and associations to generate predictions'. *Trends Cogn Sci* **11**, 280–89 (2007).

45 Rousselet, G. *et al.* 'How long to get to the "gist" of real-world natural scenes?' *Visual Cognition* **12**, 852–77 (2005).

46 Rossel, P., Peyrin, C., Roux-Sibilon, A. & Kauffmann, L. *et al.* 'It makes sense, so I see it better! Contextual information about the visual environment increases its perceived sharpness'. *Journal of Experimental Psychology. Human perception and performance* **48**, 331–50 (2022).

47 Roux-Sibilon, A. *et al.* 'Influence of peripheral vision on object categorization in central vision'. *Journal of Vision* **19**, 7 (2019).

48 Kirchner, H. & Thorpe, S. J. 'Ultra-rapid object detection with saccadic eye movements: visual processing speed revisited'. *Vision Res* **46**, 1762–76 (2006).

49 Oh, Y. *et al.* 'An insight-related neural reward signal'. *Neuroimage* **214**, 116757 (2020).

50 Tik, M. *et al.* 'Ultra-high-field fMRI insights on insight: Neural correlates of the Aha!-moment'. *Human brain mapping* **39**, 3241–52 (2018).

51 Kizilirmak, J. M. *et al.* 'Generation and the subjective feeling of "aha!" are independently related to learning from insight'. *Psychol Res* **80**, 1059–74 (2016).

52 Shen, W. *et al.* 'Feeling the Insight: Uncovering Somatic Markers of the "aha" Experience'. *Appl Psychophysiol Biofeedback* **43**, 13–21 (2018).

53 Salvi, C. *et al.* 'Sudden insight is associated with shutting out visual inputs'. *Psychon Bull Rev* **22**, 1814–19 (2015).

54 Kounios, J. & Beeman, M. 'The cognitive neuroscience of insight'. *Annu Rev Psychol* **65**, 71–93 (2014).

55 Gross, J. J. 'Emotion regulation: affective, cognitive, and social consequences'. *Psychophysiology* **39**, 281–91 (2002).

56 Critchley, H. D. 'Neural mechanisms of autonomic, affective, and cognitive integration'. *The Journal of comparative neurology* **493**, 154–66 (2005).

57 Dayan, P. *et al.* 'The Helmholtz machine'. *Neural Comput* **7**, 889–904 (1995).

58 Rao, R. P. & Ballard, D. H. 'Predictive coding in the visual cortex: a functional interpretation of some extra-classical receptive-field effects'. *Nat Neurosci* **2**, 79–87 (1999).

59 Lee, M. A. & Song, R. 'Childhood abuse, personality traits, and depressive symptoms in adulthood'. *Child Abuse Negl* **65**, 194–203 (2017).

60 Knill, D. C. & Pouget, A. 'The Bayesian brain: the role of uncertainty in neural coding and computation'. *Trends in Neurosciences* **27**, 712–19 (2004).

61 Massimini, F. *et al.* in *Optimal Experience: Psychological studies of flow in consciousness*, 60–81 (Cambridge University Press, 1988).

62 Thissen, B. A. K. *et al.* 'The pleasures of reading fiction explained by flow, presence, identification, suspense, and cognitive involvement'. *Psychology of Aesthetics, Creativity, and the Arts* **15**, 710–24 (2021).

63 Thissen, B. A. K. *et al.* 'Measuring Optimal Reading Experiences: The Reading Flow Short Scale'. *Front Psychol* **9**, 2542 (2018).

64 de Manzano, O. *et al.* 'The psychophysiology of flow during piano playing'. *Emotion* **10**, 301–11 (2010).

65 Biasutti, M. & Philippe, R. A. Editorial: 'I got flow! The flow state in music and artistic sport contexts'. *Front Psychol* **14**, 1138638 (2023).

66 Bernardi, N. F. *et al.* 'Dancing to "groovy" music enhances the experience of flow'. *Ann N Y Acad Sci* (2018).

67 Gaston, E. *et al.* 'Can flow experiences be protective against mental and cardiovascular health problems? A genetically informed prospective cohort study' (accepted).

68 Mosing, M. A. *et al.* 'Can flow experiences be protective of work-related depressive symptoms and burnout? A genetically informative approach'. *J Affect Disord* **226**, 6–11 (2018).

69 Aust, F. *et al.* 'The Relationship between Flow Experience and Burnout Symptoms: A Systematic Review'. *Int J Environ Res Public Health* **19** (2022).

70 Csíkszentmihályi, M. 'Play and Intrinsic Rewards'. *Journal of Humanistic Psychology* **15**, 41–63 (1975).

71 Deci, E. & Ryan, R. M. *Self Determination Theory* (Plenum Press, 1985).

72 McClelland, D. C. *Human Motivation* (Scott, Foresman, 1985).

73 McClelland, D. C. 'How motives, skills, and values determine what people do'. *American Psychologist* **40**, 812–25 (1985).

74 Schüler, J. *et al.* 'Implicit need for achievement moderates the relationship between competence need satisfaction and subsequent motivation'. *Journal of Research in Personality* **44**, 1–12 (2010).

75 Schüler, J. *et al.* 'Do implicit motives and basic psychological needs interact to predict well-being and flow? Testing a universal hypothesis and a matching hypothesis'. *Motivation and Emotion* **37**, 480–95 (2013).

76 Csíkszentmihályi, M. *Beyond Boredom and Anxiety* (Jossey-Bass Publishers, 1975).

77 Thissen, B. A. K. *et al.* 'At the Heart of Optimal Reading Experiences: Cardiovascular Activity and Flow Experiences in Fiction Reading'. *Reading Research Quarterly* **57**, 831–45 (2022).

78 Dewey, J. *Art as Experience* (Penguin Books Ltd, 1934).

79 Fingerhut, J. & Prinz, J. J. 'Wonder, appreciation, and the value of art'. *Progress in Brain Research* **237**, 107–28 (2018).

80 Sarasso, P. *et al.* ' "Stopping for knowledge": The sense of beauty in the perception-action cycle'. *Neurosci. Biobehav. Rev.* **118**, 723–38 (2020).

81 Kühnapfel, C. *et al.* 'How Do We Move in Front of Art? How Does This Relate to Art Experience? Linking Movement, Eye Tracking, Emotion, and Evaluations in a Gallery-Like Setting'. *Empirical Studies of the Arts* **42**, 86–146 (2024).

82 Eskine, K. J. *et al.* 'Stirring images: Fear, not happiness or arousal, makes art more sublime'. *Emotion* **12**, 1071–74 (2012).

83 Chatterjee, A. & Vartanian, O. 'Neuroaesthetics'. *Trends Cogn Sci* **18**, 370–75 (2014).

84 Schino, G. *et al.* 'Applying bodily sensation maps to art-elicited emotions: An explorative study'. *Psychology of Aesthetics, Creativity, and the Arts*, No Pagination Specified (2021).

85 Kühnapfel, C. *et al.* 'The role of the body in the experience of installation art: A case study of visitors' bodily, emotional, and transformative experiences in Tomás Saraceno's "in orbit"'. *Front Psychol* **14**, 1192689 (2023).

86 Tackett, S. *et al.* 'Transformative experiences at art museums to support flourishing in medicine'. *Med Educ Online* **28**, 2202914 (2023).

87 Aluri, J. *et al.* 'The role of arts-based curricula in professional identity formation: Results of a qualitative analysis of learner's written reflections'. *Med Educ Online* **28**, 2145105 (2023).

88 Preminger, S. 'Transformative art: Art as means for long-term neurocognitive change'. *Front Hum Neurosci* **6**, 96 (2012).

89 Plomin, R. *et al.* 'Top 10 Replicated Findings From Behavioral Genetics'. *Perspect Psychol Sci* **11**, 3–23 (2016).

90 Neumann, R. *et al.* in *The Psychology of Evaluation: Affective processes in cognition and emotion*, 371–91 (Lawrence Erlbaum Associates Publishers, 2003).

91 Gross, J. J. & Thompson, R. A. in *Handbook of emotion regulation*, 3–24 (The Guilford Press, 2007).

92 H., H. *Handbuch der physiologischen Optik*, in English Translation. Vol. 3 (1860/1962).

93 Gregory, R. L. 'Perceptions as hypotheses'. *Philosophical Transactions of the Royal Society of London*. Series B, Biological Sciences **290**, 181–97 (1980).

94 Mumford, D. 'On the computational architecture of the neocortex. II. The role of cortico-cortical loops'. *Biol Cybern* **66**, 241–51 (1992).

95 Seth, A. K. 'Interoceptive inference, emotion, and the embodied self'. *Trends Cogn Sci* **17**, 565–73 (2013).

96 Friston, K. & Kiebel, S. 'Predictive coding under the free-energy principle'. *Philosophical Transactions of the Royal Society of London*. Series B, Biological Sciences **364**, 1211–21 (2009).

97 Feldman Barrett, L. 'The theory of constructed emotion: an active inference account of interoception and categorization'. *Social Cognitive and Affective Neuroscience* **12**, 1–23 (2017).

98 Guendelman, S. *et al.* 'Mindfulness and Emotion Regulation: Insights from Neurobiological, Psychological, and Clinical Studies'. *Front Psychol* **8**, 220 (2017).

99 Okon-Singer, H. *et al.* 'The neurobiology of emotion-cognition interactions: Fundamental questions and strategies for future research'. *Front Hum Neurosci* **9**, 58 (2015).

100 Doré, B. P. & Ochsner, K. N. in *Brain Mapping: An Encyclopedia* Vol. 3 (ed. Arthur W. Toga) 53–8 (Academic Press: Elsevier, 2015).

101 Gross, J. J. & Barrett, L. F. 'Emotion generation and emotion regulation: One or two depends on your point of view'. *Emotion Review* **3**, 8–16 (2011).

102 Chenery, S. '"A visceral experience of psychosis": why one artist spent three years painting bipolar disorder'. *The Guardian* (8 June 2022).

103 Wesseldijk, L. W. *et al.* 'The effects of playing music on mental health outcomes'. *Scientific Reports* **9**, 12606 (2019).

104 Wesseldijk, L. W. *et al.* 'Gene-environment Interaction in Expertise: The importance of Childhood environment for musical achievement'. *Developmental Psychology* (2019).

105 Peña-Sarrionandia, A. *et al.* 'Integrating emotion regulation and emotional intelligence traditions: a meta-analysis'. *Front Psychol* **6**, 160 (2015).

106 Bushman, B. J. 'Does Venting Anger Feed or Extinguish the Flame? Catharsis, Rumination, Distraction, Anger, and Aggressive Responding'. *Personality and Social Psychology Bulletin* **28**, 724–31 (2002).

107 Anderson, J. C. *et al.* 'Influence of apologies and trait hostility on recovery from anger'. *J Behav Med* **29**, 347–58 (2006).

108 Wohl, M. J. *et al.* 'Why group apologies succeed and fail: Intergroup forgiveness and the role of primary and secondary emotions'. *J Pers Soc Psychol* **102**, 306–22 (2012).

109 Wohl, M. J. *et al.* 'Belief in the malleability of groups strengthens the tenuous link between a collective apology and intergroup forgiveness'. *Personality & social psychology bulletin* **41**, 714–25 (2015).

110 Philpot, C. R. & Hornsey, M. J. 'What happens when groups say sorry: The effect of intergroup apologies on their recipients'. *Personality and Social Psychology Bulletin* **34**, 474–87 (2008).

111 Hornsey, M. J. *et al.* 'Embodied remorse: Physical displays of remorse increase positive responses to public apologies, but have negligible effects on forgiveness'. *Journal of Personality and Social Psychology* **119**, 367–89 (2020).

112 Dalebroux, A. *et al.* 'Short-term mood repair through art-making: Positive emotion is more effective than venting'. *Motivation and Emotion* **32**, 288–95 (2008).

113 Rimé, B. 'Emotion Elicits the Social Sharing of Emotion: Theory and Empirical Review'. *Emotion Review* **1**, 60–85 (2009).

114 Ehlers, A. & Clark, D. M. 'Post-traumatic stress disorder: The development of effective psychological treatments'. *Nord J Psychiatry* **62** **Suppl 47**, 11–18 (2008).

115 Ehlers, A. *et al.* 'Intrusive re-experiencing in post-traumatic stress dis-order: Phenomenology, theory, and therapy'. *Memory* **12**, 403–15 (2004).

116 Ehlers, A. & Clark, D. M. 'A cognitive model of posttraumatic stress disorder'. *Behav Res Ther* **38**, 319–45 (2000).

117 Pennebaker, J. W. & Beall, S. K. 'Confronting a traumatic event: toward an understanding of inhibition and disease'. *Journal of Abnormal Psychology* **95**, 274–81 (1986).

118 Pennebaker, J. W. & Chew, C. H. 'Behavioral inhibition and electro-dermal activity during deception'. *Journal of Personality and Social Psychology* **49**, 1427–33 (1985).

119 Bedard-Gilligan, M. *et al.* 'Individual differences in trauma dis-closure'. *J Behav Ther Exp Psychiatry* **43**, 716–23 (2012).

120 Pennebaker, J. W. & O'Heeron, R. C. 'Confiding in others and ill-ness rate among spouses of suicide and accidental-death victims'. *Journal of abnormal psychology* **93**, 473–76 (1984).

121 Cooper, C. L. & Faragher, E. B. 'Psychosocial stress and breast cancer: the inter-relationship between stress events, coping strat-egies and personality'. *Psychol Med* **23**, 653–62 (1993).

122 Pennebaker, J. W. 'Putting stress into words: Health, linguistic, and therapeutic implications'. *Behav Res Ther* **31**, 539–48 (1993).

123 Pennebaker, J. W. 'Traumatic experience and psychosomatic disease: Exploring the roles of behavioural inhibition, obsession, and confid-ing'. *Canadian Psychology/Psychologie canadienne* **26**, 82–95 (1985).

124 Pennebaker, J. W. *et al.* 'The psychophysiology of confession: link-ing inhibitory and psychosomatic processes'. *J Pers Soc Psychol* **52**, 781–93 (1987).

125 Sutton, R. I. *The No Asshole Rule: Building a Civilized Workplace and Surviving One that Isn't* (Business Plus, 2010).

126 Sutton, R. I. 'Why I wrote the No Asshole Rule'. *Harvard Business Review* (2007).

127 Coberly-Holdt, P. & Braun, C. in *Conference proceedings of the adult higher education alliance 35th annual conference* (eds C. Boden-McGill, E. Oluwakemi, B. Flynn, & F. Prasun) (Adult Higher Education Alliance AHEA.ORG).

128 Farrell, L. U. 'Workplace bullying's high cost: $180M in lost time, productivity'. *Orlando Business Journal, March 18* (2002).

129 Heames, J. & Harvey, M. 'Workplace bullying: a cross-level assessment'. *Management Decision* **44**, 1214–30 (2006).

130 Harvey, M. G. *et al.* 'Bullying: From the Playground to the Boardroom'. *Journal of Leadership & Organizational Studies* **12**, 1–11 (2006).

131 Crookston, R. K. *Working with Problem Faculty: A six-step guide for department chairs* (Jossey-Bass, 2012).

132 Moss, S. 'Why some bosses bully their best employees'. *Harvard Business Review* (2016).

133 Mallick, M. 'How to Intervene When a Manager Is Gaslighting Their Employees'. *Harvard Business Review* (2021).

134 Laderer, A. 'Gaslighting explained and 17 things that gaslighters say to manipulate you'. *Business Insider Reviews* (2023).

135 Carle, M. 'Six signs you're the bully at work'. *Harvard Business Review* (2023).

136 Rakovec-Felser, Z. 'Domestic Violence and Abuse in Intimate Relationship from Public Health Perspective'. *Health Psychol Res* **2**, 1821 (2014).

137 van der Kolk, B. A. 'The compulsion to repeat the trauma. Reenactment, revictimization, and masochism'. *Psychiatr Clin North Am* **12**, 389–411 (1989).

138 Adams, T. 'Their trauma, our entertainment: what happens to documentary subjects when the cameras leave?' *The Guardian* (12 February 2023).

139 Meyer, J. 'I don't think that comedy is a safe space'. *MYP Magazine* (15 September 2021).

7. Mind Liberators – Six strategies to unwind your mind

1 Gross, J. J. & Feldman Barrett, L. 'Emotion Generation and Emotion Regulation: One or Two Depends on Your Point of View'. *Emotion Review* **3**, 8–16 (2011).

2 Fancourt, D. *et al.* 'The relationship between demographics, behavioral and experiential engagement factors, and the use of artistic creative activities to regulate emotions'. *Psychology of Aesthetics, Creativity, and the Arts*, No Pagination Specified (2020).

3 Gross, J. J. 'Emotion regulation: affective, cognitive, and social consequences'. *Psychophysiology* **39**, 281–91 (2002).

4 Lazarus, R. S. & Folkman, S. *Stress, Appraisal and Coping* (Springer, 1984).

5 Rothbaum, F. *et al.* 'Changing the world and changing the self: A two-process model of perceived control'. *Journal of Personality and Social Psychology* **42**, 5–37 (1982).

6 Proust, M. *In Search of Lost Time* (Modern Library, 1927/2003).

7 Rugg, M. D. *et al.* 'Brain regions supporting intentional and incidental memory: A PET study'. *Neuroreport* **8**, 1283–87 (1997).

8 Branigan, B. & Tadi, P. 'Physiology, Olfactory'. *StatPearls [Internet]* (StatPearls Publishing, updated 1 May 2023).

9 El Haj, M. *et al.* 'From Nose to Memory: The Involuntary Nature of Odor-evoked Autobiographical Memories in Alzheimer's Disease'. *Chem Senses* **43**, 27–34 (2017).

10 El Haj, M. *et al.* 'The involuntary nature of music-evoked autobiographical memories in Alzheimer's disease'. *Conscious Cogn* **21**, 238–46 (2012).

11 Leary, M. R. in *Shyness: Perspectives on Research and Treatment* (eds Warren H. Jones, Jonathan M. Cheek, & Stephen R. Briggs) 27–38 (Springer US, 1986).

12 Weber, R. *et al.* 'Soap Opera Exposure and Enjoyment: A Longitudinal Test of Disposition Theory'. *Media Psychology* **11**, 462–87 (2008).

13 Chang, Y.-J. & Peng, C.-Y. 'Exploring experiences of binge-watching and perceived addictiveness among binge-watchers: A qualitative study'. *BMC Public Health* **22**, 2285 (2022).

14 Griffiths, M. 'A "components" model of addiction within a biopsychosocial framework'. *Journal of Substance Use* **10**, 191–7 (2005).

15 Anschutz, D. *et al.* 'Watching your weight? The relations between watching soaps and music television and body dissatisfaction and restrained eating in young girls'. *Psychol Health* **24**, 1035–50 (2009).

16 Ahmed, A. 'New Era of TV-Watching Behavior: Binge Watching and its Psychological Effects'. *Media Watch* **8**, 192–207 (2017).

17 Sun, J. J. & Chang, Y. J. 'Associations of Problematic Binge-Watching with Depression, Social Interaction Anxiety, and Loneliness'. *Int J Environ Res Public Health* **18** (2021).

18 de Wit, L. *et al.* 'Are sedentary television watching and computer use behaviors associated with anxiety and depressive disorders?' *Psychiatry research* **186**, 239–43 (2011).

19 Boudali, M. *et al.* 'Depression and anxiety among Tunisian medical students "binge viewers"'. *European Psychiatry* **41**, S675–6 (2017).

20 Sung, Y. H., Kang, E. Y. & Lee, W. N. 'A Bad Habit for Your Health? An exploration of psychological factors for binge watching behavior'. *Semantic Scholar* (21 May 2015).

21 Nix, G. *et al.* 'Reducing depressive affect through external focus of attention'. *Journal of Social and Clinical Psychology* **14**, 36–52 (1995).

22 Doré, B. P. & Ochsner, K. N. in *Brain Mapping: An Encyclopedia* Vol. 3 (ed. Arthur W. Toga) 53–8 (Academic Press: Elsevier, 2015).

23 O'Hare, C. *et al.* 'Childhood trauma and lifetime syncope burden among older adults'. *Journal of psychosomatic research* **97**, 63–9 (2017).

24 Samanta, S. *et al.* 'Dark chocolate: An overview of its biological activity, processing, and fortification approaches'. *Curr Res Food Sci* **5**, 1916–43 (2022).

25 Shin, J. H. *et al.* 'Consumption of 85% cocoa dark chocolate improves mood in association with gut microbial changes in healthy adults: A randomized controlled trial'. *J Nutr Biochem* **99**, 108854 (2022).

26 Berends, L. M. *et al.* 'Flavan-3-ols, theobromine, and the effects of cocoa and chocolate on cardiometabolic risk factors'. *Curr Opin Lipidol* **26**, 10–19 (2015).

27 Hooper, L. *et al.* 'Effects of chocolate, cocoa, and flavan-3-ols on cardiovascular health: A systematic review and meta-analysis of randomized trials'. *Am J Clin Nutr* **95**, 740–51 (2012).

28 Boden, J. M. & Baumeister, R. F. 'Repressive coping: distraction using pleasant thoughts and memories'. *J Pers Soc Psychol* **73**, 45–62 (1997).

29 Baird, B. *et al.* 'Inspired by distraction: Mind wandering facilitates creative incubation'. *Psychol Sci* **23**, 1117–22 (2012).

30 Remoli, T. C. & Santos, F. H. 'Interactions between working memory and creativity: A systematic review'. *Psicologia em Estudo* **22**, 53–65 (2017).

31 Baas, M. *et al.* 'A meta-analysis of 25 years of mood-creativity research: Hedonic tone, activation, or regulatory focus?' *Psychol Bull* **134**, 779–806 (2008).

32 De Dreu, C. K. *et al.* 'Hedonic tone and activation level in the mood-creativity link: toward a dual pathway'. *Journal of Personality and Social Psychology* **94** (2008).

33 Boot, N. *et al.* 'Creative cognition and dopaminergic modulation of fronto-striatal networks: Integrative review and research agenda'. *Neuroscience & Biobehavioral Reviews* **78**, 13–23 (2017).

34 Ritter, S. M. & Ferguson, S. 'Happy creativity: Listening to happy music facilitates divergent thinking'. *PLoS One* **12**, e0182210 (2017).

35 Yamada, Y. & Nagai, M. 'Positive mood enhances divergent but not convergent thinking'. *Japanese Psychological Research* **57**, 281–87 (2015).

36 Smallwood, J. *et al.* 'When attention matters: The curious incident of the wandering mind'. *Memory & Cognition* **36**, 1144–50 (2008).

37 Csíkszentmihályi, M. & Sawyer, K. in *The Systems Model of Creativity: The Collected Works of Mihaly Csíkszentmihályi* (ed. Mihaly Csíkszentmihályi) 73–98 (Springer Netherlands, 2014).

38 Segal, E. 'Incubation in Insight Problem Solving'. *Creativity Research Journal* **16**, 141–8 (2004).

39 Mar, R. A. & Oatley, K. 'The Function of Fiction is the Abstraction and Simulation of Social Experience'. *Perspect Psychol Sci* **3**, 173–92 (2008).

40 Oatley, K. 'Fiction: Simulation of Social Worlds'. *Trends Cogn Sci* **20**, 618–28 (2016).

41 Helliwell, J. F. *et al.* *World Happiness Report 2022* (Sustainable Development Solutions Network, 2022).

42 Saner, E. 'Forget regret! How to have a happy life – according to the world's leading expert' in *The Guardian* (6 February 2023).

43 Sio, U. N. & Ormerod, T. C. 'Does incubation enhance problem solving? A meta-analytic review'. *Psychol Bull* **135**, 94–120 (2009).

44 John, O. P. & Gross, J. J. 'Healthy and unhealthy emotion regulation: Personality processes, individual differences, and life span development'. *J Pers* **72**, 1301–33 (2004).

45 Kalisch, R. 'The functional neuroanatomy of reappraisal: Time matters'. *Neurosci Biobehav Rev* **33**, 1215–26 (2009).

46 Zaki, J. *et al.* 'Overlapping activity in anterior insula during interoception and emotional experience'. *Neuroimage* **62**, 493–99 (2012).

47 Opitz, P. C. *et al.* 'Prefrontal mediation of age differences in cognitive reappraisal'. *Neurobiol Aging* **33**, 645–55 (2012).

48 Speer, M. E. *et al.* 'Finding positive meaning in memories of negative events adaptively updates memory'. *Nat Commun* **12**, 6601 (2021).

49 Buhle, J. T. *et al.* 'Cognitive reappraisal of emotion: A meta-analysis of human neuroimaging studies'. *Cereb Cortex* **24**, 2981–90 (2014).

50 Shiota, M. N. & Levenson, R. W. 'Turn down the volume or change the channel? Emotional effects of detached versus positive reappraisal'. *J Pers Soc Psychol* **103**, 416–29 (2012).

51 McRae, K. *et al.* 'Gender Differences in Emotion Regulation: An fMRI Study of Cognitive Reappraisal'. *Group Process Intergroup Relat* **11**, 143–62 (2008).

52 Goldin, P. R. *et al.* 'The neural bases of emotion regulation: reappraisal and suppression of negative emotion'. *Biological Psychiatry* **63**, 577–86 (2008).

53 Shiota, M. N. & Levenson, R. W. 'Effects of aging on experimentally instructed detached reappraisal, positive reappraisal, and emotional behavior suppression'. *Psychol Aging* **24**, 890–900 (2009).

54 Denny, B. T. & Ochsner, K. N. 'Behavioral effects of longitudinal training in cognitive reappraisal'. *Emotion* **14**, 425–33 (2014).

55 Dörfel, D. *et al.* 'Common and differential neural networks of emotion regulation by Detachment, Reinterpretation, Distraction, and Expressive Suppression: A comparative fMRI investigation'. *Neuroimage* **101**, 298–309 (2014).

56 Folkman, S. 'Positive psychological states and coping with severe stress'. *Soc Sci Med* **45**, 1207–21 (1997).

57 Moskowitz, J. T. *et al.* 'What works in coping with HIV? A meta-analysis with implications for coping with serious illness'. *Psychological Bulletin* **135**, 121–41 (2009).

58 Moskowitz, J. T. *et al.* 'Positive affect uniquely predicts lower risk of mortality in people with diabetes'. *Health Psychol* **27**, S73–82 (2008).

59 Shiota, M. N. 'Silver linings and candles in the dark: Differences among positive coping strategies in predicting subjective well-being'. *Emotion* **6**, 335–9 (2006).

60 Bhanji, J. P. & Delgado, M. R. 'Perceived control influences neural responses to setbacks and promotes persistence'. *Neuron* **83**, 1369–75 (2014).

61 Bhanji, J. P. *et al.* 'Perceived control alters the effect of acute stress on persistence'. *Journal of Experimental Psychology. General* **145**, 356–65 (2016).

62 Whalen, Paul J. & Kelley, William M. 'To Apply Yourself Is Human, to Reapply Divine'. *Neuron* **83**, 1227–8 (2014).

63 Tugade, M. M. & Fredrickson, B. L. 'Resilient individuals use positive emotions to bounce back from negative emotional experiences'. *J Pers Soc Psychol* **86**, 320–33 (2004).

64 Heyes, C. 'Evolution, development and intentional control of imitation'. *Philosophical Transactions of the Royal Society of London. Series B, Biological Sciences* **364**, 2293–8 (2009).

65 Heyes, C. 'Grist and mills: on the cultural origins of cultural learning'. *Philosophical Transactions of the Royal Society of London. Series B, Biological Sciences* **367**, 2181–91 (2012).

66 Brandl, E. *et al.* 'The cultural evolution of teaching'. *Evolutionary Human Sciences* **5**, e14 (2023).

67 Birch, J. & Heyes, C. 'The cultural evolution of cultural evolution'. *Philosophical Transactions of the Royal Society of London. Series B, Biological Sciences* **376**, 20200051 (2021).

68 Leder, H. & Pelowski, M. 'Metaphors or mechanism? Predictive coding and a (brief) history of empirical study of the arts'. *Philosophical transactions of the Royal Society of London. Series B, Biological Sciences* **379**, 20220427 (2024).

69 Niedenthal, P. M. *et al.* 'Embodiment in attitudes, social perception, and emotion'. *Pers Soc Psychol Rev* **9**, 184–211 (2005).

70 Wellman, H. M. *et al.* 'Meta-analysis of theory-of-mind development: the truth about false belief'. *Child Dev* **72**, 655–84 (2001).

71 Garvey, C. J. & Berndt, R. S. 'The Organization of Pretend Play'. (National Institute of Mental Health, Bethesda, MD, 1975).

72 Seitz, J. A. 'Metaphor, symbolic play, and logical thought in early childhood'. *Genet Soc Gen Psychol Monogr* **123**, 373–91 (1997).

73 Vallotton, C. D. & Ayoub, C. C. 'Symbols Build Communication and Thought: The Role of Gestures and Words in the Development

of Engagement Skills and Social-Emotional Concepts during Toddlerhood'. *Soc Dev* **19**, 601–26 (2010).

74 Malik F. 'Cognitive Development'. *StatPearls [Internet]* (StatPearls Publishing, 2023).

75 Fein, G. G. 'Pretend play in childhood: An integrative review'. *Child Development* **52**, 1095–118 (1981).

76 Garvey, C. *Play*. Vol. 27 (Harvard University Press, 1990).

77 Haddon, M. *The Curious Incident of the Dog in the Night-time* (Vintage, 2004).

78 Barret, S. 'I have autism and the lack of authentic autistic voices in books angers me'.

The Guardian (3 April 2016).

79 Aldao, A. *et al.* 'Emotion-regulation strategies across psychopathology: A meta-analytic review'. *Clinical psychology review* **30**, 217–37 (2010).

80 Dalebroux, A. *et al.* 'Short-term mood repair through art-making: Positive emotion is more effective than venting'. *Motivation and Emotion* **32**, 288–95 (2008).

81 McRae, K. *et al.* 'Bottom-up and top-down emotion generation: Implications for emotion regulation'. *Social Cognitive and Affective Neuroscience* **7**, 253–62 (2012).

82 Kashdan, T. B. *et al.* 'A contextual approach to experiential avoidance and social anxiety: Evidence from an experimental interaction and daily interactions of people with social anxiety disorder'. *Emotion* **14**, 769–81 (2014).

83 Goldin, P. R. *et al.* in *Social Anxiety* (3rd edn) (eds Stefan G. Hofmann & Patricia M. DiBartolo) 511–29 (Academic Press, 2014).

84 Schmidt, E.-M. *et al.* 'Mood induction through imitation of full-body movements with different affective intentions'. *British Journal of Psychology* (2023).

85 Ehlers, A. 'Understanding and Treating Unwanted Trauma Memories in Posttraumatic Stress Disorder'. *Z Psychol* **218**, 141–5 (2010).

86 Ochsner, K. N. *et al.* 'Rethinking feelings: An fMRI study of the cognitive regulation of emotion'. *J Cogn Neurosci* **14**, 1215–29 (2002).

87 Ochsner, K. N. & Gross, J. J. 'The cognitive control of emotion'. *Trends Cogn Sci* **9**, 242–49 (2005).

88 Banks, S. J. *et al.* 'Amygdala-frontal connectivity during emotion regulation'. *Social cognitive and affective neuroscience* **2**, 303–12 (2007).

89 Wager, T. D. *et al.* 'Prefrontal-subcortical pathways mediating successful emotion regulation'. *Neuron* **59**, 1037–50 (2008).

90 Gross, J. J. & Levenson, R. W. 'Emotional suppression: physiology, self-report, and expressive behavior'. *J Pers Soc Psychol* **64**, 970–86 (1993).

91 Lévesque, J. *et al.* 'Neural circuitry underlying voluntary suppression of sadness'. *Biological psychiatry* **53**, 502–10 (2003).

92 Beck, J. S. *Cognitive behavior therapy: Basics and beyond* (2nd edn) (The Guilford Press, 2011).

93 Sarracino, D. *et al.* 'When REBT Goes Difficult: Applying ABC-DEF to Personality Disorders'. *Journal of Rational-Emotive & Cognitive-Behavior Therapy* **35**, 278–95 (2017).

94 Clark, D. A. *et al.* *Scientific Foundations of Cognitive Ttheory and Therapy of Depression* (Wiley, 1999).

95 Ellis, A. *Overcoming Resistance* (2nd edn) (Springer Publication, 2002).

96 Beck, A. T. *Cognitive Therapy and the Emotional Disorders* (International Universities Press, 1976).

97 Hayes, S. C. *et al.* 'Open, aware, and active: Contextual approaches as an emerging trend in the behavioral and cognitive therapies'. *Annu Rev Clin Psychol* **7**, 141–68 (2011).

98 DiGiuseppe, R. *et al.* *A Practitioner's Guide to Rational Emotive Behaviour Therapy* (Oxford University Press, 2014).

99 Will, G.-J. *et al.* 'Neurocomputational mechanisms underpinning aberrant social learning in young adults with low self-esteem'. *Translational Psychiatry* **10**, 96 (2020).

100 Sträter, T. *Du kannst alles lassen, du musst es nur wollen: Neue Storys vom Meister der Sprachkomik. [Engl.: You Can Stop Doing Anything, You Just Need to Want To]* (Ullstein, 2022).

101 Southward, M. W. *et al.* 'Flexible, yet firm: A model of healthy emotion regulation'. *J Soc Clin Psychol* **37**, 231–51 (2018).

102 Webb, T. L. *et al.* 'Dealing with feeling: A meta-analysis of the effectiveness of strategies derived from the process model of emotion regulation'. *Psychol Bull* **138**, 775–808 (2012).

8. Process Over Progress – How we learn a new skill

1 Clar, J. *Atomic Habits: An Easy & Proven Way to Build Good Habits & Break Old Ones* (Random House Business, 2018).

2 Carlson, N. R. *Physiology of Behavior* (8th edn) (Pearson, 2004).

3 Hebb, D. *The Organization of Behaviour* (Wiley-Interscience, 1949).

4 Ding, X. & Rasband, M. N. 'Dynorphin, won't you myelinate my neighbor?' *Neuron* **109**, 3537–9 (2021).

5 Osso, L. A. *et al.* 'Experience-dependent myelination following stress is mediated by the neuropeptide dynorphin'. *Neuron* **109**, 3619–32. e3615 (2021).

6 Saab, A. S. *et al.* 'The role of myelin and oligodendrocytes in axonal energy metabolism'. *Curr Opin Neurobiol* **23**, 1065–72 (2013).

7 Michalski, J. P. & Kothary, R. 'Oligodendrocytes in a Nutshell'. *Front Cell Neurosci* **9**, 340 (2015).

8 Xin, W. & Chan, J. R. 'Myelin plasticity: Sculpting circuits in learning and memory'. *Nat Rev Neurosci* **21**, 682–94 (2020).

9 Bonetto, G. *et al.* 'Unraveling Myelin Plasticity'. *Front Cell Neurosci* **14**, 156 (2020).

10 Berke, J. D. 'What does dopamine mean?' *Nat Neurosci* **21**, 787–93 (2018).

11 Hamid, A. A. *et al.* 'Mesolimbic dopamine signals the value of work'. *Nat Neurosci* **19**, 117–26 (2016).

12 Harley, C. W. 'Norepinephrine and dopamine as learning signals'. *Neural Plast* **11**, 191–204 (2004).

13 Heyes, C. 'What's social about social learning?' *J Comp Psychol* **126**, 193–202 (2012).

14 Heyes, C. 'Evolution, development and intentional control of imitation'. *Philosophical Transactions of the Royal Society of London. Series B, Biological Sciences* **364**, 2293–8 (2009).

15 Heyes, C. M. 'Social learning in animals: categories and mechanisms'. *Biol Rev Camb Philos Soc* **69**, 207–31 (1994).

16 Mackenzie, N. 'From drawing to writing: What happens when you shift teaching priorities in the first six months of school?' *The Australian Journal of Language and Literacy* **34**, 322–40 (2011).

17 Burkitt, E. *et al.* 'The Attitudes and Practices that Shape Children's Drawing Experience at Home and at School'. *International Journal of Art & Design Education* **29**, 257–70 (2010).

18 Oskala, A. *et al.* 'Encourage children today to build audiences for tomorrow – Evidence from the taking part survey'. *Arts Council England* (2009).

19 Jolley, R. & Zhang, Z. 'How Drawing is Taught in Chinese Infant Schools'. *International Journal of Art & Design Education* **31**, 30–43 (2012).

20 Jindal-Snape, D. *et al.* 'Impact of arts participation on children's achievement: A systematic literature review'. *Thinking Skills and Creativity* (2018).

21 Iordanou, C. *et al.* 'Drawing and Memory: What is the Content of Children's Drawings and How Does it Differ From Their Verbal Reports?' *Empirical Studies of the Arts* **40**, 245–58 (2022).

22 Smith, C. P. *et al.* 'Learning angles through movement: Critical actions for developing understanding in an embodied activity'. *The Journal of Mathematical Behavior* **36**, 95–108 (2014).

23 McCluskey, C. *et al.* 'The role of movement in young children's spatial experiences: A review of early childhood mathematics education research'. *Mathematics Education Research Journal* **35**, 287–315 (2023).

24 Deans, J. & Cohrssen, C. 'Young Children Dancing Mathematical Thinking'. *Australasian Journal of Early Childhood* **40**, 61–7 (2015).

25 Scheiter, K. *et al.* 'Why Sketching May Aid Learning From Science Texts: Contrasting Sketching With Written Explanations'. *Top Cogn Sci* **9**, 866–82 (2017).

26 Kastner, L. *et al.* 'Designing Visual-Arts Education Programs for Transfer Effects: Development and Experimental Evaluation of (Digital) Drawing Courses in the Art Museum Designed to Promote Adolescents' Socio-Emotional Skills'. *Front Psychol* **11**, 603984 (2020).

27 Wesson, M. & Salmon, K. 'Drawing and showing: helping children to report emotionally laden events'. *Applied Cognitive Psychology* **15**, 301–19 (2001).

28 Gross, J. & Hayne, H. 'Drawing facilitates children's verbal reports of emotionally laden events'. *Journal of Experimental Psychology: Applied* **4**, 163–79 (1998).

29 Gross, J. & Hayne, H. 'Drawing facilitates children's verbal reports after long delays'. *Journal of Experimental Psychology: Applied* **5**, 265–83 (1999).

30 Købke, K. *https://kasperkobke.dk/om-kobke/* (2023).

31 Lupien, S. J. *et al.* 'The effects of chronic stress on the human brain: From neurotoxicity, to vulnerability, to opportunity'. *Front Neuroendocrinol* **49**, 91–105 (2018).

32 Mendelsohn, A. I. 'Creatures of Habit: The Neuroscience of Habit and Purposeful Behavior'. *Biological Psychiatry* **85**, e49–51 (2019).

33 Yin, H. H. 'From actions to habits: Neuroadaptations leading to dependence'. *Alcohol Res Health* **31**, 340–44 (2008).

34 Gardner, B. 'A review and analysis of the use of "habit" in understanding, predicting and influencing health-related behaviour'. *Health Psychol Rev* **9**, 277–95 (2015).

35 Wolpert, D. M. *et al.* 'Perspectives and problems in motor learning'. *Trends Cogn Sci* **5**, 487–94 (2001).

36 Chan, T.-W. *et al.* 'Interest-driven creator theory: Towards a theory of learning design for Asia in the twenty-first century'. *Journal of Computers in Education* **5**, 435–61 (2018).

37 Chen, W. *et al.* 'IDC theory: Habit and the habit loop'. *Research and Practice in Technology Enhanced Learning* **15**, 10 (2020).

38 Yamaguchi, M. & Logan, G. D. 'Pushing typists back on the learning curve: Revealing chunking in skilled typewriting'. *Journal of Experimental Psychology. Human perception and performance* **40**, 592–612 (2014).

39 Clegg, B. A. *et al.* 'Sequence learning'. *Trends Cogn Sci* **2**, 275–81 (1998).

40 Luft, A. R. & Buitrago, M. M. 'Stages of motor skill learning'. *Mol Neurobiol* **32**, 205–16 (2005).

41 Ungerleider, L. G. *et al.* 'Imaging brain plasticity during motor skill learning'. *Neurobiol Learn Mem* **78**, 553–64 (2002).

42 Wenger, E. *et al.* 'Expansion and Renormalization of Human Brain Structure During Skill Acquisition'. *Trends Cogn Sci* **21**, 930–9 (2017).

43 Sakai, K. *et al.* 'Chunking during human visuomotor sequence learning'. *Exp Brain Res* **152**, 229–42 (2003).

44 Bera, K. *et al.* 'Motor Chunking in Internally Guided Sequencing'. *Brain Sci* **11** (2021).

45 Dayan, E. & Cohen, L. G. 'Neuroplasticity subserving motor skill learning'. *Neuron* **72**, 443–44 (2011).

46 Riley, J. *et al*. 'The Benefits of Knitting for Personal and Social Well-being in Adulthood: Findings from an International Survey'. *British Journal of Occupational Therapy* **76** (2013).

47 Lamont, A. & Ranaweera, N. A. 'Knit One, Play One: Comparing the Effects of Amateur Knitting and Amateur Music Participation on Happiness and Wellbeing'. *Applied Research in Quality of Life* (2019).

48 Fabrigoule, C. *et al*. 'Social and Leisure Activities and Risk of Dementia: A Prospective Longitudinal Study'. *Journal of the Amercian Geriatrical Society* (1995).

49 Geda, Y. E. *et al*. 'Engaging in Cognitive Activities, Aging, and Mild Cognitive Impairment: A Population-Based Study'. *Journal of Neuropsychiatry and Clinhical Neuroscience* (2011).

50 Fodor, J. A. *The Language of Thought* (Harvard University Press, 1975).

51 Pylyshyn, Z. W. *Computation and Cognition* (MIT Press, 1984).

52 Barsalou, L. W. 'Grounded cognition'. *Annu Rev Psychol* **59**, 617–45 (2008).

53 Gibson, J. J. *The Senses Considered as Perceptual Systems* (Houghton Mifflin, 1966).

54 Kiefer, M. & Pulvermüller, F. 'Conceptual representations in mind and brain: Theoretical developments, current evidence and future directions'. *Cortex: a journal devoted to the study of the nervous system and behavior* **48**, 805–25 (2012).

55 Meteyard, L. *et al*. 'Coming of age: A review of embodiment and the neuroscience of semantics'. *Cortex: a journal devoted to the study of the nervous system and behavior* **48**, 788–804 (2012).

56 Koch, S. C. & Fuchs, T. 'Embodied arts therapies'. *The Arts in Psychotherapy* **38**, 276–80 (2011).

57 Koch, S. C. 'Arts and health: Active factors and a theory framework of embodied aesthetics'. *The Arts in Psychotherapy* **54**, 85–91 (2017).

58 Koch, S. C. *et al*. 'Effects of Dance Movement Therapy and Dance on Health-Related Psychological Outcomes. A Meta-Analysis Update'. *Frontiers in Psychology* **10**, 1806 (2019).

59 Niedenthal, P. M. *et al*. 'Embodiment in attitudes, social perception, and emotion'. *Pers Soc Psychol Rev* **9**, 184–211 (2005).

60 Rosen, D. S. *et al.* 'Anodal tDCS to Right Dorsolateral Prefrontal Cortex Facilitates Performance for Novice Jazz Improvisers but Hinders Experts'. *Front Hum Neurosci* **10**, 579 (2016).

61 Pinho, A. L. *et al.* 'Connecting to create: Expertise in musical improvisation is associated with increased functional connectivity between premotor and prefrontal areas'. *The Journal of Neuroscience: The official journal of the Society for Neuroscience* **34**, 6156–63 (2014).

62 Vergara, V. M. *et al.* 'Functional network connectivity during jazz improvisation'. *Sci Rep* **11**, 19036 (2021).

63 Beaty, R. E. 'The neuroscience of musical improvisation'. *Neuroscience & Biobehavioral Reviews* **51**, 108–17 (2015).

64 Wasielewski, H. 'Imitation is necessary for cumulative cultural evolution in an unfamiliar, opaque task'. *Hum Nat* **25**, 161–79 (2014).

65 Tomasello, M. *et al.* 'Cultural learning'. *Behavioral and Brain Sciences* **16**, 495–552 (1993).

66 Kirschner, S. & Tomasello, M. 'Joint drumming: Social context facilitates synchronization in preschool children'. *Journal of Experimental Child Psychology* **102**, 299–314 (2009).

67 Tomasello, M. 'The ontogeny of cultural learning'. *Current Opinion in Psychology* **8**, 1–4 (2016).

68 Kirschner, S. & Tomasello, M. 'Joint music making promotes prosocial behavior in 4-year-old children'. *Evolution and Human Behavior* **31**, 354–64 (2010).

69 Moll, H. & Tomasello, M. 'Cooperation and human cognition: the Vygotskian intelligence hypothesis'. *Philosophical Transactions of the Royal Society: B-Biological Sciences* **362**, 639–48 (2007).

70 Tomasello, M. *The Cultural Origins of Human Cognition* (Harvard University Press, 1999).

71 Snapes, L. 'The greatest pop music dance crazes – ranked!' *The Guardian* (4 January 2019).

72 Manioudaki, A. 'Vincent van Gogh Copying Other Artists'. *Daily Art* (11 July 2023).

73 'The value of Picasso's napkin'. *Good2Great: Realising the dreams of business owners* (https://good-2-great.co.uk/blog/the-value-of-picassos-napkin/).

74 Schlegel, A. *et al.* 'The artist emerges: Visual art learning alters neural structure and function'. *Neuroimage* **105**, 440–51 (2015).

75 Doyon, J. & Benali, H. 'Reorganization and plasticity in the adult brain during learning of motor skills'. *Curr Opin Neurobiol* **15**, 161–7 (2005).

76 Csíkszentmihályi, M. & Sawyer, K. in *The Systems Model of Creativity: The Collected Works of Mihaly Csíkszentmihályi* (ed. Mihaly Csíkszentmihályi) 73–98 (Springer Netherlands, 2014).

77 Getzels, U. J. W. & Csíkszentmihályi, M. *The Creative Vision: A longitudinal study of problem finding in art* (Wiley, 1976).

78 Pickersgill, J. W. *et al.* 'The Combined Influences of Exercise, Diet and Sleep on Neuroplasticity'. *Frontiers in Psychology* **13** (2022).

79 Siengsukon, C. F. & Boyd, L. A. 'Does sleep promote motor learning? Implications for physical rehabilitation'. *Phys Ther* **89**, 370–83 (2009).

80 Mindell, J. A. *et al.* 'Give children and adolescents the gift of a good night's sleep: A call to action'. *Sleep Medicine* **12**, 203–4 (2011).

81 Drago, V. *et al.* 'Cyclic alternating pattern in sleep and its relationship to creativity'. *Sleep Med* **12**, 361–66 (2011).

82 Walsh, V. 'Neuroscience and Creativity'. (TEDxAldeburgh, 2011).

83 Karin, J. *et al.* in *Dancer Wellness* (eds V. Wilmerding & D. Krasnow) (Human Kinetics, 2016).

84 Karin, J. 'Recontextualizing Dance Skills: Overcoming Impediments to Motor Learning and Expressivity in Ballet Dancers'. *Frontiers in Psychology* (2016).

85 Decety, J. & Jeannerod, M. 'Mentally simulated movements in virtual reality: Does Fitt's law hold in motor imagery?' *Behavioural brain research* **72**, 127–34 (1995).

86 Moran, A. *et al.* 'Re-imagining motor imagery: Building bridges between cognitive neuroscience and sport psychology'. *Br J Psychol* **103**, 224–47 (2012).

87 Smith, D. *et al.* 'It's All in the Mind: PETTLEP-Based Imagery and Sports Performance'. *Journal of Applied Sport Psychology* **19**, 80–92 (2007).

88 Feltz, D. L. & Landers, D. M. 'The Effects of Mental Practice on Motor Skill Learning and Performance: A Meta-analysis'. *Journal of Sport Psychology* **5**, 25–57 (1983).

89 Driskell, J. E. *et al.* 'Does mental practice enhance performance?' *Journal of Applied Psychology* **79**, 481–92 (1994).

90 Novembre, G. & Keller, P. E. 'A conceptual review on action-perception coupling in the musicians' brain: What is it good for?' *Front Hum Neurosci* **8**, 603 (2014).

91 Sevdalis, V. & Keller, P. E. 'Perceiving performer identity and intended expression intensity in point-light displays of dance'. *Psychol Res* **75**, 423–34 (2011).

92 Sevdalis, V. & Keller, P. E. 'Captured by motion: Dance, action understanding, and social cognition'. *Brain Cogn* **77**, 231–36 (2011).

93 Pecenka, N., & Keller, P. E. 'The role of temporal prediction abilities in interpersonal sensorimotor synchronization'. *Experimental Brain Research* **211**, 505–15 (2011).

94 Shin, Y. K. *et al.* 'A review of contemporary ideomotor theory'. *Psychol Bull* **136**, 943–74 (2010).

95 Stock, A. & Stock, C. 'A short history of ideo-motor action'. *Psychol Res* **68**, 176–88 (2004).

96 Prinz, W. in *Relationships Between Perception and Action: Current Approaches* (eds Odmar Neumann & Wolfgang Prinz) 167–201 (Springer Berlin Heidelberg, 1990).

97 Lahav, A. *et al.* 'Action representation of sound: Audiomotor recognition network while listening to newly acquired actions'. *The Journal of Neuroscience: The official journal of the Society for Neuroscience* **27**, 308–14 (2007).

98 de Manzano, Ö. *et al.* 'Action-Perception Coupling and Near Transfer: Listening to Melodies after Piano Practice Triggers Sequence-Specific Representations in the Auditory-Motor Network'. *Cereb Cortex* **30**, 5193–203 (2020).

99 Jarvis, E. D. 'Evolution of vocal learning and spoken language'. *Science* **366**, 50–4 (2019).

100 Patel, A. D. 'Language, music, syntax and the brain'. *Nat Neurosci* **6**, 674–81 (2003).

101 Patel, A. D. *et al.* 'Experimental evidence for synchronization to a musical beat in a nonhuman animal'. *Curr Biol* **19**, 827–30 (2009).

102 Audet, J.-N. *et al.* 'Songbird species that display more-complex vocal learning are better problem-solvers and have larger brains'. *Science* **381**, 1170–5 (2023).

103 Kleber, B. *et al.* 'The brain of opera singers: Experience-dependent changes in functional activation'. *Cereb Cortex* **20**, 1144–52 (2010).

104 Gaser, C. & Schlaug, G. 'Brain structures differ between musicians and non-musicians'. *The Journal of Neuroscience: the official journal of the Society for Neuroscience* **23**, 9240–5 (2003).

105 Mang, E. 'Intermediate Vocalizations: An Investigation of the Boundary between Speech and Songs in Young Children's Vocalizations'. *Bulletin of the Council for Research in Music Education*, 116–21 (2000).

106 Healey, E. C. *et al.* 'Factors Contributing to the Reduction of Stuttering During Singing'. *Journal of Speech and Hearing Research* **19**, 475–80 (1976).

107 Davidow, J. H. *et al.* 'Measurement of phonated intervals during four fluency-inducing conditions'. *J Speech Lang Hear Res* **52**, 188–205 (2009).

108 Colcord, R. D. & Adams, M. R. 'Voicing Duration and Vocal SPL Changes Associated with Stuttering Reduction During Singing'. *Journal of Speech, Language, and Hearing Research* **22**, 468–79 (1979).

109 Andrews, G. *et al.* 'Stuttering: Speech pattern characteristics under fluency-inducing conditions'. *J Speech Hear Res* **25**, 208–16 (1982).

110 Wan, C. Y. *et al.* 'The Therapeutic Effects of Singing in Neurological Disorders'. *Music Percept* **27**, 287–95 (2010).

111 Pearce, M. T. & Christensen, J. F. 'Conference report: The Neurosciences and Music-IV – Learning and Memory'. *Psychomusicology: Music, Mind, and Brain* **22**, 70–3 (2012).

112 Rojo, N. *et al.* 'Music-supported therapy induces plasticity in the sensorimotor cortex in chronic stroke: A single-case study using multimodal imaging (fMRI-TMS)'. *Brain Inj* **25**, 787–93 (2011).

113 Háden, G. P. *et al.* 'Beat processing in newborn infants cannot be explained by statistical learning based on transition probabilities'. *Cognition* **243**, 105670 (2024).

114 Edalati, M. *et al.* 'Rhythm in the Premature Neonate Brain: Very Early Processing of Auditory Beat and Meter'. *The Journal of Neuroscience: The official journal of the Society for Neuroscience* **43**, 2794–802 (2023).

115 Honing, H. *et al.* 'Rhesus Monkeys (*Macaca mulatta*) Sense Isochrony in Rhythm, but Not the Beat: Additional Support for the Gradual Audiomotor Evolution Hypothesis'. *Front Neurosci* **12**, 475 (2018).

116 Merchant, H. *et al.* 'Finding the beat: a neural perspective across humans and non-human primates'. *Philosophical Transactions of the Royal Society B:* Biological Sciences (2015).

117 Honing, H. & Merchant, H. 'Differences in auditory timing between human and nonhuman primates'. *The Behavioral and brain sciences* **37**, 557–58; discussion 577–604 (2014).

118 Zarco, W. *et al.* 'Subsecond timing in primates: Comparison of interval production between human subjects and rhesus monkeys'. *J Neurophysiol* **102**, 3191–202 (2009).

119 Merchant, H. & Honing, H. 'Are non-human primates capable of rhythmic entrainment? Evidence for the gradual audiomotor evolution hypothesis'. *Frontiers in Neuroscience* **7** (2014).

120 Stupacher, J. *et al.* 'The sweet spot between predictability and surprise: Musical groove in brain, body, and social interactions'. *Front Psychol* **13**, 906190 (2022).

121 Rodríguez-Fornells, A. *et al.* 'The involvement of audio-motor coupling in the music-supported therapy applied to stroke patients'. *Ann N Y Acad Sci* **1252**, 282–93 (2012).

122 Schneider, S. *et al.* 'Using musical instruments to improve motor skill recovery following a stroke'. *J Neurol* **254**, 1339–46 (2007).

123 Altenmüller, E. *et al.* 'Neural reorganization underlies improvement in stroke-induced motor dysfunction by music-supported therapy'. *Ann N Y Acad Sci* **1169**, 395–405 (2009).

124 Ripollés, P. *et al.* 'Music supported therapy promotes motor plasticity in individuals with chronic stroke'. *Brain Imaging Behav* **10**, 1289–1307 (2016).

125 Särkämö, T. *et al.* 'Music listening enhances cognitive recovery and mood after middle cerebral artery stroke'. *Brain: A journal of neurology* **131**, 866–76 (2008).

126 Scharinger, M. *et al.* 'Melody in poems and songs: Fundamental statistical properties predict aesthetic evaluation'. *Psychology of Aesthetics, Creativity, and the Arts* **17**, 163–77 (2023).

127 Kentner, G. *et al.* 'Poetics of reduplicative word formation: Evidence from a rating and recall experiment'. *Language and Cognition* **14**, 333–61 (2022).

128 Menninghaus, W. *et al.* 'Poetic speech melody: A crucial link between music and language'. *PLoS One* **13**, e0205980 (2018).

129 Menninghaus, W. *et al.* 'The emotional and aesthetic powers of parallelistic diction'. *Poetics* **63**, 47–59 (2017).

130 Tillmann, B. & Dowling, W. J. 'Memory decreases for prose, but not for poetry'. *Mem Cognit* **35**, 628–39 (2007).

131 Obermeier, C. *et al.* 'Aesthetic and emotional effects of meter and rhyme in poetry'. *Front Psychol* **4**, 10 (2013).

132 Stager, S. V. *et al.* 'Common features of fluency-evoking conditions studied in stuttering subjects and controls: An H(2)15O PET study'. *J Fluency Disord* **28**, 319–35; quiz 336 (2003).

133 Geretsegger, M. *et al.* 'Music therapy for autistic people'. *Cochrane Database Syst Rev* **5**, Cd004381 (2022).

134 Gemma, M.-G. *et al.* 'The role of music in the development of children with Down syndrome: A systematic review'. *Interdisciplinary Science Reviews* **45**, 158–73 (2020).

135 Bodeck, S. *et al.* 'Tic-reducing effects of music in patients with Tourette's syndrome: Self-reported and objective analysis'. *J Neurol Sci* **352**, 41–7 (2015).

136 Devlin, K. *et al.* 'Music Therapy and Music-Based Interventions for Movement Disorders'. *Curr Neurol Neurosci Rep* **19**, 83 (2019).

137 Di Benedetto, P. *et al.* 'Voice and choral singing treatment: A new approach for speech and voice disorders in Parkinson's disease'. *Eur J Phys Rehabil Med* **45**, 13–19 (2009).

138 Norton, A. *et al.* 'Melodic intonation therapy: shared insights on how it is done and why it might help'. *Ann N Y Acad Sci* **1169**, 431–36 (2009).

139 Schlaug, G. *et al.* 'From Singing to Speaking: Why Singing May Lead to Recovery of Expressive Language Function in Patients with Broca's Aphasia'. *Music Percept* **25**, 315–23 (2008).

140 Catmur, C. *et al.* 'Sensorimotor learning configures the human mirror system'. *Curr Biol* **17**, 1527–31 (2007).

141 Wilson, M. R. *et al.* in *Anticipation and Decision Making in Sport* (ed. A.M. Williams, Jackson, R.) (Routledge, 2019).

142 Kirchner, J. M. 'Incorporating flow into practice and performance'. *Work* **40**, 289–96 (2011).

143 Green, D. *Fight Your Fear and Win* (Broadway Books, 2002).

9. Modern Problems, Ancient Solutions?

1 Cleese, J. *Creativity: A Short and Cheerful Guide* (Crown Publishing Group, 2020).

2 Schulting, R. J. *et al.* 'Radiocarbon dating from Yuzhniy Oleniy Ostrov cemetery reveals complex human responses to socio-ecological stress during the 8.2 ka cooling event'. *Nat Ecol Evol* **6**, 155–62 (2022).

3 Rainio, R. *et al.* 'Prehistoric Pendants as Instigators of Sound and Body Movements: A Traceological Case Study from Northeast Europe, c. 8200 cal. bp.'. *Cambridge Archaeological Journal* **31**, 639–60 (2021).

4 Fullagar, R. & Matheson, C. in *The Society AWRANA* (https://awrana.org/traceology/).

5 Pfeiffer, J. E. *The Creative Explosion: An Inquiry into the Origins of Art and Religion* (Cornell University Press, 1986).

6 Conard, N. J. *et al.* 'New flutes document the earliest musical tradition in southwestern Germany'. *Nature* **460**, 737–40 (2009).

7 d'Errico, F. *et al.* 'Archaeological Evidence for the Emergence of Language, Symbolism, and Music – An Alternative Multidisciplinary Perspective'. *Journal of World Prehistory* **17**, 1–70 (2003).

8 Brandl, E. *et al.* 'The cultural evolution of teaching'. *Evolutionary Human Sciences* **5**, e14 (2023).

9 Heyes, C. 'Grist and mills: on the cultural origins of cultural learning'. *Philosophical Transactions of the Royal Society of London*. Series B, Biological Sciences **367**, 2181–91 (2012).

10 Barras, C. 'World's oldest drawing is Stone Age crayon doodle'. *Nature* (2018).

11 Henshilwood, C. S. *et al*. 'Engraved ochres from the Middle Stone Age levels at Blombos Cave, South Africa'. *Journal of Human Evolution* **57**, 27–47 (2009).

12 Hovers, E. *et al*. 'An early case of color symbolism: Ochre use by modern humans in Qafzeh Cave'. *Current Anthropology* **44**, 491–522 (2003).

13 Bouzouggar, A. *et al*. '82,000-year-old shell beads from North Africa and implications for the origins of modern human behavior'. *Proceedings of the National Academy of Sciences* **104**, 9964–9 (2007).

14 Garfinkel, Y. *Dancing at the Dawn of Agriculture* (University of Texas Press, 2001).

15 Garfinkel, Y. 'Dancing or Fighting? A Recently Discovered Predynastic Scene from Abydos, Egypt'. *Cambridge Archaeological Journal* **11**, 241–54 (2001).

16 Garfinkel, Y. 'Dance in Prehistoric Europe'. *Documenta Praehistorica* **37**, 205–14 (2010).

17 Grün, R. *et al*. 'U-series and ESR analyses of bones and teeth relating to the human burials from Skhul'. *Journal of Human Evolution* **49**, 316–34 (2005).

18 Cela Conde, C. J., Ayala, F.J. *Human Evolution: Trails From the Past* (Oxford University Press, Oxford, 2007).

19 Dorre, H. 'John Quincy Adams's Footloose Winter'. *Plodding through the Presidents* (18 October 2017) (https://www.ploddingthroughthepresidents.com/2017/10/john-quincy-adams-dancing.html).

20 Christensen, J. F. *et al*. 'Iranian Classical Dance As a Subject For Empirical Research: An Elusive Genre'. *Annals of the New York Academy of Sciences* (accepted).

21 Katz-Gerro, T. 'Highbrow cultural consumption and class distinction in Italy, Israel, West Germany, Sweden, and the United States'. *Social Forces* **81**, 207–29 (2002).

22 Chaplin, L. N. & Norton, M. I. 'Why we think we can't dance: theory of mind and children's desire to perform'. *Child Dev* **86**, 651–8 (2015).

23 Foussianes, C. 'See Rare Photos from Queen Elizabeth and Princess Margaret's WWII-Era Christmas Plays'. *Town & Country Magazine* (27 October 2021).

24 Brandreth, G. 'What the nation needs now – pantomime!' *Gyles Brandreth's Homepage* (2020) (https://www.gylesbrandreth.net/blog/2020/6/21/what-the-nation-needs-now-pantomime).

25 Parkinson, J. 'Parliament drug use claims to be raised with police this week'. *BBC News* (5 December 2021).

26 'Drogen im Parlament?: Kokainspuren beschäftigen Bundestag'. *Tagesspiegel* (1 November 2000).

27 'Kokainspuren auf dem Klo'. *Frankfurter Allgemeine* (1 November 2000).

28 'Cocaine traces at EU parliament'. *BBC NEWS* (15 July 2005).

10. Getting Started – And off you go, flow

1 Skinner, B. F. 'What is wrong with daily life in the Western world?' *American Psychologist* **41**, 568–74 (1986).

2 Pinto, D. G. *et al.* 'A behavioral test of Horney's linkage between authenticity and aggression: People living authentically are less-likely to respond aggressively in unfair situations'. *Personality and Individual Differences* **52**, 41–4 (2012).

3 Boyraz, G. *et al.* 'Authenticity, life satisfaction, and distress: A longitudinal analysis'. *J Couns Psychol* **61**, 498–505 (2014).

4 Wang, Y. & Li, Z. 'Authenticity as a Mediator of the Relationship Between Power Contingent Self-Esteem and Subjective Well-Being'. *Frontiers in Psychology* **9**, 1066 (2018).

5 Bryan, J. L., Baker, Z. G. & Tou, R. Y. *et al.* 'Prevent the blue, be true to you: Authenticity buffers the negative impact of loneliness on alcohol-related problems, physical symptoms, and depressive and anxiety symptoms'. *Journal of Health Psychology* **22**, 605–16 (2017).

6 Smallenbroek, O. *et al.* 'Authenticity as a eudaimonic construct: The relationships among authenticity, values, and valence'. *The Journal of Positive Psychology* **12**, 197–209 (2017).

7 Lenton, A. P. *et al.* 'State Authenticity in Everyday Life'. *European Journal of Personality* **30**, 64–82 (2016).

8 Bhanji, J. P. & Delgado, M. R. 'The social brain and reward: Social information processing in the human striatum'. *Wiley Interdiscip Rev Cogn Sci* **5**, 61–73 (2014).

9 Izuma, K. & Adolphs, R. 'Social manipulation of preference in the human brain'. *Neuron* **78**, 563–73 (2013).

10 Klucharev, V. *et al.* 'Reinforcement learning signal predicts social conformity'. *Neuron* **61**, 140–51 (2009).

11 Dosman, C. F. *et al.* 'Evidence-based milestone ages as a framework for developmental surveillance'. *Paediatr Child Health* **17**, 561–68 (2012).

12 Gerber, R. J. *et al.* 'Developmental milestones: Motor development'. *Pediatr Rev* **31**, 267–76; quiz 277 (2010).

13 Fenson, L. & Ramsay, D. S. 'Effects of modeling action sequences on the play of twelve-, fifteen-, and nineteen-month-old children'. *Child Dev* **52**, 1028–36 (1981).

14 Wellman, H. M. *et al.* 'Meta-analysis of theory-of-mind development: The truth about false belief'. *Child Dev* **72**, 655–84 (2001).

15 Boyatzis, C. J. & Satyaprasad, C. 'Children's facial and gestural decoding and encoding: Relations between skills and with popularity'. *Journal of Nonverbal Behavior* **18**, 37–55 (1994).

16 Boyatzis, C. J. & Watson, M. W. 'Preschool children's symbolic representation of objects through gestures'. *Child Dev* **64**, 729–35 (1993).

17 Vainio, M. & Daukantaitė, P. 'Grit and different aspects of well-being: Direct and indirect relationships via sense of coherence and authenticity'. *Journal of Happiness Studies* (Published online, 2015).

18 Wang, Y. N. 'Authenticity and Relationship Satisfaction: Two Distinct Ways of Directing Power to Self-Esteem'. *PloS one* **10**, e0146050 (2015).

19 Bonaiuto, M. *et al.* 'Optimal Experience and Personal Growth: Flow and the Consolidation of Place Identity'. *Frontiers in psychology* **7**, 1654 (2016).

20 Csíkszentmihályi, M. *Beyond Boredom and Anxiety* (Jossey-Bass Publishers, 1975).

21 Massimini, F. *et al.* in *Optimal Experience: Psychological studies of flow in consciousness* 60–81 (Cambridge University Press, 1988).

22 Csíkszentmihályi, M. *Flow: The Psychology of Optimal Experience* (Harper Perennial Modern Classics, 2008).

23 Moneta, G. B. in *Advances in Flow Research* (ed. Stefan Engeser) 23–50 (Springer New York, 2012).

24 Tschacher, W. *et al.* 'Audience synchronies in live concerts illustrate the embodiment of music experience'. *Sci Rep* **13**, 14843 (2023).

25 Wald-Fuhrmann, M. *et al.* 'Music Listening in Classical Concerts: Theory, Literature Review, and Research Program'. *Front Psychol* **12**, 638783 (2021).

26 Pelowski, M. *et al.* 'Beyond the lab: An examination of key factors influencing interaction with "real" and museum-based art'. *Psychology of Aesthetics, Creativity, and the Arts* **11**, 245–64 (2017).

27 Linden, C. & Wagemans, J. 'Presenting TaMuNaBe: A taxonomy of museum navigation behaviors'. *Psychology of Aesthetics, Creativity, and the Arts*, No Pagination Specified (2021) (https://doi.org:10.1037/aca0000413).

28 Hötting, K. & Röder, B. 'Beneficial effects of physical exercise on neuroplasticity and cognition'. *Neurosci Biobehav Rev* **37**, 2243–57 (2013).

29 'WHO guidelines on physical activity and sedentary behaviour: at a glance'. (4 May 2021).

30 Voelcker-Rehage, C. & Niemann, C. 'Structural and functional brain changes related to different types of physical activity across the life span'. *Neurosci Biobehav Rev* **37**, 2268–95 (2013).

31 Ploughman, M. 'Exercise is brain food: The effects of physical activity on cognitive function'. *Dev Neurorehabil* **11**, 236–40 (2008).

32 Cassilhas, R. C. *et al.* 'Physical exercise, neuroplasticity, spatial learning and memory'. *Cell Mol Life Sci* **73**, 975–83 (2016).

Conclusion: Art Matters

1 Tarr, B. *et al.* 'Synchrony and exertion during dance independently raise pain threshold and encourage social bonding'. *Biology Letters* **11** (2015).

2 Hickman, B. *et al.* 'Dance for Chronic Pain Conditions: A Systematic Review'. *Pain Med* **23**, 2022–41 (2022).

3 Merom, D. *et al.* 'Dancing Participation and Cardiovascular Disease Mortality: A Pooled Analysis of 11 Population-Based British Cohorts'. *American Journal of Preventive Medicine* **50**, 756–60 (2016).

4 Koch, S. C. 'Arts and health: Active factors and a theory framework of embodied aesthetics'. *The Arts in Psychotherapy* **54**, 85–91 (2017).

5 de Witte, M. *et al.* 'From Therapeutic Factors to Mechanisms of Change in the Creative Arts Therapies: A Scoping Review'. *Front Psychol* **12**, 678397 (2021).

6 Estel, S. M. & Koch, S. C. 'Wirkfaktoren von Tanz- und Bewegungstherapie im klinischen Kontext'. *Die Psychotherapie* **68**, 280–88 (2023).

7 Koch, S. C. & Weidinger-von der Recke, B. 'Traumatised refugees: An integrated dance and verbal therapy approach'. *The Arts in Psychotherapy* **36**, 289–96 (2009).

8 Hackney, M. E. & Earhart, G. M. 'Effects of dance on movement control in Parkinson's disease: a comparison of Argentine tango and American ballroom'. *Journal of Rehabilitation Medicine* **41**, 475–81 (2009).

9 Hackney, M. E. & Earhart, G. M. 'Recommendations for Implementing Tango Classes for Persons with Parkinson Disease'. *Am J Dance Ther* **32**, 41–52 (2010).

10 Lötzke, D. *et al.* 'Argentine tango in Parkinson disease – a systematic review and meta-analysis'. *BMC Neurol* **15**, 226 (2015).

11 Calvo-Merino, B. *et al.* 'Action observation and acquired motor skills: An fMRI study with expert dancers'. *Cerebral Cortex* **15**, 1243–49 (2005).

12 Cross, E. S. *et al.* 'Building a motor simulation de novo: Observation of dance by dancers'. *Neuroimage* **31**, 1257–67 (2006).

13 Orgs, G. *et al.* 'Expertise in dance modulates alpha/beta event-related desynchronization during action observation'. *European Journal of Neuroscience* **27**, 3380–4 (2008).

14 Kirsch, L. P. *et al.* 'Shaping and reshaping the aesthetic brain: Emerging perspectives on the neurobiology of embodied aesthetics'. *Neuroscience & Biobehavioral Reviews* **62**, 56–68 (2016).

15 Foster Vander Elst, O. *et al.* 'The Neuroscience of Dance: A Conceptual Framework and Systematic Review'. *Neurosci Biobehav Rev* **150**, 105197 (2023).

16 Christensen, J. F. *et al.* 'A 5-emotions stimuli set for emotion perception research with full-body dance movements'. *Scientific Reports* **13**, 8757 (2023).

17 Murcia, C. Q. *et al.* 'Emotional and Neurohumoral Responses to Dancing Tango Argentino: The Effects of Music and Partner'. *Music and Medicine* 1 (2009).

18 Koch, S. C. *et al.* 'Effects of Dance Movement Therapy and Dance on Health-Related Psychological Outcomes. A Meta-Analysis Update'. *Frontiers in psychology* 10, 1806 (2019).

19 Millman, L. S. M. *et al.* 'Towards a neurocognitive approach to dance movement therapy for mental health: A systematic review'. *Clinical Psychology & Psychotherapy* 28, 24–38 (2021).

20 Christensen, J. F. *et al.* 'A Practice-Inspired Mindset for Researching the Psychophysiological and Medical Health Effects of Recreational Dance (Dance Sport)'. *Frontiers in Psychology* 11 (2021).

21 Christensen, J. F. & Calvo-Merino, B. 'Dance as a Subject for Empirical Aesthetics.' *Psychology of Aesthetics, Creativity, and the Arts* 7, 76–88 (2013).

22 Christensen, J. F. & Jola, C. in *Art, Aesthetics, and the Brain* (eds M. Nadal *et al.*) (Oxford University Press, 2015).

Index

abstract art, 180, 224
addiction, 70–79, 170, 209
  behavioural addictions, 70–76, 166
  pleasure addiction, 75–9
  rumination and, 80–81, 83
  social media and, 78–9
ADHD, 117, 126, 155, 164, 217
adrenal gland, 21
adrenaline, 51
aesthetic experience, 231
affective aggression, 117
affective realism, 143
affective touch, 91–5
Afghanistan, 230
AIDS, 174–5
Almodóvar, Pedro, 125
Alzheimer's, 25
Ancient Greece, 37–8
anhedonia, 52, 138
anonymity, 161
anxiety, 166
  anxiety disorders, 25, 80, 83,
    130–31, 155
  performance anxiety, 218–20
aphasia, 218
architecture, 127
Argentine tango, 72–5, 163, 200,
  206–7, 258
Aron, A. P., 61
arousal misattribution, 60–61,
  64–5, 142
Art Attack (TV series), 195
arthritis, 107
arts *see* creative arts
As Good As It Gets (1997 film), 80

asthma, 107–8
attachment emotions, 51
attention deployment strategies,
  167–71
audiobooks, 126–7
autism, 179–80, 217
avoidance behaviours, 29, 166–7
awe, 128–31, 241–2
Azorin, Miguel, 188–9

Baker, Simon, 237
balconing, 63–4
Balearic Islands, University of the,
  Mallorca, 152–3
ballet, 43, 101–2, 146–9, 181, 200,
  205–6, 210, 228
Barcelona, University of, 215
Barrett, Lisa Feldman, 142,
  145, 154
Barrett, Sara, 179
BBC (British Broadcasting
  Corporation), 96, 107, 164, 170
Bechara, Antoine, 70, 76
beginner's luck, 238–9
behaviours, 19–20, 26, 36, 39–42,
  76–7, 227, 257
  adaptive behaviours, 140
  aggression, 41
  avoidance behaviours, 29, 166–7
  behavioural addictions, 70–76,
    166
  competitiveness, 40–47, 227
  creative behaviours, 87–8, 135,
    155–7
  cues, 76–7, 84

behaviours – *cont.*
  habitual behaviours, 76–8, 83–4
  learned behaviours, 104–5
  pleasure-plus, 39, 56, 69, 86–8,
    131–2, 173
  pleasure-seeking, 47–56, 227, 252–3
  risk-taking, 56–65, 227, 252
  sensation-seeking, 56–65
  see also rumination
Big Bang Theory (TV series), 179
binge-watching, 51, 166
bipolar disorder, 106, 155–6
Birds, The (Aristophanes), 122
Birmingham, University of, 43
Blombos Cave, South Africa, 224
blood pressure, 19–20, 107
body dissatisfaction, 166
body-orchestra, 11–13, 20–21, 23
boundaries, 114–32, 163, 218, 234
  people, 121–3
  senses, 116–17
  work, 117–21
brains, 2–3, 11, 13–28, 37–8, 90–91
  amygdala, 37, 90, 140, 174, 184
  anterior cingulate (ACC) 37, 90
  brain stem, 13–19, 22
  'default mode network', 24–5
  dorsolateral prefrontal cortex
    (DLPFC), 37
  fight or flight mechanism, 41, 43,
    81, 95, 98, 102, 167
  hippocampus, 37
  insula, 37, 71, 90, 95, 184
  learning, 192–3
  maintenance, 25
  negative feedback loops, 69–70
  neural pathways, 14
  nucleus accumbens, 37, 90
  prefrontal cortex, 17, 19, 22, 28,
    135, 184, 205–7, 216, 239
  'resting brain', 23–5
  sensation-seeking and, 62

'social brain', 43–4, 73, 90–100,
    227, 258
Social Engagement
    System, 98
striatum, 37
ventromedial prefrontal cortex
    (VMPFC), 28, 37
Brandreth, Gyles, 229
Bravo, Susana, 67–9
British Film Institute, 177
bullying, 159–60
Burkeman, Oliver, 4

cancer, 108
Carner, Loyle, 164–5, 186
Chang, Dong-Seon, 181–2
Chenery, Susan, 156
childhood, 176, 193–5, 207, 213, 217,
    228, 232–3
China, 79, 194
chocolate, 167–8
Church, Michael, 228
cinema, 114, 124–6, 160, 177–8
'classical' arts, 228–9, 231
Cleese, John, 221, 231, 248
cognitive change, 173–82
cognitive dissonance, 84–6
cognitive restructuring, 185–9
comedy, 160
community, 240–41
competitive arts, 42–3, 45
competitive sports, 40–42
competitiveness, 242, 252
confirmation bias, 85–6
conformism, 232–3
consciousness, 23
contingencies, 119–20
cooking, 164–5
Corfu, Greece, 34
cortisol, 21–2, 40, 43–4
Covid pandemic, 45, 49, 183
Craig, Harrison, 214

'craving', 52, 76
creative arts, 6, 86, 88, 100, 110–13, 114, 152, 148–52, 155–9
    abstract art, 180, 224
    active principles, 257–8
    choosing, 248–51
    cinema, 114, 124–6, 160, 177–8
    'classical' arts, 228–9, 231
    competitive arts, 42–3, 45
    cooking, 164–5
    dance, 20, 37, 42–3, 72–5, 146–7, 163, 205–8, 217, 222–3, 226–7, 229–30, 258–61
    disclosure through, 158–61
    drawing, 147–52, 195–6, 211–12
    emotion regulation and, 154–5, 162
    expression through arts, 146–7
    expressive writing, 107–10, 151, 158–9, 171, 202
    music, 12–13, 148, 172, 205, 217
    needle arts, 170–71, 202–3, 254–6
    paintings, 175–6, 178, 180–81, 208, 209–10, 224
    performance arts, 212–13, 218–20
    prehistoric art, 221–6
    problem-solving and, 172–3
    prohibition of, 226–31
    research and, 260–62
    science and, 259–62
    singing, 213–14, 218
    targeted distraction, 170–71
    theatre, 31, 89, 229
    'understanding' art, 180–81
creative behaviours, 87–8, 135, 155–7
creative spaces, 127
crochet *see* needle arts
Csíkszentmihályi, Mihaly, 2, 149–50, 210, 234
cues, 76–7, 84, 147–8, 186, 198–200, 245–6

intermittent pleasure-cues, 76
cumulative culture, 176
Curious Incident of the Dog in the Night-time, The (Haddon), 178–9

Daft Punk (rock band), 161
dance, 20, 37, 42–3, 72–5, 146–7, 163, 205–8, 217, 222–3, 226–7, 229–30, 258–61
    Argentine tango, 72–5, 163, 200, 206–7, 258
    ballet, 43, 101–2, 146–9, 181, 200, 205–6, 210, 228
    choreography, 259
    prohibition of, 229–30
Dancing is the Best Medicine (Christensen and Chang), 42, 152, 181
Danes, Claire, 179
Darwin, Charles, 138–9
Das, Vir, 160
Davey, G. C., 59–60
Delacroix, Eugène, 208
dementia, 203
depression *see* mental health
Descent of Man, The (Darwin), 139
detached reappraisal, 174
Devlin, Joseph T., 125, 126–7
diabetes, 175
disclosure, 158–61
distraction, 162, 170–72, 219
    distractor tasks, 116
domestic violence, 41
dopamine, 31, 49–51, 56, 77, 187
Dostoevsky, Fyodor, 27–8
Down's Syndrome, 214–15, 217
drawing, 147–52, 195–6, 211–12
Dresden University, 42
drugs, 71–2
Dumbo (1941 Disney cartoon), 66
Dutton, D. G., 61
dyslexia, 164

'Echad Mi Yodea' (Naharin), 181
education, 141, 194–5, 203, 205
Ehlers, Anke, 159
Ekman, Paul, 139
electroencephalogram (EEG), 62
Elisabeth (Sisi), Empress of Austria, 34, 36, 162
Elizabeth II, Queen of the United Kingdom, 229
Emotion Regulation Strategies, 136–7, 157, 162–90, 235, 258
   attention deployment strategies, 167–71
   cognitive change, 173–82
   cognitive restructuring, 185–9
   problem-solving, 172–3
   response modulation, 182–4
   situation selection and modification, 162–7
emotions, 18–19, 49–52, 135–44
   aesthetic emotions, 241–2
   constructed emotion, 145
   creative arts and, 155–7
   dramatic emotions, 31–2, 89
   emotion generation, 154–5
   fear, 43, 59, 80, 103–4, 139–40
   regulation of, 141, 153–5, 162–90; *see also* Emotion Regulation Strategies
   suppression of, 182–4
   toxic emotional discharge, 157–8
enculturation, 228
endorphins, 22
Epicure, 37
epilepsy, 25
eudemonism, 37–9, 53, 71, 76, 88, 132, 151
'Exam-Driven Learner', 199, 209, 219
Expression of the Emotions in Man and Animals, The (Darwin), 138–9

expressive writing, 107–10, 151, 158–9, 171, 202
extrinsic motivations, 74

facial expressions, 97–8
Fancourt, Daisy, 162, 257–8
Fei Du, 25
Ferrante, Elena, 161
Festinger, Leo, 84
FIFA World Cup (2014), 40
Fine Cell Work (charity), 170
flavonoids, 168
Florida State University, 129
'flow', 1–2, 6, 149–50, 232–56
   eight principles, 234–5
   seven 'active principles' (stars), 235–47
football, 40–41
Footloose (1984 film), 226
'forbidden fruit', 31–2
Four Thousand Weeks (Burkeman), 4
freedom of choice, 135
freedom of expression, 227
Freid, David, 165
'From a Railway Carriage' (Stevenson), 217

gambling, 76, 77
Gandhi, Mahatma, 131
ganglia, 16, 21
gender dilemmas, 188
genetic compatibility, 111
Ghostbusters (1984 film), 26–7
ghrelin, 18
Good Samaritan, The (Delacroix), 208
Gramsci, Antonio, 124
Grand Factory, Beirut, 127–8
Grandin, Temple, 179–80
Greatest Dancer, The (TV talent show), 214
Green, Don, 218–20
Greenberg, Raquel, 207

grief, 34–5
Guardian, 156, 179
Guernica (Picasso), 175

habits, 49–52
   habit loops, 197–9, 209–10, 235,
     238, 247
Hafez, 181
Hanks, Tom, 125
happiness, 98, 232
Harlow, Harry, 92
Harry Potter books (Rowling), 167–8
Harvard University, 98
Hawks, Howard, 177
health, 92, 94–9, 107–8
Hebb, Donald, 191
hedonism, 37–9, 50, 53–5
Heyes, Celia, 176
high temperature, 117
homosexuality, 108
Hopkinson, K. L., 60
hormones, 15, 17, 18
   stress hormones, 20–22, 40–46
How Emotions Are Made (Barrett), 142
Hub, Battersea, 171
human connections *see* social
   connections
hunger, 17–18, 142–3
hyperpalatable foods, 70–71

imagination, 235, 243–4, 254
imitation, 232–3
Imitation Game, The (TV series), 179
immune system, 20, 83, 92, 94, 240
immune response, 40–41, 108
   Th-1 response, 40–41
   Th-2 response, 40–41
improvisation, 205
In Search of Lost Time (Proust), 164
incentive value, 185
incubation times, 172–3
Inside Out (2015 Pixar cartoon), 137–9

insight, 144, 153
Institute for Cognitive
   Neuroscience (ICN),
   University College London, 91
Institute of Psychiatry, London, 159
intention, 245–6
'Interest-Driven Creator', 199, 203,
   204, 206, 209, 219
intermittent pleasure-cues, 76
intermittent reinforcement, 48–50
intrinsic motivation, 149–50
Iran, 114, 230
irritable bowel syndrome, 107

Jailbirds (1996 film), 214
James, William, 210
Jarvis, Eric, 213, 216
jazz music, 205, 207
Jeffrey K. Smith, 127
Johnston, W. M., 59–60
Joiner, Thomas, 129
Joy of Painting, The (TV series), 195
Jung, Carl, 130
Just One Thing (radio series), 107

Kant, Immanuel, 204
Karelia, Russia, 222–3
Kennedy, John F., 98
Kintsugi, 4, 188
knitting *see* needle arts
Købke, Christen, 196
Købke, Kasper, 195–6, 199, 203, 238
van der Kolk, Bessel, 101

L'Opéra (TV series), 101–3
Labed, Ariane, 101–2
Lambrechts, Anna, 147
Last Action Hero, The (1993 film), 132
'learned helplessness', 119–20
learning, 192–3, 205–7
Lebanon, 128
Ledoux, Joseph, 139–41, 218

Leknes, Siri, 56–7
liking-wanting principle, 87, 195,
    199, 213, 234–5
limbic system, 36–7, 184
literature, 176–7
Little Prince, The (Saint-Exupéry),
    143
Liverpool John Moores University,
    92
Llull, Ramón, 54
loneliness, 91, 94, 95–6, 98, 111, 166,
    240
Louis XIV, King of France, 228

Maiwald, Jochen, 189
Maldoom, Royston, 217
Mallorca, Spain, 53–6, 152
Marin, Sanna, 229–30
Marvelous Mrs. Maisel, The (comedy-
    drama TV series), 160, 187–8
mass trauma media contact, 60
Max Planck Institute for
    Chemistry, Mainz, 126
Max Planck Institute for Empirical
    Aesthetics, Frankfurt, 3
McGlone, Francis, 92–4
McGuigan, Ruby, 177
medical drugs, 257
meditative state, 169
melatonin, 15, 17
memory systems, 2, 12, 28, 34,
    201–3, 235
mental health, 83–4, 155–7
    depression, 25, 52, 155, 189
    see also anxiety
Mentalist, The (TV series), 237
#MeToo movement, 113, 159
mind-control techniques, 26–7
    avoidance, 29–30
    distraction, 30–32
    suppression, 26–8
mind hooks, 237, 246

mindfulness meditation, 4, 26,
    129–31
Minnesota, University of, Medical
    School, 25
mistreatments, 115
Monroe, Marilyn, 177
Montreal, University of, 43
mood induction, 59, 117–18, 182–3
Mosley, Michael, 107
motor commands, 197–8
movement, 197–8, 200–202, 204–10,
    244–5
multi-tasking, 116
multivariate phenomena, 261
muscle memory, 200
museums, 127, 242
music, 12–13, 148, 172, 205, 217
music-induced imagery, 148
Mussolini, Benito, 124
myelin, 191–2, 196, 203, 235

National Centre of Medicine and
    Science and Sport,
    Tunisia, 40
Nebra Sky Disk, 236
needle arts, 170–71, 202–3, 254–6
negative feedback loops, 69–70
neural pathways, 14, 38, 86–7, 144,
    192, 196, 216
neural transmission, 16–17, 25, 198
neuroaesthetics, 241–2
neurodiversity, 7, 164–5,
    178, 186
neurotransmitters, 77
news consumption, 58–61
Newsom, Martha, 40
Nicholson, Jack, 80
Night School, The (Daugherty), 179
North Carolina, University of, 97

Obama, Michelle, 256
obsession, 208–10

obsessive-compulsive disorder
    (OCD), 80
oligodendrocytes, 192, 196, 203
Oliver, Jamie, 7, 164–5, 186
Opening Skinner's Box (Slater), 48
operant conditioning, 47
orienting responses, 50
Other Classical Musics, The (Church),
    228
Ottley, Matt, 156
oxytocin, 61, 99, 111

pain, 27, 34, 107
    pain/pleasure, 56–7
paintings, 175–6, 178, 180–81, 208,
    209–10, 224
Palace Achilleon, Corfu, 34
Panahi, Jafar, 114, 123, 160, 168
pantomime, 229
Parkinson's disease, 25, 107, 218, 258
Pathway Prompts, 5, 196–200,
    206, 238
Pennebaker, James, 107–8, 110, 159,
    221, 246
perception-action links, 212–18
perfectionism, 6, 238, 240
performance anxiety, 218–20
performance arts, 212–13, 218–20
Perry, Bruce, 101
personality, 121–3
Pfefferbaum, B., 60
'Phoenix Circle', 254–6
physical exercise, 20
Picasso, Pablo, 175, 209
Picture With A Circle (Kandinsky), 224
'pink elephant' thoughts, 3, 20, 23,
    26–9, 66–88
pleasure-seeking, 55–6
Pleiades, 236
poetry, 181, 217
Pomona College, 131
'Porcupine Dilemma, The', 89, 96

Porges, Steven, 97–8
positive reappraisal, 174–5
post-traumatic stress disorder, 108
Poulin, Michael, 129–20
prayer, 168–70, 221
prehistoric art, 221–5
Prison Notebooks, The (Gramsci), 124
problem-solving, 172–3
Proust, Marcel, 164
psychoneuroendocrinology, 15

Quested, Eleanor, 43

Raichle, Marcus, 23–4
Rainio, Riitta, 222–3
Rattle, Simon, 217
reappraisal, 173–4, 182, 184
    detached, 174
    positive, 174–5
regulation strategies, 154
relationships, 98–9
religion, 168–70, 221, 225–6, 227–8,
    247–8
Rental Health (radio series), 96
repetition, 237–8
response modulation, 182–4
reward system, 38, 39, 44, 46, 47–50,
    52–8, 77
    'abnormal' reward system
        activation, 81
    artificial rewards, 69–71
rhythm, 213–17, 237
risk-taking, 56–9, 64–5
Rodríguez-Fornells, Antoni, 215–16
Rohleder, Nicolas, 42
Ross, Herbert, 226
routine, 236–8, 253
Rowling, J. K., 168
Rudolf, Crown Prince of Austria, 34
rumination, 39, 46, 66–7, 80–83, 171,
    182, 209
    angry rumination, 82

rumination – *cont.*
  fearful rumination, 82
  pleasure rumination, 82
  ruminative loops, 39, 46, 79, 82,
    105–6
  sad rumination, 82
running, 21–2
Ryan-Spaulding, Daniel, 120, 160

de Saint-Exupéry, Antoine, 143
schizophrenia, 25, 155
Schmidt, Eva-Madeleine, 183
Schopenhauer, Arthur, 89
Science magazine, 85
Seleoane, Sheila, 95–6
self-esteem, 186–9, 242–3
self-justification, 84–6
self-sabotage, 185–6
Selmon, Simon, 147
sensation-seeking, 61–5
senses, 49–52, 153, 164
  hearing, 164
  sight, 143–4
  smell, 164, 167, 169
  taste, 164, 167, 169
  touch, 91–5, 164
Shay, Anthony, 131
Short and Cheerful Guide to Creativity
  (Cleese), 221
'silver lining', 174–5
singing, 213–14, 218
sitting, 19–22
Skhul Cave, Mount Carmel, Israel,
  225
skill learning, 191–220, 239–40
  cognitivists, 204
  embodiment, 204, 205
  imagination, 210–12
  imitation and copying, 206–8
  memory systems, 201–3
  obsession, 208–10
  rhythm, 213–17

Skinner, Burrhus Frederic, 47–8
Slater, Lauren, 48
sleep, 16–17, 32, 107, 109, 163, 210
  disturbed sleep patterns, 17
Slimani, Maamer, 40
soap operas, 51, 166
social comparison processes, 44–5
social connections, 89–100, 110–12,
  173, 240–41
  avoidance, 166
Social Dilemma, The (Netflix
  documentary), 79
social isolation, 95–6, 110, 240
social media, 45–6, 78–9
social phobia, 182
'social prescribing', 111–12, 258
social psychology, 53
social rejection, 99–100
socialisation, 233
songbirds, 213, 216
Soul (2020 Pixar cartoon),
  162, 166
stars, 235–6
Stevenson, Robert Louis, 217
storytelling, 212, 243–4
Sträter, Torsten, 189
stress response, 20, 21–2, 26, 29
strokes, 215–16
stuttering, 214, 217
suffering, 35
survivor's syndrome', 35
symbolic thought, 225–6
synchrony, 111
Szabo, A., 60

Taforalt, Morocco, 224
Tallis, Frank, 79
tantrums, 48–9, 157–8
Targhetta, Remi, 74
technique, 205, 208–9, 238, 240
Temple Grandin (2010 film), 179–80
Ten on Ten (YouTube series), 160

Texas, University of, 107
theatre, 31, 89, 229
'Theory of Emotional Inhibition'
    (Pennebaker), 159
theory of mind, 178, 233
This Is Not a Film (2011 film), 114
TikTok, 79
To Kill a Mockingbird (Lee), 178
Today (radio programme), 164, 170
Tortella, Miquel, 197
Tourette's syndrome, 217
Tracey, Irene, 56–7
transcranial magnetic stimulation
    (TMS), 205
trauma, 82, 100–110, 115, 159–61,
    167, 188, 258
  genetics and, 103–4
  trauma cues, 102–3, 106–10
*Tree of Ecstasy and Unbearable Sadness,
    The* (Ottley), 156
van Trier, Lars, 178
Trinity University, San Antonio, 27
Turner, William, 180, 209–10
Twain, Mark, 83

unfinished tasks, 32
Universal Declaration of Human
    Rights, 176, 227
University College London, 162
US presidential elections (2004), 86

vagus nerve, 97, 167
Valkeapää, Juha, 223

Van Gogh, Vincent, 155, 208
variable ratio, 120
'variables', 261–2
vasovagal syncope, 167
Vincent, Joyce, 96
Voice of Australia, The (TV talent
    show), 214
Vrinceanu, Tudor, 43

Walsh, Vince, 209, 210, 219
Washington University School of
    Medicine, St Louis, 23
Wegner, Daniel, 27, 30–31, 166
'White Bear Problem',
    27–8, 30
Williams, Jonathan, 126
Williams, Robin, 106
Wolpert, Daniel, 200
working memory, 32–3

Xintong Jiang, 62

Yale University, 94
Yard of Sky, A (Zaghari-Ratcliffe),
    170
yoga, 129–31, 221
Yuzhniy Oleniy Ostrov burial site,
    Russia, 222–3

Zaghari-Ratcliffe, Nazanin, 7,
    123, 170
Zeigarnik, Bluma, 32
Zeigarnik effect, 51, 323

About the Author

Dr Julia F. Christensen is a Danish neuroscientist and former ballet dancer currently working as a senior scientist at the Max Planck Institute for Empirical Aesthetics in Germany. She studied psychology, human evolution and neuroscience in France, Spain and the UK. For her postdoctoral training, she worked in international interdisciplinary research labs at University College London, City, University of London and the Warburg Institute, University of London and was awarded a postdoctoral Newton International Fellowship by the British Academy.